Labor Leadership
in *Italy* and *Denmark*

JOSEPH A. RAFFAELE

The University of Wisconsin Press

MADISON, 1962

H II 6708
R 13 L

PUBLISHED BY THE UNIVERSITY OF WISCONSIN PRESS
430 Sterling Court, Madison 6, Wisconsin

Copyright © 1962 by the Regents of the University of Wisconsin

*Printed in the United States of America by the
Vail-Ballou Press, Inc., Binghamton, New York*

Library of Congress Catalog Card Number 62–14412

Labor Leadership in Italy and Denmark

To Piera and J. Mark: the future

Foreword

Research in the field of labor relations has been heavily influenced by an economic bias. And indeed this is not unjustified. Even the most confirmed non-Marxist must admit that labor organization is profoundly affected by the mode of economic organization, the state of technology, the work relationships, and the economic stability of an industry or a nation. This generalization applies not only to the occurrence of unionization, but also to the tactics and policies unions will develop.

Economic factors, on the other hand, have incomplete explanatory value. Within a single industry we can find variations in all aspects of labor organizations: admissions policies, bargaining methods, immediate objectives, and long-run goals. Across national lines we find even more such divergencies.

Industrial sociologists have proposed that, in addition to economic determinants, we must take account of small group organizations, traditions, and cultural patterns. Industrial psychologists have been more inclined to look at the personalities of leaders and of the rank-and-file members.

Research in these non-economic areas has, deplorably, been infrequent and generally small scale. Whereas economic data can usually be obtained from governmental sources, cultural and psychological data must be gotten by field study. Methodological difficulties are substantial. Particularly rare are good studies which cross national and cultural boundary lines. It is thus very gratifying to encounter Professor Raffaele's cross-cultural study of labor leaders in Italy and Denmark.

It would not be appropriate for me to attempt to summarize the findings of this extensive investigation. It does seem fitting, however, to look at this research within a somewhat broader framework.

The labor movement is composed of individual human beings. While they have in common many human attributes—hunger, thirst, love, ambition, anxiety—and many external problems, they also differ in many important ways. They differ in the way they relate to employers and to their fellows. And these differences are reflected in variations in the policies and tactics of their unions.

For the labor leader, as for everyone else, reality is determined by what he perceives. Each individual develops his own private picture of the world, and this picture guides his behavior. It is thus true that each of us lives, in a sense, in his own private universe. Events not affecting the sensory receptors do not have reality value. I may be surrounded by ultraviolet rays, X–rays, and other esoteric radiations; but unless instruments make these available to my observation, I do not know they exist; they do not form part of my reality. The color-blind man may be unable to see the difference between a green apple and a ripe one; only when he tastes them can he detect the variation.

The most important differences in perceived reality, however, do not depend on defects of the sense organs. Strong emotions may modify our precepts. When we say, "Love is blind," we mean that an emotion causes one to misperceive the loved object. Similarly, the terms "blind fear" and "blind rage" give recognition to this distorting effect. Loyalty to a group, no less than to an individual, modifies reality. The person immersed in a cultural tradition may be literally unable to see that other possible ways of behaving really exist.

As regards the union leader, he is not color-blind, nor defective in any other fashion. He tends, however, to see reality in his own distinctive way, and he guides the policies of his organization accordingly. He has no other choice. If I am driving a car, I avoid obstacles *as I see them*. The labor leader must avoid threats to his union in accordance with reality as he sees it.

This means that a study of union leaders from the point of view of their attitudes and values has great potential for illuminating the complex problems of labor relations. The craft union official "sees" certain facts which do not exist for the industrial union executive, and vice versa.

Reality is modified by exaggerating some aspects of an immediately present situation, denying that others exist, and reinterpreting many to fit into the preferred picture. Thus the politically oriented leader may magnify the extent of coöperation between employers and the government; he may deny the possibility of worker gains through direct economic action; and he may drastically change the significance of "facts" about American experience in this line, to provide support for his views. (I hope it will be understood that these are unconscious distortions, not conscious pretense.)

Virtually all economic situations are ambiguous; these inner determinants, therefore, can readily determine what is seen as the correct course of action. In a very poor economy like Italy, for example, it may be argued that the workers have no savings, hence they dare not strike; or it may appear that, having nothing to lose, they dare to take desperate measures. In the Danish situation, one leader may hold that the government is friendly and hence unions should not rock the boat; another observes that the economy is prosperous and decides his union should demand more benefits. All students of labor relations are intuitively aware of such variations; it is the merit of the present study to explore some of the deeper values which determine the kinds of choices made by particular union leaders.

Can we then allege that direct interviews with union leaders provide *objective facts* about their organizations and policies? Obviously not. The physicists tell us that no fact exists independent of an observer; and certainly the facts reported by a leader of one union may be widely at odds with those seen by another. The key point is simply this: "objective" reality is often unimportant in determining union behavior. The "subjective" reality of the leaders is always effective. Usually the leader is in fairly close touch with reality as seen by others; if not, he will not last long. But in any event, it is the facts as he sees them which guide his policy decisions. Therefore the ways of approaching and understanding reality, the attitudes and values, of union leaders must be taken into account.

It is not surprising, therefore, that Professor Raffaele finds the best conceptualization of his data making use of the term "value." This word carries not only the connotation, "This is good," but also the implication, "This one strives to achieve." In pursuit of his major values, the union leader modifies his percepts of reality and in turn shapes the policy and tactics of his organization.

The success with which Professor Raffaele has used this method will be apparent in the pages that follow. He has found that generalized value orientations do indeed affect union activity even under relatively constant economic circumstances. Thus his observations represent a needful corrective to some social philosophers, both Marxist and capitalist, who write from the assumption (sometimes unstated) that man's behavior is shaped solely by economic forces.

The usefulness of such cross-cultural studies hardly requires emphasis. In this shrinking world, where yesterday's foreigner is today's next-door neighbor, we desperately need a better understanding of national and cultural values. We must acquire insight into the realities which guide others in their behavior. Professor Raffaele has made an important contribution here. Let us hope that his work is rapidly extended to include labor leaders in many other nations.

ROSS STAGNER

Wayne University

Acknowledgments

A study of this kind is not possible without the help and coöperation of hundreds of individuals. My gratitude goes to the people in Denmark and Italy who made the study possible by their support and participation. For their generous help, I want to express particular indebtedness to Ross Stagner, of Wayne University, and Gladys L. Palmer, of the University of Pennsylvania. Their spirit of scholarship and objective inquiry was a source of encouragement throughout the course of the study, and especially during the initial uncertain phases of the pilot investigation in Italy. I want also to acknowledge the financial assistance of Drexel Institute of Technology and the Penrose Fund of the American Philosophical Society. For their help during the field investigation in Denmark, a debt is due to the late Professor Frederik Zeuthen, of the University of Copenhagen, and two of his students, Reinhard Lund and Ove Henningsen. In an atmosphere of skepticism, Professor Zeuthen's support of the project was indispensable for its continuance in Denmark. Mr. Lund was particularly helpful in the further development of the approach of the study after the initial Italian experience, including the difficult problem of preserving in the Danish language the concepts developed in English and Italian. Needless to say, as sole operator of the project, responsibility for the content of the book is my own.

JOSEPH A. RAFFAELE

Rosemont, Pennsylvania
January, 1962

Contents

Tables

CHARTS

Labor Leadership in Italy and Denmark

Introduction

Since the end of the Second World War, there has been a growing awareness of the importance of the labor question in international affairs and the need for the United States to increase its understanding of the labor movements of other countries. The balance of power in the developing countries is shifting toward labor. The ideologies which will dominate in the world are tied to the aspirations of insurgent working classes in all parts of the globe, and to the degree to which these aspirations are fulfilled. How to compare and evaluate in a tangible manner the changing labor systems of countries in various phases of development becomes a question of major importance. In making social observations, and the comparisons implicit in them, we have often shown the tendency, expressed or implied, to place countries in a scale from more advanced to less advanced, and to suggest that the latter will gradually become increasing similar to the former. It frequently seems to be assumed, too, that labor systems will increasingly approximate the British-American industrial model. In this American habit of self-adulation, not enough thought has been given to the way in which comparisons should be made in the first place. Accordingly, there is, in the study of labor abroad, a need for a method which can be applied systematically to different countries in a manner that permits the making of meaningful direct comparisons between them. In pursuing this objective, the differentiating influence of national character on labor systems is not at issue. What needs to be done is to determine how this influence can be measured on a country-to-country basis.

3

After trying many approaches, I decided that the best way to overcome the difficult hurdle was to bring together national character and labor systems by means of a study of labor leadership. This book represents an initial report on three years of field investigations designed to develop a comparative technique of studying the labor movements of countries of contrasting cultures and phases of industrialization. Italy was a useful choice as a beginning because of comparison opportunities afforded by three labor movements. While national character is a statistical abstraction, its study in a country such as Denmark has high validity and usefulness. Moreover, the disparity between Italy and Denmark made them seem an advantageous choice in the attempt to ascertain a general method which would make it possible to make direct comparison of differences.

There were a number of possible approaches: (1) economic analysis of such matters as the technology of production and distribution, the characteristics of human and economic resources, and the structure and tempo of industrialization; (2) comparison of achievements of the system, embracing such factors as the characteristics of terms of employment and the rate of improvement of living standards; (3) consideration of the laws affecting the system and the condition of labor, and the manner in which they are interpreted; (4) historical and chronological review of labor events; (5) structural analysis of the industrial relations system of different internal and interorganizational dimensions; (6) study of the origins and value characteristics of role-players in industrial relations—including employers, labor leaders, government representatives, workers, and those institutional leaders who, while at the periphery of industrial relations, exert an influence on the system—and of the perceptions these individuals have of each other and the relative differences in their power; (7) description of the activities and methods of the system, including the dynamic behavior of participants in action situations and the causes and strategy of change.

The search led to selecting the last three approaches and unifying them around the dynamics of labor leadership. While published international-labor studies have concentrated largely on the first four frameworks, it became apparent that benchmarks of comparison for such dissimilar countries as Scandinavian Denmark and Latin Italy could be better found in the last three. Behind this conclusion are several assumptions: (1) a principal factor making for differences in an industrial relations system is the mosaic of cultural values with which the participants of that system confront each other; (2) a study of labor leadership in a particular cultural context measures indirectly and economically underlying cultural, political, and economic environments; (3) relying heavily on the replies of respondents explaining how they grapple with problems provides a degree of control over the cultural biases which American students of foreign systems may inject in their observations; (4) centering a study of national character around the anchor point of labor leadership yields a large volume of data which may reveal associations between particular types of leadership and environments; (5) given descriptions of one, the other can be deduced, or the outcome of an existing system can be foretold from a particular set of existing variables.

Not all of these assumptions have been verified. Nor have the possibilities of the data collected for this work been exhausted. What began as a study consisting of a series of depth interviews of labor leaders was pushed toward an analysis of industrial relations systems. In different words, the goal of a meaningful comparative study of labor movements had to be placed in the broader context of comparative labor leadership of both organized and unorganized workers. Unfortunately, however, as one increases the benchmarks of comparison, the goal of classification of data becomes more elusive and complex. This book, therefore, is an initial exploration of how the comparative study of labor leadership provides opportunities for comparisons of industrial systems.

The basic approach to the study is talking and living with labor leaders and workers and trying to report in a systematic fashion what they do and say. My object was to develop a picture of the Italian and Danish labor movements by using the expressions of their principal players as much as possible, rather than my own, and to organize such expression of national character in a manner that would make for comparison. Although still in an experimental stage, an empirical investigation of labor leaders has promise of serving several purposes. Focusing attention on the outlook of these men appears to be an efficient way to find new trends and ebbing influences. The technique offers a manageable way to make international comparisons of the labor movements and industrial relations of different countries. Leaders can be observed in societies at different phases of development. How do the leaders of different countries conceive their role? What do they feel their obligations to be? Do they have similar traits? Are their value standards an expression of differences in the expectations of the rank and file? Faced with similar circumstances, do they behave in the same manner? Cultural differences presumably have a different impact on the objectives, methods, and values of labor leaders. Do the latter tend to become more homogeneous as economies reach similar levels of economic development? Do countries whose workers have reached similar high status-levels experience similar crises in labor organization? What factors account for ideological differences? What happens to idealistic objectives after workers achieve comfortable levels of well-being? What makes for differences in labor education and participation of the rank and file? Are there any purely voluntary associations among labor movements? Lastly, how do the labor leaders of one country perceive those of another?

The method shows promise of being capable of marshalling on a comparative basis the forces which give labor movements their special flavor. It affords an opportunity to study, on the basis of the differences among countries, the problem of the ability of labor leaders to integrate their organizations with the changing demands of labor. The study of the labor problem is thus developed out of the social climate in which it is found and viewed through the eyes and words of men seeking to control forces in the interest of those they represent.

To a significant extent, labor leaders make labor movements. An interpretation of a labor movement is a systematic explanation of the influences behind the behavior of the people in trade union organizations. These forces are shaped in part by people outside of labor unions —employers, the industrial relations public, unorganized workers. What the unorganized do, or fail to do, is an important facet of labor movement interpretations. Observing the behavior of labor leaders is an efficient and productive way to ferret out the impulses behind a labor movement. Their acts reflect prevailing economic forces, the pattern of industrial relations in their society, and the successes and failures of both the organization and the working class generally.

A study of labor leadership raises numerous questions and brings into focus many variables. What constitutes labor leadership in the first place, and how does its structuring come about? Who are the effective labor leaders in a particular society? In what manner does the style of labor leaders change with the growth of an organization? To what extent do social, economic, and power factors in the environment affect labor leadership? How do the attitudes of the community, and the existence of other power blocs with status, affect labor leadership? To what other organizations do workers belong, and what is their estimate of the relative importance of their various associations? Finally, how do labor leaders differ from employers in their society?

In this study, labor leadership is viewed as behavior rather than as a static quality. It consists of what the labor leader does and says. The behavior of labor leaders becomes meaningful when compared with that of others in their organizations and with that of the leaders of other groups with whom they have voluntary or mandatory associations. This performance is a measure of the value standards of persons applying solutions to problems which arise from their organizational environment. The effectiveness of these solutions is an indicator of the use of the emotions and intellect of both their followers and themselves. In a sense, labor leaders are a measure of the social and economic conditions of the rank and file and the spectrum of forces in their society, which they seek to control in order to find solutions and accommodations. They have to be keen analysts of their followers, their environment, and themselves—competent labor leaders are generally good executives, though the opposite is not necessarily true. In sum, the differences in the behavior of labor leaders are related to their own values and to the demands of their particular environments.

Evaluating this performance, however, can be a will-o'-the-wisp. The value standards by which these men make choices vary. They affect the shifting push and pull between short-term and long-term objectives. A possible criterion of evaluation is the relative talent labor leaders, given the social and economic environment confronting them, show in mustering a maximum of influence. This power, however, may accrue at times merely by a quirk of history, which occasionally is kinder to leaders of mediocre capacities than to those of exceptional talents. Another possible benchmark is the ability of labor leaders to carry through decisions with the maximum use of accrued influence. These factors can be viewed as a ratio of achievement over power accrual. Leaders sometimes fritter away the opportunities which accumulated influence provides them. Because of the simultaneous operation of the two variables of value standards and environment, then, it is difficult to construct universal evaluation criteria of the performance of labor leaders.

Differences in environment, of course, tend to produce differences in value standards. The values of different countries even within similar civilization groups are not alike. The eradication of an "undesirable" state in industrial relations, while having a relatively high importance in the United States, may compete for primacy with objectives arising from a dissimilar array of values in Italy or Denmark. Such differences circumscribe the conclusions which may be drawn from differences in wage changes, the scope of collective bargaining, conflict, or coöperation. They are also elusive in measuring, different sets of value criteria eliciting at times similar behavior, and dissimilar behavior resulting often from what appear to be the same value criteria. In Italy, value orientation prescribes the various labor movements in which the leaders and the led find themselves, and the perceptions of the realities confronting them. In Denmark, a greater homogeneity of values sustains a unitary labor movement and a highly integrated labor-leader–employer relationship.

In this investigation, the interviews initially sought differences among labor leaders of both countries within a framework of broad benchmarks, such as values, attitudes, role characteristics, and traits. The terms are employed according to generally accepted usage and are not used as mutually exclusive concepts.[1]

It might be argued that in relying heavily on interview technique one is bound to pick up a collection of clichés. Clichés, however, are in themselves meaningful. It is assumed, in fact, that a pattern of clichés would emerge from responses of different groups in any country. Should this not occur, it would be an indication of weakness in the inquiry, rather than validity. The kind of stereotype a respondent articulates and the factors behind it are meaningful in understanding an industrial relations system. They differ among various groups in a country, and from one nation to the next. They eventually affect the thinking of those who use them and those who hear them. Moreover, the respondent departs in course from these initial constructions, in varying degrees, providing another source of meaningful information.

Unlike other beings, humans by what they say or convey suggest to a remarkable degree the manner in which they will behave in a particular situation. If, therefore, we can systematize this language, we would then obtain a dynamic record of behavior. To be sure, the labor leader is a symbol of a political entity. He develops the incapacity to avoid introverted responses to situations confronting him. His speech

---

[1] I am indebted to Professor Ross Stagner for a lucid description of these concepts.

is political for the record, and what he conceives of as reality is the circumstances affecting his advancement of position. Accordingly, his responses to queries tend by commission or omission to be a summary of the forces he regards with respect. Nevertheless, he cannot escape at length from his individual and national character, which reveals the rules he uses to pursue goals and indeed to formulate them as well.

It is apparent that a significant cause of labor movement differences is the standards of value which labor officials possess. These values are interrelated with the values of those led in differing degrees, depending upon the nature of the relationship between the two. In the pursuit of objectives, a leader has to integrate values in a manner that constitutes success in the judgment of the workers. The relative weight assigned each set of values asserts itself in differences in leadership. Moreover, the leaders do not have quite the same traits or the same problems as their followers. They are more intelligent, more resourceful, more oriented to the success of the organization, more aware of the problem of how to remain in power. They succeed to differing degrees, according to their ability to keep close to unity the ratio of aspiration to achievement of the rank and file. In trying to reach this goal, their approach is constrained, in the long run, to be pragmatic. Their sets of values are affected by culture, social origins, the characteristics of trade union and industrial relations organizations, and the way the parties in industrial relations perceive the environment.

Values are the motivating forces which form the basis of behavior. "Value" is a dynamic idea. The term as used in this study designates the total relative estimate by labor leaders of persons, ideas, and objects, of what in them is desirable and worth striving for. Values influence methods and objectives. They create variety in outlooks toward the worthwhileness of organizations, pragmatic problem-solving, conflict, idealism, social orientation, religious sentiment, and collective bargaining demands.

Florence Kluckhohn delineates five central types of value orientation which bracket human problems and relationships and uses them to describe the different characteristics of cultures.[2] They are: (1) concepts of good and evil; (2) differences in man's relationship to his environment, ranging from subjugation to mastery; (3) differences in

[2] Florence Kluckhohn, "Dominant and Variant Value Orientations," in Clyde Kluckhohn, Henry A. Murray, and David M. Schneider (eds.), *Personality in Nature, Society, and Culture*, pp. 342–57

the importance attached to time in terms of the past, present, and future; (4) differences in the "being" and "doing" orientation of the individual, the latter, for example, being characteristic of societies which demand quick action and accomplishments; (5) the relationship of men to other men, ranging from individualism to groupism and the differences in their extent and character. These broad headings proved useful in developing specific benchmarks for determining differences among labor leaders. They suggested particular details, such as how labor officials spend their time and money, what they feel is important and unimportant, what their aspirations and ideals are, and what their views of current issues are.

Unlike "value," "attitude" is a static descriptive concept, consisting of a mental set which predisposes a labor leader to react in a predictable direction, but not with an invariable response, toward such persons and objects as employers, workers, government, and the Church. The term is also used in the abstract, to designate such attitudes as conservatism and radicalism. The distinction between values and attitudes of labor leaders is not a sharp one. Value preferences create and modify attitudes, the latter becoming efficient mechanisms in expressing the former. Whether a preference expressed by a labor leader is an attitude or a value is not crucial. The importance of these concepts is that they provide an effective instrument for the categorization and analysis of data.

By "role" is intended the organized behavior of the labor leader in the process of interacting with others with whom he comes in contact by virtue of his status and position of leadership. Demeanor and the adornments of office are a part of role. Role embraces the duties, limits, opportunities, and pressures of his job. The quality of this role is associated with the degree of status of his position and what others expect of him. Accumulated life-experience measured by such factors as religion, education, occupational origins of the family and relative differences in the extent of intergeneration upward movement, training in childhood and adulthood, father-to-son interpretation of events, the cultural value system of the community, all have an effect on role. What the labor official expects of the rank and file and what role the rank and file expects him to assume are important determinants of labor leader behavior.

Consequently, the discharge of role is a continuing summation of past experience of labor leaders. It is a convenient reference point in

developing associations between performance and the influences behind it. Regardless of country, the labor leader is constrained to
assume a role consistent with the expectations and influences of others
with whom he interacts. Further, value standards and role are not
mutually exclusive concepts, both having an effect on each other
through mutual causality.

"Trait" is another static concept, describing relatively lasting characteristics of labor leaders, directed toward no specific object. The term
includes, for example, extraversion, expression, optimism, and expansiveness. Differences in the traits of labor leaders were least productive
of meaningful interpretations of labor leadership. Traits such as extraversion and expression are abstractions difficult to separate in meaning;
they cover a variety of different sources of influence, and they have
little interpretive value. These traits are associated with such factors
as differences in education, occupations, and the attitudes of the rank
and file toward the leaders. In Italy, for example, the differences in
the extent of formal education of labor leaders had an effect on what
are usually called traits. In turn, differences in education by geography
and federation became evident. It became apparent in the investigations that these traits are not as meaningful in themselves as are the
forces and associations behind them.

A second factor limiting the usefulness of traits was that within similar levels of leadership traits are rather similar. In many ways, labor
leader traits are similar to those of employers, but generally not so
highly developed, inasmuch as a characteristic such as individualism
becomes intolerable when possessed in equal degree by the other party
at the collective bargaining table. Therefore, though traits have an
effect on the tone of industrial relations because of the way they contribute to clashes between adversaries, they are not an important source
of differentiation either among labor officials or between them and
employers. A real difference, however, is found between the labor
leaders as a group and their rank and file. Within their own union and
geographical location, leaders are more expressive, more resourceful,
and more aggressive than the average member of the group they
represent. They rate higher in the facility and speed with which they
grasp the intent of an interview question and in answering in systematic
fashion. In general, the higher the level of leadership, the greater is
this ability of expression. Trade union officials as a group evince this
characteristic to a somewhat greater degree than employers as a group.

(Perhaps in part this is a measure of candor. The former are more frank, even in stating their weaknesses. Only a small minority exercised the opportunity to remain anonymous in the written questionnaire. Indeed, some of the Italians attached calling cards of substantial proportions, on which they had written their signatures with a flourish.) Within the same level of leadership, use of conventional trait factors did not produce meaningful distinctions.

This investigation is in the experimental stage and limited in scope. The initial work, it is felt, should comprise an account of experience and a rudimentary tabulation of the more interesting portions of the data that the method is capable of amassing. Treatment of the data is based on the commitment not to associate responses with particular individuals unless such expressions can be considered a matter of public record. The study is more descriptive than quantitative, although it is felt that in subsequent investigations the concentration should be on the latter approach. In this situation, where so little is actually known about labor leaders abroad and where the sample size is small, it would be pretentious to indulge in involved statistical exercises or to create categories which would not preserve individual reactions as much as possible.

As the unit of comparison is extended to other countries, the greater amount of data will be treated to comprehensive and extensive statistical manipulation, including cross-tabulations and comparisons of labor leader profiles. With masses of information large enough, it is possible that digital computer technology could be effectively employed to obtain similarities, differences, and associations of finer quality on a quantitative basis. The critical characteristics of labor leadership could then be surmised from a systematic analysis of environmental influences. Accordingly, the present work is considered a pilot project in an area to a large extent still unexplored.

Additional refinement must be sought by continual application of the method to an increasing range of countries. With the coöperation of research centers abroad, a substantial amount of additional data has to be accumulated and treated statistically. The International Industrial Relations Center is building a repository of taped interviews of labor leaders of different countries, based on similar schedules, which are a fruitful source of raw material for further study. Periodic restudies have to be made in particular countries in order to discern what changes, if any, develop in types of labor leaders and environments. Work must also be done toward the goal of determining to what extent the value system is an independent or dependent variable.

This study makes no claim to rigid scientific conditions of control. The people on whom such an investigation must rely cannot be molded to a statistically computed random sampling. Nor can interviews be conducted under precisely similar conditions. If the study lacks aggregate economic data, no minimizing of the economic influences which exert pressure on labor leadership is intended. The differences in the labor and product markets of Italy and Denmark can be found in other publications. The absence of such data here is due to the fact that this analysis is made from another point of view. Economic influences are indirectly expressed through the presentation of the behavior and outlook of the labor leader. Labor leaders act within different types of economic forms, which affect what they do, and how and what they think. Although a legitimate part of the explanation of the factors shaping labor behavior, these forces too often are made an independent and universal variable in labor movement interpretations. Like Soviet theoreticians who make the sweep of economic history the Divinity, American labor economists have shown a similar attraction to the view that inexorable economic development is the decisive factor in social phenomena.

By undertaking to study labor leadership in its broadest sense, I have tried to avoid the criticisms brought against comparative labor studies that they do not make real comparisons possible and that they do not adequately develop associations between national character and social processes. In this investigation the one is sought within the framework of the other. It is my hope that this work will not only serve as a supplement to the results obtained by traditional analyses of the labor movements of different countries, but that it will also stimulate further efforts toward the refinements needed for a systematic analysis of labor leader behavior.

The Setting in Italy

Five labor movements and ten political parties in an economic setting ranging from moribund vestiges of feudalism to modern industrial corporations make Italy an excellent country for a study of labor leadership.

Three organizations in that country are considered to be legitimate labor movements: the "Catholics," the Confederazione Italiana Sindacati Lavoratori (CISL); the "Social-Communists," the Confederazione Generale Italiana del Lavoro (CGIL); and the "Social Democrats," the Unione Italiana del Lavoro (UIL). A fourth organization, a lay association of the Catholic Church, the Christian Associations of Italian Workers (ACLI), claims to be the sole labor movement of Italy. Its leaders are lawyers, teachers, and members of the petty bourgeoisie. They draw a distinction between trade unionists and themselves by ascribing to the former only the function of collective bargaining, reserving for themselves the political, social, and moral orientation of workers. These claims cause no small consternation to some of the labor leaders in the CISL. A fifth, the Italian Confederation of National Trade Unions (CISNAL), is organized by former Fascist officials with a corporate philosophy of trade unionism, and is not accepted as a bona fide labor movement by the three trade union organizations.[1] The members of these organizations belong to those political parties whose ideological lines best fit their perceptions and aspirations. In

[1] A sixth group, the Italian Free Workers, a splinter organization created in 1958 from the CISL of the Fiat Company, is regarded by the three major federations as company unionism.

general, the situation in Italy is more favorable for the creation of new labor movements and political parties than for the consolidation of existing ones.

One cannot discuss Italian economic organizations without considering their political counterparts. Politics and economics are intimately intertwined. The array of political forces is along inflexible economic lines. Italians use the term *politica* when they speak of either policy or politics, and they refer to economics as *economia politica*. In this fusion of economics and politics, the attitude of the extreme left and the extreme right is that government represents a means of exploiting economic interests on behalf of those who possess the power to control it.

It is unrealistic to ignore the fact that the workers of Italy have little faith in Western democracy. To understand the considerable Communist following in Italian politics and labor, it is essential to keep in mind certain political realities. One is the stalemate in making deeply felt social changes that arises from the existence of intransigent political parties more numerous than the colors of the spectrum.

Italy has eight major political parties, each with strong internal pressures to split and regenerate into more organizations. From left to right are the Communists, Socialists, Social Democrats, Republicans, Christian Democrats, Liberals, Neo-Fascists, and Monarchists.[2] The Christian Democrats are the largest party, with 42 per cent of the total vote cast. A heterogeneous economic group who call themselves "Inter-Classists," they are kept together principally by a common concern to stalemate Italian Communist power. They have been governing since the end of the Second World War, holding on to their power precariously, with the aid of parties on both their right and their left. The Republicans, the Liberals, and the Social Democrats, with approximately 1, 3, and 5 per cent respectively of the votes cast in national elections, have from time to time supported the Christian Democrats. The Republicans are a group whose antecedents were important figures during the days of Italian unification in the middle of the nineteenth century. Their modest strength lies not so much in the few deputies they manage to elect as in the respected personalities within the

---

[2] Two splinter parties, the Radicals and the National Monarchists, would raise the figure to ten. The former comprised the left wing of the Liberals, and the latter pulled out of the popular Monarchist party. There are others, but these ten are those which can be considered as having some national importance.

party. The Liberals, economic conservatives dominated by employer groups, are seeking to broaden the base of the party by attracting the clerical worker class. The Social Democrat party is influenced by liberal intellectuals and petit bourgeois elements who left the Socialist party because of its alliance with the Communists. With 23 per cent of the electorate, the Communists have the second largest party in Italy. They have an importance greater than their relative numbers. Together with the Socialists, they are the political spokesmen of a huge number of Italian industrial and agricultural workers. Many workers who do not vote for the extreme left cast ballots for the Neo-Fascists or the Monarchists, both of whom are still supported by a total of 10 per cent of the electorate.[3] Neither of these parties has any political program, but both manage to attract adherents, especially in the South, by the cult of personality and by the fascination of pomp and ceremony to the hungry and illiterate.

The relative political alignment of Italy varies also by geographical area. The Communists are strongest in the north central regions of Emilia-Romagna and Tuscany. Several factors account for their strength in this comparatively well-to-do area. The people are anticlerical, a tradition which has its origins in the existence of a Church government before the unification of Italy a hundred years ago. The stability of the combat line in this region during World War II gave the Communists precious time to organize workers. A third factor is the existence of a large body of relatively prosperous agricultural labor. It appears to be a phenomenon in economic development that the initial reaction of an exploited peasant class raised above the level of subsistence and illiteracy is a political shift to the left. Elsewhere in Italy, the Communists maintain their national voting average in the industrial North, composed of the triangle formed by Turin, Milan, and Genoa. They have similar relative strength in southern Italy, although the first stages of economic improvement for the people in that primitive agricultural society may further increase Communist strength.

The other parties show corresponding and contrasting regional dif-

---

[3] The 1958 general elections produced no significant change in the vote for the Communists, 15 and 42 per cent for the Socialists and Christian Democrats respectively, and a decline of the right wing to 10 per cent. Thus the over-all strength of the left actually increased. In a demonstration of the persisting strength of the Communists, despite the rise in per capita national income, the party polled 24.5 per cent of the total vote in the 1960 municipal and provincial elections, or an increase of 1.5 per cent over the previous election.

ferences. Generally, Socialist strength runs parallel to that of the Communists. The Christian Democrats do best in the northeast, in some regions of which they have achieved an absolute majority. The Monarchists are most effective in the economically depressed areas of southern Italy, Sardinia, and Sicily. The Neo-Fascists have their greatest concentration in Rome, Trieste, and Sicily.

Each of the four trade unions has the preponderant part of its leadership and its rank and file within one of the major political parties in Italy. The largest, the CGIL, is dominated by the Communists, with members of the Socialist party holding a few top posts. Next in size comes the CISL, with many of its top positions held by deputies of the Christian Democratic party. The minority group in the CISL is composed of Social Democrats, who hold a few leadership positions. The UIL, the smallest of the three, is the trade union arm of the Social Democrats and the Republicans. The fourth organization, the CISNAL, is the home of Neo-Fascists, principally in Rome, who yearn for the good old days, but who do not seem to be making any growth.

Americans might conceive of this fusion of political and trade union leadership if they were to visualize the American Federation of Labor and Congress of Industrial Organizations as separate labor movements, with members of the House of Representatives as their leaders. On either side of these federations would be two other labor union organizations. The one on the left, the largest, would be in the hands of the Communist and left-wing Socialist members of the House. The other, on the far right, would be administered by Fascists, also congressmen. In such a way, political and trade union leaders of labor in Italy are trying to discharge simultaneously two functions, one as politicians sensitive to the political consequences of their acts, the other as trade union leaders presumably ready to bargain collectively with employers in the interest of a particular group of workers.

Such, in brief, is the political and economic situation in Italy. Here politics is a complex game of strategy. If in the United States, where in the main two political groupings compete, one faction has to anticipate the reaction of the other, in Italy the moves of one party will be responded to by six others. The political parties of the governing bloc must bargain among themselves in order to reach a common ground on a particular issue. Outside the bloc, there exists the threat that the move of one party may cause a split in the coalition in power and the collapse of the government. The break in the formal Socialist-

Communist alliance in 1957 is a case in point. The move provoked the withdrawal of the Republicans from the coalition government and brought about a vote of confidence in the Chamber of Deputies. The right combined with the left, and the government was maintained in power by the margin of two votes.

Despite the desanctification of Stalin and the Hungarian insurrection, in the 1958 national elections the Social-Communists increased their political strength. The lack of a decline in the extreme left is to be explained by the frustration of a working class unable to obtain a labor movement powerful enough to exert an effective influence in achieving structural changes in such fields as employment, agriculture, education, administrative government, and collective bargaining. Any radical reform in these sectors is unlikely in Italy without a coalition of Socialists, Social Democrats, and Christian Democrats. To a considerable degree, the Italian government could reduce the political divisions among the working classes by its own actions if it chose to do so, and could bring about the possibility of a united labor movement. Without a break in the stalemate of reform, the Social-Communists are likely to maintain their political strength.

To imagine the sharp ideological divisions among Italians, suppose that practically all Americans were born into the same Protestant church and that an orthodox wing had organized a political party. The party professed that its policies were the implementation of the Christian principles of the one Church. One large bloc of the working class belonged to this party. A second group, however, voted for the Communists or the left-wing Socialists. Although they had been baptized in the Church, they somehow grew up to become Marxists. In the same family, in fact, one might find a minister whose brother is the head of the local Communist party. In addition, a smaller third group was detaching itself from both, professing to be both anti-Communist and anticlerical. Still another nostalgic group felt that the others were not behaving at all like great Americans and harbored the hope of imposing a dictatorship on all of them some day.

Italy, then, is a country of complexities and paradoxes. The political left is actually in the majority if the Communists, Socialists, Social Democrats, and Republicans are combined with the left of the Christian Democrat party. The government, however, is an expression of the conservative middle class, the large employers, and the Catholic hierarchy. The working classes are humanistic and poor, and their labor movement young and weak.

The particular value outlook which Italy presents gives its several labor movements both uniqueness and similarity. Italians value self-expression highly. They show a facility in developing ideas and feelings whose expression in conflict is constantly stimulating to them. They have a passion for discussion and theorization from a priori premises to particular situations. They tend to apply to social and economic situations an orthodox body of generalizations which color their perceptions of events and become a motivating force in their politics. Contending groups are inclined to apply a different set of principles and facts to the process of accommodating differences. The solutions offered by adversaries are accepted less on what merit they contain than on what school of thought is offering the proposals. This stress on initial premises was demonstrated amusingly by an observer at a debate on a political problem. As each individual rose and asked for *la parola,* the observer would note on a sheet of paper the ideological premises of the speaker and the conclusions he would draw. No meeting of minds occurred that evening, nor was anyone in the sophisticated audience expecting it.

One aspect of this purist thinking is its impatience with the technical aspects of problem-solving. A respondent who stated that socialism was the solution to what he described as the "mess" in Italy was asked why he felt that way. He was not concerned with the particulars of the *pasticcio,* he stated, because that was a technical matter of no importance to him, and neither were the special details of the new socialist state, since such technical aspects tended to obscure the basic political question. When Aneurin Bevan of the British Labour party, on a visit to Italy during the course of the field investigation, suggested that the idea of Socialist unity was an abstraction of no significance, he shocked the purists in the ranks of the Socialist party.

Into the humanistic Italian character fascism tried to transfuse a new sense of group resoluteness and determination. Mussolini depicted these qualities by the strut and tight jaw. The individualism of the Italians made the transfusion unsuccessful. To outward appearances, what is left of the experiment is the stern marble buildings of Fascist architecture, whose harsh vertical lines suggest the heroic qualities

Mussolini wanted the people to acquire. The interlude has left its traces also in a complex mass of labor legislation and in the influence of some individuals who managed to maintain their positions of power after the fall of fascism. At the end of the Second World War, the decision of the Allies not to allow a purge of leadership left control in the hands of a group that had dominated Italy during fascism. Consequently, the force of conservatism was perpetuated in government, finance, industry, and education, and its effects will be felt for many decades to come.

The new labor movement in Italy after the fall of fascism arose from the organization work of different political parties, with the help of the Allied occupation authorities. The Communists, the Socialists, and the Christian Democrats designated individuals in their town offices to organize workers in the communities into trade unions. For a while, these revolutionary forces managed to keep together within the same labor federation. They were reacting, not uniquely against employers and specific problems, but against the structure of their society. The coalition, however, was short lived. The differences between them became more intolerable than the consequences of a split in the labor movement. There ensued a series of struggles among three political camps to capture the loyalty of workers. The dominant tactic was *agitazioni,* a pressure tactic of group demonstration, whose ingredients are noise, movement, and the expression of emotion, and which uses fear as an instrument of persuasion. In this way the labor movement grew and split three ways after the fall of fascism. And, after a decade of organization, the major problem of trade-union–conscious labor leaders became how to escape the dominance of the political parties which gave them birth.

The development of Italy has been inhibited in part at least by the persistence of a society based on privilege and social immobility. The workers at the bottom, no matter how competent, find it difficult to rise toward the top. Those at the summit, no matter how incapable, cannot be dislodged. Italian history placed power in the hands of a ruling class enjoying an economic and political monopoly, men who did not reflect the aspirations and sentiments of the people they were supposed to represent. They represented no one but themselves. Two societies existed in fact. There were those who wielded power, who, in the eyes of the people, were foreigners from some other city or country and who, by a quirk of circumstances, had acquired the power to dominate and exploit them. Then there were people at the disposal of the elite, living by the sufferance and charitableness of their masters. Law and government for them were not an expression of the will of the governed, but symbols of oppression and exploitation.

Even today, the culture of Italy cannot readily be described in generalizations to be applied uniformly to all parts of the country. Italian culture is an amalgam of centuries of different civilizations, which have had dissimilar impacts on the various regions and social groups of the country. At the risk of oversimplification, a cultural line can be drawn across the girth of Italy, just north of Rome, to differentiate the industrial culture of the North from the rural culture of the South. The farther one moves from this line in one direction or the other, the more does the culture become industrial or rural. At either extreme are Milan, epitome of Italian industrialization, and Calabria, which, through heavy investment programs, has been awakening after a thousand years of dormancy. The Italians draw this line themselves, each group having a critical stereotype of the other.

To select a town in Italy as a model for the cultural and social setting of a region is difficult. The potential of Italy, when she successfully combines individualism with aggressive modernity, is epitomized by the city of Milan. Unlike any other place in Italy, with the possible exception of the automobile city of Turin, one senses a feeling of people going places. The city is one of the most attractive in western Europe, in spite of the advertising signs placed in close formation on either side of the highway, making it resemble the entrance to a carnival. In Milan are found some of the best of Italy's industrial minds. The city is over a thousand years old, but its people are more inclined to replace the rubble of ancient civilizations with aluminum skyscrapers than to make an outdoor museum of their city. The Milanese claim that whatever they build is the finest, from their magnificent specimen of Italian Gothic architecture, the cathedral in the main square, to the contemporary commercial buildings which are rising around it.

Milan, however, is not a typical Italian city. It has become the melting pot of Italy, a place of new expectations for migrating workers who settle there clandestinely, trying to escape the wretched existence of the agricultural South. They and the Milanese represent different worlds, whose men find it difficult to communicate with each other. The immigrants can be seen every day in the modern railroad station, seated on their luggage, the heirloom of many generations, absorbing a little of this modern world before going down the granite steps and outside into the city. The atmosphere in which they make the transition from being rural workers to becoming members of the labor force of a modern industrial community is a mixture of sympathetic understanding and hostility. The press has been urging the Milanese to organize a program of aid, including housing, medical care, and counseling, to help the migrants. Some of the Milanese, however, are concerned that the immigrants will bring with them their crime patterns; the rural motives of honor and *omertà*, they feel, are only an excuse for murder and barbarism.

On the train to Milan, a Milanese asked a migrant worker, a Sicilian preparing to have a lunch of bread and cheese, whether he had brought his stiletto with him. The young man, an illiterate incapable of quick repartee, remained silent. He spread an immaculately white linen cloth on his lap, cut several pieces of bread and, offering some to the Milanese, said, *"Vuol favorire?"*

The migrant workers are faced with the problem of seeking employment opportunities despite the existence of laws and administrative regulations which limit the occupational and geographic movement of workers. They sell their possessions and come as pioneers. Their first move into the industrial center is to stay with friends and avoid the public authorities. They obtain jobs illegally, since they are not on the rolls of the Department of Labor. The incentive to the employer who hires them is freedom from the payment of social security taxes. Eventually the status of the immigrant is legalized. The employer places him on the payroll as a skilled worker and intercedes for him at the local office of the Department of Labor, stating that he would like to hire a skilled worker of demonstrated ability and asking the department to issue a labor book in his behalf. The government obliges, and thereupon the worker registers with the commune as a legal resident. In this way, it is possible to break the cycle of the commune's not wanting to register him because of his illegal migration and the Department of Labor's not wanting to place him on the job rolls because of his not being a resident of the area.

Outside the heavily industrialized North, towns like Parmi and Nora are typical. Neither of these places is to be found on a map of Italy. Their names are fictitious, the first town being representative of a community in central Italy and the other of one in southern Italy or Sicily.

Parmi is a predominantly agricultural community of seventy-five thousand people, and the seat of the provincial government. Most of its people live in apartment houses. No ring of suburbs surrounds it, unlike the cities in Scandinavia. Where the town stops at the medieval gates, the agricultural land begins. The town, however, has been expanding by extending the line of apartment houses outward into the countryside beyond the walls. The surrounding province consists mostly of hills and mountains devoted to agriculture, ranging from profitable farming on the gentle slopes to a subsistence-level existence in the mountains, now being abandoned by peasants going to seek industrial employment in the cities of the North. The agricultural class, the largest group, is composed of *braccianti* (day laborers), *mezzadri* (sharecroppers), small holders, and large proprietors. Of the latter, there are those who manage their own property and those who rarely see their farms, spending most of their time in the large cities of the North. A majority of the industrial workers are employed either in a metal-fabrication plant or a slightly smaller textile mill, and in several family-owned plants. There are other job opportunities in retail services, commerce, administration, and the artisan crafts. In Parmi, accordingly, the whole gamut of economic and social classes lives together, unlike cities where suburban dispersion causes gaps in the social pyramid and loss of vitality.

The prominent citizens of the community have varying degrees of relationships with each other. Heading the government group is the provincial governor, the *prefetto,* representing the Italian government, who is appointed by the Internal Ministry in Rome. Then there is the *questore,* the head of the police, who is also selected by the Internal Ministry. With him the leader of the local CGIL has an intimate, involuntary familiarity because of regular encounters during strike activity in the community. The *questore* has in his office an extended dossier of those in the community who attract his professional interest: criminals, prostitutes, homosexuals, left-wing political activists, and labor leaders. The *proveditore agli studi,* in charge of the school system, is appointed by the Minister of Public Instruction in Rome. The *preside* of the province is elected indirectly by the people, who vote actually for the provincial councillors. This group in turn selects the *giunta,* which appoints the *preside.* The city administration is in the hands of the Communist party.

In an unobtrusive manner, the bishop of Parmi exercises considerable influence in the community. His letter of recommendation is an important requisite for job placement, and his word has weight in Rome when government contracts are being considered. Many local problems come to his attention for settlement. A group of recent college graduates publishing a political commentary has been called White Communists by the employers' association, and the bishop may have to publish an edict against the reading of their publication. Or there is the protest of the labor leader against an employer who introduced the reciting of the rosary in his plant in order to speed up the tempo of work of the women.[4]

The industrial elite of Parmi is composed of the top executives of the industrial plants and the respective heads of the industrial and agricultural employer associations. Among the former are the general directors of the two big firms and the division heads for sales, engineering, factory management, and personnel. The president of the agricultural employer association is a former general of World War I, who emphasizes his strong views on *mezzadria* by waving a black cane in the air as though leading a charge. He has been feuding with the CISL because of articles published by that organization, dealing with the condition of agricultural workers in the province, and has threatened to have labor relationships only with the CGIL. Union leaders are all agitators, he thinks, who ignore the primary objective of serving the fatherland. The top executives of the industrial plants are the highest paid in the community. Their salaries are a closely guarded secret, but as executives of medium-sized plants, they probably draw an annual salary fifteen times that of the average worker. All but one of the employers belong to the various employer associations; the exception is considered an iconoclast for having signed a collective bargaining agreement with the young leader of the CISL.

Unemployment runs to 10 per cent of the population in the city of Parmi. The sharp shifts in production of the few industrial firms in the area have the effect of creating an industrial labor force from the agricultural classes and keeping it idle for a good part of the year. Added to this cycle of production is the impact of technological change, or what the Italians refer to as *ridimensionamento*. The unemployed are immediately noticeable among the men idling on the piazza, talking

---

[4] The complaint from another plant was that the employees were required to recite a prayer before beginning the shift, including a few good words for the employer.

quietly and stopping occasionally to follow the movement of attractive women crossing the square alone. The low labor skills which these men once had have been lost through long idleness, adding thereby to the numbers of the unskilled who cause the fundamental problem of unemployment in Italy. Among the unemployed are many young men, symbols of wasted talent.

On the basis of the foreign rate of exchange, the average Parmi worker makes a fourth of the wages of the average American industrial worker. He buys consumer goods at prices comparable to those in the United States. He spends thirty-two cents for a popular brand of cigarettes, sixty-five cents for a pound of butter, and a dollar and fifty cents for a pound of coffee. Dry cleaning his suit for the important holidays costs him a dollar and sixty cents, and the smallest size of refrigerator, almost two hundred dollars. If he is a skilled worker at the metal plant or a bus driver, his basic monthly salary is $115. As a bartender, clerk, or semiskilled worker, his monthly base pay is $85; as a manual laborer, $75. He spends more than half his income on food. Consequently, he relies heavily on supplements to his wage, such as family allowances, social insurance, the Christmas bonus of one month's pay, paid holidays (of which there are seventeen), merit increases if his employer deems his conduct meritorious, low-cost housing if he can find it, and the wages of other members of the family if they have jobs.

For his newspaper reading, he can choose among papers published daily by the political parties, with local supplements. The press presents for him a critique of events, rather than objective reporting on what has transpired. Often a news article begins with condemnation or praise of a particular occurrence before delving into a report of it. The article shows the reader how one political group has merit in its position and how the other is behaving in a reprehensible manner. One of the newspapers, for example, in an article deplored the decision of a group of members of Parliament not to support their party on an issue. The matter involved Christian Democrats who had to decide whether to support the conservative policy of their party on a proposed law fixing the rights of sharecroppers or to take a position more consistent with that of their trade union members. The newspaper argued that they were elected as members of an interclass party and that, should they push a trade union program, they would become a class party no different from the Socialists. The article rejected the pursuit of self-interest as a priori inconsistent with the teaching of the Catholic Church. In general, most of the trade union and labor news is found in the Communist and Socialist newspapers, a situation roughly equivalent to relying on the American *Daily Worker* for labor coverage.

In Parmi, the outstanding annual event for organized labor is the May Day rally. At a recent typical celebration, the biggest display was made by the CGIL. Their parade came into the piazza promptly at the announced time, led by some one hundred men on motorcycles. Noise was the most important ingredient of the demonstration, and the roar of the motorcycles made a good beginning. Then came the different units of the various labor unions and the sections of the Communist party. They passed by the church, rounded the square, and took their place in front of the speakers' rostrum. The provincial labor leader shouted into the microphone the arrival of each new group as it passed the long line of bored-looking motorized police, the *celere*, at the far end of the piazza. He was like a cheerleader at a football game, announcing the virtues of each group marching toward the rostrum, and then calling out *Viva!* Each time, the crowd responded with more *vivas* and applause. Many in the crowd were *contadini* from the surrounding hills, enjoying immensely the cries for liberty, peace, and democracy. They nodded in assent to the remarks on the monopolists and American imperialists.

DiVittorio, the Communist head of the CGIL, was the feature attraction. His appearance on the rostrum was timed perfectly. As the last unit turned into the square, the provincial labor leader announced his arrival. DiVittorio held his audience spellbound. He ridiculed the cautiousness of the CISL and criticized the ACLI for celebrating May Day as the feast of Saint Joseph the artisan, stating that the day belongs to the workers. He stirred the crowd deeply.—"Capital cannot do without Labor but Labor can do without Capital."—The audience laughed at his gibes and cheered at the great expectations he stimulated in the workers. They hung on to his expressions. After he had finished, the crowd dispersed, feeling good.

Of the local labor leaders in Parmi, the most popular is Sarti, the young general secretary of the CISL in the town. To the consternation of the bishop, he has managed to attract a number of Communists into his organization. The Communists have joined because they feel he runs a better trade union organization. Some of them have sent Sarti their membership cards in the party as a token that they have resigned. Because of the following he has acquired among the workers, he was approached by a high official of the federation to run for the Chamber of Deputies on the lists of the Christian Democrat party. He refused, but it was no easy decision to make. The son of a *contadino,* he could treble his income and gain prestige if he ran successfully.

Sarti believes in making decisions with the maximum participation of his membership. He is trying to develop collective bargaining at the company level, and at a meeting of *attivisti* from different parts of the province he discussed tactics on how to achieve this goal. The group decided to talk with employers at every opportunity and to use any concession, no matter how modest, as a means of obtaining more from other employers. They decided not to use any priests in the May Day celebration, because the workers are bored with anti-Communist sermons. They decided also to resist any pressure to make promises to the *mezzadri* tilling marginal land, because of the bad repercussions from unfulfilled expectations.

The institution of *mezzadria* in Italy is many centuries old. There are some one million *mezzadro* families, principally in the region around Parmi. During the Fascist era, a system of national contracts was devised, fixing the relationship between the owner of the land and the *mezzadro* family. After the end of the Second World War, these agreements were frozen temporarily, with the effect that the owner of the land could not terminate the agreement unless the agricultural worker consented to terminate it or to quit the land. Although the government has tried since 1949 to pass a law to break the impasse, it has not yet been successful. One government-sponsored bill contained a provision under which, during the term of an agreement, the *mezzadro* could be told to leave the land only for "proper cause," the proposal stipulating what constituted proper cause for discharge. The Communists made an issue of this by suggesting that discharge for proper cause be granted indefinitely, and that the right be granted to the entire peasant class. The bitter political issue has been resolved through the attempts of the separate labor federations to make changes in the agreements with the employer associations.

The *mezzadri* say that the ideal size of a patriarchal family should be seven persons for every fourteen hectares of flat land. Under ancient custom, a *mezzadro* "man" is computed on the following basis: an *uomo valido,* a man between the ages of 18 and 65, is given a value of 100; women are worth 60; youths between the ages of 14 and 18 are valued at 50; and the old also at 50. Each unit of 100 tills two and a half hectares of rolling country or three hectares of high hills and mountains. Theoretically, when the family becomes too large in relation to the ground tilled, a branch splits and goes elsewhere in pursuit of new opportunities, the knowledge of which spreads quickly through the countryside.

At a CISL meeting, *mezzadri* from the hills surrounding Parmi described their condition of life. *Mezzadri* families average seventeen people, who have to live on 50 per cent of the produce of the land. The average farm is about seventeen hectares in size. These *mezzadri* are not opposed to mechanization, but they believe that the machines should be held in coöperatives, with the capital for them furnished by the government. In their words:

There are too many people trying to live on the land. We sell our veal at 400 lire a kilo and see it sold again in the city for 1400. It is not true that we resent the people living in the city; but we want some of the social security benefits they enjoy. Our diet consists of vegetables, soup and beans. We eat meat about once a week, the chickens and rabbits which we ourselves raise. Electricity costs 60 lire per kilowatt and it is beyond our reach. Very few of our children go beyond the fifth grade.

One *contadino* said that he had given up smoking two cigarettes a day in order to save five dollars per year. He works from twelve to fifteen hours daily, and the person who owns the land, although supposed to be his colleague, is actually his master. He had heard about the debate in Parliament on the law making it difficult for the proprietor to force his *contadino* from the land. He was not impressed with the legal niceties of the question of the rights of private property. The law should give the *contadino* something more; that is what he wants, something more.

The marginal farmsteads are inaccessible by road. One of them which the interviewer visited was a heap of stone three hundred years old, with holes in the floor, through which could be seen the cattle housed in the floor below. The *mezzadro* spoke about his condition with an embarrassed smile. He was deep in debt and did not feel it possible any longer to wipe the slate clean. The conversation passed to the feast of the patron saint, to be held the following day. The town rises up a precipitous rocky mountain, at the top of which is a sanctuary. At the religious festival, the men race up the mountain, carrying a fifteen-foot image of their saint. The *mezzadro* was going to participate. The rise was steep and had to be done in laps. Par for the course was fifteen minutes. The *mezzadro* told about amusing incidents in prior races, and the note of mild bitterness in the beginning of the conversation disappeared.

Not too far away is a model farm operated by a large Italian holding company. The farm consists of two thousand hectares, in forest, fruit, tobacco, vegetables, and wine-grape production. The difference in the faces of the *mezzadri* here is remarkable. Their average family income in two thousand dollars per year for twelve people, including a grandfather, a brother of the head of family, and his children. Their home was painted in bright colors, and the cattle were housed in separate, spotlessly white buildings. The grandfather took the investigator to see a feature of the *fattoria*, a flushing toilet. Their land produces forty quintals of wheat per hectare compared to the eighteen quintals of the marginal land. What makes for the difference, they were asked, people or capital? Their answer was land, machines, fertilizer, and irrigation.

In the less productive areas of the province, sharecroppers and proprietors entertain a mutual feeling that the other obtains the better deal in sharecropping. Neither party feels the other is an associate. The relationship is one of debtor and creditor. To make ends meet, the *mezzadro* borrows continually from the proprietor. At the end of the year when an accounting is made, the *mezzadro* always owes money, despite the lean twelve months he has experienced. The alternative to inexorably mounting debt is to quit the land and flee to the city.

The farther south one travels, the deeper the poverty becomes. There are only some four hundred miles between Rome and the southern coast of Italy, but for every hundred miles of traveling, one slips back a century. One comes at last to a society where, inside heaps of stone rubble, live silent, reserved men who work for a daily wage as low as six hundred lire—about a dollar a day—which often has to support a large family. These are men who know the equality of abject poverty. Centuries of exploitation have brutalized some of them. They and their land have been bled by the *stranieri*, beginning with the Romans. They speak rarely, are quick to take offense and to inflict harm on others. They remind one of the powerful lines of Markham. The painfully slow agricultural reform taking place there convinces one that the essential goal in development must be the creation of new men.

That is the job that has to be done. It is not merely a matter of another dollar a day or the ownership of a parcel of land.

From a distance, a Sicilian village is an attractive mass of white sitting gingerly on a hilltop. It was placed there originally for protection against foreign marauders, but its inaccessibility now makes its location highly uneconomic. The periphery, when one reaches it, suddenly becomes a heap of stones housing squalor and human shapes prematurely deteriorating in the bloom of life. Flies congregate in masses along streets which look like dry riverbeds. In front of the piles of stone sit women dressed in black, or old, broken men with impassive faces. When the road suddenly opens into the square, one sees arrayed around it the meeting places of the town: the club, the bar, the municipal building, the barber shop, and the largest edifice on the piazza, the church. In front of the only restaurant on the square, several boys in tattered clothes, whose ages range up to six, gaze with mouths ajar at the display of food. The proprietor shouts at them, asking what in the devil they want, and their spokesman answers quickly, they will return on Sunday for dinner. The town is Nora, and it is typical of the small communities of Sicily.

The primary labor problem in the South, the subsistence-level living of agricultural workers, is caused by the fact that too many people try to live on the resources of limited, fractionalized land. Most of the agricultural holdings are less than a hectare and a half in size. An Italian agricultural economist, in conversation with the investigator, estimated that five Italian peasants are as productive as one Belgian. The fierce competition for the coveted *pezzo di terra* to till pushes up the already extraordinary rent going to absentee landlords. The parceling-out to peasants of land carved out of expropriated estates under the agricultural reform law may serve only to keep the problem in temporary abeyance. The new windfall of a piece of land and a house that is habitable encourages the growth of families. Within a generation, the presence of many grown sons not inclined to emigrate to industrial centers may create again the specter of the division of agricultural land into uneconomic units and the return to abject poverty. A new landowner told the investigator that when he first married he had to go into the fields, away from a two-room household of seven adults, to obtain privacy. Now he could enjoy married life in his own home. His wife was thirty-two, and had given birth to seven children. The cattle stall at the basement level of the model house had to be utilized to provide additional space for his family. When he was asked what he would do if more children came, he answered, "God will provide."

The undernourished Sicilians are victims of a vicious circle in which low per capita income and low capital prevent each other from rising. The income of the South is half that of the North and rising no faster. Since the average income of the South is hardly beyond subsistence level, it is impossible to accumulate savings without forgoing the basic necessities of life. In such a situation, the employer is not inclined to risk his own savings, because of the uncertainty of any return and the attractiveness of plentiful cheap labor. The circle can only be broken by a massive education and investment program by the state, which so far has not been forthcoming. The accelerative effect of oil exploitation in eastern Sicily and the Southern Development Fund have caused a ripple of new industrial activity. The total development expenditures in a ten-year period, however, amounted to one-fifth of the annual investment expenditures in the North.[5]

Until World War II, Sicily was a static society in which the powerful obtained fealty from the workers in return for security at a level of subsistence. There is little *mezzadria* in the island, the people working either as *braccianti* or as tenant farmers. Even the latter, however, do not live on the land they till, as they do in the North, but travel long distances from the villages, in which they prefer to cluster. It was in this kind of isolation, with absentee lordship the dominant source of employment, that the institution of the Mafia developed. Those with power over the people were the landlords, the politicians, the Mafia, and the parish priests. The western part of the island is dominated by Palermo, the nurturing ground of the Sicilian criminal whose confreres have made a contribution to American crime. The people on that side of the island have an Arabic and Spanish cultural heritage. The eastern half is influenced by Messina and Catania. The people on that side have Greek cultural origins, and in temperament are more gentle and *mite*. The town of Nora lies roughly between the two.[6]

[5] Despite the public and private investment, per capita income of the South has declined relative to the North, amounting at this writing to approximately 45 per cent of the average for northern and central Italy. While per capita income in the South has risen, it is increasing at a faster rate in the more heavily industrial areas of Italy. See Maurice Neufeld, *Italy: School for Awakening Countries*, pp. 497–98.

[6] For a complete transcript of an interview with Danilo Dolci, the "modern Saint Francis with a college degree," see Appendix C. The same interview items were used, but placed in the context of Dolci's work among Sicilian peasants in the Mafia section of the island. The translation is a succinct document of the problems that

The small public garden in Nora is the meeting place of the old and the unemployed. The swarms of flies moving tenaciously in packs and the acrid smell of horse dung are a convenient index of the level of economic development of the town. In Sicily, as in the North, no women come to sit in such places, with the exception of the occasional elderly widow dressed in black. The men who sit there divide into three groups: the pensioners; those who are pulling strings, with the aid of the trade union or the political party, trying to obtain pensions; and the unemployed who draw unemployment insurance. They sit, talk, and snooze. The presence of an attendant cutting the grass with a hand mower arouses their interest in modern mechanics. Sitting with these men, one acquires the feeling of a world where there is neither fulfillment nor creativity, where men wait idly for death.

The Catholic and the Communist labor leaders of the town have a close working relationship. They have two major problems in common: the nature of the baronial employers, who take offense at grievances raised with them, and the character of the Sicilian workers, whose closed, reflective mentality, critical and suspicious of organized activity, makes trade unionism difficult. Collective bargaining under these circumstances is non-existent, and trade unionism performs a function which approximates that of a social welfare agency.

The Sicilian worker tends to defer to the authority of persons of consequence: politicians, professional people, trade union officials, employers, *mafiosi*, the worker who can read a newspaper to him, and the parish priest who dispenses damnation or charity. The power of these individuals derives from their ability to keep him alive before and after death. The literate worker within his group makes it possible for a group of illiterate citizens with no radios to sit in the public garden and heatedly discuss the current news. The Sicilian worker is not a group-conscious individual, in the sense of knowing how to employ

---

have to be grappled with in energizing a static society to begin the process of industrialization. Italy demonstrates that a labor leader may be someone other than a trade union official. He can be a politician, a clergyman, an employer, or a labor leader scientist such as Dolci. These men exercise leadership in the milieu in which they were born. They speak the same language, have similar values, and are accepted by those they lead. Dolci had none of these advantages initially. He went into a hostile environment and could not speak the Sicilian dialect, but he began to change attitudes and perceptions of people whose vocabulary and comprehension did not include the term "change." His function was not to champion aspirations as much as to create them, to persuade people that their lot could be improved. In the course of less than ten years, this extraordinary man has made western Sicily a unique laboratory in industrialization.

group power effectively. A person is neither necessarily good nor necessarily bad by reason of the organization to which he belongs.—*Tutti i partiti sono buoni; quel che conta sono gli uomini* ("All parties are good; what counts is the men who belong to them").—In Sicily, a Communist, a Monarchist, and a Fascist can sit down to a friendly game of cards. The principal meeting place is the political party office, the trade union, or some favorite spot on the piazza. The worker does not feel that he belongs to the same caste as the *signori* with authority. He is at the bottom of a social system in which everyone else, from the clerical employees who read and write with such facility to the *proprietari* who provide him with work for a dollar a day, is his superior.

His antisocial behavior is a compound of the influences of centuries. The alien governments which controlled him represented neither his interests nor his culture. The Mafia which began as an instrument of protection in lieu of a sympathetic government changed into a parasitic force living at his expense. The promptness with which people of authority were ready to exploit him developed in him a contempt for the common welfare, which still persists. The Sicilian value of *omertà* suggests a resignation to the inevitability of the exercise of force by the powerful and the impossibility of developing any effective organized resistance against injustice. It is futile to expect justice from government. To avoid trouble, one does not coöperate with public authority, and one settles accounts in social relationships on independent initiative. The worker's constant preoccupation with poverty has a coercive effect on his social spirit. Coöperation is difficult in a society in which human energies are devoted almost exclusively to being astute enough to stay alive.

Salvatore, a stone mason when there is any building to be done in the town, and self-appointed Communist confidant of the investigator, is typical of the Sicilians who practice the art of rolling with the changes in authority. His motto is *"Chi to dà il pane, chiamatelo il padrone"* ("He who gives you bread, call him boss"). Before the war Salvatore was a Fascist, the party card assuring him steady employment in the town. Now he was offering his services as an informant on secret matters pertaining to the political parties and the trade unions in Nora. First, he had touched the investigator for five hundred lire for what he said was a collection on behalf of a worker who had been evicted from his apartment. He never mentioned that he was the worker. It was Salvatore's view that Sicilians took Italian politics either much too seriously or not seriously at all. He cited the case of some workers who had put up posters for the Communists during the day, mutilated them at night, and offered the following morning to repair them for the party at half price, just to settle accounts with those shameless Monarchists who had scribbled the uncomplimentary remarks. Salvatore believes that a Sicilian has to learn quickly the art of snuggling up to power for the sake of survival. He told the story of the workers who were notified by their employer that Mussolini had just arrived at the railroad station. They rushed down, but no Mussolini was to be found. In desperation, they seized a porter, took away the luggage he was carrying, and bore him on their shoulders to a carriage, shouting, "Duce! Duce!"

Nora is not a marginal town by southern standards. It was suggested that the village of Fossato in the province of Calabria, at the toe of Italy, be visited on the way back to Rome. Totò, the *autista* who, wearing a white yachting cap, meets prominent visitors at the railroad station some sixty kilometers away, refers to the town as the *feudo*. It lies inside a circle of mountains, shielded by two columns of rock with an opening wide enough for an automobile to pass through. There is no road to it. The road is actually a river bed, which is dry during the dry season, but which has to be forded during the fall rain. *Contadini* were taking care of bean plants which they had succeeded in growing in the pulverized rock. The town has one source of water supply, a fountain at the entrance of the village. The rocky soil has deep fissures through which flows precious water, lost to the sea. There are no trees. The Romans, one villager said, cut them down, and they were never replaced. The streets are so narrow that no vehicle larger than a small Fiat car can reach the piazza. On them are piled heaps of dung from the horses, donkeys, and chickens that, like their owners, seem to be always idling. The streets become clean during the rainy season, but the dry spell lasts six months. During an earthquake fifty years ago, the church was damaged, and neither the exterior facade nor the interior plaster walls have been repaired since then. The village priest lives in the only wood house in the village, a temporary barracks furnished the Italian government by President Theodore Roosevelt for earthquake relief. The whole effect is one of irrevocable decay impossible to arrest. In the city where the train stops, an entire neighborhood is still housed in such barracks. The huts are two arm-lengths apart, and when the wind is right, the odor of human feces rises out of them and is wafted toward the Grand Hotel on the *piazza principale*.

The bright spot in the village is the *asilo* for the children, constructed by funds given the priest by an emigrant from the impoverished town, who went to the United States and made a fortune in building. The handling of these funds has created some animosity. The doctor feels the priest has too much power in the administration of the *asilo* and has been trying to win the other intellectual in the village, the part-time pharmacist, to his point of view.

On the day of our departure, on the way to the railroad station, the *autista* was full of ideas. He could not see why the town should not develop a seaside hotel hewn out of the rock facing the sea. A major attraction would be listening to the sound of the sea, which from that level is strikingly similar to the wind-swept Calabrian forest preserve of Canadian poplars. Totò would like to come to the United States, and occasionally pronounced the word "Mississippi" with a look of soliciting approbation. He had found a ship manifest in the sea, and could I bring back part of it to the United States, the rest to be returned personally by him? In two hours, we were back at the railroad station and on the way to Rome, or what Totò referred to, with eyes gleaming, as modern times.

A description of the cultural setting of Italy would not be complete without placing in perspective the complex role of the Catholic Church. As a journalist respondent in Rome stated:

It is erroneous to draw a picture of the Roman Catholic Church in Italy from what it is in the United States. It does not operate in a vacuum here, but in the culture in which it finds itself. The history of the Church would have been vastly different if it had not been molded in Italy by Italians. The doctrine of the Church is partly a reaction to Italian history, beginning with the struggle for unification of the country and followed by the sympathy for Mussolini on the part of the princes of the Church, who saw in him a protector of the social system. They supported him in Abyssinia and in Spain. In seventy years of activity, they have alienated workers and intellectuals and nurtured the growth of communism. There seems to be no escape from the dilemma created by the conservative force of the Church and the necessity for drastic reform which is championed by the Communists and Socialists, between authoritarian minds and the clamor for the creation of an independent spirit among the working classes.

Anticlerical sentiments are strong in Italy and strongest at the seat of the Vatican. Anticlericalism is not found solely among the Social-

Communists, who are inclined to show deference and respect for the power of the Church. It pervades the whole range of the political spectrum, existing in some degree within the Christian Democrat party itself. There is a tendency to view the Church not as a group of men of religion but as a political power bloc promoting its interests behind the cloak of religion. This anticlericalism should not be placed out of perspective, however. It must be understood in the light of the individualism and the sense of humor of the Italian people. Some of the best anecdotes circulating in Italy center around the figure of the parish priest and are passed on by those who have no quarrel with the influence of the Church. It would be a mistake to imply that no significant number of Italian males are reverent toward the Italian clergy. Indulging in controversial discussion on politics and religion is the staff of life for Italians. Life would be bland indeed if it were not possible to denounce the actions of a politician or a member of the clergy.

The respondents who spoke with the greatest restraint about the role of the Church in Italy were the Communists, while some of the most critical comments came from a priest with an important position in the Vatican organization.

The critic-priest traced the division between the Church and the left-wing forces in Italy to the famous *non expedit* of Pius IX, issued at the time of the unification of Italy. Perhaps as a reaction to its loss of political power in Italy, the Church prohibited all Catholics from participating in politics. The edict came at the moment when new political parties were rising and responding to the aspirations of the working classes. The Church, as a consequence, was placed in the role of preserving vested interests, and the Marxist parties became the champions of the common people. The Church later reacted to the results of its voluntary isolation by becoming heavily involved in political and social affairs. It organized a labor movement to compete with the Socialists, and a political party whose descendant is the ruling Christian Democrat party.

Its lay organizations among worker groups are led by intellectuals who are *capi*, rather than by the representatives of workers. They approach workers on a paternalistic basis, deciding what is best for them and what ideological outlook they should acquire. The CISL, organized by the Catholics who pulled out of the Communist-dominated CGIL, is sensitive to the activity of the Church among the working classes. The federation cannot move away too fast from the influence of the Church, the possible risk being a new form of intervention on the part of the Vatican. In the judgment of the priest respondent, by its political and social activity, the Church is slowly hanging itself in Italy, solidifying the critical attitudes of left-wing workers and alienating the middle class. In reacting to communism, Church forces tend to move further to the right, imperiling democracy by the creation of two intransigent power blocs at the political extremes.[7]

The typical parish priest in Italy has little sensitivity to the problems of labor. He is more apt to come from a peasant than an urban family, and he acquires a schooling equivalent at best to a high-school education, with no training in the social and physical sciences. His philosophy is that an employer should take care of workers by Christian charity. He accordingly fails to recognize that the working classes are tired of absolute monarchy in labor-management relations and want to participate in the determination of their economic destiny. Like the intellectuals who lead the workers, the priest does not know how to reach their hearts and perceptions. The respondent described the unemployed idling on the square in front of the village church. The priest inside does nothing. He dispenses philosophy and *carità*, not aware that charity should also include reform. If he had his way, the respondent stated, there would be a professor of industrial relations in every seminary in Italy.

Outside the industrial triangle, the farther south one travels, the more the parish priest is a central figure in the leadership of small communities. He is a regular member of the household. He does more than preside over baptism, communion, the ceremony of marriage, and the rites of death. He is counsellor in time of trouble, dispenser of jobs to the unemployed, advisor on how to vote—counsel which is especially heeded by the women of the parish. He is the local authority on matters of religion and morals, a prerogative which has a way of extending itself to much of the conduct of men in social and political affairs. He is inclined to be more impressed with the possibility of his parishioners falling into ideological error than with the virtue of developing the faculty of independent thinking. By the nature of things, the relation-

[7] A *New York Times* article of March 2, 1961, reports the Roman Catholic hierarchy advising the Christian Democrats against collaboration with the left-wing Socialists. In a letter to the secretary of the party, the president of the Bishops' Commission for Catholic Action is quoted as follows: "In the name of God, I ask you to ponder your responsibilty."

ship of priest and the faithful in matters of ideas is based on the inferiority of those of the latter.

Among the men interviewed, it was difficult to find any with indifferent feelings about the Roman Catholic Church and the part that it has played in the labor struggle. Throughout Italy, freedom-loving men are concerned with the inhibiting effect of the influence of the Church on Italian development. They express the belief that the Church in Italy discourages the creation of an independent spirit enabling men to participate in finding solutions to social problems by the exercise of their own intellects. They deplore the tendency to seek authoritarian solutions to issues on which honest differences of opinion can exist. To them, the priesthood seeks among laymen obsequious followers rather than individuals who draw their own conclusions. As leaders, they themselves feel slighted because of the tendency of Italians to look to the Church for leadership on matters which properly belong to them.

The term "*Cattolico*" actually is fuzzy in meaning. One can practice the state religion in Italy and not be accurately labeled by that term. The word actually refers to political or professional Catholics, men who in social matters try to think and feel the same way as the Pope. There are various gradations of this partisanship. As a group, these men are distinguished from unobtrusive Catholics and non-Catholic politicals who are really non-Catholic Catholics.

This religious influence is exerted more by the older leaders, and is more prevalent in some organizations than in others. It exists more widely in the Christian Workers' Associations than in the CISL, and more in Azione Cattolica than in the Christian Workers. While the leaders of the CISL are referred to as "Catholics," some of them are anticlerical in outlook. The *Cattolici* exercise more persuasion over workers in the South than in the industrial North. This is not as much an indication that the northern workers are less religious as a mark of a more independent spirit. Parish priests exercise less influence on their decisions, and their religion has less pomp and ritualistic ceremony. The black cassock of the priest is evident in the Christian Workers' Associations, but the most apparent outward sign of Catholicism in the CISL is the crucifix on the wall in the labor leader's office. It is erroneous, however, to consider any of these organizations unitary groups. The reformist views of some of the men in the Christian Workers' Associations are enough to shock their more conservative colleagues.

The political Catholic is not necessarily a man of religious sensitivity. At times he is more characteristically a believer in religious form, an advocate of religious ceremony and public demonstration of faith, or of passing laws making blasphemy and the public wearing of shorts by women violations of the criminal law. He may have a mistress and a wife, and criticize vigorously the introduction of divorce law; he may believe in the just wage, and have rather questionable relationships with his employees.

The third group comprises the *laicisti*, or, for lack of a better word, the liberals. The term is used in the American sense rather than Italian usage, which describes individuals of conservative views. The liberals find unpalatable the behavior of both the *Cattolici* and the *Social-Communisti*. They are democratic in outlook, and some of them are doctrinaire socialists whose thinking has fallen somewhat behind the swiftly changing events in Italy. They deplore the activity of the Church in social affairs and feel that the members of the CISL hang too closely to the skirts of the clergy. If the liberals belong to a labor union, it is apt to be one affiliated with the UIL.[8]

THE ITALIAN WORKER

Italian workers write on walls. They paint on buildings praises of their leaders and denunciations of their enemies, and they put up colorful posters proclaiming what they like and dislike. One evening, prior to election day, the Communists were rushing through a town in Sicily painting *"Vota Communista,"* while the Christian Democrats were following closely behind, plastering their own posters over the Communist exhortations. Everything went along peaceably until the two teams suddenly began to move in opposite directions and their paths crossed.

Making generalizations about Italian workers is difficult. It is impossible to label them neatly. Their geographical and occupational differences are greater than those of workers in America. Are the workers of Milan, Naples, or Palermo typical Italians? It would be difficult to find in the United States three cities of comparable size whose people have more cultural diversity than the Italians of these three cities.

There is little scientific study available on cultural differences among

[8] See Arturo Jemolo, *Chiesa e stato in Italia negli ultimi cento anni* (Turin: Einaudi, 1952).

Italians.[9] The Mussolini dictatorship had a ruinous effect on the development of the behavioral sciences. Though there are authors who have suggested that the Neapolitan is typical of the Italian character, the assumption is of doubtful validity. If one wanted to make a critical, unkind caricature of the Italian, it could probably be done using Neapolitan traits as a basis. Discard from them everything but the penchant for clownishness and vulgarity and there remains an unsympathetic portrait of the Italian who succeeds in amusing himself despite poverty and despair. He is the fellow who tosses his cap in the air, catches it, and exclaims, "I have just stolen a hat." The generalizations that can be made about the Italian character can be described in a series of increasingly smaller circles. The smaller the circle, the less the coverage of the generalization, and the more applicable it would be to the Italians of a particular place and social group.

Italians are often described as a highly volatile and animated people. This characterization, however, would hardly fit a sullen Calabrian agricultural laborer living at a level of subsistence. They fall, rather, into a stratified social structure based traditionally on property holdings of single families, a structure which exerts a pronounced influence on personality traits. Although the idea is breaking down, the most respected member of the community is the individual with a lot of land who performs no work. At the top of the structure is the large proprietor of either agricultural or industrial property. He is the *gran signore,* and he generally plays his role along classical lines, handling the plebeians of his estate or his plant in a diffident manner. Next in line are those who manage large plots of land for proprietors and hire peasants or rent out the land in long-term leases. In Sicily the manager is called the *gabellotto,* the confidence man of the baron. By stealing from both landlord and peasants he sometimes becomes rather well-to-do himself. Third comes the professional group. These people are, in effect, the first who have to work for a living, and in the hierarchy of workers are the most respected, as those furthest removed from menial labor. Fourth and fifth in order are the administrative and clerical bureaucracy, in which Italy richly abounds. They fall into two distinct classes: managers, or *dirigenti;* and clerks, or *impiegati.* Next come shopkeepers, small farmers, and *mezzadri.* Artisans and industrial

[9] Pioneering empirical studies in sociology have been made by Luciano Cavalli, director of the Office of Social Studies of the city of Genoa, and in psychology by Luigi Meschieri, director of the National Institute of Psychology in Rome.

workers follow, and at the end are the agricultural day laborers, the *braccianti,* or those who "sell their arms" for a day's pay. (The traditional hiring place of such agricultural laborers used to be the town piazza. There they would assemble, and employers would feel the muscle of their arms to determine whether they would be hired and what wages they would be paid.)

The industrial workers and the *braccianti* comprise the bulk of what this study refers to as Italian labor. Other occupational groups in the labor movement include clerks in retail stores and trade, government employees, and clerical workers in industry. Many such employees are found in independent unions not affiliated with any of the federations. The labor unions, particularly those of the Communists, have succeeded in organizing some of the *mezzadri,* although, strictly speaking, they are not employees. The unions have not had much luck with the small farmers, or *coltivatori diretti,* who have an organization of their own outside the labor movement. The artisans also have their own independent organization, and the employees who work for them are rarely found in labor unions.

There are few Western industrial societies with smaller worker incomes per capita than Italy. With the exception of those employed by the large monopolies, the only workers in Italy who make a wage sufficient to support a family are the skilled. The rest depend upon the earnings of their wives and children or the income they can obtain from odd jobs. Studying wages and price figures for Italy leaves one perplexed about how Italian workers manage to survive. Yet they do. Their survival power is a tribute to their ingenuity and improvisation. And the variance between statistical records and the facts reflects a society in which not telling all to government officials and getting away with it is a mark of enterprise and astuteness. Toward statistics, Italians themselves have an irreverent attitude. They tell about the town of two people, a *signore* and his *bracciante.* The signore used to eat roast chicken once a day, and thus the statistics for poultry consumption of that town was half a chicken per capita.

Italian workers improvise a miracle of survival each day. They have no weekend; no such word exists in the Italian language. There is a frenzy, a sense of unremitting pressure, that marks the lives of these frustrated workers trying to maintain their sense of dignity. They live in a world of deprivation, of constant turmoil, of competition that convinces them that whatever they acquire is achieved at someone else's expense. Struggling to exist, they are caught in the grip of a bewildering ideological struggle in which their leaders are telling them that they must make a choice among Marxism, Catholicism, and anti-clericalism. In their faces are written concern, fatigue, and resignation.

An analyst of Italian social affairs, in an interview, described Italian workers as a people with no collective aspirations. Everyone looks out for himself, everyone knows that things will be the same as they always have been, and everyone believes there will always be the oppressors and the oppressed. It is a world in which those who try to remove abuses are bores or demagogues trying to upset the balance of vested rights, where the state is something to milk under the guise of employment, something which must be supported by indirect taxes whose weight falls on the workers.

Italians, unlike the Danes, hold irreverent sentiments toward the law. It is not an instrument of benefit, but a device to extract a man's goods and to thwart his liberty of action. The result of this attitude is a game between those who exercise authority and those who through deft ways seek to defy it. Italy is a country of tax stamps. These *bolli* are affixed to hotel posters, advertising signs, and grievances processed through the Department of Labor. If an announcement of a death in the family is posted, it too requires a *bollo*. In a sense, these consumption taxes in an economy of low incomes are a mark of political astuteness in the perennial battle to foil the Italian cleverness in evading tax laws.

To workers in a town like Parmi, the community can be divided into *furbi* and *fessi*. The *furbi* are those wily enough to have others bear the burden of their responsibilities and to outwit the other fellow in any social relationship, while the *fessi* are those who eventually perform the work which has to be done and busy themselves promoting the good of the community. The difference between them is expressed in the story of a group of men carrying a rowboat on their heads. Those who, unnoticed by the others, succeed in stooping low, with their knees close to the ground, are the *furbi*, and those whose heads are touching the boat bottom are the *fessi*. Governing these two groups are the authorities, who rule with legalistic minds, men who, by worker definition, tackle a problem, define it, catalog it by basic principle, and then ignore it.[10]

---

[10] For the *furbi,* the solution to problems is never a straight line. One seeks through devious means to exert influence in order to get things done in the proper way. If a contradiction with the law exists, so much the worse for the law.

The factory worker in Italy has no reverent attitude toward work. It is the means to make money in order to subsist. He dreams of making a million in a lottery, and not working. The Nordic ethical view of work is alien to him. To produce more for its own sake is foolish. The ideal is a life of leisure, the existence of a *gran signore*. The hard worker is a fool, not a hero. The worker feels like a stranger in the plant in which he works. He has no sense of belonging to a joint productive effort, no sense of creativity and self-esteem. Out of these feelings he derives a vague conviction that if somehow he could control the management of the plant, his sense of isolation would disappear. In this quest for status and a sense of community-belonging, he has no clear vision of the precise role his trade union should play. His socialism is a sentimental reaction to poverty. It expresses a yearning for a society in which opportunity and justice exist for all, rather than for the rich only. In this sense, practically all of his fellow workers, including the Catholics, are "socialists." Hence the paradox of a country in which almost everyone is a "socialist," while power is in the hands of conservatives.

Italian public opinion polls of the DOXA organization shed some light on worker attitudes.[11] Unfortunately the responses are not classified by occupational group. On the question of what occupation workers expect their sons to prepare themselves for, 52 per cent cited one of the professions. The smallest percentage, 1, was given to the law. What was the most important criterion in choosing a job? Approximately half stated regularity of employment; 13 per cent high wages; while the rest in decreasing order cited a good employer, and opportunities for advancement. On a query concerning the kind of employment they found desirable, the greatest percentage stated a preference for working for the government. Those who were discontented with their jobs cited as reasons low pay or irregularity of employment. Was there perhaps someone who could be considered responsible for their present condition? Thirty per cent said no one in particular, everybody and nobody. Thirteen per cent blamed the employer, 17 per cent the government, and the remainder gave no reply. What was the principal reason for their discontent? The low wages in relation to the cost of living.

Asked to identify the greatest defect of Italian employers, 20 per cent of the workers questioned described them as egotists and misers. Fourteen per cent thought that they exploited workers. For 12 per cent,

[11] See Luzzatto Fegiz, *Il volto sconosciuto dell'Italia, dieci anni di sondaggi DOXA.*

they paid too little, and an additional 12 per cent felt that employers expected workers to kill themselves working for them. In 11 per cent of the replies, it was claimed that employers showed no understanding of problems of the worker, while 10 per cent stated that employers wanted to make too much money. Two per cent found no defect in employers.

The alienation of the Italian worker from his employer is expressed by an Italian psychologist in these words:

The worker does not feel secure; he is afraid of tomorrow, knows he does not communicate with management. If the worker fears unemployment, if the white-collar workers fear the same thing, management is afraid of the subterranean organization of the employees and is uneasy because he does not know exactly what the workers aspire to and what measures he would use in an emergency. . . .

If isolation is an obstacle to the development of the personality, it does not take much to imagine what would be the reaction of the workers in an emergency and why messages which preach intolerance and violence have such good luck among them . . . [12]

The alienation of Italian workers from each other is reflected in a sociological study. The majority of a sample of metal workers in the industrial city of Genoa replied in the affirmative to the question whether they believed a merger of the labor movements should be effected. However, on the matter of whether all workers should be accepted in the new labor movement, approximately half stipulated that the members of certain political parties should be excluded. The major party barred was the Socialist. One respondent stated that a complete unification of the working class into one federation would be an absurdity.

This isolation is expressed in a qualitative response in the same inquiry.

In a group of old houses, completely inhabited by workers, . . . a metal worker in his fifties tells us: "I was born here. Then everyone used to know each other, we used to go together, loved each other. After the war came politics. Now we all hate each other. You are a Communist, I am a Socialist, he is a Demo-Christian. And so we avoid each other as much as possible." [13]

To the Italian worker, a representative image of the trade union is that of a welfare agency provided by a political party in return for loyalty. A query in the DOXA study on the function of trade unions

[12] From a statement of Professor [Giuseppe] Miotto, published in *Il Nuovo Osservatore* (Rome), November 13, 1959.

[13] See Luciano Cavalli, *Quartiere operaio,* pp. 25–64.

states: "A trade union can do many things for its members in addition to defending their interests with employers and government. Here, for example, is a list of various forms of assistance which may be possible. Which two do you favor most?" The most frequently mentioned form of assistance was information on employment in various parts of Italy and abroad, followed by aid in finding a place to live, and vocational guidance.

The condition of Italian workers is such that they make poor rank-and-file union members. They have little of the ability and time necessary to practice trade unionism, and they show apathy and disillusionment toward their organizations. Fascism stunted their sense of individual initiative and stifled any belief that power rests in them. They often view their leaders, not as chosen representatives, but as an additional group of functionaries little different from government officials, who may or may not be helpful in the struggle to make a living. Poverty keeps them eternally busy in manipulating situations and people in order to survive, and generally they see their leaders only when they have fallen deeply into trouble.

The farther south, the more typical is the portrait. The idea that the union is their organization is alien to them. Least of all in their minds is the conviction that they could make a contribution toward strengthening the union organization. It is an office to go to when in trouble and a place to stay out of when matters are going well.

Workers take different types of problems to their union organization, including entanglements with the government bureaucracy. One man, unemployed for two years, complained of receiving a card from the tax office, requesting him to pay a tax for the ownership of a villa. Since he owned nothing, let alone a villa, he had complained to the government office, and was informed he would have to submit an affidavit attesting to the non-ownership of a villa, said affidavit being subject to the payment of a tax.

In the course of the day, a union official listens to many grievances. A group of workers from the local state tobacco-monopoly come in to see what can be done about their status as temporary workers. They are considered probationary day-employees, in contrast to the permanent workers with better terms of employment. They have been probationary employees for ten years, and would the union do something about their status? Another group of plant workers complain about the autocracy of their employer. There have been considerable increases in productivity and no wage increases. "He does not give *soddisfazione all'operaio*. He throws at us the 'Communist business' when there is a strike. We should not strike because it is political. . . . We know his tactics. He will succeed in talking with us for a year about a wage increase and then give us enough for another pack of cigarettes a month. . . ."

Resignation and cynicism are more characteristic of southern workers than of those in the industrial triangle. There the workers are more critical of events, and more expressive. They are more *evoluti* than those in the rural South. And they are more critical of their trade union leadership. What, they were asked, was the difference between a "good" and a "bad" labor leader? The former they consider honest, able to communicate with them, and prepared to perform his job properly. The latter is a demagogue, with no ability to map long-term strategy and objectives. What was a successful life? A happy family existence and good company, a life free from the despair of inadequate wages and constantly rising prices for necessities. If they had their way, how would wages be determined? By the ability of each company to pay after funds had been set aside to modernize and expand the firm. What were the ultimate aspirations of Italian workers? Socialism, an idealistic world of justice in which workers wielded influence. None of them was inclined to criticize the leadership of rival federations. They wanted trade union unity, and they felt that the political parties were to blame for the split in the labor movement.

The Marxist interpretation of events provides a strong thrust behind the Italian labor movement. In the judgment of many Italian workers, it has value as an instrument of interpreting Italian history. The employers, the community, and the government were more successful in fulfilling the needs of the well-to-do than those of the poor. Government was in the hands of the *stranieri*, and they used its instruments to exploit the people, who felt alienated from their society. This estrangement asserts itself now in either passive resignation or indiscriminate censuring of those who have power. The union, consequently, if useful, is a means of protection against predatory employers and government. The function of the unions—finding jobs, assisting in obtaining concessions from government, advising on vocational choices, and providing aid generally when one is in trouble—is in a sense a symbol of the failure of the community to fill workers' needs.

Generally, the lower the occupational status and degree of upward movement of Italian workers, the more revolutionary is their organization. There are exceptions, such as the Communist workers in areas once ruled by the Church who maintain their traditional radicalism despite their increasing well-being. Unless the pull of the Church is strong, the labor force at the bottom of the occupational ladder is attracted to the extreme left wing. Regardless of occupation or technical orientation, what they want is a *vita dignitosa*. For the agricultural laborer a life of dignity would require a piece of land and a house, and for the industrial worker a wage sufficient to obtain relief from the constant struggle to make ends meet and the fear of losing his job—a tragedy to him. He wants to be treated with respect by the employer, to have leisure time to enjoy his children, with whom he has an intense emotional bond, and to have the money to go down to the piazza and treat his friends at the café. A young man may simply want a job to put him in a position to make a wedding proposal. The better the job opportunities, as in the Milan-Turin-Genoa triangle, the higher the level of optimistic outlook and aspiration.

Italian workers have the impulse to associate, but they lack the psychological and physical means to practice a technical trade unionism. The pursuit of goals on a continuing basis breaks down. Sustained group control is more difficult for Italian workers than it is for Danes. They do not feel to the same extent the compulsion to modify and control their actions consistent with a vague group-myth. For the Danes, group behavior gives propriety and truth to conduct. For the Italians, no such sanction is automatically bestowed on an organization. Accordingly, though Italian workers feel that their society does not represent their interests, their outlook makes difficult pragmatic pursuit of countervailing power.

An intense legalistic sense, *senso giuridico*, plays a significant role in labor-management relationships. Italian workers, accustomed to a paternalistic society, display a characteristic described by trade union officials as a *senso di gerarchia*. Out of this willingness to submit to an intellectual hierarchy there is arising a new source of conflict. Those who have held power, the Church, the government, the idle rich, and the employer, see their leadership challenged by a new hierarchy comprised of trade union officials with rather shabby adornments of office. The orthodox relationship between paternalistic leadership and the led is fealty on the part of the latter in exchange for dispensation of charity on the part of the former. Those on the receiving end of this patronizing spirit view these guardians with mixed feelings of gratitude, fear, hatred, respect, and deference. One of the motives of a labor organization is to find for itself a legitimate role to perform in such a guardianship society.

The society in which the Italian worker lives, and in which Italian labor movements must operate, is one marked, in contrast with a country like Denmark, by the diversity and immobility of its social fabric. It is difficult, in a sense, to call Italy a society. Rather, it resembles a collection of diverse groups, armed with contrasting ideologies, whose sense of civilization keeps them reasonably together despite their lack of integration. To break this social stalemate would require the disintegration of the economic and political power of the well-to-do and the Church, greater upward social movement by the working classes, and their participation in power.

The Setting in Denmark

Coming to Scandinavia from a long stay in Italy is passing from a world of intensity and clamor to what appears to be a land of tranquillity and peace. The colored, tired facades of Italy change to somber brown brick and gray stone. The skies over the cities are lined with tall, slender bell towers rising from Gothic churches and government buildings, a contrast to the separate, softer lines of the Italian *campanili*. There is more steel, more concrete, more broad highways, more material well-being, in evidence. The people speak with a softer, bouncing cadence that contrasts with the more accented, melodic tones of Italian. The initial impression a traveler has of Italy as he goes through the countryside is of poverty and overpopulation. The first impression of Scandinavia, with its few inhabitants and large spaces, is of prosperity. If one were to turn Norway alone to the south, with Oslo as the axis, it would reach down as far as Sicily. Fifteen million people live in the expanse of Scandinavia, in comparison to more than fifty million living on the smaller Italian peninsula. Norway and Sweden reach into the polar circle, while across the short expanse of sea from Sicily is a land of Arabic culture.

One of the notable characteristics of Danish society is the considerable political and economic power of the leaders of its working classes. The shift of influence from the rich to the poor within a hundred years can be best understood in the light of the values of the Danes. Contending parties are not separated by sharp ideological differences which make the solutions proposed by one side unacceptable to the other.

No striking dissimilarity exists in the type or rate of change which each group finds acceptable. If a controversy has to be resolved on the basis of power, opposing groups show the ability to measure their relative strength and to make the concessions that would be forthcoming in the event conflict were used as an instrument of persuasion. Danish labor, by obtaining a bit here and a bit there, has managed to become a dominant force. Labor leaders have avoided approaching their goals on an all-or-nothing basis. Danish workers, through their political party, the trade union, and the coöperative movement, have become a powerful force in their society.

Smaller differences among the Danes make accommodation among groups easier than in Italy. The poor at the bottom are not as poor. The well-to-do have not created an obstacle to the eradication of poverty by insisting on the sanctity of competitive production. Both rich and poor have a similar sense of community, alien to the Italians, which makes easier the reconciliation of differences. Social differences are also narrower. In Denmark, the educational system and the relatively greater opportunities for upward movement, in comparison with Italy, provide a greater homogeneity of outlook among its people. The young sons of the working classes who do not attend a university can frequent such educational institutions as the *højskule,* with its college-campus atmosphere, gaining a sense of cultural uplift and accomplishment. Some of these boys become trade union officials, politicians, small-scale employers, executives, and supervisors. The felt disparity of the common people between themselves and those who have greater status in their society is smaller than it is in Italy. It is difficult to distinguish a public official from a worker in Tivoli park in Copenhagen on a Sunday afternoon. Although communication between such persons is not great, the smaller the community from which they come, the more likely it is that they would have some social dealings with each other.

For the Danes, life moves through organization channels from birth to death. They come into the world under the auspices of the social welfare system; after termination of schooling they discharge their roles as citizens and workers through organizations, whether as farmer, employer, retailer, or supervisor; and they reach old age and die under the protective arm of the welfare state.

The Danes are a group-conscious people. Sensitive to social status and prestige, they are inclined to make a fetish of controlling bald manifestations of inequality in these characteristics. They practice snubbing upward in order to control snubbing downward. If, for example, an individual is informed of a very personal meeting with the prime minister, he may respond by revealing his intimate association with a fishmonger. Sensitive to inequitable comparisons, they make it a point to assert their independence of the social pressures of others. In a society of watchful waiting for any hint of superiority of one group over another, the cost of individualism is social ostracism. This group-consciousness extends also to the status derived from jobs. The labor leader who surrounds himself with people who have acquired reputations as economists derives prestige from such proximity. The acme of job prestige is to be found, not in being a top employer, but in being looked upon by the community as a prominent government official.

The cultural climate of the Danish community is propitious to the group control of individual behavior. It has been suggested that the considerable restraint on aggression and independence exercised by the Danish mother on her children develops in them a high degree of social dependence in later life. The impact of such childhood experiences on Danish adult life can easily be exaggerated. Danish behavorial scientists, however, suggest that the significant degree of maternal control on the male in that country stimulates a keen need for group life and approbation in adult organizational activity.[1] Even a small Danish town may have as many as fifty active organizations.

Scandinavian society, indeed, approaches the saturation point in the number of voluntary social and economic organizations which exist, and the degree to which they reach the potential of their membership. In Denmark, and in Sweden and Norway as well, the pursuit of social and economic interests through group activity comes easily. The Scandinavian typically belongs to one organization as a producer, to a second as a consumer, to another as an expression of political interests, and to a fourth or more in his leisure activity. If one were to read down a list of the labor force, one would find each major occupational group affiliated with its appropriate organization. An individual experiencing success in moving up the list automatically leaves one organization and enters another by virtue of agreements between tandem organizations.

Strengthening the Scandinavian sense of association is an aversion to strong forms of competition. Success is not measured in terms of a

---

[1] For a summary by Danish behavioral scientists of Danish national attitudes, see Herbert Hendin, "Suicide in Denmark," *American Scandinavian Review*, XLIX (Winter, 1961–62).

competitive contest to make the most of personal strength at the expense of the weak. *Samarbejde,* rather, is the more important virtue. The individual who uses an organization to pursue personal power is not apt to be considered a hero.

To the Dane, a prominent trait of the Scandinavian character is reserve. This characteristic manifests itself in several ways. Scandinavians are reluctant to make critical generalizations on human behavior. They are apt to feel that such discussions ultimately reflect personal norms of behavior, which should remain private knowledge only. It is not common for a Dane to impugn the motives of another individual, even if his point of view is repugnant. Personal commitment is shunned. It is not proper to be asked about one's feelings. One does not probe into the influences behind the behavior of others. One should try to accommodate to the actions of others, rather than involve oneself in conflict with them; not seek unilaterally to impose one's will on others, but yield to different points of view even if the positions taken are deemed inconsistent. This reserve engenders a high tolerance for the behavior of others and an expectation that one's personal rights are to be respected. In a superficial observation of these people, it may be mistaken for hauteur and sense of superiority.

This characteristic has an importance in the social behavior of the Danes. They are more inclined to accept situations than to be highly critical of them. They eschew criticism of others. They lack that *esprit critique* which the Italians have to excess. They are not the realists the Italians are. Scandinavians are more inclined not to call a spade a spade.

The smallness of Denmark, the sensitivity of Danes to the behavior of others, and the speed with which information is disseminated act as a check imposed on the activities and accomplishments of Danes by all other Danes. In Copenhagen it is claimed that the income tax returns available for public inspection at the collector's office are as popular as a best seller. Each Dane busies himself checking the habits of his countrymen. Conspicuous consumption and ostentation are dangerous, lest the individual exhibiting them appear a ridiculous figure in the eyes of the community. In such a leavening atmosphere, stars and heroes cannot survive. The secret weapon against them is the proverbial Danish grin. It is a smile of contempt, a weapon of deflation. During World War II, Danes would go up to the tanks placed in the streets by the Germans as a display of power, and ask for a ticket in the tank lottery. A person performing pretentiously, in the judgment of a fellow citizen, may be squelched by excessive praise. The heroic image of an employer, a labor leader, or a retired general emerges with difficulty from such a climate. The bald exercise of power may lead to the isolation of the individual who exercises it. Unreasonableness and the use of threats decrease, rather than enhance, power. A blood-and-thunder contest among the leadership of different organizations is not becoming. The price to be paid for individualism and lack of restraint is too great.

These attitudes are reflected in the behavior of labor leadership. Labor leaders do not run for office, but are, in their words, "pressed into the responsibility of accepting it." They have a respect for the leadership prerogatives of other organizations. They do not exercise their leadership by organizing blocs to oppose the power of other groups. There are no Catholics to organize a labor movement directed against Marxism, nor are there Communists in sufficient number to create a dual trade-union organization. In a striking example of organization democracy, the leaders mirror the characteristics and attitudes of their respective memberships. The head of the General Workers' Union, an intelligent, sensitive individual, thinks like a laborer, despite the long-acquired prominence of high position, and shows a warm sympathy for the worker's point of view. The heads of the craft unions are difficult to distinguish from the craftsmen they lead. The national leader of the Office Workers looks like a *kontormand,* and the top leaders of the Butchers' Union work in the long white frocks of their rank and file.

Danish trade unions are old, established, and, for the most part, peaceful. Only infrequently do they arouse strong feelings in their country. Whereas the Italian labor movement originated from the thrusts of socialist and syndicalist reform movements reacting to a situation in which too many men of low skills, trying to subsist on limited land, led a harsh and frustrating existence, the Danish labor movement, according to some Danish historians,[2] grew out of the conversion of the artisan and journeyman guild structure into a more rigid class-relationship between employer and employee, each with conflict-

[2] Actually the guild system was abolished by law in 1862, and the trade unions were established a decade later. There exists, therefore, no direct link between the two systems. That the unions, however, were influenced to a considerable degree by the guilds is cited by Danish economic historians. See Frederik Zeuthen, *Arbejdsløn og Arbejdsløshed* (Copenhagen, 1939) and Georg Nørregaard, *Arbejdsforhold inden for dansk Håndvaerk og Industri* (Copenhagen, 1943).

ing interests and expectations. So long as the Danish journeyman looked forward to upward movement into the ranks of the artisans, both groups formed part of the same organization. With the coming of industrialization, however, the master became a large-scale employer, and the journeyman, an individual with permanent employee status. The masters, finding it no longer in their interest to belong to the journeyman guilds, left them, and the journeymen either converted the guilds into trade unions or created entirely new organizations. Indeed, the respective terms for labor union, *"fagforening"* and *"sindacato,"* suggest the craft-consciousness of the Danes in contrast to the industry-group–consciousness of the Italians.

THE DANISH WORKER

Danish workers are divided into what appears to be an occupational caste system of skilled workers and unskilled laborers, perpetuated by the structure of the labor movement. Originally, the craftsmen did not want the unskilled workers to belong to their trade unions. In 1897 the unskilled workers organized their own labor union, and as the separatism of the craftsmen has diminished, that of the general laborers has correspondingly increased. They are proud of their union, a strong sentiment existing among them that a reorganization of trade union structure along industrial lines would decrease their bargaining power. This influence, and the way it accrues, is a matter of difference between the two groups. Some of the skilled workers point out that the wages of general laborers, because of the interindustry nature of their organization, do not reflect the high productivity of different industries. Changes in technology, however, appear to work to the advantage of the unskilled group. They are becoming a dominant part of the work force in many plants, and there are buildings in Copenhagen which have been constructed solely by the use of "unskilled" labor.

The key to this social separation is the apprenticeship program in Denmark. It is the dominant means of entrée to the ranks of skilled workers. If a young man does not enter an apprentice program in one of the trades, he is likely to remain an unskilled worker during his job career unless he becomes an independent businessman. By contrast, in a Swedish plant, available jobs in the occupational ladder are open to anyone who has the talent to fulfill the skills required by them. In Denmark, the jobs at the top of the plant occupational ladder belong to the craftsmen in the skilled workers' trade union. Industrial unionism would tend to destroy this caste system. However, with the exception of the Metal Workers, no strong sentiment exists in either the craft unions or the General Workers' Union for all workers in one plant to belong to the same union organization.

This separatism also exists among skilled workers themselves, especially among elder workers. Among the maritime unions, incorporating the various crafts on board ship is a major problem. New ships with a common cafeteria create difficulties. The seamen say that their feeling of exclusiveness gives them a sense of camaraderie and the opportunity to "take the other crafts over the coals."

A study by Grethe Philip in 1955 of lifetime occupational movement sheds light on the extent of mobility of Danish workers. Her investigation covered some 4,000 men born in 1902 who left school at the age of 14 or 15 years. Of this number, 3,506 answered the questionnaire. Fifteen per cent of this group had left school with some kind of final examination. In 1955, of those who had not taken a final examination, 17 per cent were independent businessmen, 21 per cent white-collar workers (*funktionaerernes*), 23 per cent skilled workers, and 37 per cent unskilled workers. For those who had taken a final exam, the corresponding percentages are 25, 67, 4, and 3. Almost 26 per cent of the unskilled group had completed an apprenticeship, while practically all the skilled workers and a substantial majority of the white-collar employees and independent businessmen had had apprentice training. A considerable number of the independent businessmen come from the ranks of the unskilled. Over the work cycle, beginning at age 25, the number of white-collar workers increases from 17 to 21 per cent, the number of skilled workers decreases from 35 to 23 per cent, while the unskilled group remains relatively constant. The group in general had accumulated considerable seniority with a particular employer. About three-quarters of the white-collar group had been with the present employer for more than ten years, compared to half for the blue-collar group. The number of men who tried to become independent businessmen, about one-third, is high. The attempt is most frequent between the ages of 23 and 30, but takes place at all ages. One-sixth of the group had attained an income of 13,000 kroner annually, while 100 were making in excess of 20,000.[3]

The Danish worker, in addition to relying on his union for jobs and

[3] Grethe Philip, "Hvad 3000 Maend Uden Skoleeksamen blev til," *Socialt Tidsskrift,* Vol. XXXI, No. 1 (1955).

unemployment compensation, maintains close ties with it through the continuous interpretation of contract terms. The extensive use of piece-rate systems of wage payment in Denmark necessitates the frequent interpretation of the agreement and the setting of new rates at the local level. This function brings the membership in contact with the local leadership either directly or indirectly through the shop steward or the work leader who provides employment for the membership. The building construction industry is a case in point. Each contractor obtains workers through a work leader who is also a member of the trade union. The wage bill consists of a price set for particular types of work, such as foundations, window assembly, and staircases. Because of changes in the type of work which has to be performed, a continual haggling takes place over the price to be set for a new operation. The distinction between prices and wages, employer and labor leader responsibility, is fuzzy. Indeed, a question exists as to who precisely is the employer in Denmark. Factory large-scale enterprise tends to break down the remnants of the guild system. With the exception of unskilled labor, even factory work is often on a price basis, with a minimum of managerial supervision. This characteristic of Danish employment provides the trade union official at the local level with an important role, increases the bond between workers and himself, and widens the community of interest between the employer and the trade union.

The provision of unemployment insurance operated by the trade union establishes its role as a source of guaranteed income for workers. The connection between availability for employment and unemployment compensation does not appear to be as rigid as in the United States. Technically, if a worker refuses available employment, he is subject to a fine. Actually, it is difficult for the union leader to penalize a man he refers to as his colleague. The problem arises especially with the General Workers' Union. The attitude expressed toward the pathological unemployed is that it is better to be cared for by the unemployment insurance fund than by the welfare agencies. When the job offers coming into the hiring hall are fewer than the number of unemployed, the financial support of the emotionally disturbed by unemployment compensation becomes tolerable.

In Denmark, specific attitudes of workers were analyzed more systematically than in Italy.[4] As a result of the Italian experience, it was

[4] See Gladys L. Palmer, "Attitudes Toward Work in an Industrial Community," *American Journal of Sociology*, LXIII, No. 1 (July, 1957), 17–26.

concluded that a worker attitude survey was necessary to round out the image of the different players in a labor movement. The worker sample was developed through a "random" selection of plants, no reliance being placed on obtaining workers through the trade unions.

The material for the worker attitudes analysis came from a total of ten plants and the labor school at Esbjerg. Seven of the ten plants were in Copenhagen, and three in the provinces. Industries included clothing, brewery, metal fabrication, and soybean-processing. The material at Esbjerg was obtained during a visit in the course of the field investigation in Denmark.

Workers were asked what they expected from their jobs, what they thought constituted success in life, and what their views of trade unions and labor leadership were. In a sense, the replies are a measure of the ability to make abstractions. The replies of the skilled workers, as a group, are more lengthy and more abstract than those of the unskilled.

What are the attitudes of male Danish workers toward their jobs? What meaning has work to them? A singular feature of the responses is the almost unanimous expression of satisfaction on the part of the workers with their present jobs and pride in their work, regardless of skill level. This sentiment may in part be an expression of the bias of the sample toward large firms and enterprises operated by the cooperative movement. Differences emerge from the responses between the old and the young, the married and single, the skilled and the unskilled. The old are less concerned with stable employment and higher wages than are the young and the single. For both the skilled and unskilled, the older they are, the more they emphasize non-economic incentives. In general, the workers' image of the ideal manual job is that of the machinist who can make and maintain a piece of mechanical equipment with a minimum amount of supervision. For their sons, the ideal job is one rung up the occupational ladder from the one in which they find themselves. The exception is found in a small group of general workers who want their sons to enter government service or the professions. In broad terms, the responses reflect the series of continual adjustments the workers make between personal circumstances and environment in a lifetime of work.

More than 90 per cent of the respondents like their present jobs. The most frequently mentioned reasons are the variability of the work and the pleasant associations with management personnel and fellow workers. The remainder includes such reasons as the feeling of being part of the firm, freedom from close supervision, and good physical conditions under which to work. "I like my job because of the variability of the work, the contact with many colleagues, and the ability to learn and pass on to others." "The work is a hobby with me." "I love work; the more the better." "This company provides a *god arbejdsplads og gode forhold*." "I like it because it is independent work without a supervisor on your back." Only one out of a sample of approximately one hundred workers stated wages as the reason why he likes his job, and he is an unskilled worker in his lower thirties.

Some 10 per cent of the unskilled do not like their work. Most of them are under forty. In general, they cited as the reason the nature of their work. "I am afraid to change work; you know what you have." "No, most workers want to become self-employed." "The work is too monotonous." From a truck driver: "It does not satisfy the desire to produce."

A degree of association exists between the original job plans of workers after their schooling and their present jobs. By occupational group, a greater relative number of the skilled workers, compared to the unskilled workers, had original job plans as skilled workers. The relationship between original vocational aspirations and present position is a measure of the realistic appraisal the workers make, given the schooling under which they begin their job careers. It is not as much a measure of their occupational movement as of range of aspirations. Those with the good fortune to obtain apprenticeship training after their elementary school education have concrete ideas of a lifetime of work as craftsmen. And those with no such training are realistic about the probability of rising out of the ranks of general workers in a lifetime of work. Here again, the heroic image of the ideal worker, the machinist, emerges. Among the unskilled, those who had intended to enter different work mentioned skilled occupations, or technical and professional jobs, such as forester, veterinary, doctor. One respondent stated that he had wanted to be either a surgeon or a detective. Universally, they cited economic reasons, rather than ability, as the impediment to their aspirations. "I wanted to be independent, but there is no possibility of doing this without education." "I wanted to be a skilled worker, but there was no money in the family." "As I was born in the country, I like animals and wanted to be a veterinary. But economic conditions made it impossible." "I tried to become more than I am, but did not succeed. . . ." "I wanted to become an independent businessman, but after twelve years in a grocery I lost all interest. The wage is too small in comparison to the very long hours."

Regardless of original plans, 33 per cent of the skilled workers would go into the same kind of work if starting again. In descending order, the remainder would want to become engineers, technicians, independent businessmen, and physicians. Single choices include farmer, teacher, and boilerman in a big apartment house or institution. All of them, consequently, presented specific alternatives. By comparison, only 10 per cent of the unskilled group would go into the same kind of work. The majority of the remainder chose a skilled occupation or an independent business, while the selection for the others included office work, adviser to shop stewards on time and motion problems, haulage contractor, and "millionaire so that I could get the education I wanted."

In general, the workers transfer their original job aspirations to their sons. Approximately half of the skilled group would like their sons to be engineers, craftsmen, or independent businessmen in commerce. With one exception, the skilled workers specified civil engineering as the preferred branch in that profession. A preponderant number of the unskilled group would like their sons to be skilled workers.[5] No member of either group chose the teaching profession. General comments include such designations as "a good society-minded citizen," "whatever his ability is," "whatever his interest is." A number of the respondents stated that they want their sons to have the opportunity for an education, leaving the specific choice of occupation to the son. Some of the workers explained their choices in greater detail. A skilled worker wrote, "A job which does not consist of working with his hands, which never results in more than making both ends meet." A general worker, "A skilled craftsman because I regretted that I was not allowed the opportunity to be so." And from another unskilled worker, "An office job because it is more stable." One unskilled worker expressed the opinion that it was difficult to reply because times change so quickly. A greater relative number of the craftsmen would not object to seeing their sons remain in the same occupational level. In general,

---

[5] This attraction to the skilled occupations is explainable more readily on social than economic grounds. The wage differential between the two groups is much less significant than the wages of workers in different plants and industries. The appeal is not the negligible wage differential as much as the recognition of being looked upon as a craftsman by people in his milieu.

when the aspiration is higher than the respondent's own occupational level, it consists of the next job proximate to his own up the occupational ladder.

What Danish workers believe to be the relative importance of specified goals of workers is summarized in Table 1. Under each rank is listed the percentage of workers choosing the particular goal. The greater relative importance of supervision and higher wages is not associated with a particular occupational group. Employment security is, a greater relative number of the unskilled workers giving it first rank. The choices are associated with particular age groups. The men in their thirties tended to choose wages and a better job for their first

TABLE 1

How Danish Workers Rank Worker Goals
(Per Cent)

Goal	Rank						
	1st	2nd	3rd	4th	5th	6th	7th
Good supervision	36	20	20	18	10	3	0
Higher wages	23	26	11	23	11	6	4
Employment security	16	29	31	15	0	3	0
More health and welfare benefits	9	7	14	5	21	37	9
Better job	7	7	11	18	21	11	15
Shorter hours of work	5	7	8	11	16	20	39
Better conditions of work	4	4	3	10	21	20	33

two ranks. Those in their forties selected wages and employment security, and those in their fifties supervision and welfare benefits. The group contained only three respondents in their sixties, and all three gave supervision first ranking. The low ranking given shorter hours may reflect the gain in the shorter workweek in the negotiations preceding the survey.

An interesting question in the study of labor leadership is the extent to which the behavior and outlook of the trade union official mirror the aspirations and sentiments of the rank and file. If there seems to be a positive correlation, a study of the characteristics of labor leaders can become an economical instrument for analyzing those of workers. In probing into this matter, one of the items utilized was asking the rank and file what, in their judgment, constituted a successful life. The word "success," which the Danes have borrowed from the English language, presents difficulties. It is too middle-class for Danish worker tastes, suggesting a competitive struggle in which the shrewd and ruthless manage to reach the top. The unskilled workers are more critical of the term than the skilled craftsmen, but hostility toward it pervades even the ranks of the labor leaders.

TABLE 2

Danish Worker Concepts of Success in Life
(Per Cent)

Related to:	Skilled		Unskilled	
Sense of personal fulfillment	23		5	
Things going fine		4		3
Sense of progress		8		2
Development of personal capacities		3		0
Feeling of personal worth		8		0
Social relationships	21		21	
Good friends; respect of one's comrades		15		16
Contribution to happiness of others		6		5
Job	19		12	
Good wages		15		8
Opportunity for advancement		4		1
Job free of supervision		0		3
Economic security	14		16	
No economic worries		14		6
Steady employment		0		8
Wage sufficient not to require wife to work		0		2
Family life	8		24	
Satisfactory family life		8		8
Welfare of children; opportunity for their advancement		0		16
Good luck	3		16	
Good health	7		6	
Other	5		0	
More trade union victories		3		0
A good temper		1		0
World without suffering and oppression		1		0
Total	100		100	
Number	72		62	

The combined responses stipulate as success in life good social relationships, an interesting and well-paid job, a prosperous family life, economic security, a sense of fulfillment, good luck, and good health. The responses are summarized in Table 2. An attempt was made to draw associations in the workers' replies with the industries in which they worked, size of plant, geographical location, and occupation.

Although small sample size may be a factor, the only meaningful relationship developed is occupation.

The responses reflect differences in outlook between the skilled and unskilled. The skilled worker is more optimistic about the likelihood of personal fulfillment. He expects to derive satisfaction from challenging work and respect for his craftsmanship on the part of associates. He aspires to a house, a car, and to the possibility of owning his own business. He wants, if he cannot be an independent businessman, a job in which he can exercise his skill. Wages should be more than enough to make ends meet, and the firm should provide satisfying relationships and a minimum of supervision. The skilled worker rarely mentions steady employment, but for him that is not the problem it is for the unskilled worker. He speaks more of non-economic incentives, such as the importance of individual expression: "I want to create something for my fellow human beings"; ". . . develop the possibilities in myself"; "I want the opportunity of being an individualist at the work place."

The unskilled worker, by contrast, is more pessimistic in outlook. He tends to place more belief in the shifting fortunes of luck and adversity, which he cannot control. Circumstances, he feels, have prevented him from obtaining a better education and a dynamic job career which would have moved him up the occupational ladder in a lifetime of work. However, he expects his children to do better. He is more oriented toward a better life for his children, with an occupation better than the one he has. Some of the workers wrote that they had tried hard, had failed, and now lived with the expectations of their children's being better educated and rising into the skilled occupations. The unskilled worker shows less zeal for work and less attachment to a particular firm. He is more conscious of the need for job security. He is more inclined not to answer the item on success at all. He speaks of the successful life more in terms of cultural and social values. He tends to look at occupational differences as representing not an effort by the skilled which should be rewarded but rather the lack of opportunity for others to obtain the necessary training and have the luck to rise from their occupational origins. The argument that a substantial wage-differential should be paid for skill differences falls on deaf ears—to a surprising degree for the skilled worker as well. In the words of some of the skilled workers, "Wages should be fairly similar. It would make too much noise if one worker earns five kroner and another only three." "The wage rate should be the same or fairly similar, regardless of differences in skill. The differences should rise from dissimilarity in productivity under a system of piece rates."

Both groups, skilled and unskilled, are impressed with the power of money. In their judgment, the people with the greatest influence are, first, the rich, and then, the prominent people in the Social Democrat party. In a real showdown, however, the one with the most *penge* would be successful. Both groups express a desire to participate in management. There are several factors to explain this attitude. In part, it expresses the lingering influence of socialist orientation. As craftsmen, moreover, the Danes are attracted naturally to management problems and techniques. Both groups tend also to underestimate the complexity of management problems, and are easily misled by the readiness with which solutions come to their minds. The American story of the craftsman who did not want the job of his brother, the president of the corporation, was not particularly convincing to them.

It is difficult to draw a composite picture of the skilled and unskilled. The range of opportunities which the members of each group see facing them is not the same. Real differences exist between them. The unskilled aspire more to a job which is steady, whereas the skilled, with a broader range of expectations, place a more particularized set of demands upon it. The skilled want their craftsmanship recognized. They feel more capable of controlling their environment. They fear unemployment less because they have experienced it less, and this smaller degree of concern for the possible loss of income increases their assurance of being able to control their destinies. The unskilled, deriving less satisfaction from their jobs, look to family life as the means of obtaining a sense of fulfillment. Both want economic security, a sense of personal worth, and respect from the individuals with whom they have relationships. However, because of differences in their circumstances, the particular goals to implement these needs are not alike. Economic security to the skilled worker means steadily rising wages; to the unskilled, regular employment. As will be noted in the ensuing chapters, the differences in outlook on the part of the workers are reflected directly in differences in the pessimism, conservatism, and militancy of their labor leaders.

How do these workers expect the trade union to help them be "successful"? For the unskilled, by increasing their living standards through higher wages and providing them with steady employment, and for the skilled, by increasing wages. The skilled think the union should "obtain more advantages with each collective bargaining agreement," "take care of my economic rights," "see to it that the contract wage is paid." The unskilled mention an increase in opportunities for labor education more often than do the craftsmen, while the latter express more job-consciousness, suggesting that the trade union should help them maintain their labor monopoly. Typical comments from the unskilled include: "It should take care of my economic interests"; ". . . prevents us from being exploited by capital"; ". . . maintain solidarity among workers in order to obtain demands"; ". . . provide courses in elementary training and education"; ". . . provide good social legislation." A small minority was critical of the union. "Despite the huge bureaucracy which has to be paid, the union has not helped." The answers of the skilled include: "Help by simply increasing wages"; ". . . provide clever leadership and good results"; ". . . protect conquered rights"; ". . . be aware of the workers' daily needs and make appropriate demands." Some of the craftsmen believe success is a personal matter for which the trade union can do little. In either case, the responses ascribe a limited role to trade unionism, that envisaged by the unskilled being somewhat broader in scope.

Following are summary responses of a particular skilled worker and an unskilled worker, each typical of his group. To the skilled worker, a successful life is one in which a man has "the wages to create good conditions for [his] family and . . . a job where interesting things happen." A "good" labor leader is one who obtains the "best possible working conditions through negotiations with employers and the legislative power." He is "bad" if he is "dictatorial and reckless." As the unskilled worker sees it, "The trade union does not help the individual as such in being a success, but helps the broad masses to get reasonable conditions. It is not the task of the union to help the individual to a higher position, but it should help in obtaining jobs." A good labor leader "has a broad point of view . . . ; [he] smooths out the relationship between workers and employers and gets as many advantages for the workers as possible in a reasonable way." A "bad" labor leader "does not know how to negotiate and achieve results."

Responses to the general query on the function of trade unionism are in the range of protection which the union is to provide the members (Table 3). The skilled workers tended to restrict the function to improvement in the terms of employment through collective bargaining with the employers. The unskilled feel that it includes providing jobs for members and labor programs for those who want to participate in them. They also expressed a preoccupation with labor peace at the plant level. There is disagreement between the groups concerning the degree that policies to improve terms of employment should be consistent with the needs of workers generally. An appreciable disagreement exists over the wisdom of seeking to improve standards uniformly for all trade union organizations. One skilled worker stated that the

TABLE 3

Danish Worker Views on the Function of Trade Unionism
(Per Cent)

Function	Skilled	Unskilled
Raise economic standards	72	42
Promote general welfare and economic interests of members	50	26
Improve economic condition of all workers	22	16
Promote labor-management coöperation	8	14
Provide job security	5	20
Provide jobs for members		16
Prevent exploitation of workers	5	4
Provide labor education	5	22
Raise educational level of members	5	17
Provide education for young workers		5
Other	10	2
Assist in reorganizing society	2	2
Not make political propaganda	6	0
Not require members to support political party	2	0
Total	*100*	*100*
Number	42	50

wage policy of his organization should be such as to provide the unskilled workers belonging to another organization with greater percentage increases. In sum, an inverse relationship appears to exist between the range of aspirations and life expectations of workers and the demands which they make on the union.

Generally, Danish workers show a strong sense of identity with their trade union organizations. Like their Italian counterparts, they expect their labor leaders to express themselves well, and they are less concerned with the technical demands of trade union office than are their leaders.

Both groups, skilled and unskilled, are unimpressed with the political and economic influence of their labor leaders. Workers outside of Copenhagen, particularly the unskilled, are critical of the national leadership: "Those who should support the workers are not always awake. I am at the point of wanting an Aksel Larsen party which could stir things up." "We do not have the welfare state; we do not have that much influence." They are less conservative in their views. They want more change, more participation in management, and more *vigor* in the exercise of political influence by the labor movement. The workers in the provinces are also more critical than their counterparts in Copenhagen of the fashion in which the right to strike has been curtailed by the labor leaders themselves. "The state should not interfere in a strike so long as it is preceded by proper notice. The labor leaders have circumscribed it because of political considerations on the national level." More than their counterparts in Copenhagen, they place top government officials and employers before the trade union organization in order of influence in their country. One stated typically, "It is true we live in a democratic country, but the capitalists are still the most powerful."

The views of Danish workers on desirable labor leader characteristics are indicated in Table 4. The responses fall into several headings: (1) traits of character; (2) technical ability; (3) orientation. Stipulations of traits of character provide a portrait of the classical Danish heroic image applied to trade union leadership. The "good" labor leader is sober, honest, calm, well informed, and emotionally restrained. The unskilled workers are relatively less concerned with these qualities. Their responses are dominated by such ideas as ability to negotiate and coöperation (*samarbejde*) between labor and management. They cited, in addition, the importance of finding jobs, a matter not mentioned by the skilled craftsmen. The skilled workers, as well, stressed the importance of negotiating ability. An important facet of this ability is the demonstration of a readiness to make concessions to the point of view of the employer. Not all the workers, however, believe that negotiating ability implies the use of flexibility in principle. Some responses gave loyalty to the ideals of the working class and the "principles he believed in as a worker" as desirable characteristics of a labor leader. An unskilled worker who stated that a good characteristic is the ability to negotiate also believes that an undesirable quality is the unwillingness of a labor leader to agree 100 per cent with the workers. It is interesting to note, also, how the respondents described the relationship between trade union officials, on the one hand, and employers and workers, on the other. Here again, the view is expressed that the role of the labor leader is that of a mediator, reconciling the point of view of employers and workers. Pervading many of the replies is a disinclination to engage in conflict with the employer. A greater relative number of unskilled workers expressed this feeling directly in terms of wanting trade union officials who favor coöperation between

TABLE 4

Danish Worker Views of Desirable Labor Leader Characteristics
(Per Cent)

Related to:	Skilled		Unskilled
Character	43		12
Behaves with dignity and controls emotions		16	5
Deals honestly and frankly with others		12	2
Shows responsibility and firmness of character		9	0
Is enterprising and flexible (*sindighed*)		6	5
Technical ability	34		38
Negotiates flexibly with employers		16	18
Understands trade union problems		10	1
Secures best possible terms of employment		4	1
Protects workers from unemployment			9
Negotiates in interest of both parties		4	9
Orientation	23		50
Eschews political domination		3	12
Understands workers' problems		5	11
Maintains workers' point of view		10	24
Considers best interests of society		5	3
Total	100		100
Number	93		71

management and labor. This attitude is also prevalent in the responses of the skilled workers. They expect their labor leaders to be loyal to their employers and to show a spirit of accommodation in collective bargaining.

Table 5 lists what respondents believe to be undesirable behavior on the part of a labor leader. The reason for the noteworthy number of failures to reply to the item is conjectural. The proportion of each group who do not answer is fairly equal. Informal discussions after the interviews indicated that some workers interpreted the item as an evaluation of their leaders. The responses tend in general to be the converse of the stated desirable characteristics of a labor leader. Thus, a worker who states that a "good" labor leader keeps politics out of collective bargaining also says an undesirable characteristic of a labor leader is that he does not. Judging by the responses made, a relatively greater number of the skilled group are critical of the introduction of political considerations into collective bargaining.[6] The unskilled workers as a group are more concerned with their relationship with

TABLE 5

Danish Worker Views of Undesirable Labor Leader Characteristics
(Per Cent)

Related to:	Skilled	Unskilled
Character	33	26
Indulges in extreme and unreasonable behavior	25	20
Behaves snobbishly	8	6
Technical ability	31	26
Fails to promote workers' interests	11	3
Uses dictatorial methods	14	23
Resorts to strikes unwisely	6	0
Orientation	36	48
Introduces politics into collective bargaining	30	12
Does not support workers' party (Social Democrats)	2	6
Misuses confidence of workers	2	30
Fails to understand workers' day-to-day problems	2	0
Total	100	100
Number	36	42

the trade union official. Their replies suggest that a problem of communication exists in the large union, compared to the smaller craft unions.

In conclusion, it appears that forces in Danish society make for homogeneity and balance by a kind of law of compensation. Neither occupation, religion, nor ideology pulls the Danes apart as much as the Italians. Organized religion is not a divisive force. The Danish value of egalitarianism has a coercive effect in two ways: it makes the

[6] Politik bandlyst i Forhandlingerne kun faglige sporgsmaal.

individual who behaves much differently from his fellows appear a ridiculous figure, and it makes the narrowing of differences a highly legitimate form of social behavior. The argument that workers should have three weeks of vacation because that is what the employers are enjoying is a forceful argument in Scandinavia and a *non sequitur* in Italy. The differences in the education and the training of the participants in industrial relations are smaller than in Italy. While this is somewhat less true of workers and employers in the larger firms, the extensive opportunities in labor education available to the worker provide him with a sense of what he refers to as obtaining a higher education. Income differences are smaller, as are the differences in values between labor and management. What constitutes the pertinent facts in industrial relations problems is less at variance. The perceptions of persons and situations by labor leaders and employers are less in conflict. The tirades leveled at employers in Italy would appear ridiculous in Denmark, outside the context of the small Communist newspaper, *Land og Folk*. The stereotype of the employer as a symbol of evil would not survive the test of credulity. The feeling of solidarity in the Danish labor movement is not buttressed by the image of an exploiting employer class. Nor is it the consequence of labor leaders' fomenting a hostile atmosphere against employers as an instrument of developing organization drive. The spectacle of trade union officials of other labor movements flaying employers is viewed as a sign of weakness and immaturity. The *esprit de corps* of Danish trade union organization springs from the sense of status, the security, and the independence that trade unionism provides, and from the common pursuit of idealist goals.

Workers in Denmark have a zest for work and an enthusiasm for learning, which trade unions use to advantage in their programs of labor education. Denmark is a country where the newspaper of the General Workers' Union devotes eight of its twenty-four pages to the compilation of an encyclopedia. Such labor education provides an example of how a labor movement can assume activities not directly related to collective bargaining and use them as an instrument of strengthening the bond of organization between the leadership and rank and file. Danish workers value highly freedom from close supervision, an attitude founded on the craft tradition of work. They consider the role of the trade union essential in preserving this value. Representative comments included: "We see the employer on the first day of work and once the price is established we are on our own." "I like the trade union because you are able to work for yourself." "I like to be told the work that has to be done, then left alone to do as I see fit."

The idea that workers should have the individual right not to subscribe to the rules of organization is alien to the nature of the Danes. They have abandoned chaotic decision-making in the allocation of jobs and the determination of terms of employment for orderliness in the labor market and have apparently managed to preserve the "public interest" by the willingness to accommodate to countervailing organized influence. The complete organization of the industrial labor market by the employer and the trade union is indirectly an appraisal of the Danish attitude toward the questionable beneficence of the free play of economic forces.

Organization of the Italian and Danish Labor Movements

The trade union organization of any country reflects needs, problems, internal pressures, strategies, and objectives that are similar but not identical. Structure is shaped by the job that has to be done and the difficulties that are encountered in accomplishing it. If the labor leaders of different countries use dissimilar methods and obtain dissimilar results, it may be due to circumstances and problems which are not the same.

The differences in outlook between labor leaders in Italy and those in Denmark reflect dissimilarities in job role. The job of the Danish official is more technical than that of the Italian, more within the narrow confines of a particular craft. The Italians operate within broad interindustry groups, and the difference is reflected in the structure of the labor organization. The heart of Italian trade unionism is the multi-union Houses of Labor in the towns and cities, while that of the Danes is the trade union local. The Dane is a quasi-government official. His role is that of bureaucrat rather than revolutionary. It is difficult to determine in Denmark where trade unionism ends and government begins.

The organizations of these leaders differ by historical tradition. The Northern European concept of separate and sovereign local unions representing the members of a particular craft does not exist in Italy. There, the organization of labor movements is a historical record of the search to minimize weaknesses and exploit advantages. The low skill and education levels of workers, their class-consciousness rather than identification with a particular craft or occupation, the fact that trade

71

unionism did not arise from a guild system, as in Denmark—all these factors contribute to an explanation of the importance of organization of workers on a mass geographical area basis, rather than by craft or industry. The acute necessity of acquiring political influence to compensate for economic and social weaknesses in the discharge of the trade union function asserts itself in the structure of the Italian labor organization.

The successful conquest of political power by the Danish labor movement contrasts with the political divisions which exist in Italy. The Danes pay a price for such conquest by forgoing the bargaining power that would accrue to them if they had no political responsibilities. In Denmark, because of the similarity of collective bargaining contract dates, strikes could pile up in snowball fashion. Such a possibility places the Social Democrat party, which controls the government with the aid of small parties, in a difficult position. Under such circumstances, when collective bargaining is pushed into the political arena, at times with the assistance of the employer, the unions lose what they might be able to demand were their leadership not subject to political restraints.

For an understanding of the structure of the Italian and the Danish organizations, and the way in which the labor leaders discharge their functions in their organizations, it proved helpful to construct organization charts, to determine labor leaders' allocation of their working time, and to utilize statements of labor leaders to other trade union officials and logs recording the performance of selected officials in the course of a working day. While written trade union constitutions provide a helpful background in examining the structure of an organization, they can be misleading if reliance is placed on them alone. Paper constitutions are often statements of aspirations rather than norms of behavior. Observing the operations of a union headquarters and discussing with trade union officials their functions and allocation of working time leads to the development of a more dynamic concept of structure.

ITALIAN ORGANIZATION

In Italy two basic structures exist: the federation [1] organization which controls the provincial and town offices and converges in Rome, and

[1] The Italian term actually means "confederation," while the affiliated national organizations are generally referred to as "union federations." While the Italian terms are logically consistent, I use the term "federation" in the American sense.

the individual multi-industrial unions or *categorie,* most of which are subordinated to the federation at its different levels of organization.[2] The town and provincial offices of the federation, which bring together all the rank and file of the different unions, play a dominant role in Italian trade union organization. To develop trade-union–consciousness and strengthen organization, the federations have tried to organize plant trade union units. It is doubtful, however, whether these units will become effective so long as workers in plants are split into three competing federations. The first plant-wide collective bargaining agreement in Italy came out of a firm in which practically all the workers belonged to one federation, and the shop committee (*commissione interna*) was made impotent by the labor leader representing the federation. The typical pattern in Italy, however, is that of regional units of each federation dominating trade union activity in the provinces in which they are found.

At the bottom of a highly integrated labor movement is the town House of Labor, administering to the needs of workers in industrial union units (Chart A). With the exception of large cities, these units are weak, if they exist at all. The labor leader in charge is often a full-time worker providing his time free. He may be a young man with a political following in the town, being primed for a more responsible job by the provincial labor leader to whom he reports. Or he may have demonstrated his leadership ability by becoming a key member of the shop committee of a large plant in his commune. He does not enjoy exclusive representation in any of the plants in the commune. Moreover, when the town is not the seat of the provincial government, the number and size of work units are small, and, consequently, so is the number of workers in each of the *categorie.* For these reasons, it is difficult to find in these communes large aggregates of workers belonging to the same plant or *categoria* who are company or craft oriented. Labor-movement–consciousness tends to be maintained, and craft status discouraged from developing. The communal office is often no more than a room with chairs and tables, a place where the members socialize. No major trade union functions transpire there. The writing

---

[2] The term *"categoria"* is difficult to translate. For industrial workers, it identifies a broad industry group rather than a particular craft or occupation. Thus, workers identify themselves as chemical, rubber, or metal workers. In agriculture, they call themselves *mezzadri* (sharecroppers) and *braccianti* (day laborers). Higher up the job ladder, the terms refers to broad occupational groups, such as clerical employees, or the *dirigenti* (executives).

Chart A

Structure of the Italian Labor Movement

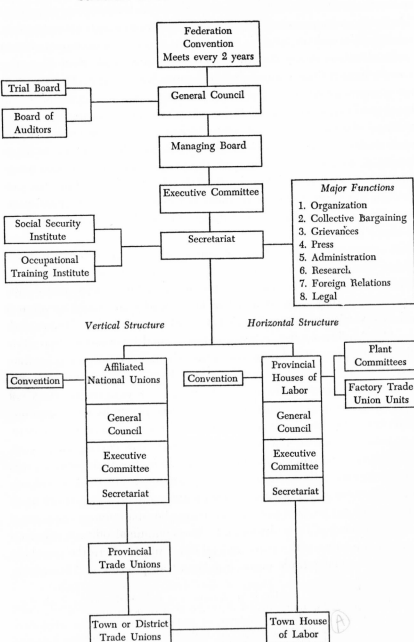

of contracts takes place in the higher echelons of trade unions, while the settlement of grievances between employers and workers is handled by the plant shop committee, which in theory represents all employees, regardless of what federation they belong to, or whether they are trade union members or not. These communal organizations, then, represent a weak base for the structure of Italian trade unionism. They provide for the provincial labor leader at the next level of organization the means of communication to the workers in the non-provincial towns.

Every commune of Italy belongs to one of ninety-two provinces, in each of which is found the seat of the provincial government. In these *luoghi di provincia* are found the power centers of the three labor movements. The relative strength of the federations at these seats of government varies from one province to the next. The CGIL may dominate in one area, while the CISL may be in the majority in another. In some provinces, the UIL is practically non-existent. Theoretically, each *categoria* will have its own organization in each provincial city. In fact, only the large labor unions, such as the Metal Workers or the Chemical Workers, are capable of carrying their own administrative units, and even they are found only in a few provinces. The general pattern is for the *categorie* to be grouped into units of industry, construction, mining, agriculture, and commerce within the same modest offices of the federation. The provincial office, consequently, is the center of both geographical and occupational representation, or what is termed horizontal and vertical structure, respectively. It represents the working part of the labor movement in Italy. For the CISL, this office was intended to become the means of developing collective bargaining on the company level. Instead, it has discharged, with different degrees of success, a consultation function for the members of the shop committees in collective bargaining; public relations duties, including relations with government officials and press campaigns; and direction of the annual election drive for shop committeemen. Organized workers, either directly, or indirectly through the communal leagues, belong to the provincial Chamber of Labor. Though the names of these offices differ among the three federations, their functions are similar. They are the heart of the labor movement in Italy.

Italian trade union government terminates in the national trade unions and the particular federations with which they are affiliated. Except in the UIL, the highest body in the organization is the General Council, approximately equivalent in the United States to the executive council of the AFL–CIO and the general executive boards of the national unions. The General Council is composed of an executive committee and members representing national unions, in the case of the federation, or major provincial organizations, in the case of the national unions. It is charged with the implementation and control of policy formulated in broad outline in convention. The UIL relies on a Managing Board as the highest body in the federation and national unions. Next in order for all three federations is a smaller executive committee which assists the secretariat in the execution of decisions formulated by the higher bodies. The members of the secretariat perform the day-to-day work of the organization. The secretary-general, equivalent to the *formand* of the Danish Samvirkende Fagforbund, is assisted by a number of secretaries, each responsible for a trade union function. In the CGIL they are elected by the Managing Board; in the CISL and the UIL, by the General Council and the executive committee, respectively. In the national unions, the secretaries are selected by the Managing Board, with the exception of the UIL, which selects its secretaries through the executive committee of each organization. The interviews conducted for this study concentrated on the secretaries in the national unions and the federations.

Some similarities exist between Italian and American federation organization. With the exception of the UIL, which has no general council, the sequence of trade union machinery is the convention, the General Council, Managing Board, executive committee, and secretariat. In the AFL–CIO, the similar bodies are the convention, General Board, Executive Council, executive committee, and the federation officers. Unlike the secretariat, American union officers are elected directly by the convention. A striking difference is the sharp distinction drawn in the United States between staff and line functions. Once the necessary functions are fixed, the Italians place in charge a secretary for each activity. In Italy there is no money for extended specialist functions. Nor is there, at the moment, the same measure of acceptance of the so-called union intellectual in a staff position, on the part of either the leadership or the rank and file. If the Italian trade unions should become more prosperous and more complex with age, it is probable that they would adopt the concept of line and staff organization.

Large communes, such as Milan, raise a special problem in organization. There, one local organization for all the members of a *categoria*, or one office for the provincial Chamber of Labor, would be too cumbersome. In such cities, where the problem is decentralization, various provincial suboffices are opened in the different industrial sectors of the city. In each of these places the *sindacati di categoria* are also likely to be housed, with a general secretary in charge of the organization. Small towns, on the other hand, may combine into one district office in order to amass a sufficiently large membership for an organization base.

The provincial leadership is usually comprised of three secretaries considered to be coequals. They are the *segretario sindacale,* the *segretario organizzativo,* and the *segretario generale.* As their titles indicate, their functions are collective bargaining, organizing, and coördinating, respectively. These leaders have a huge task to perform, with limited resources. They often attract to their offices workers who belong to no union, seeking employment or redress of grievances against an employer or the government. Some offices are housed in buildings dating back to the Renaissance period—Italy is the only country in western Europe where trade unionists can lean against sixteenth-century Corinthian columns and engage in contemplation looking up at vaulted ceilings painted with angels floating in an azure sky. The time for meditation, however, is not great. A singular characteristic of these places is bustle and confusion. These leaders have to organize and lead strikes, process grievances, train new leadership, develop trade-union–consciousness, bargain collectively with employers, deal with public officials, and cope with problems arising from such diverse economic activity as banking, insurance, construction, manufacturing, agriculture, mining, and transportation—all this on salaries no greater than that of a first-line supervisor in a medium-sized company. The administrative responsibilities of the general secretary, particularly when he is also a member of Parliament, are considerable. He has to keep in touch with the membership scattered throughout the province, and there is often only one automobile at the disposal of the whole organization. Nor is there much time or money to organize new members. Workers have to organize themselves, or are asked to affiliate when they come into the office because of a labor problem they are facing.

The next higher headquarters, Rome, is the seat of the three federations and of most of the national unions. The national unions, actually multi-industry federations, have neither the power, the resources, nor the collective bargaining function that they do in the United States.

They rely heavily on the assistance of the federation in the formulation of demands and the devising and execution of strategy. Moreover, funds tend to flow from the federations downward, rather than from the membership upward. In the CGIL, the financially independent unions include the Metal Workers, Chemical Workers, Textile Workers, Agricultural Laborers, and the Sharecroppers. In the CISL, organizations equivalent to the first three are probably the only independent ones in the federation. In the UIL, the Chemical Workers are the only trade unionists who enjoy a substantial measure of autonomy. The other national unions have to lean heavily on their federations for financial support and for assistance in collective bargaining. In their offices in Rome, a good gauge of their resources is the number of personnel in the organization, and the condition of the furnishings. The CGIL Chemical Workers, headed by a young, intelligent leader in the Communist party, have their offices across Via Buoncompagni from the United States Information Service of the American embassy, and their headquarters have almost the same respectable appearance as the bourgeois organization on the other side of the street. By contrast, the headquarters staff of the UIL Port Workers is composed of the general secretary and an office worker whom he shares with a colleague of another national union. Unlike the United States, consequently, these national unions have an intimate relationship with their respective federations. A close collaboration exists, in both political activity and collective bargaining.

The scope of the functions of the federations is greater than in Denmark. They have concluded federation-wide agreements on occupational differentials, individual and group dismissals, the functions of shop committees, cost-of-living adjustments, and the incorporation of cost-of-living allowances into the base-rate wage structure. The national unions rely heavily on their assistance in the conduct of their own bargaining. They organize national and regional meetings of workers, conciliate disputes between their provincial offices and national unions, arrange courses for trade union officials and rank-and-file members, organize May Day demonstrations, conduct organizing campaigns, create new national unions, call regional conferences on problems of a particular geographical area, and lobby in the Italian government. They also seek to involve the government in the writing of new agreements and announce the strike action of a particular national union. While an American or Danish trade unionist is apt to identify himself with the local of a particular trade union, if one were to ask an Italian worker to what union he belonged, he would be likely to mention one of the three federations.

Federation headquarters are administered by secretaries who are specialists in various functions of trade unionism.[3] The number of secretaries and assistants to the general secretary varies among the three federations. For example, the CISL office in Rome was staffed by 130 individuals, including both elected officials and administrative employees. The principal functions of the secretaries are collective bargaining, organization, administration, handling of grievances, foreign relations, legal counsel, public relations, and research. The research office is divided into six sections: economics, legislation, statistical research, industrial engineering, education and training, and library. In addition, the federations include the following offices: (1) a trial board, which is a court of last resort for disciplinary cases against individual members and disputes among different organizations in the federation; (2) an auditing board, which controls finances; (3) a semiautonomous Occupational Training Institute, subsidized by the state; and (4) a semi-autonomous Social Security Institute, also receiving state funds, which assists workers in obtaining benefits under the complex Italian system of compulsory social insurance.

There are several reasons for the dominant position of the federations in Italy. Top-heavy bureaucracy with a strong disinclination to decentralize is a characteristic of many Italian organizations. At the local level, there is lack of money and leadership. Workers are class conscious, rather than trade or industry conscious. After the fall of fascism, an entirely new labor movement had to be constructed, and both the CISL and the UIL had to build labor movements of their own from the top down after a series of secessions, beginning in 1948, from the CGIL. Because of such influences, major decisions affecting the rank and file tend to be made at the federation level.

There are no precise figures to show the relative strength of the three federations. Data based on the number of dues-paying members

---

[3] The social insurance system of Italy is administered by autonomous institutes, with the assistance of the social insurance organizations of the confederations. These institutes include the National Institute of Social Security, whose major functions concern pensions and unemployment insurance, the National Workmen's Compensation Institute (Istituto Nazionale Assicurazione contro gli Infortuni sul Lavoro), and the National Institute for Sickness Insurance. In addition to these organizations, there are special funds for particular groups of industrial and agricultural workers.

holding union cards may underestimate the actual number of adherents in each of the labor movements. The followers of a particular federation may vote for it in the shop elections without paying dues. Some find dues-paying a hardship, and some merely distasteful. To counterbalance the effect of this tendency to belong to the trade union movement without holding a membership card, there are certain factors which tend to swell membership data. Some provincial offices are liberal in the distribution of union cards to the rank and file. And in some areas, the CGIL also sells union cards to members of workers' families.

Informed Italian sources estimate total membership in the vicinity of six million, an estimate that seems to be somewhat exaggerated. The figure represents a decline of approximately 30 per cent from the peak reached in 1948. Of this figure, the CGIL is allotted 2,800,000; the CISL, 2,300,000; and the UIL, 700,000. The CGIL, therefore, is no longer a majority organization. The CISL estimates its own membership as of the end of 1958 as 2,316,000, increasing at the rate of 2.5 per cent annually. By economic sector, the distribution is strikingly even, being 26, 27, 27, and 20 per cent for agriculture, industry, commerce, and public employment, respectively. In soliciting its rival organizations for membership data, the CISL obtained an estimate of 3,600,000 from the CGIL and 1,000,000 from the UIL. These figures are scaled down by the CISL to 2,264,000 and 552,000. By economic sector, the CGIL is greater in strength in both agriculture and industry than the CISL. Comparable census figures for the United States and Italy, which could be used to compute on a similar base the percentage of the working class in the labor movement, do not exist. In Italy, figures for *dirigenti* and *impiegati* are combined by the Italian Central Institute of Statistics. Adding the combined supervisor and clerical figures to figures for industrial and agricultural workers and those seeking initial employment gives fifteen million as the approximate number representing the organizable working class. Consequently, despite a sharp decline in membership since 1948, some 40 per cent of Italian workers are still organized. (Before the rupture of the labor movement into three federations shortly after the end of the Second World War, over 60 per cent of all workers belonged to trade unions.) On the basis of figures issued by the Italian Confederation of Trade Unions on valid votes in shop steward elections in 1959, relative membership in the CGIL is somewhat higher. The CGIL polled 49 per cent of the vote, compared to 34.9 per cent for the CISL. The remaining 13 per cent represents 8 per cent of votes cast for the UIL and the rest for small trade union groups. The figures indicate a relative decline for the CISL from the peak reached in 1956.[4]

The payment of union dues in Italy is a process complex, occult, and infrequent. In principle, each worker pays for a federation card, *tessera*, and also makes monthly payments to his trade union. The *tessera* costs three hundred lire in the CGIL and the CISL, and a hundred lire in the UIL, and is renewed biennially in the first two organizations and annually in the last. The federations obtain a major portion of this sum, distributing the remainder to national unions and their own subsidiary organizations. The CGIL distributes union cards and the funds obtained therefrom through the National Bank of Labor, with the assistance of the various provincial Houses of Labor. The CISL operates in somewhat similar fashion, while the UIL uses the services of its provincial organizations directly. The payment of monthly dues is more complicated. The CGIL instructions provide for a minimum payment of 5 per cent of gross wages, and stipulate the percentage distribution of these funds to the various national union and federation organizations. The method of payment is through the purchase of stamps by the rank and file. It is estimated that monthly dues vary from 150 to 250 lire. The CISL and the UIL employ similar methods, but the average payments are much lower. For all these federations, there is close coöperation between the provincial offices and the local organizations of the national unions in the distribution and selling of stamps. The International Confederation of Free Trade Unions estimates that total dues-payment in Italy does not exceed 0.4 per cent of wages.

The task of persuading Italian workers to support their unions financially is difficult in the case of the *tessera* and prodigious in the matter of monthly dues. Estimates of payments of the latter range around 35 per cent. The federations, consequently, receive outside assistance. Of the three organizations, the CGIL is probably the most independent financially, and the UIL the least. The CISL and the UIL obtain substantial support from the International Confederation of Trade Unions. The CGIL, the CISL, and the UIL estimate their annual costs of operation at four billion lire, two and a half billion lire, and

[4] The conclusion that the CGIL remains the largest confederation in Italy is confirmed by Professor Neufeld. Comparison of three sources of data on votes in shop committee elections in 1957 shows a range of 47 per cent to 54 per cent of the factory vote for the CGIL, with the higher figure being that of the confederation itself. See Maurice Neufeld, *Italy: School for Awakening Countries*, p. 486.

one and a half billion lire, respectively. For these organizations and their affiliates, swollen treasuries are unknown, the normal state of affairs being a struggle to keep debts down to a minimum.

The labor leaders of Italy are chosen by executive boards elected by the rank and file or their delegates. In principle, each set of labor leaders at the various levels of leadership is elected by a kind of board of elders or respected men, to whom the executives are answerable. In no case do the workers choose a specific labor leader. Rather, they choose groups of men who exercise the responsibility of selecting the leader.[5] Beginning at the grass roots, for example, workers in a *sindacato* in a town or area elect an executive board and delegates to the next convention level. This committee elects the *segretari*, or the labor leaders. The provincial trade union organization, in turn, elects an executive board and delegates to the next higher convention, the assembly of the national union. The national union convention then elects its own executive board, secretaries, and delegates to the federation convention. Starting from the grass roots again, within the federation structure, all the workers in the various *sindacati* belonging to the same federation in a town or area elect an executive committee for their local Houses of Labor. Delegates from the *sindacati* and those from the local Houses of Labor come together in convention to choose the executive board of the key unit of the Italian labor movement, the provincial House of Labor. Finally, the federation leadership is elected by delegates from the national unions and the provincial Houses of Labor.

In comparison with the United States, the Italian labor leader is subject to greater control by executive boards. At the same time he is shielded to a greater extent from the shifting political pressures and sentiments that affect the quality of leadership. It sometimes happens in practice, however, that the labor leader is selected by the head of the organization to which he reports. A provincial secretary may be chosen by the federation in Rome, and may hold office until such time as he can be formally elected through the regular voting procedure. The structure of voting, consequently, may only exist on paper. In theory, however, the Italian labor movement represents a striking synthesis of maximum trade union democracy and leadership responsibility.

[5] I suspect that this practice more effectively subordinates the labor leader to the will of the executive body than is the case in the United States.

In trade union government, the Italian shop committees are an anomaly. The representatives of these committees are elected by all the workers in the plant, regardless of whether they belong to the trade union or not. Each of the three provincial Houses of Labor sponsors candidates for the plant elections if they have a substantial following of workers. In many instances, the provincial secretary gets his start as a member of the committee in the plant where he has managed to develop a following. Sometimes, he continues to be a committeeman, managing in this way to supplement his meager salary with the plant wages he draws while on leave of absence. The pattern of relationship varies from that of committeemen under the close control of the provincial secretary to that of shop representatives who are the tail wagging the dog of the trade union. In the 1958 shop elections at Fiat, for example, a committeeman led a secessionist movement from the CISL and managed to obtain 17,750 votes out of a total of 57,000 cast. The secessionist group reduced the former plurality of the CISL in numbers of committeemen to eleven by electing thirty-one of their own committeemen and announced themselves as the new free-labor movement.

The increasing prestige of the shop committees, therefore, has made them the Achilles' heel of the Italian labor movement. The CISL has tended to reject them as legitimate instruments of either trade union organization or collective bargaining. Despite the fact that they were established by mutual agreement between the federations and the employers' association, employers use the committees as a means of escaping trade unionism. They have been utilized to negotiate terms of employment above those agreed to by the national unions in nation-wide agreements. They are a divisive force among the workers. Each federation has its own committee bulletin board in the plant. Each group publishes its own paper, which more often than not indulges in vilification of rival leaders. Groups do not accept decisions made by rival groups. Unless a federation can succeed in capturing a substantial number of the committee posts and subordinate the role of the shop committee to the needs of trade unionism, the growth of effective national unions may be blocked.

Plant trade union sections are a recent innovation. Under the stimulus of developing collective bargaining at the company level, the CISL has organized such sections, in the hope of making them the new base of Italian trade unionism. These *sezioni aziendali* would be similar to the Danish *klub*, bringing together all the workers in a plant who belong to the same trade union. The CGIL has also organized plant locals, but like those of the CISL, they often exist only on paper. In the UIL, plant locals have proved to be even more ephemeral. To acquire a function which would give them a purpose for existing and prospering, they would have to dominate the shop committee. Moreover, only one section of a federation could perform effectively in behalf of the rank and file. Consequently, without the decline of the shop committee and the dominance of one federation section at the expense of the others, such trade union sections represent at best an aspiration for the future.

How Italian Labor Leaders Spend Their Working Time

The functions and relationships of Italian labor leaders differ by level of leadership and size of organization more than they do by type of federation. A description of the way specific individuals are discharging their role as labor leaders seems more significant than the presentation of a median working time. The description below presents the workday of three specific individuals belonging to the two largest federations. They were chosen for the following reasons: (1) They represent key points of leadership, one being the head of a labor movement; the second, the general secretary of a large industrial union; and the third, a provincial leader in the industrial North. (2) They represent the younger generation of labor leadership in Italy; two are Catholics, and the third is a young Communist who has risen fast up the ranks of the labor movement and the Communist party.

A pivotal Italian labor leader, the general secretary of the provincial organization, works, on an average, fifty hours a week from Monday to Saturday. If the frequent Sunday meetings are included, his workweek would run to approximately fifty-five hours. In addition to his regular workday, he holds meetings with work groups in the evening between six and eight, has dinner afterward, and then tries to catch up on his technical reading. His work is not a job but a mission. Most of his relationships are with his colleagues, of whom there may be from three to ten, and with worker and *attivisti* groups. In addition, he has relationships with government personnel, employers, representatives of employer associations, leaders of political parties, members of strategic groups in the community, and leaders of the federation.

His major responsibilities consist of holding meetings for the purpose of planning, operating, and coördinating the activity of his organization, and working alone, which involves for the most part handling correspondence and reading newspapers and literature in his field. A relatively small amount of time is spent in either the interpretation or the writing of collective bargaining agreements.

The high fractionalization of Italian social affairs makes the secretary's daily reading a considerable assignment. Every day he hurriedly glances through the newspapers of the major political parties, including *Unità, Avanti, Italia, Popolo,* and *Corriere.* In addition, there are the journals of the two rival labor organizations to be perused. Further reading includes reports of what employers are saying in the industry, and the *Bollettino per Dirigenti* published by the federation for the information of its trade union leaders. Reading on particular problems is done on a basis of subdivision of labor. With the help of colleagues, a reading list is put together, and then one individual is assigned the responsibility of briefing everyone else on the staff.

Approximately 15 per cent of the secretary's worktime is devoted to relationships with worker groups. Another 15 per cent is used in relationships with colleagues, including officials at the provincial and federation level. Most of this time is spent in daily conferences with the organization, administration, and trade union secretaries, the various secretaries of the major trade unions, and clerks discharging different functions of the office. The purpose of these daily conferences is to achieve a maximum of autonomous action within the framework of general objectives; in his words, "*Autonomia di funzione ed il massimo di collegialità e omogeneità di lavoro.*" An additional 15 per cent of the secretary's time is spent in contacts with representatives of employer associations. Day-by-day relationships with such associations are actually handled by the office in charge of trade union problems. The provincial general secretary intervenes only in those collective bargaining matters that are general in scope, not those related to particular trade union groups. Approximately 5 per cent of his time is devoted to particular employers. This relationship, however, is infrequent and irregular. It consists mostly of trying to adjust a grievance or finding employment for a member. An additional 10 per cent of his time is consumed in relationships with various public officials in government, technical, and cultural groups, or as a representative on various commissions. The remainder of his time is spent in working alone: handling correspondence, examining proposals coming before him, analyzing situations with which he is confronted, and future planning.

From the point of view of major responsibilities, a provincial leader allocates his time as follows: grievances, 5 per cent; new collective bargaining agreements, 15 per cent; outside meetings and conventions, 5 per cent; correspondence and general reading, 25 per cent; and worker conferences, 15 per cent. Other responsibilities consuming the remainder of worktime include daily coördination conferences, formulation of programs, participation in public bodies, and reading alone. Most of the working time, consequently, is consumed either in the handling of correspondence, in planning, or in conducting or participating in conferences inside the organization or with other groups. Responsibilities external to the organization are primarily with government agencies in the field of labor, such as the different social insurance agencies and the provincial offices of the Department of Labor. Time spent in the writing and administration of collective bargaining agreements is relatively small.

The factors which account for this particular configuration of work are several: (1) the importance of close supervision of trade unions in a situation of scarce economic and human resources; (2) the relatively minor contacts with employers because of the focus on bargaining at the national level; (3) the importance in Italian trade unionism of providing social welfare assistance to workers, which becomes increasingly important as one moves from industrial to agricultural areas; (4) the emphasis on the political function of increasing the strength of the federation at the expense of the other federations, through the medium of the press, literature, posters, and the various shop committees in the area.

The average workweek of a national union labor leader is fifty hours, including meetings on holidays. His fundamental responsibility consists of "directing and coördinating the activity of the union, consistent with the decisions of the convention, the central committee, the executive committee, and the secretariat." In the discharge of this function, he allocates his time in the following manner: (1) For contacts with colleagues in his trade union, he allows 15 per cent. These colleagues include members of the secretariat, central committee, the leaders of the provincial trade union offices, the members of the federation, and finally the administrative staff of the national headquarters in Rome. (2) He spends 15 per cent of his time with workers. These are group meetings, including delegations of workers coming to the national headquarters, meeting in the field, and contacts with *attivisti* in the different factories. In view of the fact that this union, even by American standards, is a large one, the extent of this direct communication with workers is unusual. (3) The processing of grievances and the collective bargaining of new agreements takes 13 per cent. Since this union is one of the very few powerful and independent national unions in Italy, this figure may not be representative of all the affiliated organizations in the federation. (4) For working alone he allows 24 per cent. This figure includes time in handling correspondence, which is estimated at 10 per cent. (5) He uses 20 per cent of his time in activity at the Chamber of Deputies as a member of Parliament. This is an estimate of time actually spent at the Parliament. (6) In contacts with employer associations he spends 5 per cent, in addition to the 13 per cent cited above in the processing of grievances and in preparation for collective bargaining. (7) Meetings other than those with colleagues inside the organization and with workers take 4 per cent. (8) In relations with business organizations, government agencies, and the Department of Labor, he spends 2 per cent. (9) In relationships with the public, he spends another 2 per cent.

One secetary-general of a federation listed the following man-to-man relationships: (1) with colleagues in the federation, national unions, and provincial Houses of Labor, 40 per cent; (2) with individual employers, 5 per cent; (3) with employer associations, 5 per cent; (4) in relations with the public, mostly government officials, 5 per cent; (5) with members of the Chamber of Deputies, 10 per cent. In terms of major responsibilities, the allocation of worktime is broken down as follows: (1) With colleagues in the federation, national unions, and provincial organizations, in discharging the function of providing *coordinamento and stimolo,* he spends 40 per cent. (2) In the collective bargaining function, 2 per cent is allocated for grievances and an additional 3 for the writing of new agreements. Total employer and employer association contacts, however, consume 10 per cent of worktime. (3) An estimated 10 per cent of worktime is spent in meetings, assemblies, and conventions of the federation and affiliated organizations. (4) Another 10 per cent of time is used as a member of Parliament. (5) Of the average workweek, 25 per cent is consumed in working alone, including the handling of correspondence, which is estimated at 10 per cent. (6) The remaining 5 per cent embraces the discharge of the public-relations function mentioned above.

It is interesting to compare this time-allocation with that of another federation general secretary who is not a member of Parliament. He also listed 10 per cent in relationships with political leaders and 10 per cent with individual employers and employer associations. In addition, he cited 10 per cent of his time devoted to contacts with workers through the medium of unions and conferences. Under responsibilities, he listed 20 per cent of his working time devoted to grievances and the writing of new agreements. The greater time devoted to collective bargaining may be a reflection of his work with weaker, more dependent, affiliated national unions.

The structure of the Milan office of the CISL provides an example of the functions of an Italian trade union headquarters in a large city. The general secretary defines his functions in terms of the seven offices over which he has executive responsibility. These are (1) technical–trade union services (servizio tecnico-sindacale), with the function of providing technical and collective bargaining assistance to affiliated trade unions and settling individual grievances of workers; (2) legal office for the assistance of the rank-and-file member; (3) research and education office for the assembling of data covering matters of interest to the organization and for the preparing of trade unionists for the performance of their duties; (4) press office, which publishes the organization newspaper and issues press releases; (5) office of plant trade unions and shop committees, which assists in the formation and operation of the trade union units and shop committees in plants of the area; (6) social assistance office, which provides aid to workers in obtaining social security benefits from government agencies; and (7) administrative office, which furnishes administrative and clerical aid to the affiliated trade union organizations.

The general secretary views his responsibility as that of executing the policies of the federation. Citing the constitution of provincial organizations, he represents the secretariat in his relationship with employers and public authorities, and with these parties makes decisions consistent with the function of the union. He prepares a report one month before the calling of the convention, subject to the approval of the General Board, and mediates disputes arising among the affiliated trade unions in the organization. For these unions he is supposed to provide a sense of direction (un indirizzo sindacale o organizzativo).

In the discharge of these duties, he is expected to encourage a maximum participation of both trade union officials and rank-and-file members.

In summary, the following observations can be made: (1) It is probable that as the affiliated national unions become stronger, the work of the federation will become increasingly that of public relations and politics. (2) The burden of political activity for those engaged actively in politics is probably underestimated by the respondents. The two members of Parliament interviewed had assumed office recently. It can be presumed that the pressure of parliamentary duties would become increasingly burdensome as these men acquired status in the Chamber of Deputies. Time spent as a deputy becomes especially onerous when Parliament is in session and the officeholder administers a union organization whose headquarters are outside of Rome. Even when Parliament is not convening, however, time must be spent in mending fences in one's constituency. For these reasons, it can be said that a prominent member of Parliament whose union organization is not in Rome is likely to be an absentee trade union executive who does not administer his office.

DANISH ORGANIZATION

Danish trade union organization has been traditionally pivoted around the exclusive association in a local union of all workers in a particular craft in a geographical area. (See Chart B.) It is more similar to American organization than to Italian, but more British than American. The skilled workers in a plant are organized, each in his own appropriate craft union. The remaining employees, the unskilled workers and the women, belong to their own organizations.[6] A particular company, therefore, has a variety of unions, whose members are covered by separate national agreements negotiated by the national union and the industry association of the employers. The workers have strong feelings for this trade union exclusiveness, the skilled employees by tradition, and the unskilled because they were not wanted originally by the craft unions and now feel capable of holding

---

[6] Some quasi-industrial unions have developed as a consequence of industrial growth. They include the Pottery Workers, Tobacco Workers, Textile Workers, Shoe Workers, and the Clothing Workers. The mixture of quasi-industrial and craft unions explains the greater number of organizations than exists in Italy. The pressures causing a consolidation of these unions are likely to create a decline in separate organizations over the years.

Chart B

Structure of the Danish Labor Movement

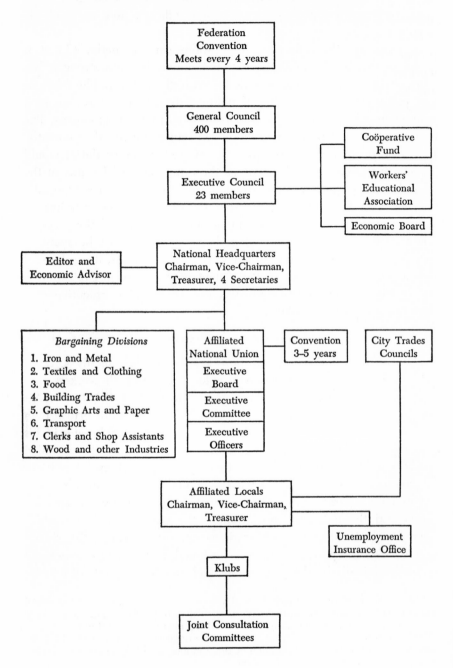

their own. Therefore, while the core of Italian trade unionism is the interunion House of Labor, its equivalent in Denmark, the Trade Union Council, is of no consequence.

The tone of the Danish labor offices contrasts with that in Italy. They lack bustle and noise, and are more expensively furnished. The portraits on the walls, of bearded former leaders who have passed away, suggest the stage of nostalgia in which the Danish labor movement finds itself. The association between the offices of the national unions and the federation does not exist in the same degree that it does in Italy. Only two of the seventy-one affiliated unions are to be found in the same building of the federation. The atmosphere of these places is not much different from the calm and tranquillity of a government office.

Comparison of different levels of trade union organization in Denmark with those in Italy raises a problem. In Italy, the two basic power centers are the federation and the provincial Chambers of Labor. Danish union structure is geared around the trade union. The decision-making body in the federation, the Executive Council, is comprised of the leaders of the dominant national unions. Consequently, for purposes of this study the Danish interviews were focused on the *formand* of the national unions and local organizations. All the major unions were covered, together with a representative group of the small crafts and at least two locals of major unions, both inside and outside of Copenhagen. In this way, some degree of comparability was obtained, the primary leadership outside the plant comprising the officials of the local organizations, and the secondary leadership consisting of the heads of the national unions. These two sets of leaders compare roughly with the general secretaries of the provincial organizations and national *sindacati* in Italy.

The mavericks who wield influence in the Danish labor movement are not the Communists, as in Italy, but the leaders of three dominant organizations: the General and Special Workers' Union (Dansk Arbejdsmands og Special-Arbejder Forbund), the Metal Workers (Smede og Maskinarbejder Forbund), and the Office Workers (Handels og Kontorfunktionaerernes Forbund). The positions they take have a significant bearing on the direction in which the Danish labor movement moves. The goals, the perceptions, and the structure within these organizations are not similar. The reconciliation of their differences provides the evolutionary force that gives direction to Danish trade unionism. The leader of the Metal Workers is sympathetic to the reorganization of the Danish labor movement into industrial-union lines, while the heads of the other two organizations take exception to this view. There are differing opinions on the issue, however, within the separate organizations. Characteristics shared by these three men are the absence of a narrow craft-guild mentality, more than average resources in money and talent, and the ability to take a position that is not easily predictable. Any new configuration taken by Danish trade union organization in the future will depend upon a reconciliation of the points of view of the leaders of these three unions. The sort of bargain that will evolve among them will be influenced by internal pressures in their organizations and differences in their astuteness in anticipating the impact of their decisions on particular organizational interests.

The typical structure in Danish trade unionism is that of the old craft union evolving slowly, and at times painfully, with the changing exigencies of technology. The major exceptions to this type of structure are the two unions of men and women workers in occupations which the crafts were not interested in organizing. The growth of the factory system is breaking down craft lines. The General Workers, so called, perform some jobs which in the United States would be called skilled operations. The existence of workers side by side in the same plant performing similar or allied operations but belonging to different unions is becoming increasingly intolerable. The two types of organization, however, are likely to persist for some time to come. Accordingly, two descriptions are appropriate: that of the craft or modified-craft type which is assimilating an increasing number of workers in its industry, and that of the huge interindustry General Workers' Union, which organizes male workers regardless of workplace, occupation, or industry. With the exceptions noted below, the functions and relationships of the latter are similar to those of the former.

The Danish rank and file are found in *klubs* brought together in the same town to form a union local. Workers in a factory belonging to the same union, or those in a specific area of the same trade, organize themselves into a *klub*. All the metal workers in a plant, for example, belong to one *klub*. In addition, a local of the General Workers in Copenhagen may have separate *klubs* for each of the occupations in which its members are found. It is here at the base that the strong occupational identity of the Danish worker is preserved, and it is here that, as chairmen of these units, Danish labor leaders often get their start in trade union leadership.

The trade union local bringing together the members of a clearly defined geographical area is the oldest unit in Danish trade union structure.[7] The local discharges many responsibilities, for while the locus of wage-bargaining has tended to move toward the federation level, local functions have not atrophied at all. The typical local labor leader, or *formand,* has a variety of duties to perform: (1) He polices the collective bargaining agreement. Constantly checking on rates being paid by employers and attending to the pay grievances of workers consume a considerable portion of executive time. (2) He assists in the writing of new agreements. In a number of instances, locals may negotiate new contracts with employers who do not belong to an industry association. Generally, their contract-writing function is limited to channeling worker demands up to the national union level. (3) He administers the unemployment compensation office. (4) He checks the progress of apprentices of masters in the local jurisdiction. (5) He administers mutual insurance funds, when they are found, including life and health insurance. (6) He conducts labor education courses for shop stewards and rank-and-file members. (7) He assists the shop stewards in the selection of rank-and-file members for factory joint production committees. While the labor leaders generally express disappointment over the results of these management-worker committees, they also emphasize their potential importance if the scope of their functions were broadened. (8) He provides jobs for the membership. In building and construction, the sole means of finding employment, for a worker, is through the union that organizes his occupation. (Similarly, the labor organizations in transportation and communication recruit workers for employers.) In manufacturing, to a lesser extent, the union is also an important source of employment. The locals can no longer call a strike or expel members without review by the national union.

The national union brings the collective bargaining function to its next higher level. It processes grievances before industry arbitration boards, and with the assistance of a federation secretary represents locals before the labor arbitration court of Denmark. In the writing

[7] As of January 1, 1958, there were 3,617 locals affiliated with the Danish trade union federation.

of new agreements, the national union leader negotiates with the representatives of the industry association in which his members are found. Demands emanating from the locals are cut down and mailed at the same time that the industry association presents its own demands on the union. In most instances, the national union takes the initiative in informing the locals what the general questions are likely to be. These consist of demands covering the entire membership, such as general wage increases, hours reduction, or new fringe benefits. The locals are then asked to submit special questions to the national union. If negotiation of general questions fails at the national union level, which is usually the case, bargaining goes to the next higher level, that of the general employers' association, with the assistance of a secretary from the federation. Movement to this third step in the federation structure has a specific deadline. In addition to these duties, the national union publishes a trade union paper, and makes periodic visits to workplaces where contacts are made with shop stewards and workers. The national union leader also has the responsibility of organizing the unorganized, in which, except for the Clerical Workers' Union, he often gains the assistance of the employers' association. He also supervises labor education courses given by his organization and follows changes in technology and their effect on the work controlled by his organization.

The scope of the functions of the headquarters federation is constantly widening. Its functions are controlled not so much by the unwillingness of the federation to increase them as by the suspicion of top strength that prevails in the labor movement. The headquarters, as of the beginning of 1959, maintained a total staff of twenty-three, including seven elected officials, consisting of the chairman, vice-chairman, treasurer, and four secretaries. The policy bodies of the federation are the General Council of four hundred members and the Executive Council, consisting of the permanent officers, two officers appointed by the Social Democrat party, and fourteen elected by the convention, among whom the leaders of the big unions are always represented. On the General Council each union has one representative for each two thousand members. The function of the General Council is to lay down trade union policy within the framework of the convention and to set up collective bargaining objectives. A smaller, twenty-three–man council is the executive body of the federation. It serves the purpose of making major decisions which the federation chairman feels cannot be made by him alone.

The unions in the same industry are brought together for collective bargaining in a group at the federation level. These bodies, called *kartels,* are similar to the departments of the American Federation of Labor. During the field investigation, a new form of interunion organization was created for the purpose of approval of new collective bargaining agreements. These eight interunion groups (the General Workers' Union belongs to all but one) are a faint glimmer of coming industrial unionism and are likely eventually to supplant the *kartels* entirely.

An important staff office of the federation is that of the editor and economic adviser. In a sense, he represents the lone intellectual in the Danish federation. A college graduate in economics, he is the editor of the federation newspaper, *Løn og Virke.* In addition, he furnishes technical assistance on such matters as time and motion study, incentive systems of wage payment, and industry rationalization.

Two outside organizations provide special assistance to the federation. The Workers' Educational Association, whose funds are derived from the federation and its affiliates, and from the Social Democrat party and other organizations in the labor movement, organizes and manages the labor education of the Danish labor movement. The association also manages the worker high schools, those extraordinary institutions of Denmark which in places such as Esbjerg assume the aspect of a university campus. In addition, jointly with the coöperative movement, the federation finances the Labor Movement Economic Board (Arbejder- bevaegelsens Erhvervsraad). It is directly responsible to the Executive Council of the federation. The board is employed to provide economic information for the purpose of assisting the labor movement in collective bargaining. Its offices resemble those of its federation employers, where the colorful modern furniture and the leisurely pace of work contrast with the atmosphere of top Italian organization.

In sum, several functions which make the federation a seat of power can be cited. In the first place, it decides general changes in the terms of employment in the Danish economy, together with its counterpart among employers, the Arbejdsgiver Forening. Three men, the chairman of the federation and the respective chairmen of the Metal Workers and the General Workers, are the key individuals who shape the bargain. Secondly, the presence of the offices of the Social Democrat party in the same building as the federation is symbolic of its influence over the party. Third is the influence it exercises over the education of workers through apprenticeship training and the labor high schools.

Lastly, the federation plays an important role in shifts in the economy because of the impossibility of the government's making major changes in policy without first consulting and obtaining the acquiescence of the top leadership of the trade unions.

The financing of this trade union structure comes from the dues of the rank-and-file members, the amount varying with the different affiliated national unions. The federation estimates that average dues for members paying full dues is 6.45 kroner per week, out of which 3.65 kroner is applied to unemployment insurance. Of the remainder, 1.53 kroner goes to the national union and 1.27 to the locals. In turn, the national union pays the federation 17½ øre per week. The collection of dues is normally undertaken by each local on a weekly basis; in a minority of cases, payment is on a monthly basis.

In dollar equivalents based on the foreign rate of exchange, the average Danish worker is paying approximately one dollar per week in dues, including money which goes into unemployment insurance. This sum represents a little more than his pay for an hour's work. Of the total dues collected from approximately 705,500 trade unionists, the federation receives roughly one million dollars per year. The largest union in the federation, based on a paying membership of 247,000, has an income of approximately $1,400,000 per year, or five dollars per member annually.

By Danish standards, the General Workers' Union is a huge and diverse trade union. Its 247,000 men in 1,304 locals include half of the male workers in the Danish labor movement. Each member belongs to one of four semi-autonomous groups covering four categories: (1) factory work; (2) construction, including buildings, roads, and railways; (3) agriculture; and (4) transportation, which includes longshoremen, drivers, and warehousemen. Their wages reflect this industrial diversity, ranging from seven kroner hourly for workers in construction, a rate comparable to that paid to a highly skilled Danish worker, to four kroner hourly for messengers. Each group elects its own officers in separate conventions after the termination of the general convention. Some locals include all four groups. Where a town is sufficiently large, however, the groups are split into four separate local unions.

Each industry group has its own chairman and governing board of about ten members elected in convention every three years. Together with the chairman, assistant chairman, secretary, and treasurer, they form the General Board of the organization. A smaller body, consisting of the permanent officers and the chairmen of the four industry groups, comprises the executive committee. With the economic adviser of the labor union, who acts as secretary, these eight men administer the organization.

The General Workers are the left wing of the Danish labor movement, in the sense of playing the part of challengers to the dominant forces in the organization. The members speak readily of their pride in their union: "The skilled workers did not want us, and now we are the biggest union in Denmark." An atmosphere of *camaraderie* and pride in newly acquired status pervades the union. In the official attitude opposing industrial unionism, there are some dissenting voices. Generally, however, the argument is that the General Workers' Union fills a need in an economy where skilled craftsmen perpetuate their position by restricting apprenticeship to their families and associates. In Sweden, industrial unions exist because a member has the right to rise up the occupational ladder in his industry solely on the basis of the talent he possesses. By contrast, in Denmark the collective bargaining agreement gives the skilled worker exclusive job rights and in this fashion perpetuates social inequality. In an atmosphere of limited job opportunities, the problem is who is to do the available work. The general sentiment is that the General Workers' Union is the best assurance that can be provided unskilled workers that they obtain their fair share of the work. In this respect, the leaders of the union point with a wry look at a new building, across the street from union headquarters, constructed entirely by the "unskilled workers" of their labor organization. In many inside industries, the General Workers, who once consisted of the helpers of the elite craftsmen, have become skilled production workers who have slowly relegated the craftsmen to a small group of repair and maintenance men.

The General Workers have an office in Copenhagen which takes care of unemployment insurance payments and labor education for all their members in the city. The head of the organization stated with pride that labor education is voluntary and that they had had even cabinet ministers as teachers, and sometimes college professors.

How Danish Labor Leaders Spend Their Working Time

The relationships and functions of the chairman of a local union vary with the extent of its collective bargaining functions, and the degree to which the union is a "leader" or a "follower" in the labor movement.

Some local unions write new collective bargaining agreements, while others are concerned only with their interpretation. Moreover, a trade union such as the General Workers' is likely to be more dynamic and pioneering in its activity than a small craft union in a declining industry. Accordingly, the following analysis of relationships and functions at the level of a large General Workers' local union is more typical of an expanding organization whose function includes the writing of agreements than of a static organization.

The chairman of one particular local union estimated his weekly working time at fifty-five to sixty hours. These hours include time spent on Sunday meetings and instruction in labor education courses, and they increase appreciably during the winter months. Of his working relationships, he estimated that 5 per cent are with his colleagues, including those in his office and those in the national union headquarters; 20 per cent with workers and their shop steward representatives; a total of 30 per cent with employers and the employers' association, with time equally divided between the two; 3 per cent with government officials; 35 per cent by himself; and the remainder in relationships with people with whom he comes in contact by virtue of political and cultural activities.

The largest percentage of time, 30 per cent, is devoted to the handling of correspondence. What he conceives of as correspondence includes the reading and dictation of letters, the writing of drafts of circulars for local distribution, and the final phrasing of collective bargaining agreements. Twenty per cent of worktime is devoted to the handling of individual grievances and 15 per cent in collective bargaining with employers. Twenty per cent is estimated as time necessary to prepare and hold meetings on official business, and 5 per cent in relations with the public. For the remainder of his responsibilities, he includes conducting seminars and lectures at the folk high schools, going to the folk high school as a "student," editing a two-page local union newspaper, and selecting and reading articles from various periodicals. He also attends seminars conducted by the Social Democrat party, and is a member of the board of the labor movement's cultural organization, Socialistisk Debat, and of the Young Peoples' Athletics, De Unges Idraet. This labor leader is the chairman of a local of the General and Special Workers' Union, whose members are in occupations ranging from longshoremen to hodcarriers and teamsters.

The scope of the activities of the chairman of a small craft local with a stable or declining membership would be less. A proportionately greater amount of time, 60 per cent, is spent in the administration of the piece-rate system and on-the-site inspection of work. Cultural activities take considerably less time and the number of weekly hours averages forty, from eight-thirty to four on weekdays, and Saturdays until noon. In either case, the chairman or an assistant, depending upon the size of the union, is helping the unemployed among the membership to find jobs.

A president of a national union, for whom a dominant function is coördination, cited a proportionately greater amount of time spent in person-to-person relationships with colleagues. In one of the largest unions in Denmark, these associates include the heads of subdivisions of the union, the chairmen of other national unions, the *formand* of the trade union federation and union representatives at the local level, and leaders in the Social Democrat party. The percentage of time spent in the discharge of the function of coördination is estimated at 30 per cent. The proportions stipulated are broken down as follows: with workers, 10 per cent; with employers and employer associations, 30 per cent; with public officials, 15 per cent; working alone, 22 per cent, and the remainder, in international relations, including trips abroad. Leaders at the national and the local level differ, accordingly, in the amount of time they spend in group activity, and in the relationships they have with public officials and at the ultimate points of power in the society.

The same union president cited as his most important responsibilities the holding of conferences in his organization and the discharge of relationships with public representatives. The percentage for the former he wrote as 50, and that for the latter as 22. In addition, he stated that very little time, a fraction of 1 per cent, is spent in the consideration of individual grievances, while 15 percentage points were cited for the discharge of the collective bargaining function with the employer. The remainder of his responsibilities includes the handling of correspondence, meetings with staff personnel, and what he described as "international connections."

A representative of the small craft unions cited the following use of worktime, including relationships and responsibilities. The workweek is fifty hours, including a half-day on Saturday. Of relationships, 15 per cent of worktime involves colleagues, including, in diminishing degree, associates in the national union office, the chairmen of other national unions, the president of the federation, and the president of the metal trades department. Twenty-five per cent is spent with workers at the national office, local headquarters, or work sites. Four per cent of worktime is spent with employers or representatives of the employers' association; 2 per cent with public officials, 10 with individuals concerned with labor education and work in the coöperative movement, and an estimated 23 per cent in working alone. Of responsibilities, the proportion of time spent in the resolution of individual grievances, 25 per cent of worktime, is relatively high. The breakdown includes 15 per cent for collective bargaining, 20 in holding meetings, 2 in public relations, and the rest in working alone. The latter involves handling correspondence, writing articles for the trade union newspaper, reading "trade and social literature," and occasionally preparing a lecture for a labor education meeting. These differences between his allocation of worktime and that of the national union president cited above reflect the responsibilities attendant upon specialized craft operations and piece-rate systems of payment. These methods of work and remuneration require a continual process of collective bargaining to determine piece rates for new jobs and to settle individual worker grievances on earnings.

No doubt, these relative percentages are not precise and may be inconsistent when a close comparison is made between those cited under responsibilities and those cited for relationships. Greater accuracy could be obtained if the investigator could sit down with the interviewee and work out the proportions more closely. It is presumed, however, that they are approximately accurate, and that the broad outlines of their differences reflect dissimilarities within the respective labor movements and between the Italian and Danish organizations. As such, they provide an insight into the day-by-day operations of labor leaders and indicate how different problems and resources are affecting their behavior.

Study of the organization of the Danish and Italian labor movements suggests the following benchmarks for comparison of the structure of labor organizations.

1) *General characteristics of organization machinery.*—The Italian labor movement is broadly based, relying heavily on regional offices of a federation to control and coördinate within its area the activities of trade unions organized on the basis of broad industry groups. In

Denmark, though a union organizes all workers of a particular craft, the labor movement is evolving into organizations which are quasi-industrial in character and behavior. Correspondingly, while an Italian union may organize workers from toolmakers to bicycle repairmen in an artisan shop, these broad groupings tend to break down administratively in particular industries. Consequently, the two countries appear to be moving in a similar direction, toward unions of quasi-industrial forms.

2) *Working-time allotment.*—The Danes spend a greater portion of their worktime in bargaining collectively with particular employers. Functions differ with the level of leadership and the size of the union. Federations tend to deal with politics and public relations more than do national unions. In Italy a greater amount of time is spent in the performance of interunion activity. The leader of a large national union is apt to spend a considerable amount of time in relations with the public and government, concerned with matters not dealing directly with collective bargaining relationships with particular employers.

3) *The tone of trade union activity.*—The atmosphere of Italian trade unionism is charged with conflict and missionary zeal; that of the Danes, marked by orderliness and systematic operation. The former is still in the stage of rebellion, while the latter is an accepted bureaucracy, serving quasi-government functions. For purposes of theoretical speculation, it will be interesting to see whether the shift from rebellion to acceptance will produce in Italy a corresponding public function for labor organization. Its beginnings may be discernible in the social security aid which the Italian trade unions dispense.

4) *Source and distribution of income.*—Danish organization is operated on the dues of its rank and file, which flow upward toward the federation and political party. The Italians are dependent upon outside sources of income, the distribution of which is made from the federations downward.

5) *The locus of organization influence.*—In Italy, the federations dominate the national unions, except for a few national unions in large-scale industries. They are responsible for the conduct of collective bargaining for many of their union affiliates. At the plant level, influence is often exerted less by the union than by the shop committee, which technically is not responsible to any trade union organization. If the national unions are able to become financially independent of other organizations, and if pressure is brought on them to provide technical

services peculiar to their own particular members in order to avoid the collapse of worker interest in trade unionism, the locus of power may shift from the Houses of Labor to the national unions. The major unions in Italy are those in the metal, rubber, and chemical industries, and the *mezzadri* and *braccianti* unions in agriculture. In Denmark, though the regional organizations of the federation are of little consequence, the federation headquarters exercises increasing influence as major decisions in collective bargaining are shifted toward that level. The national union, however, remains the dominant seat of organization influence. The particular unions which dominate the Danish federation are the Metal Workers and the General Workers.

6) *Characteristics at the bottom of the structure.*—In Italy, local organization is often non-existent. Local unions in Denmark are involved in collective bargaining and employment problems. Danish local leaders are engaged also in apprenticeship training, development of shop stewards, maintenance of quality production, and administration of unemployment compensation and grievance-processing. In Italy, there is an acute need for the federation to inspire local trade union activity. No such need exists in Denmark.

7) *Extent of left-wing dissension in the labor movement.*—The left wing of the Danish labor movement is contained within the existing organizations. It is small, and serves the function of asking for a little more in collective bargaining than the conservative leadership. The left wing in Italy has a labor movement of its own.

8) *Extent of organization of the work force.*—Labor force statistics available for these countries are not comparable. In Italy, however, the extent of labor organization is estimated at some 40 per cent of the working classes, including both blue- and white-collar workers up to the first level of supervision. In Denmark, it is estimated that some 60 per cent of the working class are in trade unions, ranging from almost complete organization in manufacturing and building and construction, to approximately 15 per cent of the agricultural workers, and a somewhat higher percentage for clerical workers. A notable difference between these countries is that in Italy agricultural and industrial trade unions are equally important, and a greater percentage of white-collar employees are organized.

9) *Source of recruitment and training of the labor leader.*—In Italy, a labor leader may come from any one of a variety of sources. He may come out of a political party, or he may be a young man with more

formal education than his rank and file, attracted to the labor movement for idealistic reasons or more simply in the quest of a job. In Denmark, the labor leader invariably comes out of the shop and is an image of the most intelligent element of the work group out of which he arises. In Italy, at the local level, the leader may be the young man whom other youths looked to for leadership as they grew up together in the same *comune*. In Denmark, he is more apt to be the most energetic of the members of a particular craft group. In Denmark there is an extensive program of labor education and training of young labor officials, which could serve as a model for trade union democracy. In Italy, the CISL has developed a program of labor leader training, including a "campus" in Florence, begun under the United States Marshall Aid program. The CGIL, to repeated inquiries, professes to no formal training program for its cadres. The Socialists in that organization, however, may force changes by insisting on a technically oriented trade unionism as an instrument for maintaining the loyalty of members to their organization.

4

Labor Leadership in Italy

A fruitful method of discerning power relationships in an Italian community is by participating in its life and determining the relationships among the leaders and the led. Workers can be asked who they think are the *pezzi grossi* of the community, and the leaders in the community can be questioned about current issues. In addition to the trade union officials, these people include employers, the mayor, the clergy, the prefect, members of the dominant political parties, journalists, and university people. The power relationships among them vary between one community and the next. It may be the local bishop, a political leader, or an employer who plays the principal role. In the large industrial centers of the North, power is too diffused to be ascribed to any one individual. Farther south, however, with some probing, it is possible to ferret out the group of individuals who are considered the key figures in the community.

Community leaders often have strong and unfavorable stereotyped views of each other. A current major issue stirring the community causes these stereotypes to gel, and builds up a web of conflict among different groups. The conditions necessary to create an alignment of points of view vary. It may be a mass layoff at the only big factory in the town, a controversial political issue, or some incident which makes individuals assume their customary ideological contrasts. Major issues which stir controversy are communism, Catholicism, and trade unionism. At such times, clashes appear to arise from an organic necessity for conflict. In one community, the prominent families, the *gran signori*, despite their differences, had allied themselves temporarily in

104

order to undermine the position of the mayor, a college professor born in the United States of Italian parents, who was considered a brazen newcomer. One has a suspicion occasionally that clashes among community leaders result from an Italian flair for improvising conflict situations to add zest to life.

To reach some community leaders, it is important to have the proper introductions. The greater the status of a person, the less likely is a direct approach to be fruitful, but a telephone call by someone of influence brings a quick response. The American embassy in Rome occasionally is helpful in making contacts. Italians respond to seats of power, although at times not without some hostility when the call emanates from the American island sanctuary on the Via Veneto in Rome.

A few failures were experienced in reaching the leadership. One involved a Communist senator. The investigator waited in his office for one hour after the scheduled appointment and then left. A second involved the general secretary of the Catholic federation in a large city. When called on the telephone, he announced himself by his last name somewhat in the manner of a herald, and advised that a personal letter of introduction from Rome would be necessary before he could be seen. If such a letter were forthcoming, he would be able to provide information, to which he alluded in a way one would refer to secrets of state. A third was the head of the employers' association in a large city of western Sicily. He granted an audience for nine o'clock in the morning at his home, which was agreed to, despite the unusual time and place. When the investigator arrived, a dour-looking, muscular individual dressed in chauffeur black showed him into the library after the precise nature of the call was satisfactorily explained. He came back after some time, saying that his *padrone* was indisposed and that another telephone call would have to be made to see whether a second appointment could be arranged.

The difficulties that arose in reaching individuals were not always unamusing. At times it seemed as though the American embassy and the Italian government were trying to outstrip each other in the new examples of bureaucracy they could muster against the common enemy —the private citizen. The American variety seems to arise from timidity and lack of imagination. It is startling to see for the first time representatives of a powerful nation behaving with warping caution. The Italian variety seems rather a blend of haughtiness and candid impatience with individuals whom they are sometimes inclined to consider more like subjects than visitors. At the American embassy, an Italian receptionist was approached, and a meeting with him after working hours suggested. He was accepted with delight, but he apparently felt it necessary to consult with his American superiors, who advised him that such a conversation with an outsider would involve taking a security risk which might have serious consequences for him. The investigator decided not to run the risk of undermining the American government by talking to the receptionist.

In another case, an Italian civil servant was asked a simple question on procedure in the Italian Parliament. He advised the investigator to write a formal letter requesting permission of one of his subordinates to provide the answer. This type of bureaucracy is more challenging. The Italian behind it is likely to be willing to participate in a battle of wits, and one can always try to play along with his sense of humor and *dignità*. After some parrying, this man ended by giving several hours of his time and inviting the investigator to dinner. Not all rebuffs had similar results. Once a receptionist at a government office advised the investigator cheerfully that the information sought could be gotten either from the staff or the director himself. Upon rushing to the office, the investigator was advised that the staff was not receiving on that day and that the director was on vacation.

Two related factors contribute to explain the busy schedule of affluent Italian government officials. One is the high degree of centralization of authority in Italian affairs. The reason for this is difficult to say. It may be the relatively low level of formal education, the poverty, the Italian individualistic character, or a combination of these elements. The other is the great use of the face-to-face meetings preferred by Italians to telephone conversations or correspondence. These meetings consume much executive time. Coming into an office, one would invariably see crowds of people with a look of resignation, waiting to see an official. Not without a feeling of guilt, one can move, on the strength of a high priority obtained by knowing the right persons, swiftly from the porter, who has a different demeanor for visitors of different social ratings, to the antechamber, the male secretary, and finally the *funzionario* himself.

Italy began her venture in a new labor movement a decade and a half ago with a shortage of trained labor leaders. The initial recruitment came from partisans fighting behind the German lines and from the ranks of young men working for local political organizations in their communities. In the South, where the inspiration behind trade unionism is more political than it is in the North, one of the difficulties has been to keep the trade union from becoming a subservient adjunct of a political party. Since the greatest opportunity for the talented son of a worker to rise dramatically up the social ladder is to become a member of Parliament, there is strong pressure on the young and talented poor, who have little ingrained orientation in trade unionism, to use their offices to further political aspirations. The dearth of trained leadership exists especially at the community and provincial level. The Catholic labor movement has had to start young men at local levels as staff employees, at a salary paid by the federation, with the expectation that some of them would eventually run for office and make competent labor leaders. The excellent material in that organization consists of men who have risen out of the agricultural class and have maintained a close contact with the rank and file without heeding the call of politics. For the CGIL the supply of leadership potential is not so great a problem, both the Socialist and the Communist parties being sources of recruitment of expressive young men with a desire to lead the working class.

A primary objective of conservative Italian labor leaders is to achieve status for themselves and their organizations in the process of reacting to the condition of the membership and to the other organizations with which they have relationships. They seek a significant role for the union within the context of the bargaining position of the employer and that of labor. If, for example, the employer abhors government intervention in labor relations, the trade union official may propose the creation of boards of conciliation. He pushes this objective in the prospect that such a proposal, while capable of serving the interests of the employer, strengthens the union as an institution and provides more returns to the membership than would be the case if reliance were placed on the use of economic power alone.

In the pursuit of objectives, the behavior of the labor leaders is conditioned by particular individuals and institutions. The differences among them are the sets of individuals and institutions whose coercive influence they voluntarily yield to in a manner consistent with their preferences. Dissimilarities are reflected in attitude stereotypes such as "labor-management coöperation," "decadent capitalism," "monopoly exploitation," and "class struggle." Moreover, since membership in the Italian trade union is voluntary, the leaders' behavior mirrors the aspirations and condition of those they are leading. These aspirations are similar among the three different sets of workers. They all speak of freedom and a *vita dignitosa;* they differ as to their appraisal of the factors which account for their situation in life and consequently the sets of individuals and institutions whose lead they are inclined to follow. Nevertheless, the behavior of all the leaders is subject to a law of increasing homogeneity as they increase their ability to change the economic and social condition of their membership.

A notable association exists between these benchmarks of behavior and measurable aspects of the life experience of labor officials. They group themselves into associations which express their value differentiations. Members of the same union are found in the same club, the same café, the same town organization of the political party. Differences between groups reflect dissimilarity of life experience, including education, occupational training, job experience, extent of upward movement, type of employer exposure, and orientation toward the Church.[1]

As a group, the labor leaders were more hostile and more pessimistic than the employers. These differences reflect the dissimilarity in the role each plays and the regularity with which each group is experiencing success.

As a group, the labor leaders show a broader value orientation than the employers as a group. The former conceive of success in terms of achievement by group effort and democratic participation of the membership in the pursuit of objectives. Personal success is described in terms of accomplishments for the members. The employers have a more individualistic orientation and prefer the unilateral exercise of decisions in matters affecting their firm. They stress legal and economic laws, whereas the labor leaders speak of broad concepts of justice. While the latter insist on a humanitarian approach to the solving of a grievance, the former in rebuttal argue that a proposal may be a violation of economic laws which cannot be broken with impunity. Agricultural and small industrial employers have a greater tendency to speak in this fashion; similarly, the southern employer more than

[1] For an account of similar findings in the United States, see Ross Stagner, "Motivational Aspects of Industrial Morale," *Personnel Psychology,* XI, No. 1 (Spring, 1958).

the executives of corporations. Arrayed against each other, these value orientations of labor leaders and employers provide the framework for their conflict relationships with each other.

The Communist trade union officials articulate a special concept of union democracy. They conceive it as a single organization of workers, the leadership of which arises spontaneously from the rank and file and moves inexorably toward the top. The leader merely reflects the needs and sentiments of workers. His personality structure has little to do with the leadership which he exercises. Although his perceptions may be somewhat more discerning than those of the workers, the quality of his leadership is an expression of the condition of labor. He interprets rather than leads and does not influence the members as much as the latter influence him. His leadership is pure democracy, pure communication upward.

This view is extended to their appraisal of Anglo-Saxon democracy. It consists of rival organizations whose ruling oligarchies compete with each other in selecting the leaders of the people. Once the democracy matures, these leaders do not arise from the masses, but are chosen by organization bosses on the basis of whether they can defeat the candidates of the rival organization rather than the basis of the needs of the people. Consequently, the behavior of leaders is not an expression of the condition of the working class at a particular moment, but rather an indication of how to develop a political machine with which to remain in power.

A charged outlook toward events, combined with the practical necessities of leading a successful organization, creates a special problem for Communist trade union officials. They have a faith in a world of abundance and enlightenment, attainable through a monolithic organization of workers. They have strong feelings about employers with whom they must deal if they are to obtain concessions for the rank and file. Laboring under an intense conviction that workers are not obtaining their share of income and power, they are forced by the practical necessities of bargaining to act in a manner not purely consistent with their sentiments. If the workers want twenty lire more in wages, to settle for less would be an act of betrayal; it would be indulging in class collaboration and renouncing the class struggle. Instead, the demand should be what the worker himself is demanding—until noble defeat.

This point of view may result in the loss of membership. Communist trade union officials are constrained to control their egalitarian spirit and to find themselves, like the "class collaboration" leaders in rival organizations, analyzing differences in plant efficiency and product markets. The outlook of the left-wing leadership does not create a problem for all to the same degree. Those in the South are less conscious of Marxist dogma and the Soviet mecca in the east. Their Communism is a symbol of the rejection of the leadership of those who have traditionally exercised power. If an organization even further to the left were in existence, they might embrace its ideology instead.

The strain caused by ideological dogma lagging behind a changing world is exemplified in the three factions within the Communist party. One, the left wing of the party, is the most orthodox and Stalinist. At the other extreme are revisionists seeking a discreet relief from the traditional shopworn clichés, while in the middle stand the forces of Togliatti, whose function is to maintain equilibrium within the organization.

The ideologies men profess are often an accident of history and environment. Those of the three labor movements in Italy are Marxism, Catholicism, and anticlerical liberalism. They are a distillation of centuries of events which have had a dissimilar impact in different parts of Italy. For the average labor leader, they represent approximations of personal outlook, and they become the expected attire of office. Their influence on behavior, however, is less than it appears to be at first blush. Ideologies suffer from a time lag. They continue to be articulated long after they have declined as a dominant influence in behavior. The Communist labor leader begins to behave in a manner not quite what would be expected of a traditional Communist. The same is true of the Catholics and the Social Democrats. Confronted with a similar situation, they behave in increasingly similar fashions. Their professed ideologies become instruments of seeking to increase their power at the expense of their rivals. If they do things merely for the sake of ideology, the membership tires of exercises in abstraction. While time and place provide them with different doctrines to employ as a thrust to initial organization of men, their interpretations eventually have to conform to the changing needs of those they are leading. If ideology affects perception of reality, the latter forces the former into more proper perspective.

Ideology, however, can strengthen the bonds of organization between leaders and workers. It can become a cohesive force which prevents the alienation of rank and file from leaders. The strong ideological outlook of employers begets an equally potent cohesion of ideas among employees. This bond of organization, to be sure, does not necessarily increase the bargaining power of the group. The creation of separate ideological blocs based on occupational and philosophical outlook may bring fewer political and economic returns than would be the case if workers were united into one organization. Such a criterion, however, is subjective, since the workers are deriving satisfaction through the association of individuals of similar outlook. For the Italians, the strong, intimate ties among the members of a group are important ends in themselves.

Some differentiation in labor leader traits was obtained among federations. The Communists are the most charged and succinct in their expressions, and the most pessimistic in outlook. Their colleagues in the CGIL, the Socialists, show more emotional control, and are more conciliatory and more flexible. Some of the Italian Communists reflect an aptitude for accommodating themselves to the contrasts between orthodox ideology and the pragmatic needs of their rank and file. Some are not too competent trade unionists, their compulsive behavior working to the disadvantage of the people they represent. Others are astute politicians, using their positions in such a way as to maintain their power. In this respect, they are little different from their counterparts in other organizations. There are those, too, who are dedicated young men of administrative ability, whose strong sense of injustice is tempered with a willingness to see how gains can be made for their people at a particular moment. Unlike some of their colleagues, they possess the ability not to fritter away an advantage by the inept tactics which result from looking at collective bargaining with employers as part of a sublime class struggle. Their description of occurrences suggests that the day-by-day pressure of trade unionism makes the Communist labor leader different from his comrade in the party structure who, divorced from the daily exigencies of leading a trade union organization, can make *pronunciamenti* on dogma.

Though the CGIL leaders articulate an ideology unlike that of their adversaries in the other two federations, the differences in the expressed ideologies of the three organizations are greater than the dissimilarity in their behavior. The extreme left wing in Italy needs a continuous series of crises on which to thrive. The left-wing leaders employ the tactic of flaying the capitalist enemy. Their poverty-stricken, uninformed adherents obtain emotional satisfaction from hearing of the sinister designs of employers and leaders of rival trade union organizations and political parties, and how these men are beaten by their leaders at every turn. However, as crises diminish in intensity and their followers become better informed and better off, talk of successful past battles falls on deaf ears. Remove the more strident battle-clichés and one finds the left-wing labor leader beginning to ask for a little more than his conservative colleagues in the rival federations. Consequently, left-wing leaders are constrained to adopt a more pragmatic approach once the faithful begin to ask themselves on sober reflection what, aside from slogans, they have obtained for the good fight. Because of the pressure of the rank and file and the possibility of greater success on the part of a rival organization, the insurrectionist character of the leadership often gives way to a systematic pursuit of concrete objectives.[2]

Italian labor leaders have some characteristics in common. Zest for work, resourcefulness, and intelligence are not exclusive characteristics of any one federation. In some geographical areas, the UIL leadership possesses some of these qualities in lesser degree; the pool of rank-and-file members out of which they are drawn, however, is smaller in number than those for the other two organizations. Italian labor leaders, even the Catholics, are influenced by a socialistic ideology learned from their fathers and from reading about the working-class heroes of the early days of trade unionism and socialism. Such socialism is rarely articulated in terms of specific economic objectives or as a full-blown Marxist philosophy, but appears rather as a yearning for an idealistic world of social justice, camaraderie, and opportunity for advancement. In addition, all of them are seeking to upset the power balance among the decision-making elite of Italy, traditionally employers, landowners, clergy, and the idle rich. In this sense, all of the labor leaders, including the Catholics, are challenging conservative forces, including those which emanate from the Church itself.

[2] The tendency of the Communists to view the working class as an abstract force is expressed in the following words of an article appearing in the Communist newspaper, *Unità,* during the field investigation: "Great and energetic struggles are now in course in all sectors of the life of the country. From postal clerks to industrial workers, from agricultural day-laborers to sharecroppers and independent farmers, hundreds of thousands of workers are involved in the defense of their rights. Discharge for just cause only, better economic conditions of employment. These are the traditional themes of a tremendous movement which has developed and which is in the process of becoming greater through new demands. The counteroffensive of workers has begun. . . ."

Respondents were asked who, in their judgment, were the three most powerful men in Italy. The responses are differentiated not as much on a federation basis as by geographical region. The South tends to look at specific individuals, while the North is inclined to think of organiza-tion rather than personal power. The farther south, the more was the respondent inclined to mention a prominent member of the clergy. In Sicily, the name most frequently mentioned as first choice was Cardinal Ruffini, primate of Sicily. Two dominant reasons are given for the choice. First, his point of view affects decisions in economic and political activity. Second, he represents a symbol of the parish priest in the community. Second and third choices are leading politicians in the Christian Democrat party. The South thus tends to view its priests and politicians as the most influential members of the community.

The farther north, the more the pattern changes. The interviewee was more inclined to mention an employer or employers' associations and was more conscious of organization power. He also found the ques-tion more difficult to answer. Those in the highly industrialized areas complained of having to select any one individual as a first choice. They were more conscious of the diffusion of power. The Pope was frequently mentioned as the symbol of the Catholic Church, while in the smaller towns the local bishop was often among the first three choices. In the large industrial cities, the clergy was not usually cited, with the exception of members of the ACLI, who expressed the opinion that the Pope is the most influential person in Italy.

The three federations were almost unanimous in the belief that Di-Vittorio, Communist labor leader of the CGIL, was the most influential trade union official. In descending order were mentioned Pastore of the CISL and Viglianesi of the UIL. A trade union official provided the following explanation:

In your country, a Meany really has little power outside his organization. He does not have a rank-and-file following. He is a remote figure to the rank and file. He cannot bargain on the basis of the support of trade unionists. In Italy, the opposite is true. DiVittorio is a symbol of the aspiration of millions of Italian workers. You have to look at the feelings of identification in their faces when they listen to him. In my country a labor official is a leader of a group of workers. In your country he is a bureaucrat as remote to the rank and file as the president of General Motors.

The North also gave the leader of the Small Farmers' Association (Coltivatori Diretti) frequent mention for first place. The reasons given for the basis of his influence read like a blueprint on how to achieve power in Italy. They are (1) by controlling the social insurance system for the small farmers, he attracts them away from the trade union federations; (2) the shift from being an agricultural laborer to becoming a small farmer increases conservatism and the kind of emotional patriotism which the head of the organization represents; (3) the organization has the strong support of the clergy as a bulwark against communism, the head of the organization being praised as an anti-Communist fighter and his colleagues referred to as the militiamen in the fight against Marxism; (4) he controls ancillary organizations, such as newspaper publishing houses and the Consorzio Agrario, a farmer coöperative which the small holders use for credit and marketing; (5) there are approximately one hundred Christian Democrat members of Parliament who gained their election through his organization and who are expected to do his bidding; (6) the organization is run by former Fascist functionaries with a long experience in bureaucratic methods and a flair for getting things done by communicating with the right individuals in and out of government.

BACKGROUND AND INDUCTION

Italian labor leaders come from a variety of social and economic backgrounds, and show a corresponding diversity in the degree to which they accept Italian institutions. The leadership at the top of the trade union organizations is dominated by traditional Socialists and Communists who practiced trade unionism before the advent of the Fascist regime and who played a major role in organizing the new labor movement after its collapse. The leaders at the bottom came from the ranks of the young men of World War II experience, including partisans, political party workers, college graduates, frustrated white-collar workers without the opportunities for fulfilling middle-class aspirations, and adventurers who have been gradually weeded out by the Catholic and liberal labor movements in which they had managed to find positions. These leaders range from the sons of agricultural workers and *mezzadri* to the children of artists and professional workers. Their education varies from three years of elementary schooling to degrees in engineering and law. They are conscious of the differences in their origins. The traditional Socialists lament the lack of old-fashioned idealism in the young, while the latter decry the lack of knowledge of modern technology in the former and their inability to grapple with the contemporary problems of collective bargaining. The partisans are proud of their war experience, while some of those from the petty bourgeoisie refer to them as good-for-nothings from the country-side who took advantage of the misfortune of war to throw over social restraints and indulge in ribaldry and unconventional behavior. Such social and economic disparity has an important bearing on the out-look of Italian labor leaders.

A spirit of evangelical zeal pervades the activity of labor leaders in Italy, in contrast with the more bureaucratic tone of Danish unionism. They speak with candor about their problems of organization under impoverished conditions, in an expressive Italian which belies the few years of formal education of many of them. They are men on the move, with a sense of mission. The opportunity for upward movement tradi-tionally provided the talented sons of the working class through politics or the priesthood has now been increased to include a trade union movement with great expectations.

A majority of the provincial labor leaders in the sample are men be-tween the ages of thirty and forty (Table 6). The members of the CGIL are somewhat older than those of the CISL, and the latter have a longer formal education. The only officials who have been to college are mem-bers of the Catholic federation.

The median age in the national union group is thirty-six. The UIL leaders are generally those who came out of the First World War, compared to those in the CISL and the CGIL, who are predominantly younger men of the Second World War. As a group, the national union officials have more schooling than the provincial leaders, the median figure for them being the equivalent of a public school education in the United States. With one exception, all were born in the industrial North. An important difference between the two levels of leadership is that the national trade union officials tend to rise out of industrial jobs. The difference may explain the job-orientation of the national leaders, compared with the political orientation of the provincial officials. By the term "political" is meant the concentration of activity designed to increase the prestige of one federation at the expense of the others on the community level.

At the federation level, the extent of formal education increases further. The CISL group has the most formal education, and the CGIL the least. Generally, the respondents in the group come from the in-dustrial North, and their median age is forty-seven. They began their trade union careers at the top, after the termination of World War II.

TABLE 6

Age and Years of Schooling of Italian Provincial Labor Leaders

Age	Years of Schooling														
	5–7			8–10			11–13			14–16			17 plus		
	CGIL	CISL	UIL	CGIL	CISL	UIL	CGIL	CISL	UIL	CGIL	CISL	UIL	CGIL	CISL	UIL
30–34		2	2	1	2	1	1	1			1			1	
35–40		2		1	2	2		4	1		1	1		3	
41–45		2		1	2		1							1	
46–50					1	1						1			
51–55							1		1						
56 plus														1	
Total		6	2	3	7	4	3	5	2		2	2		6	

One member of the CGIL group began his career with nine years in jail for trade union activity during the Fascist period. The majority of the group are active in organization work for their respective political parties.

The differences between the two major federations in upward mobility are noteworthy (Table 7). The preponderant majority of the

TABLE 7

Occupation of Paternal Grandfather and Father of Italian Labor Leaders *

Paternal Grandfather	Father				
	Clerical S C L §	Sales S C L	Skilled † S C L	Contadino ‡ S C L	Bracciante S C L
Clerical	3 1	1 1	1		
Sales		1 2			
Skilled		2	6 2		
Contadino	1	1	1 1	4 2 1	1
Bracciante				1	2
Unskilled ‖			1 2	1	
Unknown		1 3 3	1 2 2	1	1

* Not included in the table are four labor leaders of the following federations: CGIL, two whose fathers were supervisors; CISL, one who father belonged to a profession and one whose father was a landowner.
† Skilled category includes both the *operaio qualificato* and *operaio specializzato*.
‡ *Contadino* includes sharecropper, tenant farmer, and small holder.
§ The letter abbreviations S, C, and L stand for CGIL, CISL, and UIL, respectively.
‖ None of the fathers of the labor leaders in the sample belonged to the unskilled category.

CGIL leaders have working-class fathers, compared to the CISL group, who tend to come from the middle class, and who show a dichotomy in origin which does not exist for the Social Communist federation. Moreover, there has been less three-generation movement for the CGIL. For the majority of the Social Communists, the fathers and grandfathers were either production workers or peasants. The different origins of the leadership are brought out further in Table 8. The CISL leaders are predominantly from the middle class, with occupations in the clerical and professional classifications. The CGIL officials, on the other hand, rose out of blue-collar jobs. While several of the respondents in both groups entered the labor movement through political activity, a greater number of the CGIL leaders started their trade union careers in leadership positions proximate to the work place. The CGIL leaders, consequently, are more closely identified with the working class than are their counterparts in the CISL.

TABLE 8

Prior Occupation and First Position in Labor Movement of Provincial Labor Leaders *

Occupation	First Position in Labor Movement					
	Party Partisans †	Organizers	Committeemen	Provincial ‡	Trade Union	Zone Secretary
	S C L §	S C L	S C L	S C L	S C L	S C L
Engineer				1		
Teacher				1		
Supervisor	1					
Clerical	1 1	3	1 1 2	2		
Industrial worker	1 1	1	1 2		2	2 2
Agricultural worker		1			1	1
None		1				2

* One CISL official entered the labor movement from Catholic Action organization; one UIL official from Fascist trade unions.
† Organized by the respective political parties.
‡ Respondent started at that level.
§ The abbreviations S, C, and L stand for CGIL, CISL, and UIL, respectively.

CONCEPTUAL FRAMEWORK

The labor leaders' concept of their functions and responsibilities may be approached in several ways. In the first place, what, it may be asked, are the needs and incentives which form the basis for a leader's entering the labor movement? In intercountry comparisons, are these needs universal, or are they acquired in a different manner because of dissimilar life experiences? Toward which goals are these needs directed? Secondly, in what terms do the trade union officials perceive their problems and responsibilities? What do they state, when asked directly, that they feel their role obligations to be? What are the standards they use to make decisions, and how do they evaluate success or failure? What do they consider to be the qualities of an "ideal" labor leader? By these diverse approaches, it may be possible to determine needs, methods, objectives, and causal explanations of labor leader behavior.

MOTIVES FOR ENTERING THE LABOR MOVEMENT

Italian officials named their reactions to the injustices of their environment and the necessity of making radical changes as motives in entering the labor movement (Table 9). They cited either specific prior

TABLE 9

Motivation of Italian Provincial Labor Leaders for Entering
the Labor Movement
(Per Cent)

Orientation	CGIL		CISL		UIL	
Group	90		30		90	
Reformation of society		30		0		33
Identification with workers		60		15		33
Organization of political party		0		15		24
Personal	10		70		10	
Sense of mission		0		24		10
Experience of personal injustice		10		23		0
Self-advancement		0		23		0
Total	100		100		100	
Number	13		13		9	

incidents which led to the decision, or objectives they decided to pursue. There appear to be differences in the scope of the motives between the CGIL and the CISL representatives. The former articulated a greater group orientation than the latter, whose responses included expressions of frustration due to differences between job expectations and fulfillment. The CGIL leaders expressed more often the need for close contact with workers and a sense of identification with them, compared to a relatively large number of CISL responses, which have a greater personal orientation. They also placed more emphasis on the inequities of their society and their having to yield to the urge to change them.

No significant difference in the data exists among the responses grouped by levels of leadership. Among federations, the Social Communists, more often than the Catholic liberals, spoke of the injustices in their society and their zeal for reform. Not all labor leaders speak with the same sense of mission. One, in the CISL, mentioned that he had felt the need to tangle with the young Communists in the community. Another stated that he had been looking for a job, and found it in the Catholic labor movement. Those with a business-like approach to trade unionism do not come out of plant jobs, are better educated, and more likely than not to come from the South.

Representative comments from leaders in the three groups give, in their own words, the variety of their motives for entering the labor movement. Several UIL leaders spoke of an urge "to participate in the reformation of society." Among other comments from UIL leaders were the following statements:

It was a reaction to fascism. I was beaten up by the Fascists and I yearned for liberty with a passion.

Trade unionism is something you lose money and time on; you feel it like a mission, as a priest follows his. It even stifles your ability to have a career in life. Yet you do it.

I was working in an industrial plant and became very conscious of the problems of workers. It was during the period of fascism when they could not express themselves. So right after the liberation of Rome I organized a shop committee.

From the CISL came comments like the following:

I felt the need to bring freedom to Italian workers by increasing their power.

I wanted to join the effort to emancipate the workers.

I was a college graduate living in a slum area. The workers would come to me to talk about their grievances. That made me decide to join the Catholic labor movement.

I felt a sense of inferiority going to Catholic clubs and becoming aware of the social distance between the members and myself.

I was overwhelmed by two factors: the ridiculous impotence of the trade unions and the tremendous number of changes that had to be made under the impetus of trade unionism.

My initial impulse was to become a social worker rather than a labor leader. My hostility to the CGIL prompted me to organize a rival local union.

A Socialist in the CGIL reported that he felt a stimulus to do something on behalf of the workers. Why? he was asked. "It is the feeling like that you get when your soccer team kicks a goal. . . ." A Communist trade union official stated: "The huge exploiting monopolies in the chemical industry attracted me to becoming a trade union official in that industry. . . ." Another Socialist spoke of the necessity of identifying himself with the cause of the workers because it gave him a sense of selflessness and a feeling that he was fighting for ideals.

Italian labor leadership is class conscious rather than occupation conscious, reflecting the frustrations of masses of workers of low skill levels, who feel that their inability to meet their needs is due to social injustices which can be adjusted by a shift in power. The impulses behind Italian labor leadership arise out of strong feelings for justice. Generally, it can be said that the leadership arises spontaneously out of the group. The members of the group look for leadership to individuals who express well an acceptable point of view. A common characteristic of leaders of all three federations is that they are apparently the most articulate of the group from which they come. They are men with the ability to assert the sense of rebellion of their groups, and hence become the leaders of the young men with whom they grew up. A marked difference between the leaders and the led is the greater degree to which the leaders can express themselves, and the greater strength of their motivations.

CONCEPT OF ROLE

No noteworthy differences are found between the CISL and the UIL in their replies on the concept of a labor leader's role (Table 10). The interviewees of both organizations conceive their role to be one of co-

TABLE 10

Italian Labor Leaders' Concept of Role
(Per Cent)

Emphasis on:	CGIL		CISL		UIL	
Worker expression	70		35		74	
Express point of view of workers		50		15		14
Service worker needs		20		20		60
Formulation of limited objectives	20		49		14	
Organization	0		10		0	
Opposition to employer	10		6		12	
Total	100		100		100	
Number	19		21		14	

ördinating the needs of workers and developing a strategy in the "pursuit of what can be realized." In the words of one UIL leader, they have to "practice the philosophy of the art of the possible." Two in the sample spoke of their role in terms of dealing with employers: "Watch employers closely; they know their commas"; "Constantly watch the astute lawyers of the employers."

Both groups criticized the CGIL for its "impossible demands" and "demagoguery." The small differences which are apparent in their replies essentially concern the extent to which the trade union leader should modify the inclinations of the workers and lead them in the direction of objectives which he feels are in their interest. The typical attitude is that a leader is a leader because he can best articulate the needs of the rank and file and, because of better preparation, is in a better position to map out strategy for the pursuit of realizable goals. An extreme view of leadership is expressed in the statement of one respondent that his role is to determine the goals of the organization and that he expects his rank and file to follow him. The leader, in his words, is a man in whom the rank and file has trust and faith. From the confidence placed in him, he acquires power, because those with whom he deals know that his point of view has the complete support of the membership. Leadership, in this view, is loyal acceptance by the rank and file of what has been determined is in their best interests.

The statement on role made by one young labor leader is revealing. A vigorous young man in the Catholic labor movement, he is the son of a *mezzadro*, with five years of elementary education. There was a chance to observe his work for an entire week, the pace of which was exhausting to the interviewer only. In his words:

My role shifts between improvement in the organization in numbers and improvement in quality. Sometimes even numbers have to be sacrificed in immediate circumstances for the sake of improving quality in the organization. You have to have both short-term and long-term objectives. I may make a decision which may have a bad repercussion in the short term. However, if I obtain any future advantages, it was a good decision. The criterion of success is whether the organization is increasing in both quantity and quality, relative to the other organizations. My job, therefore, in approaching an individual with whom I must bargain, is first to decide what I want to obtain from him. I then find out what type of personality he has, the things that he likes. I then try to achieve my objective consistent with what he wants.

The Communist respondents articulated a dubious concept of leadership. They spoke of their role in such terms as "express the feelings of the workers"; "tie oneself to the workers and remain faithful to them"; "be a living expression of the organization." The leader is simply an expression of the sentiments of the workers in the organization. He creates nothing and brings nothing to bear in the organization. His leadership changes as the maturity and perceptions of the members change. Social problems automatically generate organizations and leaders. The leader is a mere collecting point for the needs of the workers. Although he gives these needs perspective, his personality is submerged in the expression of the workers themselves. He is close to the workers, and a mere instrument of their will. In this sense, his organization is an expression of pure democracy, since it moves constantly in whatever direction the rank and file want it to move. As the membership changes, so does the leader change.

The CISL leaders feel that such a concept of democracy places them in a difficult position. They reject the idea that labor leadership constitutes moving in any direction the workers want to go. The CISL leader, by injecting his own point of view into an analysis of a situation, runs the risk of being labeled a coward or a traitor when he resists the inclinations of the rank and file to move willy-nilly in different directions. Although in the long run he may obtain more returns to the membership, any *ad hoc* position he takes is subject to the derision of workers. Since the eventual settlement is much less than the more "democratic" demands of the CGIL, he is always running the risk of being accused of having collaborated, if not connived, with the employer.

THE PRESSURES ITALIAN LABOR LEADERS FEEL

The Italian labor leaders who were interviewed expressed in various ways the role pressures which they feel their positions entail, their fears, aspirations, and disappointments. Their comments are in a sense a record of the forces which these trade union officials feel affect their behavior in the pursuit of objectives. The comments given below, extracted from the interview transcript, are representative for the three federations.

From the CGIL:

I have to feel constantly that I am near the workers, to feel their problems. If they have no shoes, I want no shoes. You have to live with them and be subject to their will.

The Catholic Church is the principal stumbling block to a united labor movement in Italy.

I am impotent to strike unless I can obtain an agreement from the other two federations.

The workers do not respond; they are disillusioned with trade unionism because of the split in the labor movement.

The labor leaders will work for a merged labor movement only when the workers insist upon it.

We must run for political office; otherwise there will be no one in Parliament to promote the interests of workers.

The fear of unemployment prevents them [workers] from becoming trade union conscious, and that makes my job very difficult.

The top leaders do not want trade union unity and that is why you do not have it.

We have made mistakes; we have been inflexible; but we now are trying to behave in such a way as to make it difficult for the other two organizations not to want a merger.

CISL and UIL collect little or no dues from workers and that makes our dues-collection problem difficult.

When I was twelve years old I knew what I wanted to do: fight for the workers.

The workers have been exploited for so long they do not care anymore.

Can you tell me how you can induce employers to respect collective bargaining agreements when I am made to feel inferior to them?

Italian employers do not bargain; rather, they bestow concessions.

My philosophy of Marxism does not allow me to believe the possibility of collaboration with employers.

This work is a felt mission, springing from the desire to change society. We become labor leaders as a result of struggling side by side with the workers. Our job is to tie ourselves to them and remain faithful to them.

A social problem generates organization automatically, and this presupposes leadership. A leader is merely the collecting point for the needs of workers. He merely gives them perspective. The more enlightened the workers become, the more enlightened the leader becomes. Only to a limited extent can he bring about this enlightenment.

From the UIL:

I feel free as a labor leader in the UIL. I do not feel the burden of an outside organization on my back. I am ideologically free. Besides, as a Sicilian, I am not opposed to dealing with rival organizations, despite our differences. I judge a man by who he is as an individual rather than by what organization he belongs to. I think a labor leader can best do his work under these circumstances, not be controlled by an outside organization but be able to deal with other men despite differences in points of view.

None of the free federations is free: they are all controlled by outside organizations.

I cannot do my job well. The workers are too fatalistic.

A man who is both a labor leader and a politician is in conflict with himself.

The low level of education of the workers makes my job difficult.

You have to behave in such a way as to inspire trust and confidence. Then you have power. The organization acquires a *spirito di forza,* and you can shape the direction of the organization.

Southern workers are weak in organization. Give them a wage above subsistence level, and they subject themselves to the paternalism of the employer.

The workers are more sensitive to the pressure of the employer than they are to mine.

They [workers] cannot think for themselves.

From the CISL:

The Communist agitators in the CGIL force us to take actions we are not inclined to take.

Some of us are influenced by Catholic paternalistic philosophy of the rich having to give to the poor. That is not collective bargaining.

The Communists want a dictatorship; so we have to practice a trade unionism which weakens their organization.

They [workers] do not understand the nature of group power. They think I have power because I am a *signore.*

Only the exceptional among the college graduates in the labor leadership will succeed. They have difficulty in communicating with workers.

They [workers] are closed inside themselves; they have no faith in society.

Workers are easily swayed by emotional appeals and promises which are easily forgotten.

The low level of education makes trade unionism very difficult.

They behave exasperatingly in a manner so as not to offend the employer.

I feel a sense of mission in doing something for the working class.

The workers do not make a distinction between their trade union and political leadership; so how can we?

I am afraid to cause divisions among the workers deeper than they are already.

I have constantly to fight this Arabic mentality of taking the world as it comes.

I never ask a worker what he believes in; I ask him what he needs.

A fundamental fact you should remember is that in Italy sovereignty and authority do not rest with the people. They come from the top. The government, the employer, the Church, even sometimes a labor leader, determine what is best for the common people and how they should behave. For this reason, workers have no sense of initiative or responsibility. Why should they? They do not feel they have to participate in the institutions which control them. They spend their time thinking how much they can exploit the other fellow. As children, they should be taught how to think for themselves and to work with others.

The democratic labor leader in Italy is in a very difficult position. He is caught between the effects of Communist leadership and the intransigent attitude of the employer. The Communists conceive of leadership as leading the workers wherever they want to go. In this atmosphere, by injecting your own point of view after analyzing the situation, you run the risk of being called a traitor and a coward. The employers compound the difficulty. A strike is a personal affront to them. They feel their dignity violated. They make unilateral concessions to workers, which would be appreciated more if they were forthcoming as a result of union participation.

The matter of role obligations was approached in somewhat different fashion in the written questionnaire. Two queries were juxtaposed against each other: What obligations and attitudes did the labor leader feel obliged to assume because of his role as labor leader, and what did he think the workers expected of him? Responses to the latter question reflected differences in the level of leadership. The provincial officials wrote about employment, wages, and camaraderie. Representative responses follow:

They expect the possible and impossible. The former consists of a knowledge of labor problems and the capacity to guide the worker in making a decision. The latter consists of protecting him from unemployment and employer coercion.

They want a commitment not based on opportunistic motives but something which can be seen through.

They expect me to be a loyal friend and never to take an authoritarian position. They also like to hear me speak with conviction on issues which interest them.

They expect me to protect them from the bosses [padroni].

By contrast, the federation leaders characteristically gave more abstract responses. One of them wrote: "They want a decisive struggle for the accomplishment of objectives without indulging in demagoguery and party politics."

The responses on what the leaders feel obliged to do also reflect the differing problems of different levels of leadership. Responses from provincial leaders include the following:

Stimulate workers to suggest what they are disposed to do in order to reach objectives . . .

Decentralize the work as much as possible to obtain a maximum of participation, while maintaining control at the same time . . .

Take a position in the interests of workers, even though it may not be particularly popular . . .

Stimulate workers continually to make them understand that they, and not the leaders, are the protagonists of trade unionism . . .

Persuade the workers that we are the guiding spirits, not tugboats . . .

Do the possible, consistent with the policies of my federation . . .

I try to avoid getting a worker into difficulty because of my decisions, and to be reserved and loyal in meetings with them. It gives them a sense of assurance.

Following are the comments of federation officials:

The initiative I take depends on the probability of success. My subsequent behavior depends upon what happens after I have made the decision.

I feel obliged to explore all possible alternatives before resorting to the use of agitation.

The responses of the local leadership seem to reflect more interest in particulars, more concern with the problem of communication and worker participation and the defense of immediate interests, than those of leaders at the federation level, which are more abstract and more free from indications of worker pressure.

A significant comment on role obligations is revealed in the thinking of a CISL trade union official on public pressure. He drew a distinction between two types of relationships with public authorities. These relationships exist on a basis of collaboration when problems requiring administrative interpretation are to be dealt with, and they are on a basis of conflict when interests not protected, or insufficiently protected, by law are involved. Relationships with the employment office, the Social Security Institute, the Institute of Industrial Accidents, the labor office, and the Bureau of Employment Standards should be handled only by a representative of the federation. Since the scope of this relationship is seeking information or exerting pressure, the trade union official should always be accompanied by representatives of the trade union involved, or by a group of workers directly interested in the matter. The intervention should be on the basis of allowing these government offices to take action without precluding the possibility of the trade union's taking further action if deemed necessary.

In this view, relationships with the general public are of paramount importance. Public opinion should be influenced in cases where trade union action creates a public inconvenience and the public is not directly interested in the trade union action. A public utilities strike, for example, should be preceded by promotional activity to make the public aware that the position of the workers is justifiable and that the employer is uncomprehending or hostile. Relationships with the public could be a means of exerting indirect pressure on the employer. Consumers of a product should be informed of the conditions under which it is being produced by the workers. Toward this objective, the provincial press office should be used by the member trade unions.

PROBLEMS, RESPONSIBILITIES, AND OBJECTIVES

What do Italian labor leaders feel are the most important problems confronting them? According to their responses as summarized in Table 11, there are four chief categories: organizational, economic, po-

TABLE 11

Italian Labor Leaders' Views of Their Most Important Problems
(Per Cent)

Related to:	CGIL		CISL		UIL
Organization	44		59		33
Lack of trade-union–consciousness		14		38	27
Split in trade unionism		30		0	6
Weakness of collective bargaining power		0		14	0
Religious influence on unionism		0		7	0
Economics	38		23		33
Provision of jobs for members		24		23	33
Need for improving terms of employment		10		0	0
Low level of industrialization		4		0	0
Employers	14		4		20
Anti-union policies		14		2	20
Paternalism		0		2	0
Politics	4		8		7
Domination of unions by political parties		0		8	7
Political division of workers		4		0	0
Other	0		6		7
Invidious comparisons by workers in small plants		0		2	7
2000 years of exploitation		0		2	0
Excesses of local unions		0		2	0
Total	100		100		100
Number	21		43		15

litical, and those related to the employer. Pervading the responses is concern for the deleterious impact on trade unionism of the existence of a large mass of unskilled unemployed, relatively frozen within their communities, either by volition or by government-imposed restraints. The impact of unemployment, in the judgment of the respondents, is felt in the following fashion: (1) it enables the employer to lower the standards set by trade unionism, and results in loss of organization prestige; (2) it promotes fear of employer retaliation for trade union activity; (3) it prevents the existence of large groups of industrial workers who have developed enough job security to want to take the step of determining on a group basis the conditions of employment. In sum, the trade union leader tends to see the problem of the worker as his problem, but to a certain extent in terms of the organizational difficulties it raises. To him, a measure of success of the organization is the degree to which it can provide job security to its members.

The farther south the respondent, the more inclined he is to view unemployment as his major problem, in its impact on the mentality of the worker and that of the employer as well. In Sicily, a CGIL leader stated:

Unemployment and subsistence wages make trade unionism a parlor game. After the unification of Italy, the northern bosses agreed to consider Sicily autonomous under the control of the landed aristocracy. In return, the island became a colony for the manufactured products of the North. The Sicilian workers never felt they were part of the Italian nation. There has been some industrialization since the end of the Second World War. The per capita income of the North, however, is rising faster than that of the South. The state should intervene directly and develop power, steel, all the basic production. In other sectors, it should develop private initiative. It should not be aiding the big monopolies as the government is now doing. If we can get a competitive industrial economy in Sicily, we can then develop trade unionism.

Following is a summary of the point of view of a UIL leader in Sicily:

We have a kind of slave market here in Palermo. Every morning all the wretched unemployed swoop down to the _____ shipyards and sit on the ground. Then the boss shows up, a character looking like a member of the Mafia; he walks through their ranks saying "You, *Si*," and "You, *No*." Those who obtain a job for the day will be able to fill their stomachs that night. This procedure of course is illegal, but it is done anyway.

It is impossible to approach the worker here on the basis of mere trade unionism. He will not respond. We are dealing with a mass of subhumans, not with enlightened industrial workers. Let me give you an example of how they react. In Naples, all three federations got together in an unusually coöperative strike effort against a large employer. The strike failed because the workers began to ask themselves why they should try to improve their terms of employment, which were already much better than those enjoyed by the majority of their fellow workers. They were comparing themselves not with those who were achieving high aspirations but with those who were at a level of subsistence. We are forced to start from a problem which the worker feels and align this feeling with objectives of the organization in a manner that would produce a sustained will to achieve them.

We have to develop a trade-union-consciousness among workers before we can begin to have a successful labor movement. In the same large city of Naples, where some eight hundred plants should elect shop committees by law, only sixty shop committees are in existence. Our problem is to develop a daily habit of trade unionism. We must support economic development programs with the hope of seeing the growth of large-scale production. We have to obtain the acceptance of collective bargaining by law. We also have to support training and education programs designed to raise workers out of the level of illiterate common laborers.

A CISL official in Sicily stated:

The two problems affecting my organization are the sulphur mines and the *feudo*. The mines provide most of the industrial employment, and at the moment one-third of the 4,500 miners have no work. The industry is subject to sharp recurring crises in demand, approximately once every ten years. The Korean War stimulated production, but then the market collapsed as stocks from the United States came into distribution. During good times, industry does not modernize because of the lack of an incentive to reduce costs, and during bad times it cannot. CISL succeeded in the passage of legislation to provide incentives for capital investment, guarantee sulphur prices, and provide wage subsidies to miners. For the first time in Italy, a law was passed stipulating that employers had to respect a collective bargaining agreement.

The second problem is created by the existence of the *feudo*. These barren stretches of land are principally in wheat production. The peasants work the land for 600 lire per day, and work approximately 150 days per year. They travel as much as seven miles to reach their place of work, the fortunate ones by mule, the rest on foot. The Mafia, which has been in decline, developed in the *feudo*. Actually, it is composed of the *campieri* who are the guardians of the estates and the big city criminals in Palermo. They gain power through the direct and indirect support they receive from the influential members of the community. I mean the priests, the employers, politicians, and judges who fail to back up the common people when they become subject to the pressures of the Mafia. The Mafia call themselves friends. The people of the community call their leaders the friends of the friends, *gli amici degli amici*. In the city, the Mafia indulges in smuggling cigarettes for resale at prices below the government monopoly price and controls the distribution of fruits and vegetables. In Palermo, you cannot operate such a business either at wholesale or retail without paying off the Mafia. In trade unionism, the Mafia shows up in defense of the interests of the employer. The worker may be advised to settle for less to prevent matters from becoming unpleasant. A CGIL trade union leader was killed here, and his murder never solved. The solution to the problem is to break up the *feudo,* encourage industry, support the peasants, and develop new leaders in the community.

The problem faced by Italian labor leaders is building a labor movement among workers whose attitudes are shaped by such conditions of life. A trade union official in the South, to the question about the rural orientation of workers, commented: "The workers have a serf complex; their minds are poisoned against society and it is difficult to persuade them to express themselves. They have no desire to join in the struggle. We have to increase our strike activity in order to give them a sense of battle." A CISL leader reported: "A *contadino* came to me suggesting a training course on how to live in the city before he would venture to go. They have been bossed for centuries by employers, politicians, and priests. They have serious inferiority complexes."

The respondents, however, do not complain of a communication problem with their workers. Only one expressed difficulty in putting his point of view across: "I have difficulty in persuading the *contadini* to my point of view. The sharecroppers want solutions as sharecroppers, and I am convinced the only solution is to eliminate the feudalistic system entirely."

Concern with environmental situations which inhibit the growth of the trade union organization is prevalent among labor leaders in all parts of Italy. In central Italy, a CISL official stated:

There is a lack of dynamic large-scale industry in this area. The baronial mentality of the employers and the low level of education on the part of workers combine to make it difficult for democratic trade unionism to survive. Workers come to my office only when they run into trouble over some term of employment or a layoff. There is a large group of Communists in this area, principally due to the fact that the Church used to govern here. They had a strong following among the *contadini,* and they make a modern type of trade union impossible.

All groups recognize that the ultimate solutions are primarily political in character, but the CGIL leaders go beyond those of the other federations in the extent of government intervention which they advocate. General sentiment expressed by the groups includes the necessity of freeing trade unions from political dominance. One top leader of the CGIL stated that no conflict need exist if a labor leader performs a dual role: it is possible for an individual to be active as a trade union leader and as a Communist party member and keep both functions separate because he is subject to different pressures in each role.

Respondents from the CGIL showed a greater tendency than those of the other groups to see their problems in abstract terms. They have to join with the workers in their emancipation. They show less faith in "private enterprise" and see a better world to be gained in national planning and the direct government operation of key resources. They say with feeling that they have had more government sanctions directed against them than have any of the other federations. Some CGIL leaders have been imprisoned for their activity; others have died. Generally speaking, Communist members in the South are less doctrinaire in their expressions than those of the North.

The statements of the CISL and the UIL leaders are more technical, directed to particular ends:

Workers have to be taught the nature of costs to see the reasons for wage differences.

We believe in a program of labor-management coöperation, but the employers do not want it.

The threat of the southern workers coming up here has to be met by organization and training as quickly as possible.

We have to develop a training program to make the workers feel free and proud before we can have a successful labor movement.

Responses of the national union leaders reflected the differences in their role, compared to that of the provincial leaders. They stressed problems peculiar to their industries, including the weakness of their bargaining power in the writing of national agreements. "When I bargain with the employer, I have not got the strike weapon in my pocket. . . ." "We cannot strike because the unemployed will take over the jobs. . . ." The Social-Communists emphasized the split in the labor movement as a cause of organization weakness: "The split in the labor movement necessitates spending our time slandering and competing against each other."

The level of technical awareness is greater at the national union level. Trade union officials in agriculture view themselves as advisers in production and sales, and in purchase of tools, materials, and equipment. There is general unanimity among the three groups that the solution to the problems of the *contadini* and the *braccianti* lies in shifting them to the status of independent farmers. The agricultural day-laborer, in particular, is a victim of seasonal employment. His wages range from a thousand lire per day in the North to six hundred in the South, and he is fortunate if he can succeed in working for two hundred days during the year. His wages, unlike those of workers in the industrial sector, are commonly bargained on the provincial level, while fringe issues, job classification, and other general terms of employment are covered by a national agreement. Coöperative societies which seek to bring men and work together in orderly fashion have been founded by political groups. National leaders tend to talk more of such goals than of ideological differences. Two of the CISL group even spoke in terms of admiration of their Communist counterparts.

One Communist trade union official, in his evaluation of the situation, reported:

Trade unionism in agriculture is not having the same crisis as in industry. The *contadini* make better trade unionists because of a longer tradition. They work hard and love their work. They have a spirit of independent action and are not afraid of the employer. The CGIL *contadini* are friends of the CISL *contadini*. Communism and Catholicism do not keep them apart. They have a sense of solidarity and a will for action.

His counterpart in the CISL stated:

The important problem is how to emancipate the *contadini*. They represent the last vestiges of feudalism in Europe; they should be converted into independent farmers. The 350,000 *mezzadri* families can be protected by establishing by law the right of discharge only for just cause. You cannot resolve their problem today by long-run solutions. That is why we may appear to be inconsistent on issues.

A second CISL national union leader described the problem in broader terms:

There is a lack of realization on the part of the workers of how power accrues in an organization. Italy is a country of tremendous social problems, millions of protesting workers, and puny reform legislation. You had the first two characteristics twenty-five years ago and came up with the New Deal. I think the difference is in the low educational level and the resignation of the Italian masses. They are made promises by politicians, promises which are not kept. The workers read little or nothing, and are easily swayed by emotional appeals.

The CISL and UIL groups stressed also the importance of raising the level of education and training. In their words:

Our whole school system from the elementary school to the universities is antiquated. They have not kept up with the changes which have occurred in the world.

All Italians should be kept in school at least until they are fourteen.

The gap between the end of schooling and the beginning of a job career is enough to make a worker an illiterate by the time he begins to work.

Leaders at the national level are more conversant with the problems of their respective industrial sectors than are provincial leaders. They spoke of differences in capitalization, cost components, volume of production, average wages, and collective bargaining strategy. The head of the metal workers in one of the federations expressed fears which the leaders in the smaller unions or the provincial organizations are less likely to experience: the workers do not seem to understand his position; their demands are unreasonable. The reasons for his concern make a subject for interesting speculation. They may be the problems of a conservatively educated labor leader heading a large organization of comparatively enlightened workers conscious of their self-interests. The metal workers are the most mature and militant group among the industrial labor force in Italy. They are a key group in the economy and receive the highest base wages, fifty cents per hour, on the average, based on the current rate of exchange. The interfederation rivalry for their loyalty, moreover, is intense. The CGIL union is headed by one of the most competent young trade union leaders in that federation.

The query on problems brought forth expressions on worker attitudes presenting difficulties for leadership.

From a Communist official:

They are afraid to become trade union members because of job insecurity. They are disgusted with the labor movement split. They have low wages, long hours, high accident and sickness rates.

From a CISL leader:

The membership is introverted and inexpressive—the result of twenty years of fascism. The relations between employers and workers are deplorable. There are no relations. Why should workers increase their productivity if they do not share in its benefits? Between 1952 and 1957 productivity in my industry rose 120 per cent. During the same period, the national contracts increased wages 5 per cent, while actual wages on a company basis rose 15 per cent. The latter includes mostly unilateral wage increases which employers in my industry give workers and which some day will blow up in their faces.

From a UIL leader:

Workers are the worst kind of employers. They can only conceive of their own problem and do not have the capacity of placing it within the context of the reality around them. They do not understand that if their leader has power, it really comes from them and not because he is a big shot who can talk to the boss.

On the federation level, respondents cited the split in the labor movement and the lack of trade-union–consciousness as factors which make their jobs difficult. The CGIL official in the collective bargaining office spoke of the lack of meaning in national bargaining when employers unilaterally grant wages well above the minima stipulated by the agreements. A UIL official lamented the lack of competent organizers. A summary of the responses of three officials, each prominent in his respective organization, is given below. Each is a prototype: for the CGIL, the revolutionary with a record of arrests who has now acquired respectability as a top official in the labor movement; for the CISL, the left-wing orthodox Catholic, well educated, disturbed by the influence of the Church in social affairs; and for the UIL, the somewhat less formally educated leader, anticlercial, who has a strong stereotype of CISL members as servile followers of the clergy.

From the CGIL leader:

The workers should assume an important role in the direction of the economy. They must participate not only in the distribution of income, but also in its formation. Once they become conscious of the nature of income, they would be in a position to develop it, not for the private profit of a few, but for the common good of all. Our greatest problem is the loss of collective bargaining power due to the split in the labor movement. The employers play one federation against the other. The CISL organization at Fiat does not really bargain. Management bestows on them the privilege of being talked to, but CISL calls it bargaining. I grant that my organization made a serious mistake by not realizing national collective bargaining was a meaningless thing to the rank and file. What has evolved at Fiat, however, is not collective bargaining. The workers cannot go on strike. If the people there did not dance to management's tune, Fiat would close the faucet on them. The situation represents a failure in trade unionism and collective bargaining.

What should our objectives be? They should include company-wide collective bargaining and coöperation among federations at the plant level. Every year in the shop-committee elections we present to management the spectacle of workers fighting against each other. We should nominate men on the basis of technical competency and then present workers with only one list of candidates, instead of three. The winners would then represent all the workers in the plant. We could also take unified action on the national union level. It is on the provincial level of organization that political differences have a sharp impact. As to political objectives, I see no conflict in role for the labor leader who is a member of Parliament as well as a trade union official. Workers need their representatives in Parliament. If they do not have them, no one will promote their interests in the government. We should also work for a united Socialist party. It will take time. The Social Democrats, although small in total number, are very influential on the provincial level, and, unlike the Communists or Socialists, can exercise influence with effective results. Because of this factor, they bargain from strength for socialist unity.

We should also have a planned economy, with representatives of workers participating in the making of policy decisions. Investments should be controlled, and agricultural rent eliminated entirely. We also have to force employers to acknowledge the responsibility that workers have in increasing productivity and to share in the determination of the division of the income of the enterprise. We also have broad social objectives. The institutions of Italy have to be made more democratic. And we have to raise the low cultural level of Italian workers through education, training, and leisure activity. We shall try to achieve these objectives by developing powerful organizations and by putting unremitting pressure on employers and government.

From the CISL official:

Our broad objective is social progress. Our particular objectives are to institute collective bargaining at the company level and to isolate the Communists in the labor movement by gathering all the democratic forces into our organization. By our collective bargaining policy, we expect to achieve rising wages without inflation. As for the Communists, we are convinced they want to alter the structure of the Italian government and economy, although the majority of their own workers prefer democracy. If we could pull these workers away from the CGIL, we would have isolated the Communist and Fascist forces in Italy. We believe in the possibility of collaboration with the employer and reject the idea of the inevitability of class conflict. Unfortunately, however, employers have not accepted the idea of joint responsibility in productivity. They conceive of profits not in terms of collaboration with labor but as a gain directly in proportion to the exploitation of the worker. Even when they do accept the idea of collaboration, they become paternalistic and insist that what they have to offer should be granted unilaterally.

Our objectives have to be pursued by a clear separation of trade unions and political parties. The unions should place themselves in a position of influence over the political parties, not the reverse. Practically, workers want to mix politics with trade unionism, and they expect their labor leaders to be their political leaders as well. Our constitution prohibits our line officials from holding executive positions in political parties. Ideally, labor leaders should not be politicians. At the moment, however, such a combination is useful, in order to obtain the reforms necessary to make collective bargaining work. The effect of a single labor party would be to weaken the over-all political influence of the workers, which at the moment asserts itself through the parties in power. I must also grant that the Communist party has made a contribution by developing in workers a consciousness of their interests.

Our method in employer relationships is to anticipate and move toward realistic goals. Through the study of economic facts we have to determine what can be obtained at the moment and devise a strategy to obtain it. Excessive demands are not wise generally, except with some employers. Demands can be used as a means of increasing employer efficiency in the interest of workers. In broad terms, the objective of trade unionism is to promote the interests of workers, not to be the instrument for achieving the objectives of a group of political theoreticians. The fundamental objective of the CGIL is political power.

We, of course, have our problems. We do not believe in compulsory trade unionism. Accordingly, the solicitation of monthly dues is a painful process. We shall, however, adhere to our faith in trade unionism as a voluntary association. In the meantime, we must work toward the goal where 100 per cent of our members are paying their monthly dues.

From the UIL official:

The fundamental objective of trade unionism is guardianship of the economic, political, and social interests of the working class. The concept of ACLI [Christian Associations of Italian Workers] is an artificial one. You cannot separate the various interests of workers into different organizations. They have an integralist idea of the human being.[3] He belongs to God, or more specifically, to the Church. Out of this concept comes the affirmation of the right to exercise direction of the worker in the different organizations to which he belongs. In this view, the trade union has a technical function restricted to writing collective bargaining agreements. For the other functions, there is the ACLI to provide the worker with his ideology, the parish church, and the Christian Democrat party. I reject this authoritarian concept of guiding workers. The trade union should be a democratic instrument for promoting the interests of labor, not something which authoritarians deem it should be. The Communist party is also integralist. They have their own separate organizations, which put together embrace the total behavior of the individual.

The CISL leaders, like the ACLI officials, are also lay leaders of the Catholic Church. The only difference between them is their idea of the function of trade unions. They are an instrument, by inadvertence perhaps, of the establishment of a clerical state in Italy. We in the UIL have a lay concept of trade unionism. We see it as a device to serve the needs of workers. We also believe that the way to combat a clerical state in Italy is by a counterforce, such as a united socialist party. We can coöperate with the CISL on collective bargaining policy, even with the CGIL. Unity with the CISL, however, can come about only by a mutual abandonment of respective positions on Catholic integralism and socialism.

The goal we seek in government legislation is fundamentally industrial development. You cannot have trade unionism without economic growth. I am opposed to an industrial relations law, however, which the other federations want. A law protecting collecting bargaining agreements and extending them automatically to all workers, including the unorganized, would be a blow to trade union organization.

On the matter of the relationships between trade unions and political parties, I do not think there should be any ties between the two at all. This business of one man being both a trade union official and a member of the Chamber of Deputies is a mistake. In Italy, the political party is the supreme

[3] Catholic integralism refers to a concept derived from the thought of the French philosopher Jacques Maritain, who conceives of the life activity of man as an organic whole based on strict precepts of Christian morality. All aspects of life, be they spiritual, political, social, or economic, are in harmony with each other and are to be regulated by Christian principles. The term has acquired a special flavor in Italy by its reference to the inflexible attitude of Catholics not only toward Marxism but to the Social Democrats as well.

authority. Your congressmen in the United States can take independent positions. In my country, a man who does will be thrown out of the party and will not be able to run for office any more. Look at the way Pastore has to behave for the government backed by Fascists. What will the workers think of such a spectacle? A politician cannot be a successful labor leader in Italy.

However, I do believe that in the interests of the working class, there should be a broad-based socialist party. All workers, including the Catholics, are socialists. The Church is destroying the power of workers by combating it. The workers are not Marxists. Their socialism is an idealistic reaction to human misery and organized privilege in Italy. If we could collect all these people under a man who is not the leader of a political party, we would have a great force for reform. It would break the political stalemate caused by the juxtaposition of Social-Communists on one side and Catholic Church on the other. And I might add that we have a conviction that your government supports reaction in Italy and thereby stifles the aspirations of the Italian working class.

We should limit the strike severely as a method of achieving our goals. It should be used every ten years instead of every ten days. The workers are tired of strike action. The right to strike, however, should not be taken away, not even from government employees. Government is a big, and not particularly good, employer in Italy.

The respondents were asked, in the written questionnaire, what they considered the most difficult problems they had faced. The responses are summarized in Table 12. Because of the failure of the CGIL officials to answer this question, responses could be tabulated only for the UIL and the CISL. Problems of organization are given greater stress by the CISL than by the UIL. The UIL is more concerned with problems arising from economic pressures. Difficulties involved in getting collective bargaining accepted on the company level are a dominant concern of the CISL; they run like an undertone throughout the responses to the question. The diversity of these expressed concerns contrasts with those of the Danes, which are concentrated predominantly on the problem of unemployment.

In the few written responses submitted by respondents of the CGIL, the question of the most difficult problem faced by the labor leader is not answered directly. One prominent Communist labor leader omitted the question but answered the rest of the questionnaire. The others answer in terms of the impersonal play of forces with which the labor leader swings and sways, rather than in terms of the impact of the personality of the trade union official and his own responsibility and influence in shaping the course of events. The response of a Socialist member of the CGIL is typical and is quoted in its entirety:

All problems are difficult. It often happens that we find ourselves in the position of having put together all the elements of a given situation, which appears in perspective in a particular way. We are convinced, and we do our utmost to have these elements understood by the masses. To understand them, however, is not always easy. Too many factors are at play in the behavior of workers, such as, for example, unemployment. In such a state of affairs, the situation could rush headlong into crisis and the workers find themselves suddenly in very serious circumstances, caught by surprise, only because they had not sufficiently grasped the situation and simply thrust it back. This could happen in all sorts of circumstances, like the split in the labor movement in 1948 and the attack against the CGIL after the 1953 elections. How can such a situation be resolved? There are no formulas, but certainly a strong effort should be made for unity, for orientation and discussion; to have faith in the basic struggle and give immediate problems a long-term view.

I have found myself in the position of having to resolve thousands of diffi-

TABLE 12

Italian Labor Leaders' Views of Their Most Difficult Problems *
(Per Cent)

Related to:		CISL		UIL
Organization	42		18	
Lack of trade-union–consciousness		27		12
Split in trade unionism		5		0
Organizing under Communist influence		5		6
Lack of funds		5		0
Economics	29		43	
Adverse impact of unemployment		3		25
Grappling with change		16		0
Achieving uniform standards		8		12
Combating effects of inflation		2		6
Politics	5		14	
Political domination of unions		0		7
Weakening the Communists		5		7
Employers	20		25	
Anti-union policies		6		25
Strike-action failure		14		0
Personal relationships	4		0	
Rejecting assistance from those with vested interest		2		0
Solving wage dispute between an employer and future son-in-law		2		0
Total	100		100	
Number	37		32	

* Because the CGIL leaders did not respond to this item, that organization is not included in the table.

cult situations. Strikes which run the risk of being broken by employer action and by the police, who in our country always protect them, are a case in point. In these circumstances you have to run risks. I have been arrested more than twenty times. Listen to this. It happened this spring on the four-teenth or fifteenth of April, during the regional Chemical strike. I was in charge of directing the struggle in front of the _____ plant, one of our weakest firms. With an automobile and a loudspeaker, from four o'clock in the morning, I was urging the workers not to enter the plant. Then the police prohibited me from continuing. They did not have the right to do so; but in my country questions of rights are worth little under such cir-cumstances. The police thought that my expulsion would deal a serious blow to the situation. The workers were beginning to waver; they were all in front of the gates. The siren was about to blow. Would the psychological effect, habit, fear, predominate? I do not remember this precisely, but as soon as the siren blew, I drove the automobile at maximum speed toward the plant, blowing the horn constantly. The police finally stopped me. The workers did not enter. The strike was 95 per cent successful. What happened to me perhaps does not interest you. It has no connection with your question.

The question of the most pressing problems of the labor leaders was approached from another perspective. They were asked: "In your judgment, what is the major obstacle to the growth of trade unionism in Italy?" There are no noteworthy differences in the responses to this question from those to the question on the most pressing problems. All three groups stressed the low level of organization-consciousness, low industrialization, high unemployment, anti-union employer policies, and the lack of collective bargaining power which is the consequence of such conditions. The problem faced by Italian labor leaders is funda-mentally difficulty in building dynamic, successful organizations. Their ability to do so is predicated on full employment and an expanding economy.

A CISL provincial labor leader presented a detailed labor educa-tion program designed to cope with the problem of low trade-union–consciousness. To achieve a habit of trade unionism, he suggested, it is necessary to increase the workers' sense of organization and to provide them with the education necessary to discern goals clearly and move systematically in their direction. Specifically, labor education courses should include techniques of wage payment, economic principles, methods of group action, industrial management, and grievance pro-cedure. From such education and training will emerge the development of goals and objectives, through the diagnosis of actual problems facing the organization and the membership.

The selection of men to attend such courses would normally depend upon the objective of the particular course. Preference should be given to the younger workers, but the actual selection would be left to the individual conducting the program. Ideally, all workers would enroll in at least the basic trade union courses, and further work would be done by smaller groups formed according to interests and abilities shown in the basic courses.

The success or failure of such courses would depend on the efforts made after they have terminated. The leadership should be responsible for observing the effects of the labor education program and for using effectively the skills imparted by it. The workers should be made aware that the usefulness of the program is measured only by the changes in the behavior of the individuals who participated in it. If no results are gained by the program, the trade union officials in the organization should ascertain the reasons and make appropriate changes.

The labor education program should be based on the fundamental principle that trade unionism rests on the ability to analyze situations. Consequently, although instruction would differ with changing circumstances, the course content would follow these general lines: (1) economic and social environment in which the organization is operating; (2) characteristics of the labor market; (3) plant problems, particularly those which affect the worker, including such items as the structure of the organization, its financial position, and method of operation and personnel policies. To become proficient in the actual analysis of situations, the participants should be taught the following steps: (1) determine precisely the nature of the problem; (2) collect the facts pertinent to the problem, examine precedents, listen to the opinions of interested parties, and determine the difference between the situation as it stands and the situation as it should be; (3) ascertain precisely what were the causes of the present situation.

The differences in the replies on labor leaders' responsibilities could not be pulled apart significantly by federation. They are summarized with all three federations combined in Table 13. The term *coordinamento* appears frequently in the responses. In general, a provincial labor leader tends to see his responsibility as one of controlling the activities of the various trade unions attached his own office. Coördination is explained in the sense of providing guidance in order to avoid mistakes, determining realizable objectives, and seeing that the various affiliated unions are pursuing consistent goals. The provincial leaders feel also that they have a propaganda responsibility to discharge by making speeches and writing newspaper releases. The heads of the national unions appear to view their responsibilities as those of executive officers discharging and controlling policies formulated by superior bodies, such as the convention or the executive board. The low level of ideological responses is explained as follows: "We are forced to inject ideology into trade unions because of the Communists. The indispensable requisites of trade unionism, however, are members and the servicing of their needs."

TABLE 13

Italian Labor Leaders' Concept of Their Responsibilities

Related to:		Number
Organization	46	
Control and coördinate trade unions		15
Increase trade-union–consciousness and militancy		11
Attract new members to organization		6
Be in constant contact with workers		5
Provide workers with assistance as they need it		3
Increase influence of workers		3
Develop class-consciousness		1
Weaken the CGIL		1
Raise efficiency of shop committeemen		1
Collective bargaining	8	
Improve terms of employment periodically		4
Enforce collective bargaining agreements		2
Develop collective bargaining policies		2
Total	54	

To the query on long-term objectives, the overwhelming number of responses from provincial trade union officials is political in character (Table 14). The stress on political solutions is dominant, those of the CGIL being most radical. The question did not restrict the answer to any particular sphere. It asked: "In your judgment, what, if any, are the major long-term objectives trade unionism should seek in order to improve the condition of Italian labor?" CISL officials express the greatest aversion to legislation as a solution to the labor problem. A collective bargaining law should be passed only to give agreements legal sanctity. One leader expressed the thought that using the American method of exclusive representation for one union would have the effect of favoring the CGIL. Another expressed his opinion of law in this way:

"The government of Italy resolves a problem under the law strictly on the basis of what group is the most powerful in the particular area. There is no such thing as justice under the law. Justice is the point of view of the most powerful."

TABLE 14

Objectives of Italian Provincial Trade Union Leaders
(Per Cent)

Nature of objective	CGIL		CISL		UIL
Political	86		66		65
More public investment		39	0		0
Socialist state		15	0		0
More private investment		0	13		0
More recognition of trade unions		8	19		40
Improved social insurance		8	14		0
Limitation on landholding		8	3		0
Minimum-wage legislation		0	3		0
Reformation of employment exchanges		8	0		0
No new laws		0	14		25
Economic	14		14		25
Shift of labor from agriculture to industry		0	0		25
Rise in economic level of workers		14	0		0
Company-wide collective bargaining		0	14		0
Organizational	0		20		10
Development of trade-union–consciousness		0	20		0
Unification of labor movement with UIL		0	0		10
Total	100		100		100
Number	13		24		8

The CISL expressed the fewest reformist goals; the CGIL, the most. No internal consistency appears in the CISL and the UIL objectives. One CISL leader wants nothing to do with political parties, while another believes in the founding of a new labor party. The Socialist aspirations of the UIL do not appear clear. One official of that organization complained that state socialism stifles trade unionism by pushing up decisions into government levels, while another stated a belief that the effective solution to the myriad of problems confronting Italy is a socialist society.

The extent of government intervention espoused by the CGIL ranges from the public control of new power, steel, and fuel to a radical reform of Italian society through the creation of a socialist state. In contrast with the other federations, none of the CGIL members expressed doubts about the efficacy of government control in Italy. One stated that any criticism of the way the government is handling its numerous state enterprises is not valid, since the present government is not socialist. Another stated that while the present constitution has many idealistic objectives which the Communists believe in, they have never been implemented by law by the Christian Democrats, who do not intend to do so.

Amplification of some of the statements follows: "By advocating a class-conscious labor movement, I mean that the UIL is critical of the CISL idea of class collaboration, which resembles the Fascist idea of the corporate state. I do not mean by the idea the Marxist concept of the inevitability of class conflict. Rather, I have in mind a trade unionism divorced from the Catholic idea of employer-employee collaboration. What that Catholic idea in Italy would mean is company unionism." A member of the Communist party, discussing the reformation of the employment exchanges in Italy, voiced one of the rare expressions of criticism of the Church heard from that group. In Italy, he stated bitterly, a job recommendation from a bishop is second only to one from a cardinal. On the objective of company-wide collective bargaining, one official stated that it is an excellent way to pit one employer against another in obtaining concessions.

CRITERIA FOR MEASURING SUCCESS

In the written questionnaire, labor leaders were asked what criteria should be used to measure the achievements of trade unionism. Responses, compared by federation in Table 15, fall into several categories. (1) Increase in the influence of the trade union organization is an important criterion of success. A preoccupation with the ineffectiveness of trade union power pervades the expressions. The unions need more power, in terms of legislation passed and in representation on official bodies making decisions which affect the economic and social life of the country. Greater influence over the employer, through increasing the ability to modify his decisions affecting terms of employment and eliminating his manipulation of trade union organizations, would mean greater achievement. Increase in influence is also expressed in terms of freedom from the dominance of other organizations, including political parties and the Church. (2) The extent to which the worker participates in economic and social affairs generally, and his trade union in particular, is another consideration. (3) Improvement in the economic standards of workers is an indication of the success of trade unions. Actual improvement in employment terms represents a small minority of the responses. This outcome is a measure of the immediate

TABLE 15

Italian Labor Leaders' Criteria for Measuring Success of Trade Unionism (Per Cent)

Criterion of success	CGIL	CISL	UIL
Vitality of organization	24	56	48
Unity in labor movement	8	8	9
Decrease in political dominance of unions	0	0	7
Increase in collective bargaining power	0	8	0
Increase in number of collective bargaining agreements	8	12	7
Ratio of dues-paying members to potential	0	0	5
Number and influence of shop committees	0	8	7
Successful labor legislation	8	12	5
Creation of new jobs	0	8	8
Worker participation	42	20	17
Economic and social affairs	8	8	9
Trade union affairs	34	12	8
Improvement of standards	25	16	33
Difference between gains and costs	0	0	7
Extent and rapidity of improvement of workers	0	16	13
Economic improvement of country	25	0	13
Other	8	8	2
Structural changes in industry and agriculture	8	4	0
Maintenance of democracy in Italy	0	0	0
Development of sympathetic public	0	4	2
Total	99 *	100	100
Number	12	26	53

* Percentages were rounded.

and pressing problem of increasing organizational strength before the attainment of other objectives. Noteworthy in the replies is the diversity of the criteria and the insistence that there is no single benchmark for the evaluation of a labor movement.

One UIL respondent suggested at length criteria of success, all of which involve the extent to which trade unionism in Italy can over-come what he believes are its principal obstacles: (1) the lack of a democratic spirit in the country, due principally to the twenty years of Fascist dictatorship and its encouragement of paternalism; (2) the low level of economic activity, which provides opportunities for Communist agitation, and fosters a wage policy based on political demagoguery, especially among the poorly educated and the under-employed, producing a mass of workers who oppose everything and propose nothing, who know what they are against but not what they are for; (3) the passivity of democratic workers disillusioned by the split in the labor movement and the introduction of party politics in trade unionism; (4) the niggardly and reactionary mentality of the em-ployers. The particular emphasis of this UIL official was on the de-structive effect of the Fascist era on the development of a habit of democratic group participation in social and economic affairs. As a consequence, the new labor movement in a period of ten years has had to be manned at the rank-and-file level with men not sufficiently equipped to perform their jobs adequately.

Another UIL respondent stated that environmental factors have to be stressed in making an appraisal of a labor movement. In Italy, these influences include (1) the level of industrialization, including the characteristics of the economic mix in particular geographical areas, which shapes the level and type of industrial employment, and involves the characteristics of the workers being attracted to these jobs, the pressure or absence of an urban mentality, and the power of the em-ployer; (2) the extent to which communism is exercising an influence in particular labor market areas; (3) the prevalence of the mentality crystallized during the period of Fascist power.

The representativeness of the CGIL responses is not known because of the failure to obtain a substantial number of returns from that organization on the written questionnaire. The available answers por-tray the vision of a united mass of workers moving inexorably in co-hesion toward the achievement of social and economic objectives. The comments of a young Communist labor leader are quoted verbatim:

The criteria which can be used in measuring the successes of Italian trade unionism can be summed up only by taking into account its three phases, beginning with the period of trade union unity. From 1945 to 1948, the united labor movement was a great propulsive force for general progress, not only for the workers, but for all the Italian people. From 1948 to 1956 came the period of employer discrimination against the *attivisti* of the CGIL, causing serious damage to the labor movement and a sharpening of the division among the workers. During the last two years there has continued a certain discrimination against the *attivisti,* but at the same time a greater movement of the workers in the direction of unity has occurred.

The first consideration in measuring the success of trade unionism should be the importance that the action of workers has for Italy, in the application of the constitution and in the modification of the economic and social condition of the country. The Italian labor movement and the action of workers, in particular, have been a powerful stimulus for the realization of some modifications of the social and political structure, such as the agrarian reform, despite its limitations; industrial development in the South; and general governmental development plans.

Industrial workers have also obtained, since 1946, wage escalation based on the cost of living; the right to elect shop committeemen; the writing of collective bargaining agreements applicable to all workers in the particular industries they cover; new social laws, such as those on women workers; apprentice training; improvements in pensions; compensation for accidents and industrial illnesses; the extension of sickness insurance to pensioners and small farmers; and other victories of a social character.

The second consideration is the general improvement in trade union action, the strengthening of the unity of workers at the shop, and the better ties among the labor organizations themselves—for example, the action of the metal workers for the reduction of the workweek, as the result of an agreement achieved through the combined action of the three federations. Trade union action at the plant level finds the workers constantly united, and as a consequence improves their standard of living and their conditions of work.

The third is the level of debate among the workers on various questions and grievances. Presently, problems are being fully debated and discussed, not only in operational terms and for immediate goals, but also in terms of political economy, long-term prospect of work, defense of trade union freedom and democratic liberties, and the development of the economy of the country, tied together with the increase of wages for the working class and the Italian people generally. In sum, the needs and aspirations are three: (1) the guarantee of trade union and democratic liberties in the plants and the banishment of reprisals; (2) the guarantee of employment; (3) the improvement of wages.

In a subsequent revision of the written questionnaire, the respondents were asked this question: "Once a decision has been made by you on a trade union problem, what do you use as the basis for judging the success or failure of the results?" The replies to this item are similar to those to the query in the oral interview on what constitutes success for a labor leader. Because of the small number of responses, the replies have not been tabulated. The answers given by the leaders of the CISL and the UIL imply certain practical limits within which these men anticipate success. They expressed their responses in terms of permanent improvements gained, relative to the price paid for them by the workers. CISL leaders also mentioned as a positive return of a decision the strengthening of the organization in the eyes of the workers. No mention was made of the idea that benefits accrue in the course of the action itself. The CGIL leaders stated that the satisfactions derived by workers in the course of action itself are to be considered part of the benefits. The worker is always right in the trade union action and the employer always wrong; and the action is never a complete failure so long as workers are reacting positively toward it, a manifestation of principle consistent with previous statements that the expression of worker sentiments is an overriding principle in trade unionism. The noteworthy difference, consequently, between the CGIL statements and those from the UIL and the CISL lies in the idea that conflict has intrinsic advantages as a method of expression, compared to the idea that conflict is an instrument of advantage when the price paid for it is less than the improved terms of employment that ensue from it. Representative comments from the CISL and the UIL and complete responses from the CGIL are given below.

From the CISL:

The relationship between the asking price and the gain . . .

Because of our poverty, whether the gain necessitated a loss of pay . . .

The reaction of the affected workers to the decision and the consequence derived from the decision . . .

Whether the decision continues the sequence of continual gains . . .

If workers remain convinced that without trade unionism the result would have been worse and that no other organization could have done better . . .

If the action produced a lasting gain not at the expense of other workers . . .

If the decision is not a compromise to prevent a worsening of the situation . . .

If previously fixed objectives have been reached . . .

If the objective is reached or, failing this, the reaction of the workers to the failure . . .

From the UIL:

If 50 per cent of the objectives were obtained . . .

If the solution is really a fundamental one for the workers and the benefits will have an impact on the future . . . If the decision is an expedient and does not resolve anything either in the present or the future, then there has been a failure of leadership.

There is success when the decision has benefited the workers without precluding the possibility of plant expansion if economic factors are propitious for such expansion. Another criterion is whether the decision has the effect of increasing the acceptability of the trade union organization.

From the CGIL:

The success or failure of a grievance action can be judged in the first place by the manner in which the action of the workers has been prepared, how the struggle [*lotta*] has been conducted, and what tactics have been employed.

At times a trade union action, even if a good one, may not be satisfactory when the action has not been conducted well. The same good action may be termed excellent if the preparation and discharge of the action produces satisfaction to the workers because of both the results and the action taken.

The results of a trade union action cannot be judged in terms of absolute value; they should be evaluated instead in relation to the action conducted by the workers and the general circumstances under which the controversy unfolds and is resolved. You must also take into account that sometimes failure of an action undertaken under unfavorable circumstances could lay the foundations for a future success and that not always in a struggle between workers and bosses [*padroni*] can the right gain the victory.

There is no technical way of making an appraisal of a struggle over a trade union problem. In the renewal of a labor agreement, a comparison could certainly be made between the initial demands and the gains made in the agreement. Even in this case, however, you must keep in mind that these initial demands represent long-term objectives which, if not first obtained, will be achieved in a subsequent encounter.

One should consider that some objectives are always affected by external realities which are taken into account in preparing a trade union action, but which often have an impact greater than that anticipated. Examples of this are the lack of trade union unity, external events, and disequilibrium between geographical areas in both trade union power and the economic situation.

Complete failure occurs only when, given the proposed plan of attack, the workers do not react positively. In such a case, however, the mistake is to be found in the plan of attack. A political error was made, the plan probably being unpopular or undemocratic and therefore either rejected or misunderstood by the workers.

A revealing record of the successes and the failures which the Italian labor movement has encountered in the pursuit of its objectives may be found in the statement of the general secretary at the 1958 annual press conference of the CISL. It provides benchmarks which the Italian trade union movement, speaking through the top leadership of the CISL, has suggested as a means of appraising its efforts. A paraphrase of the salient points follows. (1) Despite the average 5 per cent increase in wages of collective bargaining agreements signed by the unions affiliated with the federation, the real wages of workers actually have fallen. (2) The policy of collective bargaining at the company level has had no significant success. (3) In the agricultural sector, rapid mechanization has raised additional new problems, but the equivocal position of the CGIL has caused some delays in solving them. (4) In the matter of collective bargaining law, the CISL continued to oppose any law which establishes trade unionism by force of law and would rather see unions remain voluntary associations. (5) The strategy of industry-wide strikes serves no usefulness in the development of collective bargaining at the company level. The only way this important goal can be reached is by trade union unity, and such unity cannot be obtained merely by bringing together the various political factions in the labor movement, as the CGIL has suggested. (6) Enrollment in the federation has risen from 2,180,000 to 2,300,000, while trade union dues payments have risen 12 per cent over the past year. (7) A loss of a little more than 1 per cent was sustained in the percentage of seats in the *commissioni interne*. The division of these seats now stands at 35.5, 48.7, and 8.2 for the CISL, the CGIL, and the UIL respectively.[4] This loss may be explained partly as a falling-off from the significant gains which the CISL had made in a period of economic expansion, and partly by the effects of the CGIL policy of telling workers that the CISL has lost interest in the work of the *commissioni interne*. The policy of the CISL is to make the federation members of these commissions subject to its affiliated trade unions. (8) The organizational goal of the CISL is to strengthen the structure of trade unionism. To accomplish this objective, the federation intended to strengthen the trade union units in each plant and subordinate regional conventions of the trade unions to those of trade union local organizations, and to organize trade union structures for multiplant firms and generally encourage action on the plant level. (9) The CISL looked forward to an important role in the construction of international unions necessary to grapple with the problem of eliminating differences in the terms of employment in the different countries participating in the European Common Market. (10) The federation favored the reorganization of the various independent social assistance agencies into a single system of social security. (11) The federation recommended that any plan for the reform of the educational system should consider the impact of technological change on the labor market and that the coöperation

---

[4] In the 1959 elections, the valid votes cast were distributed 34.9, 49.0, and 8.1 per cent respectively.

of the trade unions should be solicited in its formulation. (12) The federation supported the promotion of competition in wholesale markets of food and deprecated the politics in government which so far had prevented the passage of this reform. (13) The federation characterized Italian agriculture as backward and irrational in structure. To enable it to compete successfully in the Common Market would require state intervention to provide financial and technical assistance, especially in the sharecropping sector (*mezzadria*). (14) The need for occupational training was emphasized. The CISL was prepared to participate in a program financed jointly by employers, workers, and the state to prepare workers for the demands of the market place. (15) The CISL urged the control of company savings in order to regulate investment in a manner that would produce an expanding economy. (16) Maintaining that a state can never pursue the objectives which government must seek without an efficient administration, the federation urged the reform of public administration forthwith. (17) Urging a new orientation for southern development, the CISL stated that the government had never made clear whether such a program should leave to private operators the responsibility of economic development, or whether a centrally directed planning agency should integrate or replace private initiative with public enterprise, whichever was necessary. It advocated that the latter be done by means of a coördinated plan of economic development. In the area of general economic development, the federation said, the Vanoni plan [5] had not been realized in a manner consistent with the needs of Italian society; the CISL had proposed a wage policy consistent with such development, but had had no response. The federation took the position that the economic policy of the Italian government should be geared, in general, to the responsibilities assumed in its participation in the European Common Market, and stated that it intended to propagandize the need to push the Common Market toward unity, especially in the political sphere. (18) The operations of the new National Council of Economics and Labor should be watched closely, lest it become a system of encouraging increasing government controls in areas which could best be left to negotiation between interested parties. (19) Parliament and the government were

[5] The Vanoni Plan, named after Minister of the Budget Ezio Vanoni, contained a series of assumptions and forecasts for the ten-year period 1955–64 and had for its objective the absorption of Italy's unemployed and underemployed, through an annual average increase in the national income of 5 per cent.

asked for a courageous policy of economic development and absolute defense of democratic liberties. The trade unions, on their part, promised to provide the stimulus for a government program and to serve to control its execution, defending their freedom to criticize and negotiate, whatever the government. Referring to the cabinet minister post held by the former general secretary of the CISL, the federation stated that, while it welcomed seeing a friend in government, his presence did not at all compromise the position of the union in promoting the interests of workers with government, free from the special interests of political parties. (20) From the coming convention of the Socialist party, the CISL hoped for a declaration of democratic intent, not only in the political field, but in the trade unions as well. A serious view of autonomy from the Communist party cannot be expected, it was remarked, when trade union officials of the Socialist party participate in an organization dominated by the Communist party, which is tied to an international organization connected with Moscow. To the executives and *militanti* of the Socialist party was directed the hope that they would soon find themselves united with their fellow trade unionists, including those of the TUC, the German DGB, the AFL–CIO, and the Italian CISL. (21) The CISL looked forward to a year of democratic trade union unity, working for the unification of all the democratic trade unions with the CISL. The CISL expressed sincere aspirations for united trade unionism, neutral on the ideological level and democratic in its application and technique. Any discrimination on its part, the statement went on, would be exercised only against the so-called Fascist and Communist unions, dominated by ideologies and practices which deny the very principle of the existence of the free trade union and the liberty of association. In the words of the general secretary: "If we have not realized this trade union unity, we are not to blame. We have tried everything. In the face of diffidence, fear, prejudice, personal interest, dishonesty in attributing to us characteristics and objectives which are not ours, we have persevered in making an appeal to unity."

WHAT ITALIAN LABOR LEADERS CONSIDER
DESIRABLE LABOR LEADER CHARACTERISTICS

Characteristics given first preference by Italian labor leaders as those of a "good" labor leader, given in Table 16, fall into the following categories: (1) intellectual qualities, such as intelligence, keenness of mind, or clearness of ideas; (2) leadership characteristics, such as the ability to inspire faith in workers or win the esteem of colleagues; (3) social orientation, including such characteristics as strong class-consciousness and emotional involvement with the working class; (4) moral traits of character, such as honesty; (5) technical capabilities. The characteristic of honesty is not used solely in the narrow sense to describe those who refrain from using trade union office for personal

TABLE 16

First Preferences of Italian Labor Leaders among Characteristics of
Good Labor Leaders
(Per Cent)

Nature of preferred trait		CGIL		CISL		UIL
Intellectual	0		44		17	
Intelligence		0		44		3
Sense of proportion		0		0		14
Leadership	0		6		24	
Influence over workers		0		6		7
Influence over colleagues		0		0		7
Ability to communicate		0		0		10
Moral	0		19		21	
Honesty		0		19		14
Spirit of sacrifice		0		0		7
Social	80		25		14	
Dedication to workers		60		19		14
Democratic spirit		20		0		0
Sensitivity to social problems		0		6		0
Technical	20		6		24	
Comprehension of labor problems		20		6		21
Ideological and practical preparation		0		0		3
Total	100		100		100	
Number	5		16		28	

gain, but in a broader application to portray the individuals who exercise candor and frankness with their colleagues and the rank and file. These first preferences include only the primary qualification stated by the respondents. The responses are too few to allow any interfederation comparison of first preferences. It is probable, however, that the Social-Communists would emphasize a strong orientation to the working class, while the CISL–UIL group would mention more frequently technical preparation and qualities of personal character. The Catholic group would be more apt to stress the latter qualities than would the UIL as a group.

In Table 17 all the responses on the characteristics of a good labor leader are tabulated. The CISL–UIL group stressed leadership ability

TABLE 17

Opinions of Italian Labor Leaders of Characteristics of Good Labor Leaders (Per Cent)

Nature of preferred trait	CGIL		CISL		UIL	
Intellectual	19		41		35	
Intelligence		19		29		15
Sense of proportion		0		6		12
Zest for work		0		0		6
Initiative		0		6		2
Leadership	23		19		40	
Ability to communicate		9		8		16
Self-control		14		3		10
Ability to motivate		0		8		14
Moral	5		15		11	
Honesty		5		13		5
Spirit of sacrifice		0		2		6
Social	43		14		6	
Dedication to workers		29		8		6
Sense of humanity		9		0		0
Democratic spirit		5		6		0
Technical	10		10		8	
Comprehension of labor problems		5		6		6
Ideological and practical preparation		0		2		1
Knowledge of production methods		0		0		1
Knowledge of psychology of workers		5		2		0
Total	100		99 *		100	
Number	20		38		89	

* Percentages were rounded.

and character traits as well as technical ability. One CISL respondent stated: "The presence of static technical and character traits produces an outcome in the labor leader which is crucial, namely, the inspiring of faith in his leadership, the respect of employers, and general public esteem. These are important goals. . . ." The Social-Communists are less concerned with the approbation of other economic groups. A prominent Communist trade union official listed, in order of importance, the following characteristics: (1) absolute dedication to the cause of workers; (2) the capacity to understand and evaluate the various situations which evolve in the world of labor—such as the changing aspirations of workers and the extent of their will to action (*la volontà effettiva di azione dei lavoratori*)—and the ability to discern what tactics to use in a particular situation and how to time his action properly; (3) clearness of ideas, including the ability to give the fullest expression of the point of view of the worker through the exercise of democratic leadership; (4) a uniform policy toward all problems which are of interest to the working class; (5) the ability to obtain complete unity of action on the part of workers. The posture the CGIL takes on its concept of leadership is again apparent. Making a decision not palatable to workers may be considered an act of courage by the CISL–UIL group, but it is an undemocratic act to the CGIL group.

The ability to analyze a situation is a common value, but the goal-criteria to apply after the analysis is made are not. Similarly, the knowledge of problems was stressed in different ways, in terms of general economic problems or of particular ones which workers bring to the trade union organization for solution. The term "intuition" used by some of the officials describes the ability to comprehend a situation quickly. The responses reflect also differences in leadership level. Thus the federation leaders spoke more often of the ability to synthesize different types of activity, and were more critical of the characteristics of rival federation leaders than were the national or provincial officials.

The characteristics of a competent labor leader were described in a statement addressed to colleagues by a CISL general secretary in the industrial North. He should be able to control his actions in a manner that would make predictable what these actions will be. He should possess a loyal, open spirit, and a comprehension of men and reality, capable of adapting himself to the most disparate situations without sacrificing the principles of the labor movement. The temperament of the innovator should dominate his behavior, not that of an individual tied to rigid and traditional schemes. His behavior should be exemplary, such as to command prestige in the eyes of workers. He should also be able to lead men on the basis of maximum participation of those being led. Lastly, he must be capable of profiting from his experiences, the manifestation of which should be shown in his conduct.

POLITICAL ATTITUDES

To develop for the purposes of this study an estimation of the attitudes of Italian labor leaders toward the relationship between trade unionism and politics, in the interviews respondents were asked questions based on the following items: (1) In your judgment, what should be the relationship between trade unionism and politics? (2) Which political party do you think best represents the interests of workers? (3) [Asked of CISL and UIL respondents] What contribution do you feel the Communist party in Italy has made in the interest of workers? (4) Who has more political power, employers or trade unions?

Inasmuch as the contemporary labor movement in Italy was founded by the left and center political parties after the collapse of fascism, trade unions have inevitably been deeply involved in politics. In the judgment of the top leadership, however, criticism of the Italian labor movement as being too politically oriented is not warranted. Political influence is indispensable because it serves as a supplement to inadequate bargaining power and as a means of obtaining structural changes in the economy through the passage of legislation. The concessions gained through political influence are not obtainable through the use of economic pressure alone. When a labor leader is also a member of Parliament, immediate advantages accrue to the membership. He can use his stature in the community as a "fixer" and "trouble-shooter." The employer is more apt to listen when a *deputato* is on the telephone. If the unions are heavily committed in the political arena, it is because they have no other choice. The problem they face is how to organize in a manner that would maximize their economic influence without weakening their political power. A major concern expressed by the labor leaders was how to overcome the dependence of unions on political parties without, at the same time, destroying the political influence of the working class. Even the Social-Communists expressed an aspiration of this nature. They stated that the Communists had given up their policy of using trade unionism as a transmission belt for the party (*cinghia di trasmissione*). The CISL and the UIL expressed doubt of their intentions. One facet of the problem is striking. Although all the federations have prominent members in either the Senate or the Chamber of Deputies, each emphasized the manner in which the others are dominated by political parties. One CISL member of Parliament stated candidly that he felt the constitution should prohibit elected politicians such as he himself from holding trade union office. However, he felt that the dearth of labor leadership in Italy and the fact that the politician could use his position in promoting the interests of workers would make such a prohibition of questionable value at the moment. In general, despite the short period since the founding of the new labor movement, there was, the investigation revealed, a strong desire on the part of the leadership to dominate rather than be dominated by political parties.

The UIL officials were the most sanguine in their affirmation of the necessity of divorcing trade unions from political parties. Their criticism, however, may be a reflection of the greater success which the CGIL and the CISL have had in getting their people elected to Parliament. Some of the respondents of these two organizations, although they are a minority, expressed the need to have a labor party modeled along British lines, which could be influenced by the labor movement. The CGIL respondents did not feel that any new party was necessary. The other two groups expressed the feeling that there is involved an issue of whether to choose the British or American solution in combining trade unionism and politics. Representative summary responses from the three groups are given below.

From the CISL:

We need to separate the political structure from the trade union structure. The political parties founded the labor movement, but now it is time for the movement to divorce itself from them.

You cannot separate politics from trade unionism. Solutions to the pressing problems of the workers are to be found by exercising an influence in Parliament and government. The only way to obtain a political voice is by the labor movement's electing its own members. You Americans make a mistake when you criticize us for making a mixture of politics and trade unions. That is not the issue. The problem is how best to perform both functions. People in Europe vote along class lines. If we did not enter politics, we would be ruined. In your country, collective bargaining offers most of the solutions to worker problems. That is impossible here because we have no collective bargaining power. Government is not democratic in Italy. It represents the interests of the most powerful groups. That is why we cannot abandon what we are doing.

Workers should organize a united trade union movement and then seek to influence political parties. In the meantime, we should not concern ourselves with the niceties of theory. The employers do not. If we did not have members in Parliament no one would look after us.

I wish American professors would stop telling us how politically conscious we are. They show their ignorance of our problems when they do.

Unions by their essence are political. That is not the real problem. The problem is how to achieve maximum trade union power and political power at the same time. The trouble is that the labor leader who is also a member of Parliament cannot split himself in two. In Italy, the political party governs. As a member of Parliament, he owes his allegiance to the political party to which he belongs and which put him in office.

From the CGIL:

Complete separation is ideal but not practical. There would be nobody representing the workers in Parliament.

I believe in independence with qualifications. If there are parties which promote the interests of workers, the relationship between such parties and the trade unions becomes inevitable because of the common objectives of both organizations.

It is absurd to think of non-political trade unionism. The leaders of the CISL and the UIL belong to parties, and why should not the Communists do so too? The union on occasion must take political action. Trade union leadership can be separated from political leadership even when both are performed by the same individual. As the former, what the leader does is conditioned by the need and desires of the rank and file. His power rests with them. As the latter, he is just one member of the party central committee. The party makes no decisions on trade union matters. We have been accused of starting political strikes at the instigation of the party. The Togliatti strike was begun by the workers. The Belgian Catholics have pulled political strikes, and we did not object to them.

From the UIL:

There should be a complete separation between political parties and labor unions. A man who is both a labor leader and a politician is in conflict with himself. As a politician, he must follow the dictates of the party. In Italy there occurs the sorry spectacle of a labor leader in Parliament having to vote with the Fascists because the government wants him to. Look at the position it puts him in, in the eyes of workers.

The labor movement should free itself of political parties but exert political influence on them.

The sentiments expressed are colored by the positions of those expressing them. The members of Parliament interviewed tend not to see any conflict in their dual role, with the exception of one CISL respondent. The CGIL vigorously defends its position. One leader of that organization stated that an intelligent young man rising out of the working class in Italy, if he has ambition, is faced with two alternatives: try to become a bishop or run for Parliament. The problem is created partly by restrictions on upward movement in Italy, where a political career affords opportunities for a sudden improvement in one's social and economic position.

To the question on which party represents the best interests of workers, the dominant tone of the responses of the UIL and the CISL was that no such party exists in Italy. Even respondents from the CISL, an organization often criticized for working on behalf of the governing party, were critical of the Christian Democrat party. One member of Parliament belonging to the Christian Democrat party does not believe that his party represents the interests of the working class.

A minority of the CISL and UIL respondents cited their own party as best representing the workers; those in the CISL, the Christian Democrat party generally, and those in the UIL, the Republican or Social Democrat party. The Communists and Socialists cited their own parties, respectively, with one exception, a Communist who believed all three parties of the left (including the Social Democrats) answer the question.

Representative responses from the CGIL include the following statements:

There is no such party. If Socialism became democratic and moderate, a new Socialist party combining all the left forces would be the best party of the working class.

None, not even the Christian Democrats. That party is supported by the masses and governed by the rich and the Church in their own interest.

It depends on specific individuals in the various parties. The Communists unfortunately have convinced the masses that they represent their interests.

None. The Christian Democrats are too heterogeneous a group.

None. If the Communists lost about two million votes it would then be possible to organize a labor party.

A CISL member of Parliament made a plea for the Christian Democrat party as being realistically the only organization that could be made a workers' party.

Our democracy is based strictly on a party system. The only way to obtain political support is to have deputies in a political party coming out of the trade unions. The primary responsibility of such a deputy is not to his constituents but to his party. The working class, therefore, can obtain political power only through strong conviction on the part of workers that the center parties serve only the interests of the bourgeoisie. The labor-oriented deputy in the center party has to fight this constantly in order to maintain his following. The success of the labor deputy lies in developing a following from the different trade unions. In this way he may succeed in becoming independent of both the local party organization and the Church. This is the only means to resolve the paradox of a tremendous number of voters of the working class having no voice in their government. . . . It may also dissipate the feeling that the workers have been denied power in their society for no justifiable reason.

The majority of the CISL and UIL respondents stated that they believe the Communist party has made a contribution to the cause of workers. Those answering in the affirmative gave the following reasons: (1) The Communists have reawakened the masses drugged by twenty years of fascism. (2) They organized workers even during the Fascist regime. (3) They have broken reaction in Italy. (4) The party has developed a will to indulge in struggle (*volontà di lotta*). Provincial officials of the CISL were more inclined to recognize the contribution of the Communists than were their colleagues on the national and federation level. Those in the South were more apt to concede a contribution than those in the North. Only one federation leader granted some contribution, and he felt that the Communists no longer have any realizable constructive objectives. One top federation leader in the UIL stated that the party has been instrumental in spurring needed reforms. Negative responses included the following statements: "They use the workers for their own political ends." "They have failed to obtain badly needed reforms in the practice of collective bargaining." "They have worsened the condition of workers and now want labor unity because they are losing their members."

During the early phase of the field investigation, the CGIL respondents were asked the same question. It was dropped when it became evident that the Communists were being piqued by the query. The reply below is typical:

We have been instrumental in reform here in Italy, as the other federations would concede. We aroused and wakened the masses, and gave them the courage to fight for their interests. If it were not for the Communist party, there would be collusion between employers and trade unions. You cannot infer the objectives of the party by seeing what they are elsewhere. We believe we can achieve reform under the Italian constitution. The party has abandoned the idea of the union as a chain of transmission. It is the only party in all of the capitalist countries that has done so. Our party is the most effective force for democracy in Italy.

On the question of who possesses more political power—the employers or the unions—the lower the level of leadership, the more frequently the respondents selected the employers. With no exception, the provincial officials expressed the judgment that it is the employers who have the greater political power. One of them asserted that the employers' industrial association controls both the Parliament and the government. Another stated that the power of the employers accrues not so much from what the Parliament does but from what the Parliament fails to do, and that the real power they exert is in the way the government is administered. This view is shared by a UIL leader who expressed the opinion that the employers' effective power comes from their intimate relationships with top-level government bureaucrats and the assurance which such a relationship brings that government will be administered in their interests, regardless of what the Parliament does. The CGIL responses include both similar comments on the influence which employers exercise on the executive branch of the government and opinions in the traditional Marxist vein that those who own the tools of production control the government. In this view, the will of the majority is a mirage. The effective behavior of government, in terms of what it does or fails to do in the society, is controlled by employers and their representatives.

Disaffection toward a labor movement subservient to political parties is apparent. The Communist leaders themselves concede mistakes in the use of the trade union in the pursuit of political objectives. A general disengagement, however, has its risks. The initial effect would be to shift the political balance of power toward the right, because of the preëminence of the political party in the Italian democratic process. Political action takes place through a coalescing of views of those in control of political parties, rather than of individuals acting with a certain amount of political freedom. A disassociation of trade union leaders might have the effect of shifting the party from which they withdraw away from trade union interests. Consequently, the problem of the labor leader is how to keep outside political influence from dominating his organization, without throwing away his influence on the government.

One possibility is to remove the deputies and senators from leadership positions in the trade union movement. By belonging to rival political parties, they create strong divisive forces among the federations. It is unlikely that a united labor movement could be achieved without such a step being taken first. The CISL politician–labor-leaders are in a particularly difficult position. They belong to a party in which the well-to-do and the Catholic hierarchy combine to create a strong conservative influence. In either alternative, were they to remove themselves from trade union organizations or from the Christian Democrat party, the outcome is uncertain. While the presence of these politicians places them in a position to obtain concessions from the rank and file, they are beholden to their party organizations. There are no primary elections in Italy, the candidates being chosen by the party organizations. If it is difficult in the United States for a political candidate to run against the organization candidate, in Italy it is virtually impossible to do so. Consequently, the price these labor politicians pay for their presence on party lists is strict party discipline, with the exception of those few who manage to acquire stature sufficient to exercise some measure of political independence. To expect a unification of the labor movement under such circumstances would be equivalent to anticipating a merger of two American labor federations, one controlled by the Republican party and the other by the Democrats.

The figure of the labor-leader–politician raises paradoxes in Italy. He believes it is his rival and not he himself that is controlled by the political party. DiVittorio, the deceased former secretary of the CGIL, as a Communist deputy was a political outcast, and as a trade union leader was respected by both the industrial relations public and employers. The employer respondents in the investigation ranked him as one of the best labor leaders in Italy. The reason for their choice is important. He understood the nature of collective bargaining, they stated, and he could be trusted to keep his word. To cite another example, the membership of the general secretary of the CISL in the Christian Democrat party presents a situation analogous to a hypothetical situation in which the leaders of the American labor movement in its period of protest were running for political office in the conservative Republican party.

ATTITUDES TOWARD THE ROLE OF THE CHURCH
IN THE LABOR PROBLEM

Italian trade union officials were asked whether the Church has a role to perform in the labor problem. Those who answered in the affirmative were asked what the role should be. Approximately half of the CISL respondents stated that they believe the Church has a proper function to perform. Except for two individuals who answered in the negative, the remainder gave a qualified answer in the affirmative. Without exception, the UIL group felt that the Church should stay out of the field of labor entirely. The CGIL also answered in the negative, but in a more diffident manner. Some stated that, like it or not, the Church is a powerful influence in labor matters. Some of the respondents raised the question of the labor priests in Italian plants, the split in attitudes toward them falling along similar lines. Noteworthy is the number of CISL members who expressed concern over the role of the Church in the labor movement. They are afraid lest the clergy or the ACLI usurp what they believe to be their proper function in labor leadership. They are sensitive to the criticism leveled at their organization that it is influenced by the clergy. One of them told the story that a priest who wandered into the Rome research office of the CISL was urged to remove his cassock before venturing forth again.

The sharpest differences between the CISL and the UIL found in the study center around the Roman Catholic Church. The members of both organizations have critical stereotypes of each other, of people who fawn on priests, on the one hand, and of professional priest-baiters, on the other. The stereotypes are much stronger than the reality from which they are drawn. The CISL officials are not influenced as much by the Church as the UIL leaders think they are, and none of the latter appears to have the impulse to throw stones at religious processions any more.

Summarized below are a number of statements which reveal qualitative differences among the groups.

From the CISL:

Priests unfortunately do not understand social problems. They have a restricted mentality. The tragedy in Italy is that a man who assumes leadership in social problems without the close guidance of a priest may be considered by the Church as having fallen into ideological error. This attitude weakens non-Communist leadership.

The role of the Church should be limited to religious assistance to workers —console the sick and the poor. It is not true the priests are working for us. The *Cappellani del Lavoro* [labor priests] have a legitimate role. It should be limited, however, to promoting spiritual welfare of plant workers, and not interfere with trade unionism.

Yes, it does have a role. The Church should affirm the justice due to workers, and its specific functions should include education and assistance.

Yes, to appeal to the conscience of the employers.

Yes, by asking the employers to implement Christian principles. It is not true we are influenced by the Church; it is all UIL propaganda.

The Church should have a function in industrial relations, but the *Cappellani* should stay out of trade union and labor-management affairs.

No. Priests intervene too much as it is.

ACLI has a proper function to teach Christian principles so long as they keep out of trade unionism.

The Catholics themselves are to blame for alienating the workers from the Church. Can you appreciate the tremendous step it takes for an Italian to give up the Church and become a Communist?

From the CGIL:

They [the clergy] have a role anyway. There is nothing to discuss.

Catholic unions as Catholic unions have a proper role in Italy. They have a right to express an ideology. What confuses me is the CISL. I do not know what their ideology is, nor do I think they themselves do.

No, not the clergy. But we recognize the right of Catholics to organize. Our position against the clergy is due to their tremendous political power. In Italy a bishop has more power than a provincial governor.

No, the Church is the biggest obstacle to progress in Italy. They do not prepare Italians to strike out and solve their own problems. The priests find tolerable the characteristics of Arabic fatalism and intellectual dependence which the masses show.

From the UIL:

They should take care of souls only [curare le anime]. We are suspicious of their political ambitions.

Priests have a stifling effect on the development of a labor movement. The Church cannot countenance a movement of workers with independent leaders. They prefer men subservient to their thinking. They do not tolerate compromise. You follow their point of view or you are not a good Catholic. They talk a lot about human dignity but do not tolerate it. How many intellectual giants are there in Italy who are also devout Catholics? We have many problems, but the Church stultifies thinking by its sweeping generalizations on every kind of human conduct. The Pope makes a pronouncement, and then instead of solving our problems we spend our time arguing how the generalization is to apply to particular cases.

The Church weakens its own influence by becoming involved in social and political problems. Workers tend to react to an action by the Church as to a political move. They become cynical. They are convinced the Church is playing politics. Listening to a political sermon is maddening because you cannot get up and talk back.

On the national level, the responses produced a similar range, from sympathy on the part of CISL members to neutrality and hostility from the CGIL and UIL groups. CISL leaders continued to express concern over the possible usurpation of their functions by the ACLI and the labor priests. Two of them expressed the view that priests do not have the competence to solve problems on the basis of the generalizations they have learned in the seminary.

One CGIL official stated his position in this fashion:

We Communists respect the ideological heterogeneity of the Italian peasants. They vote for the Communist party and go to church too. They formulate their demands under Communist and Socialist leadership, and then march down to the local priest or bishop and present them formally. Consequently, they recognize the clergy as part of the total aggregate of the community on whom responsibility falls for the redressing of grievances. Many of the priests are from *mezzadri* families, with brothers who are Communist leaders. It would be a tragedy if the Church were to force these people to make choices between Catholicism and Communism. It would tear families apart.

One UIL leader expressed the view that the Church is responsible for the split in the labor movement. The Church tends to force divisions along ideological lines, while trade union officials, if left alone, are constrained to take a practical look at worker problems. He mentioned the ACLI's interfering with the May Day celebrations of the trade unions on the excuse that Joseph, the father of Christ, was a carpenter.

Among federation leaders the pattern of responses is similar. A federation CISL leader gave an opinion that the Church has a role to perform simply because Catholicism is the state religion of Italy. One member of the CGIL stated that the Church has an important function in dispensing jobs in Italy. On the whole, the responses of the CGIL and UIL federation officials are less intense than those of leaders at the national and provincial levels. The federation leaders appear to show greater ability to control their emotions on a matter which stirs Italians deeply.

THE PROBLEM OF A UNITED LABOR MOVEMENT

In the course of the study, the question was raised of what the trade union officials thought of the possibility of a united labor movement in Italy, and how they believed such unity could be achieved. Those queried agreed unanimously that it would be a good idea if the federations were united. *"Auspicabile"* was the common response; it was something to be wished. Table 18 summarizes replies to the query whether unification could be achieved within five years. The Social-Communists were the most optimistic. With the exception of two officials in Sicily, none of the CISL respondents believed it possible with the CGIL. The UIL group is somewhat less pessimistic in this respect. Everyone agreed that the split is weakening his collective bargaining power. Neither the CISL nor the UIL expressed any readiness to make concessions for the sake of unity. The implication was that labor unity could be achieved at the expense of the CGIL, by attracting its members to their own organizations. CGIL respondents expressed the view that their organization is ready to negotiate and is willing to see a new organization created, rather than proceed on the basis of having one organization absorb another.

TABLE 18

Attitudes of Italian Labor Leaders toward Unity in the Labor Movement

	CGIL	CISL	UIL
Impossible with either of the other two federations	0	2	2
Impossible with CGIL	—	2	1
Difficult with UIL	1	1	—
Difficult with CISL	2	—	1
Possible with UIL	0	5	—
Possible with CISL	0	—	8
Possible with CGIL	—	0	2
Possible only by all joining CISL	0	2	0
Possible only by all joining UIL	0	0	2
Possible with both CISL and UIL	9	—	—
Total	12	12	16

A sudden collapse of the CGIL would have a serious effect on trade unionism and collective bargaining in Italy. It would remove a militant kind of unionism with a venerated tradition, increase the likelihood of employer domination of union representatives at the plant level and weaken the counter pressures against management. It would probably also cause a considerable number of workers to drop out of the organized labor movement. Such a view is privately expressed by labor leaders in both CISL and UIL.

Following are representative comments on the question of unity.

From the CISL (South):

It is possible with the UIL but not with the CGIL as long as the Communists are in control of that organization. CGIL must accept four basic principles: a free society, gradual reform, liberty, and the abandonment of the idea that the union is a transmission belt for the party. In the meantime, I am willing to try to do business with them.

From the CISL (North):

It is difficult even with the UIL. Many of their people remember the time they used to throw stones at religious processions.

The greatest difficulty is at the top. The top leaders talk too much about contrasting ideologies.

From the UIL:

It is impossible to collaborate to try to achieve unity. Each federation clearly knows that the intent of the others is to grow at its own expense. Because of our character of ideological purity, a merger will probably cause another split anyway.

It is difficult because the top three leaders of the three organizations are not free men. CISL is influenced by the way the Church may react to unity. CGIL is influenced by the Communist party, and UIL is controlled by the desire to become stronger before talking about merger. The workers want unity but the leaders do not.

The top leaders are too dominated by political parties to move in the direction of unity. The biggest stumbling block is the Communist party and the Catholic Church. The Church would prefer seeing the workers impotent to a rapprochement of the CISL and the CGIL.

From the CGIL:

We are willing to create a new organization but CISL and UIL want unity by destroying us. They cannot do that however; there are just too many Communist workers.

As the power of the employer increases, we will have to unify or see the destruction of the labor movement. Unity at the top is difficult because of the differences in political parties. You cannot have unity without Communist workers. In some towns of Italy, it would mean a labor movement with zero membership.

The responses on how the unification would come about distribute themselves in the following fashion. Similar responses within the three groups are incorporated.

From the CISL:

When CGIL abandons its totalitarian ideas and removes itself from the influence of the Communist party . . .

CISL and UIL will unite first; then the Socialists in the CGIL would come into the organization.

By isolating and weakening the CGIL and drawing workers away from them . . .

By replacement of the present leaders of the Communist party . . .

By the death or resignation of all the top leaders . . .

By CISL absorbing UIL and CGIL members . . .

By beginning joint action at the plant level . . .

From the CGIL:

When the workers themselves decide to have unity . . .

When the other federations stop trying to steal our members . . .

By starting a unified collective bargaining policy . . .

From the UIL:

When the workers decide to have unity . . .

By Socialists coming into UIL, and the UIL becoming the converging point of a new labor movement . . .

By the workers in the other federations joining up with UIL . . .

Representative comments expressing Italian labor leaders' perceptions of each other are given below.

From the CISL:

UIL thinks we all are priest-lovers.

The Church would prevent having relationships with CGIL.

When the CGIL gets into trouble in a strike they come running down to us pleading for help to bring it to a successful conclusion. They send us worker delegations, and if we turn them down, they call us traitors.

It will take them [CGIL] at least a generation to change.

We coöperate with both of them when it comes to an important collective bargaining issue.

The UIL people in town are maligning us because we have had successes in organization.

From the UIL:

We have sharp debates with the others but we coöperate whenever joint action is necessary.

I feel free belonging to UIL, but the people in the other federations do not. There is no burden of another organization on my back. I resent the way CISL gets American help. All things from Uncle Sam come to Italy courtesy of CISL or the Church, and sometimes the Christian Democrat party.

As a Sicilian, I approach their leaders as individuals, rather than as members of an organization.

CISL is paternalistic . . . influenced by the Church . . . confused . . . controlled by priests . . . dominated by the Christian Democrat party.

We are the only free trade union movement in Italy.

From the CGIL:

They are trying to steal our members.

We know both of them collect little or no dues from the membership. It puts us in a difficult position with our members. CISL is favored by the provincial governor, who uses his influence to promote their interests. They have the support of the government and we have not. We have made mistakes by agitating too much and taking inflexible positions in bargaining. But we are now changing our policies in a way that makes it very difficult for CISL and UIL to reject unification.

We have made mistakes by calling too many strikes, but the others play politics too. By raiding us they are destroying the labor movement.

We are willing to change our structure, but you cannot change Communists if they want to remain Communists.

CISL has a confused ideology which weakens trade unionism. I prefer ACLI; at least I know what they are for. CISL believes you can practice trade unionism by borrowing a technique from another country.

Both federations have picked up strength at our expense by conniving with employers to use discharge and merit wage increases as weapons. But they are playing with fire; it will ruin the labor movement.

The statements above do not exaggerate the extent of the rivalry among the leaders of the three organizations. It is sharpest on the provincial level, where labor leaders indulge in vituperation of each other in newspapers and *manifesti.* They have called each other liars, thieves, and enemies of the working class. The violence of the exchange varies from one province to the next. The larger provincial organizations publish weeklies and biweeklies in which their officials exchange *polemiche.* In addition to the provincial newspapers, there are those published by particular trade unions or different factions in the shop committees. In the plants where these committees exist, bulletin boards are posted with the unflattering estimates which each federation makes of the other two.

The stated policy of the CISL is that any form of alliance with organizations directed and controlled by Communists is prejudicial to the interests of the workers. It accuses the CGIL of tending to make a political issue of every trade union action. In an article appearing in the federation newspaper, *Conquiste del Lavoro,* it cites comments from the Communist newspaper *Unità* in support of its analysis. On the proposed legislation governing labor-management relationships in agriculture, the so-called *patti agrari,* the paper is quoted as saying: " 'The aspirations of millions of peasants are against the reactionary line of *Fanfani* '" [the Christian Democrat Prime Minister]. Other quotations include: " 'From Genoa to Naples, energetic worker reaction against the blow of *Fanfani* against state-controlled industry . . .' "

" 'Strike for IRI [state-controlled industry] in Genoa and against the policy of government and the employers. . . .'" " 'It is up to the party to elaborate and realize agricultural policy, and orient militant comrades in the trade union organizations. . . .'" The article concludes by stating that talking about unity with the CGIL will be possible when that organization can show the same independence of the Communist party that the CISL has shown in regard to the government and the democratic political parties. In another article printed in a subsequent issue, the view is presented that the split in the Italian labor movement is not something imposed by the leadership as much as it is a natural development to provide an alternative to a trade union organization whose methods and principles are repugnant to workers.

In view of the voluntary character of trade union membership in Italy, trade union officials were asked for their views on compulsory union membership. The CGIL respondents were unanimously against it, stating that it would be a violation of liberty. Approximately half of the CISL officials gave either a qualified or direct affirmative. The latter is an expression of criticism of workers who enjoy the benefits of trade unionism without paying dues. A majority of the UIL group feel some form of compulsion is in order. They stated: "We cannot strike because the non-union members take over the jobs. . . ." "It will increase our political and economic power. . . ." "The workers at least should be required to pay their dues. . . ."

The responses should be viewed against the backdrop of compulsory membership in the so-called unions which existed during the days of fascism. The differences in the replies are also in part a reflection of differences in organizational stability and financial position among the three organizations. The general feeling, however, that pervades all three groups is that a trade union should be a voluntary association; the leaders feel that having in their organizations a worker who was compelled to join is a distasteful idea. It is the job of the trade union official to sell trade unionism to the worker and to persuade him to join the labor movement voluntarily. If workers were compelled to join, the trade unions would inevitably become state organizations.

RECEPTION OF THE AMERICAN LABOR MOVEMENT

In the course of the investigation, Italian labor leaders were asked about their attitudes toward the American labor movement. Favorable comments are listed, with all three federations combined, in Table 19.

Among the favorable comments, the dominant theme was organizational efficiency. The financial resources available make possible the development of a technical approach to problem-solving. Next in order of frequency is admiration for collective bargaining power and the influence that trade unions exert in the United States. In this respect,

TABLE 19

Favorable Comments on the American Labor Movement by Italian Labor Leaders

Related to:	Number	
Organizational characteristics	22	
Obligatory checkoff of union dues		6
Research and information facilities		4
Union-shop clauses		3
United labor movement		2
Courage in combating corruption in unions		2
Huge financial resources		1
Financial support of strikers by non-strikers		1
Autonomous industrial unionism		1
Disbursement of strike benefits		1
Trade-union–consciousness of workers		1
Trade union philosophy	13	
Technical approach to collective bargaining		8
Freedom from domination of political parties		4
Acceptance of increased productivity		1
National influence	5	
Influence in society		2
Influence in production process		2
Influence in economic activity		1
Collective bargaining	9	
Collective bargaining power		3
Use of arbitration in contract interpretation		2
Collective bargaining at plant level		1
Respect for collective bargaining agreements		1
Precise collective bargaining agreements		1
Ability of union to obtain company data		1
Total	49	

there are no noteworthy differences among the three federations. All three are impressed with the power of American trade unionism, although they differ in their preferences as to the objectives toward which this influence should be used. The obligatory checkoff is admired actually for the money it provides to build an effective organization. Italians are not inclined, however, to take the other side of the coin, compulsory union membership.

Respondents from the CGIL are somewhat less sanguine about the favorable aspects of the American labor movement. Favorable comment is concentrated on the financial resources available for strike action and the ability of American workers to shut a plant down completely during the course of a strike. In addition, in answering the item, the CGIL respondents tend to conjure up in their minds characteristics of American workers rather than leadership and organization.

TABLE 20

Criticism of the American Labor Movement by Italian Labor Leaders

Related to:		Number
Labor-leader power	16	
Concentration of power		7
Corruption		4
Ability of leaders to violate will of rank and file		2
Power of labor leaders over workers		1
Use of bureaucracy to maintain power		1
Brutality in organizing workers		1
Philosophy	18	
Business unionism		4
Lack of idealistic orientation		4
Bargaining policy which excludes unorganized		4
Company rather than industry orientation		1
Confusion of socialism with communism		1
Political inactivity of workers		1
Belief in collaboration with employers		1
Bargaining policy which creates worker elites		1
Overemphasis on technical aspects		1
Organization characteristics	6	
Huge bureaucratic apparatus		2
Lack of worker participation in trade union		1
Separation of leaders from rank and file		1
Political factions in unions		1
Failure to organize those who need it most		1
Other	5	
Lack of knowledge of Italian trade unionism		2
No understanding of European problems		1
Failure to champion aspirations of working class abroad		1
Discriminatory intervention in affairs of foreign unions		1
Total		45

Major forms of criticism center around the following points: (1) excessive power of trade union officials; (2) the lack of an idealistic orientation for the labor movement; (3) corruption among trade union officials; (4) the tendency to behave like a business rather than a labor movement. The dominant tone of the criticism is an indirect expression of the conviction of the respondents that the trade union should be an idealistically motivated organization, with a close camaraderie between leadership and rank and file. Responses are summarized in Table 20.

The extended comments of two prominent CGIL members are noteworthy.

I hesitate to answer the question. The reports we have on American trade unionism are contradictory. I prefer not to believe that corruption and gangsterism are a general phenomenon, even if the problem is apparently serious enough for Congress to intervene. There is something profoundly incomprehensible to us in the political and social system of the United States because of what the workers find tolerable in it. It must be that the high standard of living is preventing a violent rupture of the system. In our country, considering the employers we have, such tolerance would not last too long. Are the American workers really convinced that they should refrain from political activity? Maybe they are, because of their high living standards.

American workers lack an awareness of the grave international issues of our time, such as the H-bomb, international tensions, international trade; they are indifferent to the fight of workers against colonialism. Their concept of collaboration between labor and management excludes a correct opinion, on their part, on the permanent contrast of interests that exists between the working class and the capitalist.

Excessive discretionary power of the American labor leader was criticized in terms like the following: "A state of dictatorship exists in some of the trade unions. . . ." "The labor leaders use brutality in controlling the rank and file. . . ." "They use the bureaucratic machine of the trade union to entrench themselves in power. . . ." "They use the organization for their own interests. . . ." Sixteen responses in Table 20 consist of variations of the same idea.

A second type of criticism is that directed by members of the CGIL and the UIL organizations at collective bargaining on the company level. The officials of the UIL felt that company-wide bargaining exists at the expense of the unorganized in the rest of the industry. A CGIL official expressed his criticism in the following manner: "Company trade unionism breaks the unity of workers in the same *categoria* and isolates the weaknesses of workers, not permitting those with greater economic power to exercise pressure in behalf of the weak." The criticism of *affarismo* relates to the image of the American labor leader operating a profit-seeking business rather than a trade union. The term is difficult to translate. A colloquial expression such as "the fellow in pursuit of a fast buck" would be an appropriate rendition of the term. Another frequent complaint was that the American labor movement lacks an idealistic orientation. "I wish the American trade unions were less technical and more romantic. . . ." "The lack of ideals in the American labor movement makes it difficult to keep the workers organized. . . ." These expressions, like the favorable comments above, are indications of the Italian labor leaders' own problems, aspirations, and values.

A simple definitive answer on why corruption exists in some labor movements and not others is difficult. The difference may be one of definition or extent of public exposure, but that is doubtful in the case of Italy. The drama, the players, and the environment are different from the United States. The minor transgressions in Italy arise from the dread of unemployment, the deep desire of the Italian worker to be treated with respect, and the master-servant character of the employer-employee relationship. In return for a secure job, a trade union leader at the local level may become less militant and more docile to the expressed or implied company point of view. The collective bargaining function is even more removed from the Italian rank and file, and the grievance procedure in its initial stages is in the hands of employee representatives rather than the trade union as such. However, the Italians are stirred by a sense of struggle which welds together the leaders and the members. For the American rank and file, Mr. Meany is often a rather remote person, hardly more than a name. It would be interesting to see what percentage of the American trade union membership could name the president of the federation by his full name. In Italy, a Catholic Pastore or a Communist DiVittorio is a kind of savior, a symbol of deep aspirations and hope for the future. Each one in his own way is the image of utopian trade unionism. Watching an Italian audience of workers listening to them, one sees an expression of intense satisfaction on their faces. These leaders arouse deep excitement. They are heroes dedicated to the conquest of the enemy in behalf of the workers. The workers' choice between a Pastore or a DiVittorio is one of selecting the kind of leadership that best fits their perceptions and sentiments.

Moreover, the trade unions of the Italians are voluntary associations in fact as well as in name. In the United States, the automatic mandatory enrollment of workers in trade unions through union shop clauses has hidden below the surface the problem of communication between leader and rank and file. If the production worker were left with the choice of joining or not joining a union, he would probably decide not to join. He may not feel that the union is a vital link in the fulfillment of his needs. Fifteen years of job security make him inclined to think his aspirations can be fulfilled without a union. He expresses this sentiment through such responses as "I get nothing from my union dues"; "The union elections are rigged so I do not bother."

The Italian rank and file elects to join voluntarily. Their leaders are selected indirectly by a board of elders to whom the elected officials must make an accounting. They do not have the free rein some American labor leaders have. The unions in Italian towns, more than those in the depersonalized metropolis of the United States, are a social and political way of life. Workers are intimately associated with each other, with strong community loyalties; and their leaders cannot detach themselves from the people of their town, nor do they desire to do so.

There is another reason for the difference. Competition for material goods is a strong motive in the United States. An employer who achieves success in business at the possible expense of the weak may be considered a hero. American trade union officials are also offspring of their culture. A few have found themselves in a good position to reap fortunes and have yielded to the urge for material acquisition. When their acts accumulate with impunity, the habit becomes routine. Some of them, when matters were going in their favor, glowed from the blandishments and praise of politicians and college professors singing their praises in after-dinner speeches. Without the moral compulsion of social restraint, they found it easy to yield in successive stages to values in which actions are good so long as they lead to more money and more popularity.

THE PRESENT CRISIS IN THE ITALIAN LABOR MOVEMENT

To what extent is the present crisis in Italian trade unionism a crisis of leadership? There has been a decline of trade union influence, which can probably be halted only by efforts on the part of Socialists and Catholics toward a united labor movement. Worker participation in organization activity has been falling off from the peak caused by the surge of aspirations attending the fall of facism. In prominent firms, company-dominated employee organizations are blossoming out. It remains to be seen whether organized labor will meet this challenge successfully.

By standards suggested by the leadership itself, the Italian labor movement has not had notable successes. Membership in trade unions barely keeps up with the increase in the labor force. Its influence in collective bargaining is small. The trade unions can boast of having obtained a cost-of-living criterion for wage determination, which has probably served to depress wages rather than raise them.

What is the reason for such failure? The explanation lies partly in the greater economic and political power of employers, who have values different from those of the working class. The inability to redress this imbalance of power is a fault of the top leaders themselves, whose contrasting political identities are more important to them than the resolution of their differences. Nor do politicians running the legislature transform themselves into trade union technicians when they live by the sufferance of rival political parties.

The dominance of the federation in Italian trade union structure tends to emphasize ideological differences at the expense of the increase of bargaining power with particular employers. The regional representatives of the federations are more politically conscious than the leaders of the national unions. Since the provincial organization is the core of Italian trade unionism, political power-play is enhanced. Each federation leader states that trade union unity is difficult because of the conduct and the ideological position of the other federation leaders. These positions are sometimes set aside when a serious dispute takes place with an employer. The workers themselves tend to force the fusion of union energy. The data suggest that the more educated and urbanized they become, the more conscious they are of the use of organization as a device against a particular employer, rather than employers as a group versus the labor movement, each with an inflexible ideological outlook. They become more aware of the possibility of developing benefits on the plant level. Accordingly, it is likely that the dominance of the federations may be progressively weakened as the condition of labor rises, and the primary energies of leadership are directed more toward the improvement of the condition of specific labor groups rather than dissipated in organizational rivalry based on ideological differences.

In Italy, much of the labor leadership rising out of the working classes is channeled into left-wing political parties, the clergy, or labor organizations isolated from effective power. Many who start in the labor movement use it as a stepping stone to a political career. Although the Communist-dominated CGIL has considerable leadership potential, dynamic labor representatives with the revolutionary zeal warranted by the condition of labor in Italy, officials who maintain close relationships with the rank and file, its ideology has the effect of reducing the returns it is capable of providing its membership.

Another factor weakening labor leadership in Italy is the psychological-economic state of the working class. Italian workers display more often a sense of fatality, turning their backs to inequities in their society, than a driving ambition to pursue constructive measures for reform. Such conditions do not foster the organizational drive essential to recruit a force of workers who have the competency and willingness to participate successfully in joint efforts to reach goals in the face of difficult obstacles.

Effective labor leadership is further inhibited by the stalemate which exists in power positions in the political and economic spheres. In the face of a left-wing working class, which actually represents the majority of the electorate, the government has shown the tendency to move to the right and become a rallying force for conservatism. A move by the government toward the left would be in the interest of the Italian working classes. The presence of these contrasting forces provides latent opportunities for a political explosion whose aftermath may be the failure of Italian democracy. This stalemate is a consequence of the convergence of various forces, including the survival of Fascist power, the intransigence of the extreme left, the conservatism of the Italian Catholic Church, the split in the labor movement, and the attitudes of the Italian employer.

A break in this stalemate would probably have to wait for the slow impact of a massive program of social and economic change. The sort of reform which is needed would involve such factors as agreement upon a wider common area of political and economic objectives among organized labor and development of an educational system which would educate and train young Italians until the age of sixteen and provide them jobs thereafter to avoid deterioration in their skills. The long-term consequences of such education and training would probably be an increase in a pragmatic approach to problem-solving, instead of one stemming from fixed ideological premises. There is need for a political party which could legitimately compete for power with the Christian Democrat party without creating a political crisis of insurrectionist proportions. The only realistic possibility is a right-wing socialist party, provided the Church ceases to lump together Socialists and Communists in the same category. A massive system of public investment is also necessary to provide full employment and increase the power of trade union officials. Another essential is the sort of economic atmosphere that would encourage increased production and productivity and discourage adherence to a policy of short-run maximization of opportunities on the part of both employers and workers. An inhibiting factor at present is the existence in the labor movement of a horizontal structure led by men whose technical qualifications are essentially those of political strategists, functioning in the initial organization of masses of workers. The continuance of such a structure mitigates the development of a trade unionism which fulfills on a recurrent basis the needs of particular workers in particular plants. In this respect, the Italians can draw a lesson from the initial successes of the Knights of Labor and the IWW in organizing protest, and their subsequent failures and collapse.

The need for a large minority political party capable of offering real opposition to Christian Democrats is urgent. The existing stalemate stultifies a prime requisite of dynamic democratic government, the ability to remove from office those in power. However, the Italians are warned constantly by the Church that they either accept the Christian Democrats or face dire political consequences. The effective consolidation of a large minority party may take many decades. The Socialists want to eat their cake and have it too. They make a strong class-conscious appeal and at the same time expect people of diverse economic and social groups to recognize a common political bond. They need to shift from insistence upon organizational purism to acceptance of groups who hold different points of view.

Whether a labor party similar to that of the Danes can emerge in Italy is problematical. The Socialist forces would have to attract some of the Communists on their left, Social Democrats, and left-wing Catholic reformists in order to become a party that could realistically aspire for power. Such an amalgamation is unlikely in the near future. A realignment of this nature might push right-wing forces in Italy toward the Christian Democrats, a result which could give that party an absolute majority for the first time since taking power.

More likely than a Socialist consolidation is a partial merger of the labor movement. A common area of agreement may be found on the federation level on such matters as social insurance, employment, training, and the Common Market. There is little basis in reality for the stereotyped attitudes which the CISL and the UIL have of each other. The extreme CISL view of the UIL leaders as godless Marxists is as exaggerated as the UIL vision of the CISL members as men holding meekly to the *sottana* of the clergy. There are anticlericals in the CISL and practicing Catholics in the UIL. Applying the prerequisites for the merger of the American labor movement to Italy, one sees that the elimination of the top contending personalities has been partly achieved. The death of the leader of the CGIL at the time of the split and the acceptance of a cabinet post by his CISL counterpart have removed two of the three top leaders. Second, the federation which split from the parent organization would have to be declining in strength. Here the picture becomes reversed. Both the CISL and the UIL are claiming dramatic growth. Third, an outside threat must be sufficiently strong to override personal ambition and to force consideration of a merger. This prerequisite exists in Italy. The federations are faced with disillusionment on the part of members and an inability to widen the scope of collective bargaining into areas which would give substance to trade unionism. A two-way merger is much more likely than a fusion of three. The probability of a working agreement with the CGIL would increase if that organization managed to elect a Socialist instead of a Communist as its general secretary. Under the pressure of the successes of rival organizations, the CGIL top leadership announced in 1960, at its fifth national congress, a movement away from trade unionism as an instrument of subverting Italian society and a change to the practice of using collective bargaining as a means of achieving small but tangible successes in raising the conditions and terms of employment. Whether the leadership at the bottom of the organization will modify its behavior to be consistent with this announced view remains to be seen. Too close a rapprochement between the CISL and the CGIL, however, might be instrumental in the organizing of still another labor movement.

The American policy of avoiding relationships with the labor leaders of the Communist-dominated CGIL may need reëvaluation. It cannot be demonstrated that such a policy of withdrawal from different ideologies has the effect of weakening them. Many individuals in that organi-

zation are willing to be exposed to different points of view. The Socialists have shown an increased tendency for flexibility and a readiness to
compromise with forces on their right. A hands-off policy has the effect
of perpetuating a weak Italian labor movement and isolating a considerable segment of Italian labor from Western points of view on
labor movement objectives.

The Italian labor movement is displaying a growing independence
from political parties and the Church. A principal factor in this development is the desire of labor leaders to build power organizations of their
own and decrease outside pressures on their organizations. This development constitutes a gauge of the growth of an independent Italian
labor movement. It would facilitate the unity of the labor movement,
were it not for the special problem such a divorcement raises for the
Communists on one side and the CISL on the other. Italian trade
unionism, moreover, is acquiring a technical orientation. Trade union
officials are beginning to speak of productivity, rising real income, incentive systems, and job evaluation, seekings ways and means to
strengthen the *raison d'être* of their organizations.

The promise of a new trade unionism and improved industrial relations in Italy lies in its young leaders. Not old enough to have been
influenced by fascism—except for having suffered for its mistakes—
they are assuming posts in trade unions, communications, and business
organizations. They tend to approach problems from an empirical point
of view. They not only talk about democracy, they practice it. This
group may be the wedge which will successfully insert itself between
the inflexible positions of their elders and provide trade unionism and
industrial relations with a different outlook.

Labor Leadership in Denmark

Differences in the organization of trade unions in Denmark from that of unions in Italy raise a problem of comparability. Generally, Danish trade unions are smaller and are constructed on a vertical, rather than horizontal, basis. This dissimilarity creates a problem of comparison which was resolved by the approach of interviewing most of the leaders of the national unions and a "sample" of local unions in Copenhagen and in the provinces. With a sample constructed in this way, the stature of the Danish respondents is roughly comparable to that of those in the Italian group. In addition, a maximum range of exploration is provided, to determine on what basis the greatest differentiation could be found among the Danish labor leadership, whether by size of union, type of industry, or level of trade union organization.

In Denmark the strategy for winning acceptance of the investigation had to be more elaborate than in Italy. Their cultural climate makes the Danes suspicious of attitude surveys and skeptical of their practical value. In some quarters of the Danish labor movement, the study was referred to as "sociological," a term akin to blasphemy. (Just prior to the investigation, an American professor of sociology had created a stir in the press by conducting a survey of sex attitudes among college students.) In such an atmosphere, it was considered important to fix a plan of procedure that would not foreclose the availability of respondents from within the ranks of the labor leaders. In Italy, the study was begun without soliciting the official sanction of the heads of the federations. In Denmark, because of the advice that the trade union movement was closely knit and centralized, it was decided to seek the approval of the federation and the employers' association.

It was suggested that a groundswell of approval be developed around them in a manner that would preclude the possibility of an adverse decision. The project was explained to staff people in the federation and the trade union research organization, Arbeiderbevaegelsens Erhvervsraad. It was felt that if the "intellectuals" of the labor movement were first persuaded of the value of the program, the persuasion in due time would carry on up to the line officials. If approval of trusted lieutenants were first obtained, a favorable response would be forthcoming.

The initial outcome of this approach, however, was the creation of an impediment to the investigation by the intellectuals. Comments coming back to the headquarters of the study were that the questions made little sense, were often repeated, would not be answered truthfully. Labor leaders would not want to be psychoanalyzed, it was said, and the responses would damage the position of trade union officers vis-à-vis the employers with whom they dealt. One comment filtering down to headquarters was of particular interest. The statement was made that a Marxist interpretation of a labor movement made a "personality analysis" of the type contemplated by the study a useless enterprise. Labor movements were determined by external forces, and the personalities caught in their grip were molded by them. The failure to understand or accept the scope of the project on the part of the staff people, or their insecure positions in their organization, consequently, threatened to impede the success of the study.

The aftermath of this thinking was that, while the federation would not give the project its official sanction, it would not place any obstacles in its way. If trade union officials who were approached as interviewees communicated with the federation, they would be advised of this position. The employer association then took the position that, because of the attitude of the federation, no official coöperation could be given the project.

Without exception, the national union leaders who were approached were cordial. They were told that the interviewer was interested in knowing what their problems and duties were. Those interviewed included, paradoxically, the members of the executive council of the federation who had refused to take official cognizance of the study. In some instances the interviewers were invited to lunch and dinner, which provided a further opportunity for frank discussion. As in Italy, some of the respondents found the interview fascinating. The questions intrigued them, and only in rare instances did they decline to answer them. There was little evidence of the mental reservations with which the members of the staff had been concerned. Toward the end of the field investigation, there was an opportunity to talk with the president of the federation. Although he had stated in his initial remarks that he was "amazed by the project," he announced at the end of the interview that the federation was at our disposal. Consequently, the method of building the labor leader sample which evolved in Denmark was the same as the one used in Italy. An introduction to one trade union official became the basis of interviewing others. The importance of the thinking of staff members in these matters was overestimated.

If the prototype of the Italian labor leader is a revolutionary, that of the Dane is a quasi-government official. Danish trade union officials are unglamorous administrators working unobtrusively in a pragmatic fashion. The transition from manual labor to positions of power is made without ostentation. The tone of their relationships with employers is polite, and occasionally in the familiar "thou" form. The rough accents of class warfare of a generation ago are gone. In a way, the change is symbolized in the renaming of the federation newspaper from *Workers* to *Wages and Work*. And the next step, in a story making the rounds in industrial relations circles, is that the journal of the employers' association, *Employer*, will be changed some day to *Work and Wages*.

The point where trade union function terminates and government begins in Denmark is not clearly defined. Young men beginning as shop stewards may eventually rise to become members of Parliament or trade union officials discharging functions jointly with members of government. They experience a considerable stability in tenure of office. One president of a large Copenhagen local stated that only once in twenty years had anyone run against him, and his rival received no votes. He cited his case as not unique, saying that the machinations to obtain power typical of other labor movements, with their manifestations in leadership instability and irresponsibility, are uncommon in Danish trade unionism.

The competition for positions of leadership, then, is not intensive. When found, it exists mostly at the local level. National leaders are replaced either because of death or voluntary resignation. At the local level, competition is drawn along political lines. A trade union local commonly divides into three factions: Social Democrats active in the party, Communists, and a third group of neutrals, so called, who view the political rivalry of the other two groups with some disfavor. The active Social Democrats generally provide the leadership for the organizations. The sense of solidarity in the Danish trade unions precludes the possibility of machinations by a minority sufficiently strong to unseat the conservative leadership. If a labor leader is performing his work conscientiously, sentiment is likely to be strong that he should be kept in office.

BACKGROUND AND INDUCTION

A striking characteristic of Danish national leaders, in contrast to the Italians, is the greater homogeneity of background and way of entrance into the labor movement. Without exception, the respondents arose out of working-class jobs, terminated seven years of public schooling at the age of fourteen, and started their trade union careers in the shop. The median age for the group is fifty-five, and the range from forty-five to seventy-two. The dominant pattern of movement in the trade union hierarchy is shop steward, local executive board member, local president, member of the executive council of the national union, and national union president. Many of the leaders began their organization activity as members of the Socialist youth organization. They differ according to whether or not they enter an apprenticeship program after leaving school. This event in their lives determines whether they become craft union leaders or officials in the General Workers' Union, and produces a marked influence on their future outlook. The national leaders, accordingly, have their start either as craftsmen apprentices or general laborers, and it is not extraordinary for them to have their first responsible trade union position at the age of nineteen.

MOTIVES FOR ENTERING THE LABOR MOVEMENT

What motivates these officials to seek trade union office? To be sure, they derive a sense of power from their work. They are spurred also by a sense of idealism and a desire to shape a better life for the people in their organization, and in doing so to derive status and prestige within their own social milieu. The salaries of the national leaders do not amount to twice the wages of the average skilled worker, and those of the local leaders may be only a little more. They are not paid on the basis of equitable comparisons with the salaries of management, and many of them have the competence to treble their income, if they so desire. Of course, their motivations are not alike, even for Danes. The differences among them spring partly from the character- istics of the occupational group from which they arise and partly from the uniqueness of individual personalities. One would expect excep- tional men to lead the Metal Workers' and the General Workers' Unions. Tradition and the characteristics of the men these unions organize stimulate the rise of outstanding leadership. Exceptional leaders, however, such as the incumbents of these two unions, do not necessarily come with regularity. It is rare for two outstanding labor leaders to follow each other in succession.

TABLE 21

Motivation of Danish National Trade Union Leaders for Entering the Labor Movement

Orientation	Per cent	
Group	75	
Trade-union–consciousness in home environment		29
Support of older labor leaders		25
Interest in improving general condition of workers		21
Personal	25	
Experience of personal injustices		17
Sense of mission		8
Total	100	
Number	24	

To the queries on motivation, the majority of the responses showed a group orientation, while a minority reflected the evangelical spirit which pervaded the Danish labor movement in its early stages (Table 21). The respondents were either first-generation labor leaders or the architects of Danish trade union organization. A noteworthy number of the responses on the reason for entering the labor movement empha- sized the influence of the home environment (Table 21). A father or relative active in Socialist politics or trade unionism had stimulated the interest of many respondents in doing organization work or joining the Socialist youth organization. Initial enthusiasm was nurtured further by an older trade union official who "paced them ahead." There was a strong tendency in the replies, as in those for other queries, for the respondents to relate their choices to the desires of the people around them. They stressed repeatedly that they had simply elected to behave in the manner expected of them by the people of their community. They did not run for office, but rather accepted it at the urging of their comrades. The typical statement was, "You show an interest, and your colleagues ask you to accept an office."

Questions posed at the beginning of the interview related to what the respondents thought was the purpose of their organization and what they considered their responsibilities as labor leaders. Some differentiation is obtained in the replies to the latter, and very little in those to the former. The question of the purpose of the trade union evoked almost universally a reference to the union constitution, while responses to the query on responsibility centered mainly on organizing workers in a particular craft or industry and raising their standards. The initial comments, consequently, had a greater official orientation than did those of the Italians.

CONCEPT OF ROLE

An important theme running through the responses of the labor leaders on role concept was the crystallizing of objectives and the guiding of members toward them (Table 22). As one respondent stated:

The labor leader stands as a midpoint between objectives and methods as he sees them and the sentiments of the members. He must assume that the members do not have at their disposal the means to look ahead. The average member does not know the possibilities. It is not enough to sit and wait for the members to propose something. The difference when you have intelligent members is that communication is made easier, and hence the job of striking the midpoint is made easier.

TABLE 22

Danish National Trade Union Leaders' Concept of Their Role

Emphasis on:	Per cent
Mediation function	29
Limited economic objectives	32
Organization	32
Socially oriented objectives	7
Total	100
Number	28

The concept of the labor leader as a mediator standing between the employer and the rank and file is a noteworthy point of difference from the responses of the Italians. In the words of the respondents:

The labor leader at times has to act contrary to the desires of his members. He has to get the members to understand that it has to be so and so. To do this, he examines the conditions in the industry and makes the best of possibilities. The goal is the best possible understanding between employers and the workers. The time has passed when the labor leader had only to thump the table; he must know about problems before he can perform his task in orderly fashion for his members and society.

It is not enough to sit and wait until the members propose something; you ask for their sentiments and you have to tell them your opinion. You guide them by advising on risks and possibilities. You develop the broad lines of action that are to be taken, and you reconcile the point of view of the workers with that of the employer.

The responses of the officials reflect security in their positions of leadership and an orientation in outlook beyond that of the trade union each leads. "I do not have to be concerned with a minority group undermining my position. . . ." "We have to look beyond the immediate interests of the trade union. . . ." The two points of view perhaps are related. A membership reluctant to follow a minority trying to undermine the leadership is not likely to foster among its leaders an outlook that is an expression of political insecurity and instability.

The following typical responses culled from the written questionnaire reflect role obligations trade union officials are constrained to assume:

I have to set an example in both public and private conduct and behavior.

Be at the disposition of the members whenever they need me . . .

Be well oriented about everything that may have significance to the labor movement . . .

Lead a respectable life consistent with the principles I fight for in my work . . .

Discharge my responsibilities to the federation and to the other national unions . . .

On the question of what the workers expected of them, they stated:

Fight for their cause [*kamper for mein medlemmers sag*] . . .

Know how to interpret their thoughts and demands . . .

Use my influence in their behalf in the circles in which I move . . .

Show the ability to see beyond the tip of my nose . . .

Be equal to the employer in negotiation ability . . .

Be independent in my positions . . .

Be able to see all the possibilities in a situation . . .

Get them the highest real wages possible . . .

Be friendly with them and show the desire for teamwork.

THE PRESSURES DANISH LABOR LEADERS FEEL

The following quotations taken from the interview transcripts reflect the pressures behind the behavior of the Danish leadership.

I try to discuss matters with the leaders of the minority before a formal meeting. In that way, they remain silent and no conflict occurs.

You have to become reconciled to the idea that you inevitably will have a falling-out with some of the members of the union.

Electricians are individualists, and that makes my position difficult during the course of negotiations.

Danish workers abide by the collective bargaining agreement religiously and that makes contract enforcement easier and relieves the pressure on the labor leader from the employer.

I cannot avoid being influenced by the atmosphere that exists among the members. It is my job as a labor leader to know how to work against the current of sentiment. It is of greatest importance. This must be done by displaying technical knowledge, rather than through drama and oratory, on which we Danes place little value.

While my role is to tell the members what is possible, there is always the possibility, too, of losing an election.

My membership is reasonable and understanding and that is the only thing a leader can ask.

The labor leader must see to it that the agreement is kept by both the employer and the workers.

You cannot be on good terms with everybody among the members. We are not paid like kings. Our salary is little better than that of a craftsman.

The workers want employment security and rising wages, in that order, and you have to do something about it.

You cannot avoid at times acting contrary to the desires of the members.

Workers should educate themselves more to think about problems which are affecting the organization.

You have to take care of the members, consistent with the needs of society.

I do not consider my job as work but as striving toward a goal.

The labor leader has to act in such a way as to create respect for his organization on the part of both the members and those outside the organization.

Danish workers are purposeful organization people. In negotiations with the employer, you can always stress that the agreement will increase orderliness and good labor relations.

You must keep your word with the employer.

My responsibility is to see that the workers produce good handicraft work. But that is not a difficult task. The workers are proud of being skilled workers. They are changing in some ways. The drinking used to be bad, but now they take milk for lunch. They want their children to be nicely dressed, and to rise up the occupational ladder.

You should not have ambition as a labor leader, and you should keep your word. You do not run for office; the workers ask you to stand for office, and you do not ask why you were elected.

PROBLEMS, RESPONSIBILITIES, AND OBJECTIVES

The reactions of Danish labor leaders to queries on their problems and objectives indicate the conservative forces pervading their organizations. Many of the respondents were at a loss to state what their problems were, and reacted with a puzzled look when they were asked. They have succeeded in controlling entrance to the employment covered by their trade unions. In the electrical industry, for example, the ratio of apprentices is kept to approximately one for five craftsmen, and the rolls of apprentices include ten-year-old boys who must wait four years before acceptance. The children of the trade union members have first right to the apprenticeships that are available. The union officials control the apprentices and the craftsmen of their trade unions. Consequently, complete organization and the control over the question of who should get the available jobs made an expression of problems difficult. The leaders spoke frequently of the problem of unemployment, but in a vague fashion. They also mentioned the necessity of extending piece-rate systems to more workers. The issue of craft unionism versus industrial unionism had to be prompted by the investigator, in the majority of instances. In a parody of a famous remark on the American labor movement, one trade union official stated that it would take a hundred funerals of Danish union presidents and vice-presidents before industrial unionism would come to Denmark. Danish labor leaders do not appear to be faced with any serious problem of communication with the rank and file. "We are not afraid of our members. We do not have to worry what they think of us. We live in small communities where all of us are in regular communication with each other. The single member knows constantly what is going on in the trade union. Everything is an open record. We know each other well."

If historical, official trade union records are valid statements of intent, a shift has apparently occurred in traditional objectives. Danish labor leaders, with the acquisition of economic and political power, no longer express themselves on the nationalization of industry and the redistribution of income. Part of this disinclination, to be sure, arises from a desire to appear as a united bloc in the eyes of the public and to defer to the leadership prerogatives of other officials in the labor movement. A small minority, most of them Communists, still expound upon the blessings of nationalization. The impression one gains, however, is that socialization and redistribution of income are concepts that have lost their magic, and have been replaced by the goal of a fair share of increased productivity.

TABLE 23

Danish National Trade Union Leaders' Concept of Their Responsibilities

Related to:		Per cent
Organization	43	
Organize the unorganized		16
Assist workers as they need it		16
Increase influence of national union		8
Subordinate union to the labor movement		3
Collective bargaining	43	
Provide members with job security		13
Improve terms of employment periodically		11
Enforce collective bargaining standards		8
Obtain best possible adjustment of grievances		11
Industry	14	
Work with problems of the industry		8
Act with responsibility toward employers		6
Total	100	
Number	37	

Success and power are matters which call for exercise of restraint. The use of personal strength in a competitive struggle to reach the top is an abhorrent idea, or at least one which gains no praise. Nor is the quest of the lion for the lion's share a proper mode of conduct. And the comment in industrial relations circles is that not until recently would a Danish trade union leader dare to be seen driving, or worse, riding in, a black automobile.

Responses of Danish labor leaders on their responsibilities (Table 23) indicate the following major concerns: (1) strengthening the organization; (2) improving the condition of the workers; (3) promoting the health of the industry. In comparison with Italian responses, neither the strengthening of the organization nor the improvement of the position of workers is unique. What is different is the expression of responsibility to the employer: "It is my responsibility to strengthen the relationship between the employers and the workers"; "The union has to be concerned with the improvement of the productivity of the industry"; "We must act with responsibility toward the employer and the other members of society."

The typical response to the query concerning the most difficult problem the respondent had faced as a labor leader is a description of a moment of crisis in the collective bargaining of a new agreement, such as an impending work stoppage or one in the process of being terminated. Among the responses were the following:

The oil and gas strike of 1956 . . . The consequences of shutting off oil and gas were so great that they gave innumerable problems. External to the organization, we had to determine what exceptions could be made and what public opinion should not be estranged. Inside the organization, these exceptions, agreement in the political sphere, and results had to be explained and defended to the membership.

The collective bargaining of 1958 . . . We were seeking higher wages and shorter hours, despite the flat rejection by the employers and a law restricting the workers' right to strike. But it went through all the same.

How to adapt to technological change . . . In this instance, the change made possible the use of unskilled labor on a job which was previously done by highly skilled labor.

Trying to obtain unity among the trade unions in implementing the policy of the Social Democrat party . . .

The responses reflect the size and type of union, and the level of leadership.

To the query on their most important problem, the majority of national union leaders cited unemployment in the industry or in the economy generally. Most of the respondents who gave this answer asserted that the existence of unemployed workers in their industries is a threat to the maintenance of trade union standards. Other problems expressed relate to specific objectives of the particular labor organization. The head of the women workers cited the attempt to get equal pay for equal work; a craft union leader complained of members of other unions performing the work belonging to his union; and the *formand* of a union that prefers obtaining wage increases through the operation of the incentive system expressed the desire of extending the piece-rate method of payment to more workers in the union. Several respondents stated that they have no problems.

This difficulty in encouraging the expression of problems contrasts with the experience in Italy. Beginning the discussion by asking what were obstacles to the further development of trade unionism created difficulties for the craft-oriented leaders. They cited the high level of organization as a criterion of success and expressed puzzlement as to how greater development could be obtained. One craft union official said: "We have no problems; we are almost 100 per cent organized. You have to stay in the union if you want a job. When we hear of unorganized workers, we ask the employers' association to tell the particular employer to get the workers to join the union." The more broadly oriented group spoke of the problems of full employment, the search for a common market for the Scandinavian countries, and the new responsibilities for unions in increasing production and preparing union members for jobs under new technology.

In contrast to the Italians, who stated objectives in terms of aspirations, the objectives of the Danes were described in terms of maintaining standards already achieved. The existence of unemployment, for instance, poses the problem of how to maintain the standards already gained for the membership. Or there are strong political forces trying to undermine the influence of the trade union by seeking to take away its unemployment insurance function. One trade union official stated that Samkob, the consumer durable goods coöperative, is causing increasing political opposition on the part of employers to the coöperative movement. Another labor leader stated that seasonal unemployment in his industry reached a high of 65 per cent, creating a difficult problem of policing the collective bargaining agreement with small employers. In sum, the Danish respondents expressed concern about maintaining their influence and prestige; the Italians, about increasing the power of their organizations.

Except for the Communist leadership, the nationalization of industry appears to be a dead issue (Table 24). Two dominant reasons were given for this shift in political objectives: the outcome of socialism in Soviet Russia and the conquest of political power by trade unionism. Both of these developments have created doubts as to the efficacy of nationalization in reaching working-class objectives. Production for use, it was stated, is realizable through increased activity in the coöperative movement, particularly through the elimination of the wholesaler function. How this would be done was rather vaguely described. The tone of the replies indicated objectives constituting an evolutionary conversion of the economy toward production in the common interest, with employers and trade union officials viewed as the trustees of the production power of the country. The transfer of ownership is to be obtained, not through nationalization, but by a distribution in the interest of the general population. This concept was expressed by the leaders of the large organizations and the quasi-industrial unions. The senti-

Table 24

Objectives of Danish National Trade Union Leaders

Related to:		Number
Economics	15	
More coöperation and no socialization		5
More health and welfare benefits from employers		4
A society of production for whole population		2
Increased employment and productivity		1
Equal pay for equal work for women		1
Improved conditions for all workers, not one union		1
More job security		1
Education	3	
Higher cultural level of workers		2
Incentives for workers to increase education		1
Politics	3	
Better social insurance system		2
Better social security for the aged		1
Other	7	
Improved employment terms through collective bargaining and politics		4
Means of persuasion other than strike		3
Total	28	

ment is also an indication of the level of maturity of the Danish workers, who do not require their leaders to maintain a contrived atmosphere of antagonism toward the employer and society generally as a justification for trade unionism. The unions are to assume their share of responsibility for increased production in the interest of the consumer. In a sense, the idea represents a strategic retreat from initial objectives, with the advent of responsibility in the assumption of power.

Another facet of the responses is the de-emphasis of increased wages as a goal in collective bargaining. Along with this follows the curtailed use of the strike. One trade union official expressed this point of view in the following fashion: "There is no sense in a struggle on wages. Under a system of piece rates, you can actually raise wages during the course of the existing agreement. We therefore place the emphasis on health and welfare benefits." These benefits are to be gained either through government or collective bargaining, depending upon shifts in economic and political power.

Expressed differences in objectives appear to reflect differences in the type of trade union organization. The leaders of small craft unions tended to state that no change in objectives has occurred. The goal is still a matter of increasing terms of employment for craftsmen. Officials of the larger and quasi-industrial unions expressed a broader outlook. The data also suggest that the older labor leaders articulate a more limited and traditional view of trade union objectives than the younger officials.

CRITERIA FOR MEASURING SUCCESS

Table 25 summarizes responses of national union leaders to the question of what constitutes success for a trade union official. A noteworthy number of the respondents were critical of the use of the term "success."

TABLE 25

Danish National Trade Union Leaders' Criteria of Success

Success related to:	Number
Favorable reaction from members	8
Pleasure of fighting for demand and winning	6
Dynamic organization	4
Confidence of membership	4
Personal satisfaction in work	4
Acceptance by members of formulated objectives	3
Confidence in one's own capability	2
Low number of grievances	2
Satisfactory coöperation with employer	1
Total	34

The word has a middle-class connotation of competition among people trying to reach the top of the heap; hence it is offensive to the Danish egalitarian spirit. In the view of the respondents, men should act collectively in the common interest of the group to which they belong, rather than pursuing individually their own personal goals at the expense of others. This point of view is genuine and not propagandistic, and it contrasts with the more individualistic and optimistic outlook of the majority of the employers. These dissimilar perceptions of life are a major source of difference between employers and trade union officials.[1] The term also jars the labor leaders' sense of social restraint. Success, in the judgment of one respondent, is something reserved for opera singers. A Dane who performs his role with too much prominence and display would appear absurd in the eyes of the members of the community. This value of restraint appears again in their image of foreign trade union officials. To the Danes, the American trade union officer who practices collective bargaining with bluster and blast is immature rather than heroic.

The same expression of the propriety of social modesty appears in other statements:

You never ask yourself why you are elected, nor do you run for election. The members choose you if they have confidence in you and respect for you.

The job of the leader is a position of trust, to which personal ambition and success are foreign.

Success is derived from the satisfaction of seeing the members content with their newly acquired gains.

Some of the labor leaders expressed the view that other leaders are somewhat more ambitious and vain: "The younger officials are aspiring to a political career or a position at the federation level"; "Some are social climbers and would like to see their pictures in the newspapers."

In the judgment of the labor leaders, what is the most important goal of the workers which can be used as a benchmark of successful achievement? The preponderant number of the responses cited improvement in job security and economic standards. "Improve the standard of living"; ". . . better living conditions and social welfare"; ". . . more wages and shorter working hours." One respondent ranked worker goals in the following order of importance: "Job security, influence on the operation of the work place, higher wages, and political and trade union unity among the workers." The national leader of the General Workers' Union listed as goals better labor and public education, and the head of the Metal Workers cited the opportunity to rise up the occupa-

[1] See discussion of Ross Stagner, "Some Problems in Contemporary Industrial Psychology," *Bulletin of the Menninger Clinic*, XXI, No. 6 (November, 1957).

tional ladder. What is the method of achieving these goals? In general, the respondents stated it could best be done by exerting influence in the political and economic arenas. Representative responses included:

By strengthening the influence of the labor movement in Parliament and by bargaining collectively . . .

By exercising industriousness, thriftiness [sparsomlighed], and cleverness . . .

By working toward coöperation [samarbejde] . . .

By getting influence at the plant level through the joint production committees and by obtaining through collective bargaining a wage system which gives more consideration to the efforts of the individual . . .

From the replies of an official of a large quasi-industrial union:

The methods are multifold. In a given situation, you choose the best-suited goal, in the light of the possibilities afforded by the political and economic situation and the situation in the trade union.

From the *formand* of a craft union:

By getting the employer to use a greater amount of the profit of the business for social welfare benefits, such as employment, sickness, and old age insurance . . .

The term *samarbejde* appears in these responses, as it does frequently throughout the transcriptions. This ability to work together with other power groups in Danish society is a mark of success which the community commends. If the Danish trade union official coöperates successfully with the employer, he is performing an act of sociability; for his Italian counterpart, on the other hand, such behavior might be considered traitorous. In the words of one respondent: "The man who proposes compromise and coöperation with opponents has a greater chance of obtaining votes than the man who proposes a fight, because the people know that coöperation has solved problems before. There is a strong tradition in favor of the peaceful settlement of differences." Of course, equality in the political and economic power of adversaries in Denmark is a fact. Which factor is cause and which effect is difficult to say.

In the pursuit of these goals, the labor leaders were asked, how do you determine whether a particular decision has been a success or failure? From a majority of the respondents:

By determining whether the result produces satisfaction or dissatisfaction among the members . . .

After the decision has been working for some time, ascertain whether workers are still concerned with the question; if they are not, the decision is surely correct.

On big questions you find out easily enough by the reaction of the members; on other questions, close coöperation and knowledge of the members makes it comparatively easy to avoid mistakes.

In certain cases by making an investigation to determine the consequences of the decision . . .

One respondent stated that he could not answer the question because decisions are a matter of joint determination, and their interpretation subject to independent judicial control.

The technical and administrative orientation of the Danish national union leaders is reflected again in their answers to two queries on trade unionism. What criteria, they were asked, could be used in evaluating the success of Danish trade unionism? Most of the replies concentrated on the standard of living of Danish workers. Several replies indicated that the percentage of organization of workers is an appropriate benchmark for evaluation of the efforts of Danish trade unionism. What is the most important function they are discharging in their trade union? The daily management of the affairs of the union, or put in another way, the performance of the administrative work of the labor organization. And the particular nature of this administrative work is the settlement with employers and the employers' association of problems arising out of the employment relationship. The craft union leaders mention "working with the trade." In the discharge of this function, it is important to believe in teamwork and to have a knowledge of the "mentality" of the trade.

WHAT DANISH LABOR LEADERS CONSIDER
DESIRABLE LABOR LEADER CHARACTERISTICS

Among the characteristics of the ideal labor leader, the first preference by far is negotiation ability. The commonly mentioned term is *forhandlingsevne*. "He must be capable of negotiating an agreement. . . ." "He should have a detailed knowledge of the collective bargaining agreement. . . ." "He must show flexibility in bargaining collectively with the employer. . . ." The president of the most powerful trade union in Denmark stated: "We should possess a clear view of the problems that are being handled and have enough flexibility in coöperation and negotiation technique." Other replies include "stubbornness," "upright character," "sobriety," "a strong will to work," "a knowledge of the character of human beings," "the ability to defend one's opinions with the employer and with the membership," and "knowledge of the industry." Two craft union leaders stressed the importance of policing existing collective bargaining agreements. In sum, the replies of Danish leaders are oriented toward technical aspects of collective bargaining, while those of the Italians emphasize moral values of the labor leader.

THE ISSUE OF INDUSTRIAL UNIONISM

Whether to reorganize the labor movement into industrial unions is a sensitive issue among Danish trade unionists. Denmark is the only Scandinavian country which adheres to the craft form of labor organization. The critical point of view in this issue is that of the General Workers' Union. It is reflected in the account a member of that union gave of on-the-site construction facilities for workers. "When a building goes up in Denmark," he stated, "there is one barracks for the skilled workers and a separate one for the unskilled workers. It remains as a symbol of the fact that the skilled craftsmen do not wish to associate with us. Now that we have become powerful, they have asked us to join their unions, but now we do not want to associate with them." Some of the respondents in the General Workers' Union, despite the lingering sense of the historical split between skilled and unskilled workers in the labor movement, spoke favorably of industrial unionism. Among some of the craft leaders themselves there exists a concern that craft organization impedes economic development and presents an obstacle to the upward movement of unskilled workers. They grant that keeping the unskilled workers outside the craft unions was a serious blunder. The leaders of the Office Workers and the Women Workers expressed some critical concern about industrial unionism. By age group, the younger men in secondary positions of leadership appear to be more favorably disposed toward the organization of all the workers of an industry into one union. The comments of the national union labor leaders are given below.

Favorable comments

Small craft unions will gain because of better administration in large unions.

Personal interests will make any conversion difficult.

Difficult to persuade workers of different crafts to belong to same union . . .

Best way to cope with technological change . . .

Will increase bargaining power through better preparation . . .

Will raise average wages because wages of unskilled are geared to them . . .

Makes it easier for labor movement to coöperate with government . . .

Will improve terms of employment for the skilled . . .

Unfavorable comments

It increases the bargaining power of the employers.

Not good for my union; will take fifty years to achieve . . .

It will take work away from the skilled to the unskilled. The latter will then make more wages because the pace of the craftsmen will decrease.

No advantage to the craftsmen in building construction . . .

No committal

Will dilute the skill of the craftsmen . . .

Dignity of work will be lost.

Craft work gives men freedom from supervision.

Do not see any advantage to be gained . . .

POLITICAL ATTITUDES

Trade unionism in Denmark, as in Italy, cannot be understood divorced from its intimate relationship with the political alignment of the country. A major difference between the two countries is that organized labor in Denmark does not dissipate its political strength, but concentrates it almost entirely within the Social Democrat party. Although there are a few Communist trade union officials in the national unions, the federation leaders are Social Democrats who work closely with the party hierarchy with offices in the same building. The Social Democrats control the government, with the aid of small parties. The employers assert their political influence for the most part through the Conservative party, while the organized farmers dominate the Liberal party. Teachers and newspapermen as a group lean to the Social Democrats, and the rest of the electorate distributes itself in no particular pattern among all the political parties. A characteristic of this array of political grouping is that the Social Democrats do not have an overwhelming balance of power. The necessity of mustering coalitions to push through policies gives the employer and farm groups an effective check on what organized labor can do in politics.[2]

The bargain in the economic arena in Denmark is inseparable from that in the political arena. Fringe benefits are as negotiable in Parliament as in collective bargaining with employers. The decisions of employers and labor leaders are affected by political and economic forces which are not divisible. Paradoxically, the political restraint imposed on labor leaders because of their intimate relationship with the Social Democrats serves to increase the bargaining power of the employers. The Danes, however, like the Italians, see no clear distinction between politics and economics.

An additional factor giving employers compensatory influence is their greater degree of centralization. The powers of the employers' association are less permissive than those of the labor federation. The more rigid disciple exercised by the Dansk Arbejdsgiverforening to prevent company-wide collective bargaining agreements makes it difficult for a trade union official to negotiate on the basis of whatever the local traffic will bear. In negotiations, therefore, the labor movement may be faced with a possible shutdown of the economy, depending upon how the employers dominating the association react to the union proposals. Thus the phalanx which the employers can array in collective bargaining and the commitment of the labor leaders to the government to avoid political embarrassments serve to reduce the level of union collective bargaining power. Although the trade unions call the tune, the employers can determine to what extent it should be played.

It is difficult to say how much influence leaders of the Social Democrat party and trade union officials have on each other. The latter generally say that the influence is mutual and that neither organization dominates the other. Some workers and local union officials said that the party has a dominating influence on trade union policy and has nullified the use of the strike as an instrument of collective bargaining. It is probable that in a major contest between employers and trade

---

[2] In the national election held in May, 1957, based on proportional representation, the single-house Folketing seats were distributed among the political parties as follows: Social Democrats, 70; Social Liberals, 14; Conservatives, 30; Liberals, 45; Justice party, 9; Communists, 6; and minority parties, 5. The Communists split in November, 1958, into two groups. Aksel Larsen, the party chairman for 27 years, was attacked for revisionist ideas and Titoism, and expelled from the party. He founded a new party, Socialistisk Folkeparti. Knud Jespersen, a trade union official, became the new chairman of the Communist party. The split grew out of the Hungarian revolt. Its effect, apparently, is to give dissident Social Democrats a more respectable alternative organization.

unions, when the chips are down and the outcome is protracted conflict, trade union officials would have to yield to the needs of the party.

In Denmark, political left-wingism is part of the unitary trade union movement, in contrast to Italy, where it has its own labor organizations. The political factions in the trade unions are the Social Democrats, in most instances in the majority; the Communists; and the so-called neutrals, who look with disfavor at attempts on the part of the first two groups to inject political issues into trade union affairs. Communist strength is dominant in a few trade unions, such as the Seamen, the Typographers, the Carpenters, and some of the locals of the General Workers' Union. Consequently, its concentration cannot be explained on the basis that a particular occupational level is attracted to the party. Some of the national union officers granted the contribution the Communists have made to trade union leadership, although a few stated that their role is to engender unrest, in accord with the thesis of the Third International. Where Communists sit on executive boards, the national officers of the trade unions stated that their relationship with them is constructive and harmonious. The responses of the Danish Communists were less consistent with traditional Marxist ideology than were those of their Italian counterparts. They differed from the Social Democrats in being more critical of employers and expressing a more vigorous view in favor of the use of the strike. Their presence as the left wing of trade unionism does not appear to make much of a stir either inside or outside the labor movement.

A factor explaining the low level of political controversy within the trade unions is the eschewal of major political issues. The practice of standing up and being counted within the individual trade unions is shunned in favor of the maneuvering of the federation leadership in the Social Democrat party. Labor leaders are expected to work quietly, without publicity, in smoke-filled rooms, with party representatives, in order to obtain concessions. Leaders of the national unions rarely express themselves in public on political and social affairs, but concentrate their efforts instead on the details of administering their organizations. The labor leader who would use a trade union meeting to make a political pronunciamento might be considered rash. Because of such discretion, despite the considerable top support the trade union movement provides the Social Democrat party, only a grumble or two was heard from the Communists that their party is not being supported in the same manner.

This approach of the trade unions to politics stems in part from the desire not to interfere with what is considered to be the proper domain of other leaders in the labor movement. In the judgment of some of the trade union officials, the party is having a difficult time putting together a stirring political program. Many of the leaders no longer believe in nationalization as a panacea to the labor problem. As organization men par excellence, they have a sense of propriety which makes them disinclined to express views on difficult matters that are the proper concern of a different arm of the labor movement.

This attitude toward politics indicates also the sensitivity of trade union officials to their dependence on the party. A departure from the semblance of neutrality might weaken the support of part of their rank and file. There is also prevalent to some degree among workers a belief that deference in collective bargaining to political exigencies has had the effect of curtailing the ability of the trade union to promote their economic interests. The consequence of this sensitivity to the dominance of the trade unions by the party is a disinclination to discuss trade unions and politics.

The Social Democrat party is represented in the trade union federation, and the federation has representation in the executive council of the party. The majority of the respondents could not say which organization is dominating the other. One criticized the use of trade union newspapers by the Social Democrat party to conduct political campaigns. Ten members of Parliament are also trade union officials, and more of the latter aspire to political office. By the time a trade union official has developed a political following, however, he is too advanced in years to start a political career, or he has become too involved in trade union affairs. With the exception of the ten members of Parliament, the two sets of leadership in the labor movement are staffed by different individuals.

Respondents were asked whether they saw any conflict in this relationship between party and trade union. The overwhelming majority see no conflict of interest:

> We would not have reached our goals without coöperation with the Social Democrat party.

> We can work easily with the Social Democrats because the same people are involved.

> It is a means of guaranteeing the gains made in collective bargaining.

There may be conflicts of interest, but they are resolved internally, without publicity.

In our type of democracy, it is easier to influence one political party than it is to act as a pressure group on the men of different political parties. It is a means of obtaining what you cannot get in collective bargaining.

Such a relationship is a means of determining whether political conditions are favorable for a wage increase.

The majority of the rank and file are not concerned with the ideological question of close association with the party, but look at the matter in terms of the advantages in such an association.

It is a way of communication upward into the government.

Two respondents were critical of the relationship. One stated that trade unions are too subservient to needs of the party, and the other criticized the Social Democrats for vagueness and slowness in getting things done.

Some conflict of interest is conceded if an individual is both head of a trade union and member of the Folketing. The policy of a trade union is by nature more narrow than that of the political party. There may be a conflict of opinion, but it does not often happen. When it does, the problem of labor leadership is made more complex, for a choice must be made; and the job of persuading constituents in both camps is difficult. However, the view was expressed that it is the job of the leaders to anticipate trends and to prepare the membership for the reality that confronts them. The members expect them to do this by constantly presenting new ideas, suggestions, and opinions. In this way, irreconcilable differences between the political organization of workers and the economic organization can be kept to a minimum. For some officials, the question of conflict of interest is too academic. They shrug it off by pointing to the gains made by workers by virtue of the existence of a labor party.

Nor do they see a conflict of interest between the furtherance of collective bargaining and the control of plants by means of the coöperative movement. Unions indirectly, through the purchase of securities, control such diverse businesses as retail stores, baking plants, fuel distribution, canteens, banks, building construction, plumbing fixtures manufacturing, and a brewery whose product was displayed exclusively during the interviews. The question was raised whether such a relationship produces a situation in which union representatives bargain with other union representatives on the control of labor costs. The labor federation, it was stated, had agreed that it would not seek terms of employment better than those for the top third in the industry, and that grievances arising out of interpretation of the terms of employment would be settled without resorting to strikes. There are two strikes on record, but neither was supported by the federation. To the question of what workers obtained from such coöperative enterprises which they could not get otherwise, the response cited improved terms of employment, in some instances. The basic purpose of such enterprises, however, is to create a downward pressure on the prices in an industry and to improve the quality of goods and services. By achieving such results, these enterprises are promoting the interests of the working class.

The trade union movement has managed to achieve a delicate balance of power among the various organized economic blocs. The Social Democrats fall just short of a majority in the Folketing, the marginal difference representing their inability to allay fears of increased socialization, should they reach a majority. The trade unions no longer find the offices of the Social Democrats the avenue to automatic concessions. Organizations have a way of developing institutional needs of their own, and the Social Democrat party appears to be no exception. The economic interests represented by the political parties are rather sharply defined into those of employers, farmers, and organized workers. However, the necessity incumbent upon the Social Democrats of gaining support of the unorganized portions of the electorate in order to remain in power provides employers with an effective instrument to control the demands of trade unions in collective bargaining. They compensate for the economic power which they cannot muster in collective bargaining by making the issue a political one and forcing the Social Democrats to exert pressure on the trade unions.

Trade union leaders view this finely balanced political and economic power as a matter of organized votes counterbalancing organized money. The men they mentioned as having power in their society, whether in government or private industry, are those who control either money or votes. People with influence are the finance minister, the head of the national bank, the prime minister, or large employers. Power in the society is evenly distributed, because those with the *penge* are checkmated by those with the votes. "Employers have more money, but we have more votes." "We control financial power by mustering together most of the votes of the workers into the Social Democrat party."

More than among the Italians, power is construed in terms of organizations rather than individuals, of blocs counterbalancing the influence of other blocs. An individual exerts influence in a country by controlling an organization whose decisions inevitably affect a large number of people. The non-organization man is an ineffective voice crying in the wilderness. A minority of the respondents introduced into their comments meaningful nuances. Influence depends on particular situations and issues which cause shifts in the power of different blocs. Moreover, the voice of a single individual without any group support could exert considerable pressure in a situation. In general, however, there are no noteworthy differences of opinion among national union leaders on how power accrues. Nor do they disagree in their assessment of the relatively equal power of employers as a group and the organized labor movement.

The judgment of national labor leaders on the contributions of the Communist party to the cause of workers is concentrated in the little-to-none range. Some drew a distinction between Communist leadership in the trade union movement and that in the party, praising the responsibility of the former and criticizing the recklessness of the latter. It was apparent that the majority considered that the Communists pose no threat to their trade union leadership, and they were either tolerably disposed toward the party or mildly critical of it. Adverse comments included:

They vote against an improvement because they want still more, with the result they may get nothing.

They have a policy of maintaining dissatisfaction.

They actually bring about a decline in collective bargaining power by causing a stiffening of the position of the employer.

They cause splits in the ranks of labor.

They have a policy of asking for a little more than anybody else.

Representative non-hostile comments included:

Their function is to "keep the bile" [maintain dissatisfaction] and in that way gain improvements.

Their propaganda activates the non-Communist groups.

They act as a pressure group on the Social Democrat party.

The latter comment is typical of those who feel the Communist party is making a useful contribution to the interests of the working class.

PERCEPTION OF THE AMERICAN LABOR MOVEMENT

Among favorable comments on the American labor movement, the dominant response cited the high standard of living of American workers, which the Danish labor leaders imputed to the efforts of American trade unions. A number of the responses reflected situations in their own trade unions.

The high standard of living is to be admired.

The considerable fringe benefits which have been obtained under collective bargaining . . .

The ability to strike under a collective bargaining agreement without being heavily fined . . .

The way in which many trade unions try to solve problems without any consideration of the employer's point of view . . .

The lack of a prejudiced attitude toward workers' increasing their productivity . . .

The lack of a strong dividing line between the skilled and unskilled workers . . .

Two of the national leaders declined to answer, stating that they did not know enough about American trade unionism to comment.

Unfavorable comments center on corruption and the political outlook of the American working class. "There is corruption in the American labor movement. . . ." "Some American labor leaders are half gangsters. . . ." "They do not know how to handle themselves in trade union activity in which money is involved. . . ." On the matter of politics, a noteworthy number of respondents commented on what they described as the lack of political intelligence on the part of American workers. "They are unable to reach goals because of a lack of political intelligence." The tone of these responses is one of perplexity why the working class, by what it fails to do, yields political power to other groups in its society. Two respondents commented on the low caliber of the American labor press, and an equal number stated that they believed American trade union officials show an inability to understand foreign labor movements. Additional comments included:

It is shocking that they [labor leaders] should suggest that war production be increased in order to solve an economic crisis.

They have a lack of respect for collective society.

The great difference in the wages of the skilled compared to the unskilled . .

Their lack of fight for social good to help the old and the sick . . .

Four respondents declined to comment on the question. One of them stated: "I have no right to criticize, because each labor movement has to work consistent with its own structure and nature."

THE LEADERSHIP AT THE LOCAL LEVEL

The sample at the local level comprises shop stewards and presidents of locals inside Copenhagen and the provinces. The shop stewards were asked what their responsibilities were and what difficulties they were having in the discharge of their functions. Correlative with these questions were two on what the workers and the employers expected of them as shop stewards. The local presidents were asked the same queries as the national leaders. The object was to determine what were the differences, if any, between the local and national leadership and what factors might account for the dissimilarities.

The machinery of shop steward representation in one plant of several hundred employees which was visited is typical of industrial firms of this size. Each trade union selects its own shop steward by vote of the membership, and the stewards in turn jointly select a chief shop steward out of their number. The stewards are assisted by eighty representatives, in order to maintain a maximum of person-to-person contact, and they rely for written communication on bulletin boards in the plant, on which are posted notices coming from the union local office. In addition, each separate *klub* meets at least once a month, while the joint *klub* for the entire plant meets once every quarter, with additional meetings for special occasions.

Shop stewards expressed role obligations and pressures peculiar to their position as the immediate representatives of the workers vis-à-vis individuals who are also their employers. Although they desire to promote the interests of the workers they represent, those who come to them with grievances expect more than they can possibly produce. They feel caught between their knowledge of the problems of the employer and the pressure from workers more aware of their demands than of the difficulties involved in meeting them. Their predicament could be eased by labor education programs for workers and by improvement of the human relations skills of management. They feel the job of the shop steward could also be made easier by the cementing of good relations between management and the workers and by the achievement of stability in relationships which would result from shifting from individual solutions to those based on the common interest.

The major responsibility which the shop stewards expressed is the maintenance of good relations between the employer and the workers.

The responsibility first and foremost is to make the relationship between workers and employers as good as possible.

There has to be peace and order. It happens, as you know, that workers sometimes say "Stop" in the plant. You have to take care that it does not happen on small things.

On the correlative question of functions, representative answers were:

When the comrades come and say something, then you have to go to management. First I go to the supervisor, and we agree whether I should go to the top or whether we can settle the problem between ourselves. We discuss whether the demand is reasonable, and sometimes we do not agree.

If a worker cannot agree with management, I must come in and mediate.

When a new employee comes to the firm I talk with the manager on where to place him.

My job is to represent an individual worker when he feels his piece rate is not enough. Also general conditions of work. Certain workers, for instance, have long lunch hours, which they readily would do without because they cannot go home.

Replies to queries on worker and employer expectations are suggestive of pressures on shop stewards. The queries on expectations evoked the recurrent theme that the role of the trade union official is that of mediator.

The employer expects that I see the problem from his viewpoint also. He wants a man who "smooths things," who takes the sharp edges off the viewpoints of the workers. I have to settle the differences.

You have to try to satisfy both sides.

The workers expect me to get the best possible results out of the demand.

They do not understand the point of view of management. They have to be taught.

You cannot make a solution simply to please a worker. It will lead to trouble.

The employer expects me to smooth things out. It is not possible always to demand and demand.

The local union president is the link between the shop stewards operating at the plant level and the national union. His role is to maintain the flow of communication upward from the membership through the shop stewards to the national union and downward from the national office to the individual work places. The response of the *formand* of a large local of the Metal Workers' Union outside Copenhagen described the way this function is typically discharged.

First, I sit on the executive board of the national union and in that way maintain a close contact. Also, whenever a grievance rises to the national level we have contact. Correspondence and the shop steward courses bring us into communication with each other. Regularly, therefore, there is always correspondence going up and down, which in turn reaches the shop stewards, who use plant bulletin boards to get the communication to the membership. Whenever we have trade meetings for any of the skilled classifications, someone in the national office comes to visit us. If on any other occasion we want the chairman or the secretary, they come here. In the other direction, all the shop stewards in this area are on the executive board of the local. You must make certain that every board member has a function. We have shop steward meetings once every three months, and the membership is invited to attend. We are in constant contact by the dissemination of stenciled material, which is sent to all the firms. Here at the local office, most of the workers we see are the unemployed. If a worker is dissatisfied at the shop steward level, however, he can always come to the local. The local also participates in the firm *klub* meetings. Whenever a problem on piece rates comes up, it is solved by the local office. The shop steward can leave work any time without losing his salary. And of course there is also the trade union newspaper. Under such a system of constant communication, it is difficult for any conflict to arise. If it does arise among the executive board members, I will go directly to the members.

Table 26 summarizes local trade union leader expressions on reasons for joining the labor movement. Like the majority of national union leaders, most of the local leaders stated that the decision was a

TABLE 26

Motivation of Danish Local Trade Union Leaders for Entering
the Labor Movement

Orientation	Number	
Group	10	
Trade-union–consciousness in home environment		5
Support of workers		5
Personal	5	
Sense of mission		4
Experience of personal injustices		1
Total	15	

response to group pressure. "It is not a voluntary choice that you make; you develop an interest in trade union affairs, and then if you show competency your fellow workers appoint you as their spokesman. . . ."

"I was asked to take over the position of shop steward; I did not seek the position. . . ." The expression of intense personal convictions which led to joining the labor movement is associated with the age of the respondents. The four responses with a marked personal orientation were those of trade union officials in their late fifties and sixties. They entered the Danish labor movement during its evangelical days, and they were more inclined than their younger colleagues to express themselves with feeling.

TABLE 27

Danish Local Trade Union Leaders' Concept of Their Responsibilities

Related to:		Number
Organization	7	
Assist workers as they need it		3
Organize the unorganized		1
Maintain communication with membership		3
Collective bargaining	6	
Enforce collective bargaining standards		5
Improve terms of employment periodically		1
Industry	3	
Act with responsibility toward employers		3
Total	16	

The local leadership is less concerned with size of organization than are the national union officials (Table 27). The local presidents placed more stress on maintaining close associations with the members. There are two dominant responsibilities in the pursuit of this objective: the policing of the collective bargaining agreement and the defense of legitimate employer objectives. Typical statements included:

I have a responsibility to both employers and workers to see that the work done is of high quality and that workers have the opportunity to make the highest piece-rate earnings possible.

I look after the interests of workers in their relations with employers; but sometimes I have to explain to workers why they cannot get more.

My responsibility is to maintain as close a contact as possible with the members and try to obtain periodically a little improvement in employment terms. I also have a responsibility to the employer.

Statements on role reflect the same concern with the closeness of the relationship with the rank and file (Table 28). Expressions are more concrete and less abstract than those of the national leaders.

I was forced to study labor legislation because the members expected me to interpret it for them.

I must be firm with the members and assume responsibility for the decisions that have to be made.

In negotiating with the employers, I first tell the members and the shop stewards what we think of proposing, and they give their opinion. It is important that the proposals be formulated in this way.

I wish the Danish workers were a little more interested in the pattern of culture and a little less in a wage increase and that they would be less impressed with advertising and middle-class ambitions.

I work entirely for the members. The trade union official who does the work during his leisure time may be more interested than the paid functionary. Some of them are *pamper*.

You have to solve members' problems on the basis of what is good for the members, not what is good for the Social Democrats or the Communists. It is criminal to exploit situations for a political party.

TABLE 28

Danish Local Trade Union Leaders' Concept of Their Role

Emphasis on:	Per cent
Mediation function	44
Limited economic objectives	3
Organization	50
Socially oriented objectives	3
Total	100
Number	15

A considerable portion of the local sample stated that they believe that the labor-management program in Denmark has been unsuccessful. The only respondent who stated it has been a success felt that the program had improved physical conditions of work and that workers had obtained information on what was going to happen in the organization in the future. Those who considered it unsatisfactory gave answers like the following:

Management lacks frankness in economic matters.

The right to direct and distribute the work is too one-sided.

Management cannot reconcile itself to the demand of the trade union movement on sharing influence in the plant.

It is unsatisfactory; there is a lack of understanding on both sides.

Marked differences from the opinion of the national officials exist in local leaders' estimates of the collective bargaining and political power of employers. In part, this dissimilarity reflects differences in problems and role of the two sets of labor leadership. The primary leaders closest to the membership cannot isolate themselves from the shifting pushes and pulls of day-by-day trade union events and employer-employee relationships. The secondary leaders have different types of problems. They deal with ultimate sources of power and are more politically conscious. Their relationships with those outside their organizations are more formal, more ritualistic, and less turbulent.

The preponderant majority of the local union officer respondents believe the employer has the greater collective bargaining power. A typical expression is that the fellow with more money has the greater bargaining power.

It is the employer; he sits on the cash box.

Everybody says it is the trade unions, but I do not believe it.

It is the employer; he has more money. And also because the politicians have taken away from us the right to strike. The socialist government, so called, by interfering in a dispute helps the employer. So whenever we strike, the government sides with the employer.

It is the employer, because it costs too much to fight for five ore.

It is the employer, of course. All they need to do is say No, and then the issue ends up in Parliament, where working men's opinions are not greatly valued.

The three respondents who believed the trade unions have greater bargaining power tend to view collective bargaining influence as political power. "It is the workers, because they all belong to one political party. . . ." A variation of the "money is power" theme is the expression that whoever possesses the means of production possesses the greatest power as well. However, the general comment is the former: *Penge er jo magt.*

The same sentiment is expressed about political influence. The respondents were almost unanimous in feeling that the relationship between trade unionism and politics should involve the close support of the Social Democrat party. "We must stick together and support the Social Democrat party. . . ." "Trade unionism belongs naturally to the Social Democrat party. . . ." "The only possible relationship is with the Social Democrats. They failed us in 1956, but I hope it will not happen again. . . ." Only one respondent expressed a different view. "We should support any party that is willing to support us. . . ." Despite this expression of political solidarity, the local leaders were also almost unanimous in the belief that the employers have the greatest political power in Denmark. In a political contest between the two groups, it is felt that the government, by inadvertence perhaps, actually supports by its actions the side of the employers.

The majority feel that employers are favorable toward trade unionism.

When talking about employers, a distinction has to be drawn between the chief executive of the company and the shareholders. The former is generally in favor of trade unions. When such an employer does not belong to the employers' association, that makes it even better for the trade union at times. Being alone, he cannot take a work stoppage for too long. They also like to hire the most skilled workmen and are willing to pay more for them. Another advantage is that in this situation you are dealing directly with the employer, rather than the employers' association, and the relationship is good. Most of the employers here in _____ do not belong to the association.

Other qualifying comments include:

The exception is sometimes the small employer. They are sometimes not favorable to us, but we do not tell them that we know it.

They are favorable because the union provides the only means by which there can exist a legal relationship [*retsforhold*] between the parties.[3]

They are favorable because when they have a complaint to make they can turn to the union.

On the function of the strike, the sentiment expressed is similar to that of the national leaders: it is a pressure weapon which should be used with discretion. The differences are in the greater expression of disillusionment on the part of the local leadership with the way politics has forced a curtailment of its use. Among the comments were the following:

The purpose is to stop production; but the government has curtailed its use.

Its purpose is to obtain from the employer a concession which would not be forthcoming otherwise.

It should be used when compromise is not possible, and the state should not interfere.

To force through demands, but at times we strike for a lot of nonsense . . .

To see to it that demands which we consider reasonable [*forsvarlige*] [4] are carried through . . .

[3] The term connotes a relationship based on justice.
[4] The term means "capable of being defended," a significant commentary on Danish attitudes.

One respondent stated his belief that the strike has a political function, such as to avert a war or to subvert a foreign occupation, in addition to the general use of selling labor as expensively as possible.

The majority of the local respondents expressed the opinion that the Communist party has made no contribution to the cause of workers. "They make the most noise and do the least about the labor problem. . . ." "They do not have a real point of view; they only oppose. . . ." "They have done harm in both trade unionism and politics. . . ." A minority felt that the party serves the useful function of stirring the Social Democrats into action. "They keep the other fishes alive. . . ." One respondent felt that the Communist party has made an effective contribution. "The comrades in the party have made an effective contribution. It must not be forgotten that it was the revolutionists that organized the labor movement. I myself was locked out for two years by the employers. They are elected to office not in order to get money but to do a good job. . . ."

The majority also expressed favorable attitudes toward industrial unionism for Denmark.

It will make our strikes in industry less absurd.

It would give us more power if all the unions in the industry were together.

It will serve to level the distinction between the skilled and unskilled and facilitate the work of organization for both the employer and the trade union.

I am in favor; but we should not lose contact with the members because of industrial organization. The problem of skill-pride is also difficult to overcome; you cannot prevent a skilled worker from feeling he is a professional, compared to other workers.

Four of the respondents were not favorable to the idea. Their comments follow:

Building construction is performed on a craft basis, each with separate employers; it will not work in that industry.

We would be split up and then, as unskilled workers, lag behind the skilled workers in improved terms of employment.

It will decrease the relative wage of the unskilled workers because they will become the helpers of the craftsmen. The skilled workers want to have industrial unionism to prevent us from doing skilled work.

I am afraid that the destruction of the craft unions will lead to loss of interest in trade unionism by the members.

All of the officials from the General Workers' Union in the sample expressed unfavorable attitudes, while a majority of the craft union leaders are favorably disposed to the conversion of the labor movement into industrial unions.

Expressions on objectives are more plant oriented than those of national union leaders. The most commonly expressed goal is achievement of a greater degree of industrial democracy. "We should have more influence in the management of firms, the employment of new workers, and the discharge of our members. . . ." "We should have greater industrial democracy; profit-sharing is of no interest to us; it does not achieve industrial democracy, which to me means more union control in the firm. . . ." The respondent who feels the Communist party has made a significant contribution to the cause of Danish workers also believes one trade union objective should be the distribution of the whole share of the enterprise to workers. By "share" is meant net income after an allocation to capitalization, and by "workers," everyone working for the organization, including management. Remaining objectives include job security, more fringe benefits, and equal pay for equal work for women. The respondent who expressed the latter objective believes such a goal would serve to increase job opportunities for men and is therefore commendable. The respondent who stated that a full share should be distributed to workers also stated that time and motion studies should be operated jointly by management and the trade union. Another respondent stated: "Objectives change. We are not the idealists the founders were. The pressure for change from the labor movement diminishes. As the top leaders acquire influence, they become more conservative than the local leaders. . . ." The findings sustain this view of differences in conservatism-liberalism. The local leadership generally expresses more willingness to strike and has more orthodox socialist objectives, both in the political sphere and in the control of plant operations.

Generally, the local representatives had the same difficulty in stating what the problems of the union are as did the national union leaders. The response is similar: "We have no problems; we are 100 per cent organized." Those who expressed the existence of a problem in the union gave answers like the following:

Our problem is the low wages of some of our members, but we have gotten nowhere because of the opposition of our employers. The solution is a solidaric wage policy, but it is difficult to get all the unions to agree.

The employers think that only they know about time study and rationalization of work. They do not understand you cannot solve these things by dictation. Our people should be educated on these subjects, and the employer should pay for the education.

My problem is the lethargy of the young.

My problem is how to obtain participating influence in the organization [*medinflydelse*].[5]

Other items used did not bring enough responses to constitute an adequate sample. Nine respondents answered the question on success. The majority of them expressed the feeling that success is achieved through the satisfaction of doing a good job for the members. "I get satisfaction by doing an interesting job for the members and knowing all the men personally. . . ." "I am a success if my members trust me and express satisfaction with the results I obtain. . . ." One respondent in this group stated: "The important thing is for all to live well—that children get warm clothes. Today, when a man walks down the street, you cannot see whether he is the son of an unskilled worker or a manager. And that is most important for me. . . ." The group which did not answer stated that they have never sought success, or that it is a question of private ambitions, such as the building of a firm, and that the working class does not seek success.

Only seven respondents answered the query on the American labor movement. In their answers, they mentioned the industrial form of organization, the greater financial resources, and the greater ability to strike as favorable aspects of American trade unionism. Unfavorable responses concerned the power of American trade union leaders, corruption, and the salaries of American officials. "The trade union leaders have dictatorial power. . . ." "The high salaries of American labor leaders are not pleasing [*utiltalende*]. . . ." "They have a desire for power. . . ." "The differences in the wages of trade union members are too great. . . ." Consequently, the same pattern of responses, together with a noteworthy disinclination to be critical, is found among the local leaders and among the national union officials.

Characteristically, throughout the interview, national and local leaders alike evinced a high respect for the prerogatives and responsibilities of different leaders, even those outside the bargaining organizations. The axiom was frequently expressed that you do not criticize the efforts of another individual in the labor movement if you cannot assume the burden of responsibility of your point of view: "We were taught in the youth movement that you do not criticize without taking the responsibility for the criticism." In this way, a sense of cohesion is maintained

[5] The word literally says "coinfluence."

among the trade union, the coöperative movement, and the political party. The respondents were reluctant to evaluate the efforts of those with whom they had no direct association. This attitude toward leadership increases the tolerance for contrasting points of view and makes accommodation easier. It strengthens group cohesion and stifles the development of divisive forces which assert themselves in erratic and irresponsible leadership.

Generally, Danish labor leaders have a low estimate of drama and oratory in trade unionism. They have small regard for table-thumping and emotional outburst. This is not to say that a competitive spirit does not exist among them. They too are concerned with any change in the relative position of their workers, compared to those of other trade unions, as the result of collective bargaining negotiations. Such inter-union rivalry is controlled by a disciplined employer association, which seeks to prevent dissimilar changes in the terms of employment, lest they become the basis of whipsawing tactics against particular employers.

Danish trade union officials are pragmatic, rather than purist and sentimental, in their approach to objectives. However, they do not consider a social-economic system sacrosanct by its very existence. The president of one of the two dominant trade unions summarized this philosophy as follows: "If the people who own the capital in a country cannot hire all the workers under constantly rising terms of employment, then we will not recognize a liberal [laissez-faire] society that tolerates such a situation. We will go ahead and change it."

They are willing to sacrifice the immediacy of more money for job security and safety of employment. They believe American workers are too production and money conscious, and not appreciative enough of a tempo of work which would allow the diversion of their energies to cultural pursuits. They look askance at the work schedules of other Scandinavian countries, which include night work and seven-day shifts.

The trade union officials of Denmark see no conflict between their goals and those of "society" or the "public interest." To them these abstract terms mean the middle class. In their view, if the workers were poor, the middle class would be poor, too. The members of the middle class may act as an obstacle to the achievement of worker goals, but in a rather ineffective way, because of their individualism and egocentricity. In a theory which resembles the American percolation-theory of prosperity, in reverse, they argue that, by helping the working class, the middle class benefits indirectly.

The threat to Danish trade union stability comes from the impact of technological change on an essentially craft type of union structure and the ensuing clash of interest between the general workers organized across industry lines and the small craft organizations. The problem is an internal one within a united labor movement, however, and a sense of solidarity and restraint prevents it from erupting into conflict.

Danish trade union officials do not live in an atmosphere of conflict, as do the Italians. Neither they nor the workers they represent are as aggressive and frustrated as their counterparts in Italy. There is little in their environment that would encourage an aggressive attitude. The battle for recognition of the union as a partner in the joint determination of employment terms and a legitimate organization wielding influence in society was fought and won a half-century ago. The Italians are still fighting for recognition. With the exception of the union of clerical and sales workers, Danish labor leaders do not have the problem of workers outside their organization posing a threat to the union. The trade union controls not only the distribution of the available jobs but also the unemployment insurance for those who have no jobs.

The relationship between Communist and non-Communist in the Danish labor movement does not present the same difficulties as in Italy. They share leadership in the same union. They do not differ as sharply in philosophy and objectives. They are the loyal opposition in the locals. They demand more than what the labor leader in power is asking for, especially when he is a Social Democrat. In the political arena, they do have differences. The Communists advocate socialization, while the Social Democrats have tacitly abandoned the program. A substantial number of the Communists are "Titoists," individuals who are disinclined to see the party swing and sway to the shifting tune of Soviet international politics.

With trade union status and influence has come conservatism. Through the union, workers achieve respectability in their communities. The labor leaders provide them with jobs, unemployment compensation when they are not working, cultural activity, including extended labor education programs for their leisure, and the means of expressing themselves politically in an effective manner. Consequently, the union is for workers not simply the instrument of obtaining more wages periodically, but also the key to asserting themselves in the community. The area of controversy between employers and labor leaders is of no great consequence. Employers accept trade union officials as instruments for impressing their point of view on workers and, in their words, rationalizing the labor market. In two matters only are there appreciable differences in outlook: the organization of clerical employees, and the extension of the coöperative movement into areas which some employers believe are in their domain. The battle over their respective prerogatives has subsided to an occasional grumble from an employer. The labor leaders themselves are in a nostalgic stage, and the less conservative bearded men of bygone days whose portraits line the walls of their offices are those who fought for recognition a long time ago and won.

CHAPTER 6

Group Images of Labor Leaders and Employers

EMPLOYERS

Several objectives were sought in the employer interviews: employers' images of labor leaders, the influences they contribute which affect labor leader behavior, and factors which may account for these influences. The study of these environmental factors was developed by discovering the background and characteristics of employers, including the structure of their organizations and the cultural climate in which they operate. The employer "sample" reflects the geographical and industrial patterns of each country.

THE ITALIAN EMPLOYER

In Italy the respondents were concentrated in the industrial triangle formed by the cities of Genoa, Turin, and Milan. In diminishing degree, the group included employers down the boot of Italy, including Sicily. The economic sectors represented are metal manufacturing, food processing, wood products, clothing, chemicals, and agriculture. Among the respondents were directors of provincial employer associations, personnel directors, and a management consultant. Company size ranged from small, family-owned firms to multiplant corporations.

The prototype of the Italian employer is that of a man running single-handed a family-owned firm. His appearance and behavior are characterized by labor leaders as baronial. He is handsome, impeccably dressed, quick-witted; he moves fast, talks rapidly and quietly, and maintains a disquieting reserve with his employees and their representatives. He is disinclined to handle his labor relations directly with the representatives of his employees, preferring instead the counsel of the employers' association, to which he is a steadfast adherent. He has little confidence in the ability of labor leaders and refers to them as "orators and politicians," alluding not only to men holding or aspiring to political office, but to individuals who can do no more than indulge in "endless talk with no meaning." He considers himself a person of responsibility and ability, aware of the problems of running a successful organization. His orientation is directed toward the profitable operation of his plant, and he feels resentment against the labor leaders for burdening him with "global" problems which are not of his creation. He does not believe in government intervention unless he runs into difficulty and voluntarily seeks such aid. Accordingly, he professes a faith in *l'iniziative privata*, subject to restrictions he himself would dictate. He shows little faith in government, believing that it might be better to have two legislatures, one housing the orators and the other staffed with professional people like himself, who would have the responsibility of shaping policy.

The stereotype is that of a man with a limited outlook, as far as the possibility of expanding his organization is concerned. He has had to operate in an economy where the general order of things has been monetary instability and political turmoil. The maximum profits of the present are more attractive than the hopes of greater sales in the future. His acceptance of fascism during the Mussolini regime makes him suspect; it places him in a defensive position, wherein he becomes culpable even for the scarcity of economic resources. He does not feel particularly successful in communicating his problems to his employees. In fact, employer-employee relations can be summed up in a word: non-existent. In attitude surveys, employees have called him a miser, egotist, exploiter of workers, and a man who treats workers like beasts of burden. Nor is he unaware of the ideological intentions of some of the labor leaders on the other side of the collective bargaining table, who would prefer, he feels, to see him liquidated.

Confindustria, the employer association to which most of the industrial employers belong, is a closely knit organization capable of bringing together in its conventions ten thousand employers and employer representatives. The large paternalistic monopolies of Italy—Fiat (autos), Necchi (sewing machines), Olivetti (business machines), Edison (power), Marzotto (textiles), and Montecatini (chemicals)—have pursued policies independent of Confindustria. A few middle-sized firms, preferring to develop their own labor relations policies with the local representatives of their workers, have also declined to follow the line of the association, which advocates national uniformity and solidarity. Most of the other employers, however, pursue a course of channeling their trade union approach through the employers' association. Consequently, Confindustria, with its national headquarters on the same piazza where Mussolini used to make his speeches, represents one of the most powerful economic organizations in Italy.

In the sample interviews, the median age of the employers was fifty-five. More than 90 per cent had a college degree, either in law, engineering, or economics, in descending order. Two had degrees in chemistry, and one in agriculture. Ninety per cent had fathers who came from either the professional or employer class. The fathers of the remainder were clerks or salesmen, and one had been a skilled worker. The 10 per cent who had experienced upward movement were in the industrial North, rather than the rural South.

Except in the North, where there are beginning traces of the growth of a professional executive class, a major difference among Italian employers is the degree of their paternalism. In the South and in Sicily, the baronial authoritarian type is common. He dispenses favors unilaterally to his employees in a spirit of *noblesse oblige,* and he views the very existence of a labor leader as a slur upon his moral intentions. Another type is the technical autocrat. He is professionally competent and operates his own organization. Although his employees fear him, they have an admiration for his efficiency and are not unwilling to seek his help when in trouble. If such aid is solicited, the employer feels morally obliged to meet it. This variety of paternalist is willing to deal with labor leaders, provided they do not take away his prerogatives as the *padrone* of the plant. The third type, the democratic paternalist, provides extensive welfare benefits to his employees and does not demand fealty in return. The difference in his philosophy is evidenced in the behavior and attitudes of his workers. They work with less fear and obsequiousness, and there is no look of intimidation on their faces. The sample suggests that with the expansion of plants, Italian employers shift from autocratic to democratic paternalism.

The small employer is likely to be an authoritarian paternalist. His problems, however, are not quite the same as those of the owners of large plants. He complains of the shortage of working capital, the uncertainty of his market, and pressures from trade unions with a global outlook beyond his interest and comprehension. He complains of the shortage of skilled workers, and he is afraid of hiring new employees because of the violent reaction which a future layoff might produce. The orientation of the trade unions to affairs outside the needs of his small plant forces him to seek the protection of the employers' association as an effective bulwark against trade unionism.

The traditional image of the Italian employer is apparently beginning to break down. Some of the respondents were planning to expand their markets because of the prospect of increased sales under the Common Market. There is a growing interest in new techniques of merchandising. An employer of a medium-sized firm proudly played back a "singing commercial" for his product and asked if it did not sound like the ones in the United States. It undeniably did. There are also new influences at work in industrial relations. A few of the large firms had personnel directors whose fathers had been industrial workers. When the top executive is not the owner or the original founder, or when the plant is big, the respondent tends to show more flexibility in his approach to industrial relations. He is more willing to discuss new proposals with the union and even adopt some of them if he can be persuaded that they are in the interests of his organization. He shows less inclination to participate in a contest over property rights as long as the trade union official approaches him in a diplomatic, professional manner. Two employers in the sample had joined with a trade union in signing a collective bargaining agreement, a rare phenomenon for Italy.

Concept of Responsibilities

Employers were asked initially to describe their major problems in operating their organizations. A common response was high costs, of which labor expense is a major component. They complained about the law requiring them to hire inefficient labor. The maintenance of marginal workers is a social problem, they feel. It should be met by society rather than by the employer, who should be helped to increase his productivity instead of being handicapped by having to hire inefficient employees. In fact, an increase in productivity is the ultimate solution, they feel, to the problem of caring for such workers. They also lamented the hostile attitudes of the workers. Workers have a persecution complex, one employer stated, in explaining his attitude. If they find twenty lire less in a pay envelope, they rush to the trade union representative instead of taking up the error with the supervisor.

Other problems expressed include the following: (1) Skilled workers have a relatively low status in Italy. The skilled worker is being badly treated because of political pressures to provide a living wage for the mass of unskilled laborers. The lowest grade of clerical employee makes more money than a skilled industrial worker. (2) Italian employers, complained some of them, ". . . are too conservative. They are afraid to take capital risks. . . ." "We have a way of doing a little of everything instead of specializing. . . ." (3) Labor leaders ". . . are politicians rather than technicians. . . ." "They do not understand the problems of employers. . . ." "They are ambitious demagogues. . . ." (4) The government ". . . has an authoritarian outlook. . . ." "We should participate in government the way employers do in the United States. . . ." One employer cited the preponderance of individuals from the South in government. They bring to their jobs a legalistic frame of mind, and seek to resolve problems by a strict application of the letter of the law rather than by a humane approach. This "byzantine" application of badly conceived law engenders a loss of faith in government by those victimized by it.

Respondents were asked whether employers have functions and responsibilities different from those in the past. All answered in the affirmative, with the exception of three whose responses did not indicate what functions and responsibilities they had in mind (Table 29). The dominant replies divided responsibilities roughly between providing job security and expanding production on a continuing basis. The responses on serving the public interest were vague. One employer stated a belief that such an objective should temper that of making money. The other was not too clear on how the public interest should be served. The personnel directors believe that the employer should provide employee education. They do not believe that Italian education develops a sense of social awareness and responsibility, and by inference they suggest that this deficiency applies to the employers also. In their view, workers have an orientation toward specific individuals, and the concept of group responsibility is a meaningless abstraction to them.

The small sample does not allow the drawing of definitive associations between these attitudes and such environmental factors as plant size, location, and policies. However, it appears that the northern employer tends to take a more particularized pragmatic approach to problems than does his counterpart in the South. This factor is especially apparent in those who operate large plants. In the small firm the industrial relations function is practically non-existent. One employer who had inherited a successful chemical firm from his father genuinely did not know what the interviewer meant by "collective bargaining." In the small firm the approach to industrial relations tends also to be legalistic. That is to say, a particular problem is juxtaposed against a law which appears pertinent to the case. The labor leader's point of view in fact serves as an obstruction to the justice to be obtained from

TABLE 29

Italian Employers' Views of Their New Responsibilities

Related to:	Per cent	
Employees	54	
Maintain jobs		29
Educate workers		14
Understand workers		7
Improve terms of employment		4
Plant	35	
Expand production		21
Provide funds for new investment		7
Increase plant productivity		7
Economy	11	
Serve the public interest		7
Raise standards of depressed areas		4
Total	100	
Number	34	

the application of law. Nepotism as a policy of recruiting workers and management personnel is also common. In one medium-sized machine tool plant, three nephews of a childless employer were the production manager, sales manager, and superintendent of the organization. In many of the firms, an employee-service program akin to the welfare function in personnel administration is discharged by an outside agency, either a labor priest or a welfare worker belonging to the Patronato Assistenze Lavoratore, a social welfare agency supported by employers. Two large employers have a welfare organization of their own, which the employees assist in operating. The very big companies have a comprehensive industrial relations department divided into two basic

units: a *servizio del personale* and a *servizio sindacale,* corresponding
to the personnel and labor relations functions, respectively, in the
United States. The operation of such departments is apt to develop
professional attitudes in the handling of labor matters.

Responses on the purpose of trade unionism (Table 30) reflected the
education and role of the interviewees and the trade union environment
with which they are confronted. The personnel directors and the management consultant were concerned with the development of the capacities of workers and their cultural level. Respondents with production responsibilities complained of the lack of concern on the part

TABLE 30

Italian Employers' Attitudes toward the Purpose of Trade Unionism

Nature of purpose	Per cent	
Economic improvement of workers	*58*	
Improve employment terms consistent with employer needs		36
Improve employment terms		22
Labor-management relations	*18*	
Improve relationships		12
Help increase productivity		6
Social and cultural improvement	*18*	
Raise cultural level of workers		12
Develop worker capacities		6
Purpose should be fixed by law	*6*	
Total	100	
Number	33	

of trade unions for the growth of the firm. There was general disappro-
bation of joint interunion action, and of the political orientation and
the ideology of labor leaders. The objection to ideology was directed
toward, not its articulation, but its use as a part of union tactics against
the employer.

Some of the employer responses on the purpose of trade unionism
suggest the objective of trying to prevent the development of a single
powerful union federation in their organizations. To achieve this goal,
an employer might support one federation at the expense of the others.
Such manipulation is aided by the readiness of each federation to increase its strength in the firm at the expense of the others and by the
inclination of workers to shift their support according to what they

believe to be the sentiments of the employer. The showdown may come when an employer is convinced that a particular federation poses a threat to the successful operation of his enterprise. At that point he may be willing to engage in a contest with no holds barred. One employer stated: "The _____ federation almost ruined us. They indulged in unannounced demonstration strikes, invaded the administrative offices, and committed acts of sabotage. Their objective was to ruin capitalism by ruining us first. We went ahead and broke them instead. . . ." Consequently, the position of the employer stiffens if the ideological outlook of the union is translated into conduct directed against him. In a show of strong pressure from any one union, the existence of three rival trade union organizations provides him with the opportunity to meet the challenge successfully.

TABLE 31

Critical Attitudes of Italian Employers toward Labor Leaders

Subject of criticism	Per cent	
Goal orientation	69	
Promote own ambitions		25
Do not grapple with unemployment problem		22
Are politically ambitious		19
Have no long-range point of view		3
Technical ability	22	
Are technically incompetent		14
Lack flexibility		8
Employer relationship	9	
Cause deterioration of relationship		6
Demand more than employer can pay		3
Total	*100*	
Number	34	

Attitudes toward Labor Leaders

Employers are critical of the broader orientation of labor leaders, and of their lack of education and training (Table 31). Among the criticisms were:

They are political agitators without any interest in the welfare of the company.

They use workers for political purposes.

They seek more than what the company can pay.

Their demands have little to do with the needs of the workers or the needs of my firm.

They are not trained to do a competent job.

They do not know how to resolve a problem with an employer in their own long-term interest.

They do not understand that industrial relations decisions must be consistent with the law. Collective bargaining is too deeply involved in the law to have it interpreted by uneducated trade union officials. Labor problems are fundamentally a matter of the law; yet they want answers based on power rather than logic.

They have no long-range point of view; they are unable to anticipate the consequences of their decisions.

Their purpose is to vilify employers.

If they have a grievance against me, why don't they tell me face to face instead of publishing it in the newspapers?

A portion of the responses blame trade union officials for pursuing their own ambitions, rather than using the needs of the workers as criteria of behavior: "They all want to become members of Parliament and be *onorevoli*"; "They do not promote the interests of workers, but are primarily concerned with their own rival ambitions"; "Their primary goal is personal power, not worker improvement."

One employer praised the local CGIL official as a thinker, not an agitator, and a man who possesses many admirable qualities. The rival CISL provincial secretary, the young, aggressive son of a *mezzadro*, had succeeded in persuading another employer in the community to sign a company collective bargaining agreement, much to the consternation of the employer association. Another employer felt caught between the "hate" politics of the Communists and the Catholics toward each other. "Why," he asked, "should I not try to use them in my own interest? Every politician and labor leader in Italy is playing his role in such a way as to promote his own interest. . . ." A third employer expressed an economic viewpoint not uncommon among the operators of small firms. "If a worker gets a hundred lire an hour," he stated, "he should not ask for ten more, since it only increases costs. When the labor leader supports him in this position, he is only promoting his own political ambitions rather than the interests of workers. . . ."

The interview touched upon the characteristics of a "good" labor leader. The replies stressed technical proficiency. Representative comments included:

He must be technically competent, and should have been a worker himself, which is not true of many trade union officials.

He should be a good seller, able to understand his client, the man on the other side of the collective bargaining table.

He must have a sense of proportion and know how to anticipate the impact of what he does.

He would be astute if he showed the employer a knowledge of plant problems.

When asked who they thought was the most outstanding labor leader in Italy, the employers consistently mentioned DiVittorio, the Communist general secretary of the CGIL. The reasons stated were that he knew how to bargain collectively and that he could be trusted.

Views of Workers

Italian employers were asked the following question: "Studies suggest that workers in Italy have strong feelings of hostility toward employers. Do you believe this is so? How would you account for it?" The preponderant majority gave qualified agreement. A minority agreed and an equally small group disagreed with the statement. Whether by chance or not, the two employers agreeing completely with the statement are sons of poor fathers. One stated as a reason for such feelings the inability of employers to treat workers as human beings; the other cited management's inability or unwillingness to work side by side with workers. The qualifications expressed by the majority have to do with the impact of Marxist propaganda and politics generally. One employer blamed the hostility on the Marxist philosophy of workers juxtaposed against the Malthusian economics studied by the employers. Other comments included:

It is caused by politicians who never held a job in industry.

There is always hostility to supervision, even in convents.

Italian workers are more aware of what society owes them than of what they owe to society.

It is due to envy.

It is due to the normal conflict of interest and the individuality of Italians.

The fault is the lack of understanding of each other on the part of employers and workers.

Italian employees do not want to listen to the point of view of the employer. They interpret his behavior from a political point of view. The assumption of responsibility to the company is alien to them. They have no

sense of social responsibility. Their religion gives them a paternalistic outlook. If they have a large family, their reaction is, "Who will take care of
me now, the employer or the government?" It does not occur to them that
they create the circumstances in which they find themselves. Their motto is,
"Gli altri ci penseranno."

The hostility is due to the personalization of the employment relationship.
We are Italians, not Scandinavians. The Italian employer takes offense at
collective demands. It is like a slap in the face. It is difficult for collective
bargaining to work under such circumstances. He feels that he is doing his
best and finds intolerable a situation in which people who have no knowledge
of his plant are making demands on him. The conflict therefore is not an
economic pressure game, but an emotional conflict. The solution to the
impasse lies in whether technical preparation on either side can reduce this
cultural characteristic.

It is a political reaction. They are mad at employers as a stereotype, not
at any particular one.

It is a manifestation of the fear of unemployment and the conviction that
they will always be workers.

It is propaganda in which the low wages due to low productivity are
propagandized as being caused by exploitation.

It is propaganda feeding on ignorant workers.

Ignorant labor leaders are the cause; if they prepared themselves to meet
with the employer, they would actually increase their bargaining power.

The following comment is that of an enlightened autocratic paternalist:

I look upon this matter of hostility quite differently from the way other
employers do. I give my workers a maximum of freedom from supervision.
If a worker knows what his responsibilities are, he will work hard. I assume
that all my workers want to put their best effort into production. My job is
to provide them employment in a pleasant atmosphere. "Keep smiling" is
my motto when I go through the shipyard. If a worker is ill and needs
money, he gets it. I have never fired a worker in my life and am proud of the
record. The workers can come to my office any time to see me. They do not
have to go to the union. I concern myself with their diet and hygiene. I insist
they bathe after work, and I provide them with an ample hot lunch for
nothing. Every year I hire twelve boys and train them. Those who have the
capacity I send to college. The cornerstone of employer-employee relations
is mutual understanding. I split half my profits between new investment
and bonuses for the employees. My workers are very loyal to me. When my
son was almost killed in an automobile accident, they came to me with
tears in their eyes to express their sympathy. They went to pray in church
for me, their Jewish employer.

In discussions of the ways in which the relationship between employer and worker could be improved, the majority of employers in
the sample indicated that they feel it can be done by raising the edu-

cation and training level of workers. Other methods include the following: (1) encourage worker participation in determining terms and conditions of employment; (2) convince the worker he is a collaborator and not a slave; (3) stop using incentive systems as a device to reduce wages; (4) decrease labor costs going to government and use the money to increase wages; (5) encourage worker recognition of the employer as the one who provides him with a livelihood; (6) refrain from expecting gratitude and obedience from workers; (7) provide workers with steady employment; (8) act in more humane fashion; (9) have workers become cost-conscious; (10) persuade workers that they and employers have mutual needs; (11) avoid humiliating workers; (12) have workers show more responsibility toward the company; (13) pay workers more if they work harder.

Attitudes toward the Role of the Church

Italian employers were asked the same question as labor leaders on the proper role for the Church in the labor problem. None of the respondents expressed any enthusiasm for the Church's playing an active role. The majority are inclined to believe that the Church plays too active a role already. "She should limit herself to the teaching of broad moral principles only. . . ." "She should get out of labor politics too; it is damaging the interests of the Church. . . ." "She forces adverse political reactions such as Communism. . . ." Three employers defended the function of the labor priest as similar to the welfare function of the personnel organization of an American firm, or the work of public welfare agencies found in Anglo-Saxon countries. Because of the decline in parish activity of the Catholic Church, it is felt that the welfare function formerly dispensed there can now be performed by priests coming to plants. Several employers feel the Church in Italy makes too many day-by-day decisions which inevitably run into conflict with the points of view of those outside the Church. The clergy have not only become advisors on how to vote, which means in substance support of the Christian Democrat party, but play a dominant part in placing men in jobs. In the view of the employers, the result of this influence is a nation of Catholics with little respect for the clergy.

Italian Labor Leaders' Perceptions of Employers

Trade union officials were asked: "In your judgment, are the employers favorable to trade unionism, do they merely tolerate trade unions, or would they like to see them destroyed?" Without exception, the provincial officials in the CISL–UIL group stated that they felt the employers tolerated unions. All the CGIL officials felt that the employers would like to see the unions destroyed. One respondent in the latter group excepted the government-operated plants, which in his view tolerate unions. Another in the same group believes that employers would like to destroy only the CGIL and use the other organizations to promote their interests. The responses of the national leaders were notably different. With few exceptions, all expressed the view that the employers would prefer seeing the trade unions destroyed. The CGIL leaders were somewhat less pessimistic. The Communist head of one national union stated that the employers tolerate unions because they cannot do otherwise. The federation leaders divided evenly between those who believe the employers want the unions destroyed and those who think they tolerate them. A CGIL official stated that it is his belief that they want company unions which they can control. Two in the CISL–UIL group stated that the question centers around the particular industry and that no generalizations can be made covering all the unions.

The basis for the differences is a matter for speculation. In all probability, they are associated with the amount of collective bargaining which the trade officials perform. The role of the provincial secretary is more political than the role of the national union leader, who is more trade union oriented. The frustrations attending the latter function may have a bearing on what the particular respondent feels is the extent of the anti-union attitude of the employer which he faces in collective bargaining.

Table 32 is a summary of the differences, if any, that the provincial officials see in employers. Some of the respondents expressed preferences for particular employers who, in their view, exercise the smallest amount of aristocratic leadership. In the CISL–UIL group, Valletta (Fiat Motor Company) is preferred as one of the best employers. Marzotto (textiles) is cited as one of the worst. While CGIL respondents believe some degree of difference exists among employers because of the economics of different industries, they are inclined to view their general characteristics as being caused by the capitalist system. They appear to find it difficult to reconcile their image of the large employer as a "bad monopolist" with the fact that he may be offering the highest terms of employment. Preferences in the CISL–UIL group are an expression of the rejection of paternalism as industrial relations policy.

A CISL official stated: "They differ in the extent of their paternalism. Valletta says, 'I am the boss of the machines,' while Marzotto says, 'I am the boss, period.'" Another respondent of the same organization stated that the motto of Italian employers is, "I do, I say, you obey." (*Io faccio, Io dico, Voi Obbedite.*) "Valletta typifies the progressive employer. He seeks to expand his plant and pay high wages. On the other hand, Marzotto is the prototype of the reactionary. He is paternalistic and expects workers to show gratitude for his efforts in their behalf. . . ." One UIL member described the latter group in the following fashion: "They have simple economic brains. The less they give workers, the more money

TABLE 32

Italian Labor Leaders' Views on How Italian Employers Differ
(Per Cent)

Differences related to:	CGIL	CISL	UIL
Economics of industry	27	38	50
Attitudes toward unions	33	46	25
Personality	0	15	13
Attitudes toward working class	17	0	12
No real differences	22	0	0
Total	99 *	99 *	100
Number	19	14	9

* Percentages were rounded.

they make. If you make a hundred lire on the first unit you sell, the second unit should be worth the same money. They act like barons. One of them fired a worker for removing his coat. . . ." The CISL–UIL groups in the South without exception expressed the belief that there is no progressive type of employer in their geographical area. However, it is felt that this situation will change as the plants in the South become larger in size and become staffed with professional managers.

Additional probative comment indicates that on the matter of employer policies which tend to weaken trade unionism, there are some differences by federation. CGIL leaders charged that their members in particular are discriminated against, in order to weaken their organization because it is the most militant of the three. The UIL complained of employer propaganda to weaken trade unionism generally. The CISL asserted that employers simply ignore national collective bargaining agreements, and fix terms of employment on an individual basis. They also find that the paternalism of the employer lessens the possibility of developing an independent spirit among the workers.

Table 33 summarizes responses on what Italian trade union officials feel is the responsibility of the employer toward workers. The language of human relations, present in the CISL and UIL to a small degree, was absent in the expressions of the CGIL. "He should treat the workers with respect. . . ." "He should learn how to handle human relations. . . ." The CGIL leaders see little prospect of the employers'

TABLE 33

Italian Labor Leaders' Attitudes toward Employers' Responsibilities
to Workers
(Per Cent)

Responsibility related to:	CGIL		CISL		UIL
Attitude toward workers	43		47		40
Respect dignity of workers		12		47	40
Give workers voice in management		31		0	0
Economic responsibilities	31		48		50
Improve wages and conditions of work		0		29	10
Accept role of unions in improving efficiency		31		19	40
No individual responsibility; it's the system	25		5		10
Total	99 *		100		100
Number	16		22		10

* Percentages were rounded.

changing their attitudes toward workers under the existing system. A Communist of that organization stated: "Employers commonly exploit labor by taking away part of the income that rightfully belongs to the workers. The difference among them is one of size. A large employer often even exploits small employers from whom he buys materials and supplies or those with whom he contracts out part of his production. The system requires him to do this. . . ." This concept of exploitation was prevalent in the responses of the CGIL. The idea appears to be that the portion of income derived by virtue of differences in economic power is considered to be exploitation. If those who expressed this view believe that such exploitation can be diminished by a unified labor movement and collective bargaining, they did not so state.

With one exception, all respondents expressed the view that the employer has more collective bargaining power than the trade unions. The single dissenter stated that the question of relative power depends upon the industry and the time in which the bargain is made. By "time" is meant economic factors which might cause a sudden shift in favor of the union position. A CISL member stated that the collective bargaining power of the unions could be increased if the federations bargained jointly, with one spokesman representing the entire group. However, he added that such a prospect is unlikely. As a group, the provincial secretaries expressed the nuances of collective bargaining less often than the national union and federation leadership. The responses of the former reflect partly the political orientation of their jobs and partly the successful resistance by employers against the shifting of the locus of collective bargaining down to the provincial and plant level.

THE DANISH EMPLOYER

Danish firms are predominantly small. According to Census of Industries figures of 1948, approximately half of the manufacturing firms hire from zero to a maximum of five wage earners. Of the remainder of the 102,303 firms, 10,000 had from six to twenty employees; 2,800 employed within a range of twenty-one to one hundred; and some 500 firms had employees in excess of one hundred. Twenty-three per cent of Danish employers belong to the employers' confederation, and they employ approximately half of the wage earners. Employers belonging to the coöperative movement do not affiliate with the employers' association. For purposes of the study, firms hiring up to twenty wage earners are considered small; from twenty-one to one hundred, medium-sized; and over one hundred, large. The sample includes all three groups, including two organizations belonging to the coöperative movement.

In eight of the twenty-five firms, the plant manager is also the owner of the firm. The median age of the group is fifty-six, and the range from thirty-eight to seventy-two. The majority of the employers have college educations, mostly in civil or mechanical engineering, in contrast with the Italian group, whose college education is in either liberal arts or law. There is also a notable degree of upward movement, when the positions of the Danish employers are compared to those of their fathers. More than half of the fathers of the sample group were industrial workers or farmers. Most of the owner-operated firms were built in two generations, the father having begun his job career as a craftsman. For the remainder of this group, the firm was developed from zero in the lifetime of the present incumbent. The "rugged individualist" philosophy which appears in the sample is found among those employers who built their own organization in a lifetime of work.

Danish employers can be grouped into two broad types. The first, the owner-oriented employer, is generally the founder of the company, or his son. He is conscious of his rights as sole decision-maker in the organization. He dislikes interference from persons he believes technically less qualified to run an organization toward which he feels a high personal attachment. The second, the professionally oriented employer, is the head of a firm considered large by Danish standards, and has a less emotional attachment to the company. To him, union representatives are an additional factor to consider in making decisions in which the overriding criterion is what has to be done to achieve the primary objective, a dynamic organization.

Both eschew display of wealth through conspicuous consumption. While cynical Danes explain this behavior as an outcome encouraged by the tax system, others explain this modesty as the Danish cultural characteristic of social restraint. While the Italian employer gives the impression of belonging to a different social class from that of his workers, the Danish employer plays the part of the industrial leader who has risen out of the craftsman class, representing the most intelligent and competent in that group. If he is placed in the same room with union representatives, it would be difficult to tell them apart, in contrast to the Italian employer, whose appearance and demeanor would be more easily distinguishable.

Top executives of a large Danish firm are concerned with achieving acceptance from each other. The common pyramidal picture of a company organization does not accurately depict the diffusion of decision-making in Danish organizations. Each top executive has allocated to him a particular phase of management, and his relationship with the others is that of an equal. To be sure, the difference, compared with corporations in other industrial societies, is not great. But the dissimilarity, however small, makes an important difference in the tone of relationships inside Danish firms and with other organizations. In the competitive struggle for higher positions in the organization, the winner in any given round has the task of selling himself to the loser, or runs the risk of being isolated for not doing so. This encourages a rule-by-consent, which permeates the union-management relationship. The atmosphere does not lend itself to power struggles, either in the organization or in labor relations.

For most of these executives, the local and national union leaders are rather remote figures. The collective bargaining of new agreements is handled generally through the industry associations, so that the executives' contact with trade unionism is with unobtrusive shop stewards, and to a lesser degree with the presidents of local unions. A relationship with higher-level union representatives may occur in the rare instance when a grievance arising out of an existing agreement has to be taken to the industry level for settlement, or when a new contract has to be negotiated.

With the exception of a few rugged individualists who have managed to build large firms within their lifetimes, Danish employers accept the group determination of the terms of employment. The minority who are not amenable to dealing with trade union representatives are also not too keen about adhering to the policies of the employers' association. The majority, however, subscribe to the objective of national uniformity in the formal terms of employment. They prefer presenting themselves as a solid phalanx to labor, agreeing among themselves, even on such details as the use of newspapers in employee recruitment. There is a saying current in Denmark that you can never catch one of the parties indulging in behavior which is not a conscious interpretation of a particular rule. In a sense, Danish employer organization is another link in the successive chain of organization of productive labor in the economy. It represents the last in a series of associations through which an individual can progress in a lifetime of work.

In Denmark, the relationship between labor and management is not disturbed by conflict over vital issues. Collective bargaining on the company level is not a subject of controversy. The practice of industry-wide bargaining in Denmark has been flexible enough to serve the needs of trade union officials, employers, and workers at the plant level. By contrast, in Italy labor leaders have not succeeded to any great degree in tapping differences in firm productivity in a manner that would not challenge the existence of the trade union as a national institution. To be sure, the concept of productivity in individual firms is a somewhat vague idea for some Danish employers and trade union officials. The employers express themselves on the virtue of increasing productivity, but are not precise as to the role of workers and their organizations in increasing productivity, and are equally indefinite on how such increases should be translated into higher real wages. Some of the trade union officials, for their part, while accepting in principle the idea of increasing productivity, have to contend with the egalitarian spirit of Danish workers, when translating the abstraction into specific firm-by-firm policies. Consequently, the subject tends to be relegated to after-dinner speeches, and its latent possibility for controversy has not materialized.

The greatest resistance to trade unionism among Danish employers is directed against the organization of clerical employees. Strong opposition comes from large industrial organizations and from firms using office employees exclusively. Some of these companies have their own company unions and use terms of employment as a means of discouraging organization by the Clerical Workers' Union affiliated with the Danish federation. The employer association recognizes the union, but its collective bargaining agreement with it is disregarded by a number of prominent employers. The opposition to clerical organization is in part politically inspired. Although employers accept the idea of industrial workers' supporting the Social Democrat party, they are reluctant to see a strong clerical workers' union within the structure of the labor movement cause a decrease in their political influence.

The Danish employer who heads a firm belonging to the coöperative movement is in a unique position. As such, he is technically an employee of the trade union movement. He does not belong to the employers' confederation. He generally has risen out of trade unionism and feels he must make his firm a model of labor relations. On the other hand, he expresses his problems in the universal employer language of controlling costs and increasing sales. By granting his employees new types of fringe benefits, he sets a basis for demands made on the members of the employers' association.

Most Danish supervisors belong to one of eight foremen unions. In an agreement between the employers and the trade union federation, employees promoted to supervisory ranks are automatically moved from the trade unions into their own organizations, bringing with them their seniority and their vested rights in their pension fund. The dominant functional activity of these organizations is training, and they cannot bargain collectively for their members. In the metal association, one of the largest, whenever the workers in the trade union obtain a wage increase, the supervisors receive a percentage increase. They can ask the association to represent them in individual negotiations with their employers for further merit increases. In this way, regardless of the degree of upward movement, economic organization of the Danish workers remains with them throughout their job careers.

A major problem expressed by supervisors is a felt loss of status. The employers, they claimed, treat the shop steward with more respect than they do their own supervisors.

They go to him in order to determine what changes have been made in the terms and conditions of employment rather than to us. We have no office, while the shop steward does. In the United States, a worker generally addresses himself to the supervisor when he has a complaint to make against management. In Denmark, he goes to the shop steward. Moreover, the joint production committees further decrease our prestige by allowing the worker representatives to smoke cigars with top management. Lastly, we are not really the deputies of top management. They do not consider us as such.

These are typical complaints. Supervisors want to be given more authority and to hold more frequent meetings with top management. If they quit their jobs, it is not because of low wages but because they lack the authority commensurate with their responsibilities in controlling work standards. It is difficult, they say, to exercise control over workers who know the supervisor possesses no authority. The job of a supervisor no longer brings any significant difference in returns—other than the opportunity for the wife of a foreman to brag about the title of her husband.

Concept of Responsibilities

The dominant expressed objective of the respondents in the employer group was expansion of the firm. In some instances, the statement was qualified by an expression of the desire to produce goods of high quality at the cheapest possible prices, or by the suggestion that the purpose of business expansion is to create job security for a maximum number of employees. These qualifications were expressed more often by plant managers of large firms than by respondents from small, owner-operated enterprises. The responses are summarized in Table 34.

Expressions of major problems differentiate by size of company. The large employer is concerned with the maintenance of a skilled, contented work force at a minimum of labor turnover. The small employer has the problem of finding liquid capital and maintaining his sales. The large employer articulates more often a concern over rela-

TABLE 34

Danish Employer Objectives by Size of Firm
(Per Cent)

Nature of objective	Large	Medium	Small
Satisfactory relationship with employees	50	38	38
Expansion of firm	33	25	12
Production of quality goods	0	25	37
Keep firm going	0	12	13
Profitability	17	0	0
Total	100	100	100
Number	9	7	8

tionships with managerial personnel and workers in his organization than does the manager of the small organization. Representative comments included the following:

It is difficult to maintain company loyalty among workers, as in the United States.

Workers do not associate improved terms of employment with increasing responsibility toward the company.

My major problem is to see that the employees want to belong to the organization and that they give their best effort to it.

Making young workers show responsibility . . .

Finding dependable female workers . . .

No problems; only two cases in the labor court in the past eight years.

Communists have taken over the union local and the effect has been that new employees are Communists too; we have been trying to combat this by off-the-street employment.

How to determine what the true feelings of a worker are, not what he says, is my problem.

The difficulty here has been labor turnover; out of a work force of four hundred, we lost two hundred in one year; the trouble is poor supervision.

The preponderant majority of employers in the sample believe that their responsibility toward workers is to provide job security and a "good" work place. The item does not scale, the differences being expressed in what constitutes a good *arbejdsplads*. The term is used either with reference to safe conditions of work or an atmosphere such as to make the employees "happy." Two employers stated that they had no responsibility toward workers because it had been removed by collective bargaining and the law of labor standards. What was the best way to improve the condition of workers? Almost unanimously, they cited an increase in productivity. One owner-manager stated that the goal could be achieved by fighting alcoholism among the workers and by combating the labor unions, which place obstacles in the paths of workers who are inclined to increase their tempo of work. Another employer-owner stated that it could be done by being more productive and not trying to take money from the rich, and the plant manager of a large organization expressed the hope that workers would interest themselves in the economics of the firm.

Like the Italian employers, the majority of the Danish respondents believe that employer functions and responsibilities are different from what they used to be. There are no discernible differences by size of company in affirmative replies. The affirmative responses are concerned with the problem of maintaining a prosperous firm under continual trade union pressure which increases the cost of labor. Also included in this category are the new responsibilities of providing employment security for the worker and the maintenance of a stable work force. Affirmative responses included:

> How to reduce prices and at the same time increase wages . . .

> How to meet the ever-increasing demand for more wages and fringe benefits . . .

> There are greater responsibilities due to more capital to take care of.

> Preserve industry in Denmark and reduce waste by instilling a sense of duty in workers . . .

Negative replies included:

> I have always considered the welfare of my workers of prime importance.

> It is still the same: to make the company prosperous, although the method of coöperation has changed.

Attitudes toward the Purpose of Trade Unionism

Among Danish employer opinions on the purpose of trade unionism, the bulk of the responses are divided equally between emphasis on improving the terms of employment of workers through collective bargaining and emphasis on promoting coöperation between the employer and workers. The latter is the expression, which recurred throughout the study in Denmark, of the worth of *samarbejde*, an important value in Danish ethos. The man who proposes compromise and coöperation with opponents achieves greater public acclaim than the individual who proposes a fight.

Representative responses on the purpose of trade unionism included the following comments:

Bring about a smooth coöperation between employers and workers . . .

Improve terms of employment without ruining society . . .

Represent the employees in collective bargaining . . .

Express worker needs and help reconcile them with needs of the firm . . .

Develop mutual trust and confidence . . .

Get workers to understand management methods . . .

Act as a control on workers . . .

Organize workers, with the exception of clerical workers . . .

See that worker effort equals the demanded wage . . .

Stick to trade union problems, not political ones . . .

Following is a quotation from a large employer in the provinces:

The purpose of these trade union organizations was originally to fight for wages. Their work has changed considerably. Much has to be done on both sides to teach workers about employer problems. The purpose of trade unions should be to make the rank and file sensible about new management methods and explain time studies to them. The trade union movement has done something by establishing shop-steward schools. There is still some misunderstanding, however, between workers and employers on these matters.

Responses on the weaknesses of trade unionism reflected differences in perspective between employers and trade union representatives. The former felt that the labor official is too prone to yield to immediate pressures which are manifestations of irrationality on the part of workers. Rather than assume the burden of control over these pressures, the labor leader follows the line of least resistance by passing them to the employer. Criticism was also leveled at some aspects of collectivism. Although employers accept the group determination of the terms of employment, they complain of the control of output and the stifling of individual initiative which results from trade union insistence upon uniformity of earnings among employees. Their comments included:

They do not allow the exercise of individual initiative among workers; they do not like to see some workers making more money than others.

They are always making demands. They demand a nursery because there is one at the Carlsberg brewery, in spite of the fact that I have no women employees of child-bearing age. They demand shower rooms, which then are not used.

They have a stranglehold on jobs. Their source of power is their control of the available jobs.

It is absurd to have so many unions in one plant. We cannot provide workers with the opportunity of a better job because of union restrictions as to who should do the work.

They are inclined to adopt a policy of grievances applicable to all workers. It is easier for the shop steward to press the foreman on concessions than to tell the worker there is no merit in his position.

The labor leaders and the leaders of the Social Democrat party are afraid to tell workers that they have a responsibility to increase productivity and eliminate deliberate restrictions on output.

The intelligence level of the shop steward is declining as the standard of living rises, because of the increased preference of the competent workers for family and leisure activity.

The trade unions have changed. Twenty years ago, the trade union leaders used to drink a lot. In the ten years I have been here, I have never seen a drunken labor official. The General Workers may be an exception. When we bargain with them, the conference room is laden with beer. What motivates a labor leader? A good salary for one thing. Then there is the possibility of being a politician in the town where he lives or in Parliament. Or he may become a cabinet minister or a prime minister and dance with the queen and eat with the king.

Attitudes toward Labor Leaders

The belief that part of the role of the labor leader is to induce workers to accept the employer's point of view is manifested in the employers' responses on the qualities of a good trade union leader. Above all, a good labor leader possesses flexibility, fairness, and common sense. He should be technically competent, and should have the ability to persuade the members to follow his leadership. Emphasis on this element of control appears frequently in the responses: ". . . ability to control the members"; ". . . get members to abide by his decisions"; ". . . prevent grievances which have no merit from coming up in the grievance procedure." The employer, consequently, prefers a strong labor leader, and he expresses impatience with the official who shifts his position because of rank-and-file pressure.

Danish employers were also asked what they thought were the differences among labor leaders. Principal differences cited centered on flexibility, political outlook, intelligence, and technical preparation. A labor leader lacking in flexibility is one who shows the disinclination or the inability to accept at least partly the needs of management at the plant level. Responses included:

It is not a matter of political affiliation, this flexibility; I have a Communist trade union representative who is very flexible.

The differences in flexibility are really an expression of the workers who choose the leaders. Another factor is, the higher the level of leadership, the greater is flexibility.

They differ in courage. Some of them are afraid profit-sharing plans may make the workers love their company too much.

Some of them are very clever [klog]. Mr. _____ is very shrewd. He declared, for example, that the workers could not get any money for Christmas because of the short week. He therefore stated that it was a social question rather than an economic one. The latter, of course, is the pertinent one for the employer, but it was difficult to reject the demand.

The differences between them are simple; they are either Socialists or Communists.

They differ in the security of their positions.

They differ in their attitudes toward increased productivity.

To a considerable extent, the way the Danish employer views the labor leader is a mirror of reconciled attitudes of employer and workers toward each other.

Views of Workers

Danish workers, unlike those in Italy, have no strongly hostile feelings toward employers. Employers were asked what they believed to be the reasons for this lack of hostility. They gave a social explanation, an economic interpretation, and an analysis of mutual acceptance of trade unions, which in substance reverted to social and economic factors. Comments offering a social explanation were expressed in such terms as the following:

We are a quiet, peaceful, and socially controlled people.

We are relatively highly educated, and there are smaller differences in the education and training among us.

We talk the same language and understand each other's problems.

We do not fight each other; it is against our temperament, despite the fact we may have differences in interests.

It is difficult to get into an argument with people who are not strangers.

We are lazy; we like to have things run smoothly to avoid clashes of intellect.

The economic interpretation concerns the high standard of living of the Danish worker, and more specifically, the smaller dissimilarity between his plane of living and that of his employer:

We do not appear to each other like kings and paupers.

The Danish workers have a high standard of living; so what should they be hostile about?

The institutional explanation has to do with the acceptance of the role of the labor movement:

The organized trade union and the political power of workers have brought about mutual respect.

We accept the trade union official as performing a necessary role in controlling the behavior of workers.

It is the social interpretation, however, which dominates the responses explaining the difference between Italy and Denmark in worker hostility.

Among critical employer attitudes toward workers, a dominant one emphasized what is considered an unwillingness to accept the company point of view.

They do not understand the economic problems of the firm.

They feel they have job rights and no responsibilities.

I pay them above the union scale but they deliberately restrict their output. If someone produces more than the minimum set by the workers, he is coerced and required to give them the difference.

I would like them to refer to the company as "we," but for them it is "they."

It is easier to talk to the shop steward than it is with them.

They should try to be more productive and not try to take money away from the rich.

They are irritating when they make an elephant out of a mosquito.

One employer described his attitude toward workers in the following terms:

Danish men are born either conservative or socialist. The former is creative, ambitious, has a strong impulse to acquire money and prestige in business. The latter is a collectivist, and not especially ambitious. He quickly becomes a pessimist and a socialist when he sees the limits of his intelligence and opportunities. His socialist mentality consists of splitting up into shares the opportunity created by others, the conservatives. I am proud, however, that in Denmark we have succeeded in integrating these two contrasting mentalities.

The Meaning of Success

Success for the Danish employer is associated with the creation of a company and watching it expand. The large employers tended to associate the running of a dynamic organization with a contented work force, while the small employers spoke more often in terms of achieving economic independence. Most of the respondents regarded success as a sense of improvement vis-à-vis their particular situations.

It is a sense of continuing improvement in one's firm and standard of life, compared to those in my profession.

A sense of having created something . . .

When the workers say they like working for my company—but I do not like the word "success"; it reminds me of an opera singer.

Keeping the factory operating continuously and having labor peace . . .

A happy life; some employers want medals and others, more money.

Like most employers, a better plant, rising wages, and a good return on investment . . .

It is the satisfaction derived from running a plant well.

We want a sense of improvement, as all human beings do.

A prosperous company, a sound economy, and happy employees . . .

Danish Labor Leaders' Perceptions of Employers

In contrast with Italy, the image of the employer does not engender strong feelings in the Danish labor leader. He regards employer responsibility toward workers as a contractual one, not one based on a morally inspired paternalism. Asked what they feel is the responsibility of employers toward their workers, Danish labor leaders overwhelmingly cited that stipulated by the law and the collective bargaining agreement. One labor leader, after apologizing for his "impertinence," stated that Danish employers do not have too great a responsibility. Only in two instances was any hostile sentiment expressed. "The Communists say that they are all bad. I nearly believe the same. The employers in the _____ industry belong to a very strong association which directs all the attitudes they take against us. . . ." "Some employers adhere to the spirit of the agreement, but some of them see what they can put over on us by stressing the commas. . . ."

This view of the employer is related to the more limited role which the Danish trade union officials ascribe to the managerial function.

The "good" employer provides a satisfying climate for work and a minimum amount of supervision. The responsibility for the quantity and quality of work is just as much the worker's and the trade union official's as it is the employer's. In fact, under ideal circumstances, the good employer tells the worker what has to be done and then lets him do it in his own way. In sum, he allows his employees to work on their own responsibility, pays the wages prescribed in the agreement, adheres to the law, and provides physical conditions of work which create a "pleasure in work."

The majority of the national trade union officials believe the employers are favorably disposed to trade unionism. Their comments included:

The employer sees us as an instrument of achieving personal goals.

There is considerable cohesion between employers and trade union officials. They accept collective bargaining as being in their interest.

The trade unions provide them with the opportunity of complaining about worker behavior.

They use the union as a means of rejecting worker demands by pointing to the collective bargaining agreement.

They prefer settling terms of employment with one party only.

The trade union protects them against unfair competition.

Thus the labor leaders feel that employers accept group determination of the terms of employment as much as they do. The concept of uniformity of employment terms is also in the interest of the employer, who sees it as an instrument of protection against other employers and as a means of placing the onus of an aberrant worker on the trade union official. The semblance of uniformity of terms of employment in a written collective bargaining agreement is in the interest of both the employer and the union.

Several officials believe employers merely tolerate trade unions or are opposed to them. One of these officials leads a union that meets strong resistance from employers for recognition. The others lead unions in the maritime industry, an economic activity traditionally characterized by an individualistic employer philosophy and a strong sense of protest on the part of the workers.

In sum, Danish labor leader perceptions of employers are of individuals with functions severely circumscribed by law, custom, and collective bargaining. These limitations have their origin in the guild system of control of the relationship between masters and journeymen. The Danish employer is not a remote figure, but an individual with whom decisions are shared in production and distribution of earnings. Labor leaders view him more as a collaborator than as an adversary in a situation wherein a gain for one is a loss for the other. Consequently, the sharp image of usurper of prerogatives and enemy of the working classes, found in Italy, is, but for a very small left-wing minority, not to be found in Denmark.

In Denmark, insight was sought into the problem of trade union corruption by an inquiry on the causes of its absence. By asking Danish employers and industrial relations personnel what factors they believed accounted for its absence, a record was developed indirectly of the conditions which nurture its presence. They stated that the problem was negligible or non-existent in their country, unless one blew out of proportion the acceptance of a dinner engagement or petty cases of embezzlement of unemployment insurance funds. As a factor explaining its absence, they relied heavily in their statements on the close contacts between leaders and rank and file in an atmosphere of idealism and camaraderie. The importance of labor education in trade union activity was an expression of this socializing process between officials and members. The following factors were cited: (1) smallness of the Danish community and the difficulty of living isolated from the stream of community life; (2) existence of locals small enough for members to know each other personally; (3) importance of other values in life besides money; (4) feeling of group solidarity that pervades the ranks of workers; (5) lack of opportunity to reap substantial benefits from corruption; (6) close communication between leaders and rank and file; (7) critical surveillance by Danes of any evidence of increased consumption by a member of the community; (8) high level of education and social awareness. The most common responses referred to the smallness of the community and the highly coercive pressures in Danish society. The social explanations by far outweigh economic interpretations of trade union corruption.

Comments from the industrial relations group included:

There is too much pressure from the rank and file that the labor leader live in the same style of life as the worker. In your country, the workers may think it is smart and clever for a trade union officer to amass money, Here he had better not be seen in a shiny black car.

The country is small and we are nearly one big family. The trade union organizations are small, and that makes contact with the labor leader easier.

The members are too close to the operation of their union.

The rank and file is better educated.

There is little opportunity for corruption.

There are strong moral feelings against it.

The cars and houses of labor leaders had better not be so big. It would cause criticism.

There is less cultivation of smartness in consumption and high income than in your country.

There is just too much compulsion from a variety of community sources on the labor leader.

He is afraid to indulge in conspicuous consumption.

The basic motive of the Dane, envy, does not permit it. He is constantly checking on the consumption habits of others.

Tradition makes the trade unions fine and honorable institutions, and the labor leaders naturally conform to this tradition.

The people in Denmark act as a control on each other.

It is part of the Danish characteristic of seeing any extreme position as ridiculous.

Labor leader corruption exists where corruption in the society is commonplace.

The responses of employers were in somewhat different perspective. They cited the inadvisability of conspicuous consumption in a country such as Denmark, and the proximity of members of the Danish community to each other. They also specified the democratic sensitiveness in Danish trade unionism.

In their labor education the rank and file and the leaders come together in the same classroom and the former is quite often the teacher; this creates respect for each other.

Danish workers are much more interested in the working of their trade unions.

It is fundamentally a problem of maintaining close communication between leaders and rank and file.

The presidents of the local unions are members of the executive board of the national union. The national union officers know many of the members by their first name. They knew each other when they were both apprentices.

In sum, the employers tended to stress the greater participation of the membership in their organizations and the greater flow of communication between themselves and their representatives.

A comparison of the characteristics of Danish and Italian employers suggests the following "employer" variables exerting an influence on the labor movements in those countries: (1) the extent to which the employer rejects the role that the labor official seeks to play in industrial relations; (2) the prevalence of a legalistic approach to the solution of industrial problems, which serves to inhibit the effective remedying of problems in a particular context; (3) the degree to which the employer is critical of the technical competency of the labor official; (4) the existence of pressures created by the plant-orientation of the employer, compared to the trade-union– and labor-movement– orientation of the labor official; (5) differences in education, or more important, differences in opportunity for higher education, between employers and the working class; (6) the relative inability of the working class to move up toward occupations and roles whose prestige value is closer to that of the employer class; (7) the extent to which employer and employee dissimilarities are social and economic rather than functional and technical; (8) the degree to which the employer views trade unionism as an instrument in the frustration of his goals.

In these benchmarks, Italy rates "more." The significant dissimilarities of national temperament have their impact on the employer–labor-leader relationship. Italians are inclined to view a labor problem against an abstract, idealistic, and rigid principle, whose interpretation may produce conflict. Danes operate in a more democratic atmosphere, marked by the acceptance of the power and status of the labor leader, and a tone of restraint in group relations.

The differences, however, should not obscure the similarities. In both countries, the employer is aware of the needs of his plant and critical of the broader orientation of his employees. Small employers, or those who have built large organizations in a lifetime of work, are jealous of their prerogatives of making their own decisions concerning what they consider their personal creations. Big or small, employers are sensitive to differences in technical competency and resentful of the political consciousness of labor officials.

THE INDUSTRIAL RELATIONS PUBLIC

The third group of respondents in the study comprises the industrial relations public. They are individuals who, while not members of either party in a particular country, either are exerting an influence in industrial relations or have the potential to do so. They make their point of view felt through mass communications media, influence in government, or their proximity to political parties and workers. The occupations they hold differ from one country to the next, depending upon the maturity of the industrial relations function and the extent of public interest in the labor problem. They include lawyers, mediators, arbitrators, labor market experts, teachers, social scientists, journalists, politicians, government employees, and writers. In Italy, the "sample" included journalists, university professors, high school teachers, Catholic Actionists, writers, politicians, priests, and government officials. Their political affiliation ranged from the Liberty party on the right of the Christian Democrats to the Communist party on the left. In Denmark, with the exception of members of religious organizations, the group was approximately similar. In Denmark, the members of the clergy, in contrast with Italy, exert little or no influence on trade unionism and labor relations. The Danish group included arbitrators, but in Italy the use of labor arbitration as a means of settling grievances which arise out of existing collective bargaining agreements is relatively unknown. The use of this industrial relations public helps to place the labor leader in perspective in his society, and furnishes culturally oriented benchmarks of what constitutes outstanding labor leadership. At the time the study was going on, it also provided interpretive guidance and helped to create a groundswell of interest. With the increasing maturity of industrial relations there arises a corps of individuals whose income or part thereof derives directly or indirectly from the increasingly complex relationships arising out of large-scale industrial employment. Consequently, the composition of this sample group shifts from social critics to technical labor specialists of different types.

Interviews of an industrial relations public have these purposes in view. What does the public conceive the function of the labor leadership to be? What is their estimate of the job they are doing? The items used center on attitudes toward trade unionism, estimate of the relative influence of the parties in industrial relations, and estimate of the labor leaders. As the result of the Italian experience, additional items were used in Denmark, but all of them fall into these three headings. If these basic groups ferret out particular issues within a country, additional items are used to probe into them.

In sum, the development of an industrial relations sample group provides the following advantages: (1) through the configuration of the group, a measure of the stage of the industrial relations system and status of labor unions in a particular country; (2) interpretive guidance from informed individuals in the sample group; (3) opportunity to ferret out issues industrial relations spokesmen are dealing with at a particular time; (4) estimates of the relative economic and political influence of the parties in industrial relations; (5) middle-class perceptions of organized labor; (6) a critique of trade union methods and objectives, and proposals for changes; (7) insight into the differences among labor leaders; (8) clues to possible shifts in industrial relations practices. In brief, the inclusion of such a group offers the opportunity of placing the trade union and industrial relations system of a country in proper perspective.

The Italian Industrial Relations Public

There is no "informed public opinion" in Italy. There exists, rather, the opinion of the professional politician expressing the needs of a particular political party. And there is that of the social critic, the book writer, and the newspaperman, all of whom tend to perceive situations through the eyes of a political party. And the views of these informed publics use the same political framework in their estimate of the Italian employer. Thus Italian public opinion becomes a heterogeneous series of relatively fixed political positions. In some degree, the university professor is an exception to this political intransigence. He tends to be more objective, although on a particular issue he is likely to side with the position of the employer. What accounts for his latent pro-employer sympathies? The employer, after all, is a technician, legal minded, shrewd, and possessing *le belle maniere*. If the professor becomes relatively well-to-do, he may also acquire the same mentality of looking down at menial work. For these reasons, even to those striving to be objective, the Italian employer is more likely to present a heroic image than the Italian trade union official.

A factor limiting the size of the industrial relations public in Italy is the lack of a substantial and influential "third party." Such a group appears in a country *pari passu* with the emergence of influential trade unions and a voluntaristic method of group determination of conditions of employment. In Italy, arbitration has not become a commonly accepted means of settling labor disputes. The major newspapers, owned by the political parties, show a disinterestedness in industrial reporting. For a comprehensive day-by-day coverage of events in trade unionism and labor relations, one has to rely on the papers of the Communist or Socialist parties.

Noteworthy attitudes toward trade unionism and industrial relations are uncovered in the very process of constructing a sample group. For instance, there appeared to be a lack of interest on the part of teachers in Italy when they were approached in connection with the study. They come from middle-class and petty bourgeoisie groups, who, except for such people as labor law professors, know little about collective bargaining, and care less. The most closely related subject taught in the universities is labor law, offered in both the faculties of jurisprudence and economics. No separate departments in business administration or in the behavioral sciences exist. The study of industrial psychology and sociology is just developing in Italy, compared to Denmark, where it is advanced. The labor law course is closer to a theoretical analysis of the rights of labor under the statutes than to a study of contemporary industrial relations. Courses in labor economics, industrial relations, and personnel administration, as such, are not to be found in the government universities. Consequently, the labor law professor in Italy comes closest to the area of interest of an investigator of labor problems. The solutions he sees generally are not voluntaristic ones, but rather those which lie in the passage of additional laws.

Italian professors have a legalistic orientation toward the labor problem. Asked what the employer-labor relationship is, they are inclined to state what it is and should be under the law. As a group, they are more sensitive to the revelation of subjective preferences. A query on what, in the judgment of the interviewee, should be the function of trade unionism is countered with the reply that such a question seeks to reveal personal philosophy. This legal orientation carries over to their views of the split in the labor movement. The thought of the evolution of three sets of collective bargaining law is not a neat idea to contemplate. The constitutional guarantees in Italy of a just wage should be implemented by law specifying criteria for wage determination which would assure a worker a *vita dignitosa*. In sum, what is morally just should be expressed through the nobility of the law.

Italian students themselves express little interest in contemporary industrial relations problems. The educational system tends to separate the rich from the poor early in their educational careers and exposes them to dissimilar training experiences, which crystallize the differences in perceptions that clash later in adulthood. It provides for the educated elite an intensive training in the classics and physical sciences on the precollege level and specialized professional training at the university, which differentiates them further in outlook from the leadership which arises out of the working classes, self-taught from contemporary experiences.

An attitude survey of Italian high school students reveals their disinterestedness in the labor problem. The sample included boys and girls in the sixteen-to-eighteen age group, whose fathers come predominantly from clerical, managerial, and professional groups. Sixty-six per cent replied in the negative to the question whether they interested themselves in the labor problem. Responses included: "I feel superior to the workers. . . ." "It is a problem for the Russians to solve. . . ." "The worker is treated well enough. . . ." "If they want a raise, they should work harder. . . ." A second item was designed to reflect the value preferences of the respondents by asking them what they would do with a sum of money which they did not need. The forced choices included (1) take a trip abroad; (2) rebuild a plant; and (3) maintain a trade union. Half of the group preferred taking a trip abroad. Three per cent would aid a union, and 40 per cent voluntarily stated that in no case would they aid a labor union. These sentiments should be interpreted on the premise that the sixteen-to-eighteen-year-old Italian is a more mature individual than his counterpart in the United States.[1]

Asked for its estimate of the relative economic and political influence of the parties in industrial relations, more than half of the Italian group stated that the former depends on changing circumstances and that bargaining power shifted with the industry and with time. The preponderant majority of the group, however, believed that the employers had greater political influence.

They [employers] have succeeded in preventing the implementation of the constitution by the passage of laws.

The employers have more influence in the administration of government and in the passage of laws; the union, in forcing the government to intervene in labor disputes.

Employers have an influence on choices for strategic public posts, by working through the bureaucrats of the political parties. These posts are filled primarily by people who owe their allegiance to the Christian Democrat party.

[1] See discussion of Pier Giovanni Grasso, *Gioventù di metà secolo.*

Political influence is wielded by the dozen or so monopolies in Italy. They see to it that the government does not do anything which runs against their interests.

The influence of the employer is financial, while that of the union is in controlling votes. This creates a stalemate and conservatism. The majority in Italy does not govern. The passage of law by the majority is nullified by the minority after its passage.

The majority feel that employers tolerate unionism. None stated that the employers favor trade unionism. Three of the thirty-five respondents feel they would like to see the unions destroyed. Comments representative of the majority included the following: "They are too shrewd to be eliminated entirely. . . ." "They object to the political orientation of Italian trade unionism and to being presented with problems over which they have no control. . . ."

TABLE 35

Critical Attitudes of the Italian Public Group toward Labor Leaders

Subject of criticism	Per cent	
Goal orientation	51	
Are politically ambitious		24
Do not grapple with unemployment problem		24
Have no long-range point of view		3
Technical incompetence	15	
Employer relationship	34	
Are subservient to employers		12
Are not as shrewd as employers		12
Cause deterioration of relationship		7
Demand more than employer can pay		3
Total	100	
Number	32	

Table 35 summarizes critical attitudes of the Italian industrial relations public toward labor leaders. The dominant responses are similar to those of the employers. The trade union officials, it was said, use their positions to pursue political ambitions rather than to strengthen trade unionism and collective bargaining. Or they lack a technical preparation in approaching the complex problems arising out of the employment relationship. For both the employer and the public groups, the latter comment is a typical reaction of technicians in their respective fields looking at the political figure of the labor leader, evaluating him as a technician. Their view contrasts with that of workers, whose judgment of the primary qualification of their representative is that he "can talk to them" and can deal with the "big shots" (*pezzi grossi*) in positions of power in Italian society.

Responses on the biggest weakness, if any, of trade union leaders are associated with the replies on the purpose of trade unionism (Table 36). That is to say, those who are critical of the political consciousness of union officials are inclined to state that the purpose of trade unionism is to improve the terms of employment of workers through the

TABLE 36

Attitudes of the Italian Public Group toward the Purpose of Trade Unionism

Nature of purpose	Per cent	
Economic improvement of workers	57	
Improve employment terms		38
Provide social welfare service		13
Eliminate unemployment		6
Labor-management relations	9	
Help increase productivity		3
Bargain collectively		3
Improve relationships		3
Political ends	28	
Promote passage of labor legislation		13
Participate in government		3
Help preserve liberty		6
Make capitalism work		3
Do away with capitalism		3
Social and cultural improvement	6	
Total	*100*	
Number	34	

collective bargaining process. This association also exists for those who believe trade union officials lack technical preparation to perform their jobs. There is some evidence also that the replies reflect the political orientation of the respondents, although it was not possible to ascertain the extent of the relationship.

Statements on the weakness of Italian trade unionism invariably turned to the characteristics of Italian workers themselves. Their qualities, it is felt, are not propitious to the growth of a militant, independent trade unionism. The views of the Italian industrial relations public on the qualities of Italian workers which reflect themselves in the tone of labor leadership in Italy are indicated below. The dominant responses center around (1) fatalism, by which is implied a disinclination to change and control their situation in life; (2) greater political, rather than trade union, orientation, which makes them inclined to view the labor official as a political representative; (3) lack of faith in the representativeness of government and attendant disillusionment about the worthwhileness of group activity. Representative comments included the following:

Italian workers are too fatalistic; they complain and do nothing about their situation.

They are more conscious of their political leadership.

Their poverty and ignorance make them politically conscious.

They have little faith in government.

Southern workers isolate themselves from society.

The struggle over the plant committees has disillusioned workers.

They have no faith in employers.

They are afraid to cause further divisions among themselves.

They do not know how to express their needs.

They want socialism, by which they mean justice.

Their depressed condition makes it difficult for leaders to arise from their ranks.

They need a living wage in order to practice trade unionism.

Their intellectual laziness makes them victims of agitators.

They criticize without understanding problems.

The majority of the respondents felt that the Church plays an excessive and unfortunate role in the employment relationship. A minority felt the Church should play a positive role, either because of the threat of Communism or because of the necessity of implementing Christian principles in the employment relationship. One member of the clergy in the group believes that the Catholic Church could possess a greater sensitivity to the problems of workers. "Our priests are philosophers; few of them understand workers and their problems. . . ." Negative responses included: "The priests use religion to support the ruling political party. . . ." "Italian priests are ignorant. . . ." "They have too much power already. . . ." "They use money and jobs to control workers. . . ." "Industrial relations should be based, not on Christian charity, but on the idea of equality. . . ."

"They are too conservative. . . ." "They should only practice religion. . . ."

Since the group, more than its counterpart in Denmark, was critical of the state of affairs in its country, the respondents were asked whether they would propose any changes. The replies are associated with what a particular respondent believes to be the purpose of trade unionism. As noted in Table 37, the dominant responses emphasized more education and training for workers and structural reform of society, as well as a shift in the orientation of the labor movement away from the dominance of political parties. Again, the political orientation of the respondent appears to be expressed in the proposals for change. Thus,

TABLE 37

Italian Public Group Proposals for Change

Type of change	Per cent
Structural reforms of society	60
More education	34
Less political dominance of unions	6
Total	100
Number	32

the Socialists and Social Democrats spoke of a planned society and a socialist state, while the more conservative respondents expressed the necessity of increasing public control within the existing political framework of Italy.

The Danish Industrial Relations Public

To the Danish public group, the employers are rather acceptable fellows. They are neither heroes nor villains. They are favorable toward trade unions (which is sensible), with the exception of a few rugged individualists. They are practical realists not inclined to make a fight. The consensus is that the employer association is stronger than the trade union federation because of the more rigid discipline it exercises over its members. They are more flexible; more informed; more realistic; they lack ostentatiousness; they are ready to compromise with a point of view different from their own. They are realists, aware that different employees represent different costs, but willing to meet at least partially the trade union need of standardization of employment terms. The public group is less suspicious of the political intent of employers than of that of trade union leaders. Employers are not abstractions which can be easily disliked as such, but specific individuals, many of whom have risen out of employee ranks. In sum, the Danish public group finds the characteristics of employers somewhat more to their liking than the sum of those of the trade union officials.

The image which the Danish industrial relations public has of the trade unions in its country is that of a conservative organization which raises no strong feelings one way or the other. It was difficult to find an informed individual in this group who was inclined to consider the trade unions either a menace to, or the saviors of, Danish society. Even the unorganized middle class, the bearers of anti-union sentiment in the Western European democracies, are either indifferent to, or somewhat suspicious of, the intent of the labor movement, rather than hostile. They are not inclined to see any distinction between the collective bargaining activity of labor leaders and their involvement in politics. The term "labor movement" connotes a political organization, the almost universal reaction being that when one joins a trade union, one also joins the Social Democrat party. The general indifference to trade unionism is manifested by the absence of polemics in trade union and industrial relations reporting. A new settlement is considered topical, bringing an across-the-page headline in the newspapers. Generally, however, there is little labor reporting, and what does exist has none of the controversial tone found in the Italian press. In general, the attitude of the industrial relations public in Denmark is one of enlightened detachment. The strongest criticism, if that word can be used, came from those with a professional interest in industrial relations and had to do with what they called the antiquated structure of the craft unions and the power they wield in the control of jobs.

The majority of the Danish respondents do not believe that trade unionism runs counter to the interests of society. In their country, the excessive pressures of one group generate counterinfluences from another. Respondents stated:

What are the interests of society? You cannot speak of the interests of society or the public, but rather of those of different groups, and then the problem becomes a matter of weighing the impact of a group relative to its numbers. All groups in society may give a country a certain rigidity and expose it to conflict. The trade unions have their share of responsibility for unemployment and inflation. Sometimes groups use their power to excess in promoting their interests and cause a burden to fall on people, including those whom they represent. But the concept of society is vague.

Trade unionism, of course, runs counter to the interests of other groups in society. That is the purpose. The "interest of society" is an almost meaningless term.

A critical view of the impact of trade unionism on unemployment was expressed as follows:

Labor leaders express concern about unemployment and put forth proposals to eliminate it. However, they often behave in such a manner as to create unemployment in their own industries and in those outside of their jurisdiction. Consciously or unconsciously, they make decisions whose effect is to curtail employment. They get away with it because those who suffer the consequences of unemployment either have no vote in the union or are not aware of the fact that the decisions of their representatives cause a loss of their jobs.

Respondents were asked what attributes of the Danish character give trade unionism and industrial relations a flavor different from that of Italy. The most frequently mentioned characteristic is the Danish concern for pragmatism and orderliness, and the abhorrence of engaging in a fight. "We are a skeptical people not addicted to hero-worship, with a desire for orderliness, practicality, and common sense in social affairs. Our sense of humor sees as ridiculous hero-worshiping or the taking of extreme positions. . . ." This produces at the same time both a desire to demonstrate one's independence and the will to coöperate. Equal stress is placed on the penchant for organization. In the words of respondents:

There is a high democratic participation in social affairs. However, the relationship between the different Danish groups is not as natural as it is in the United States. We are less straightforward and more stiff. We are inclined to leave intergroup relations to the top leaderships. We are not democratic in the sense of fluidity between the members of different groups. Americans are more independent of their leaders and less inclined to follow the leader. The Danes are better organization people. Perhaps, the principal factor that accounts for these differences is the greater social mobility in the United States. The Danes organize, elect their leaders, and then follow them unimaginatively.

Apart from the political problem of socialization versus private initiative, Denmark is a highly coöperative society. It lies in the temperament of the people. We squabble about things; we talk much. When a Danish worker comes into a workshop, you are at once like a family. We have found work for Danish workers in Swedish plants, but it is not successful. There were difficulties in the way the Danes are accustomed to talk together, whereas it takes a long time for the Swedes to talk. We have clashes of interests, but many interests in common.

Danish responses on the purpose of trade unionism are, in the main, on a political-economic base. The basic purpose of trade unions is to serve the economic interests of the members, which will lead them to both bargaining collectively and engaging in political activity in the pursuit of objectives. "The basic purpose of the trade union is to create better economic conditions, to give the workers a greater share of the values which are created; but also to raise the whole class culturally. However, my attitude when I was a trade union leader was that the members should take care of their responsibilities, or I would have nothing to do with the matter. There are no trade union leaders who want to take up a problem when the members are wrong."

The responses have a less moralistic and reformist tone than those of the Italian public group. They stressed more the improvement of the economic condition of workers. The group was unanimous in believing that the standard of living of Danish workers would be worse if there were no trade unions. A majority felt that the close relationship between the trade unions and the Social Democrat party is a legitimate discharge of the trade union function and saw no objection to the intimate ties between the two organizations. In sum, while the group expressed the acceptance of the economic and political objectives of the labor movement, they were critical of particular methods and their consequences.

Replies fan out from simple statements emphasizing the collective bargaining role to answers describing other purposes of trade unionism. These range from raising the cultural level of workers to the improvement of relationships at the plant level. "The union should represent the entire political, economic, and cultural interests of its members. . . ." "They should seek to stabilize the relationship between management and workers. . . ." "They should democratize relationships at the plant level to increase the status of the worker and reduce paternalism. . . ." "The union should educate the worker and not only raise his economic standards. . . ."

Responses on the weaknesses of trade unionism concentrate on what is described as the antiquated craft-structure of the labor organizations. The craft form is a bar to economic progress, it was stated. It encourages in the trade union organizations a restricted mentality, which views the purpose of unionism as one of preventing change in the pattern of jobs and controlling the individuals who have such jobs. "Our trade unions are imbued with a restricted mentality. The philosophy of the union is that the employer provides the jobs, while the union controls how the jobs should be performed and who should

perform them. In my judgment, this gives them too much power. . . ."
Another weakness cited is the control of unemployment insurance by
the trade unions. "The administration of the unemployment insurance
fund by trade unions makes it difficult for the trade union official to
unveil membership abuses of the fund. Often unemployment is like
a vacation, with the worker drawing almost all of his regular wage."
Another sentiment is that trade unionism should provide a more as-
sertive and vigorous type of worker guidance. "The unions suffer from
excessive democracy, or, to put it another way, from leadership irre-

TABLE 38

Critical Attitudes of the Danish Public Group toward Labor Leaders

Related to:		Per cent
Character	20	
Behave snobbishly		10
Indulge in extreme behavior		10
Orientation	44	
Do not communicate with workers		35
Emphasize politics		6
Do not communicate with middle class		3
Technical ability	35	
Adhere to craft unionism		19
Lack adequate preparation		10
Push up costs		6
Total	99 *	
Number	38	

* Percentages were rounded.

sponsibility. The leaders would give the members a pill if they wanted
it, even though it would prove lethal in the long run. . . ." Critical
expressions related to labor leadership also concentrate on the craft
structure of union organization (Table 38). The price the craft union
leaders force the country to pay is counted in terms of higher costs,
unemployment, the prevention of upward movement for workers, and,
paradoxically, the slowing of upward wage movement that would
occur in the absence of craft unionism. One respondent stated:

They have created a craft structure and a system of collective bargaining
which prevents the unskilled from rising up the occupational ladder and
gears the terms of employment to the employer who is economically weakest.
They really do not know how to bargain collectively, but play by ear, and
are confronted with more fully informed employer representatives. When

wage costs are equalized among employers, there occurs the phenomenon of employers' quitting the employer association in order to raise the standard of employment of their workers. Workers tolerate this situation because they are not aware of plant and industry differences. To some extent, the piece-rate system gears wages to plant productivity, but technological change will tend to convert wages on a time basis.

Differences in labor leadership discerned by the group are associated either with qualities inherent in the labor leader or with circumstances in his environment. The first category includes innate capacities and the extent of preparation for positions in the trade union movement, and the latter embraces pressures stemming from his own union or outside organizations. The major differences among leaders concern flexibility, range of social awareness, intelligence, extent of training, and courage. Other differences include the extent to which leaders mirror the sentiments of the rank and file, the degree of conflict they enjoy, the degree of conservatism they show, and the reasonableness of the demands they make. Some of the respondents stated that the differences among labor leaders are due to the characteristics of the industries in which they are found, that is, the economics of the particular industry and the types of workers it attracts. The term "flexibility" connotes the ability to discern changing situations and the willingness to adopt new forms of conduct not necessarily consistent with prior behavior.

Among the representative comments were the following statements:

There are three basic types of labor leaders. There is the craft union mentality, which predominates in trade union organizations in Denmark, that has the astuteness to exercise a frank policy of trade union monopoly. The second type comprises a handful of labor leaders, two or three perhaps, who control the economy-wide decisions in behalf of the labor bloc in Denmark. They possess greater perceptive ability and social awareness and tend to lose the craft mentality if they possessed it previously. Finally, there is the bumbling, unobtrusive variety who assert themselves by an adroit ability of stick-to-itiveness. They all have one characteristic; they are all honest.

It is difficult to discern their differences, because in their exposure to the public they behave for strategic reasons like a power bloc, expressing similar ideas and avoiding any semblance of difference in their opinions. They are compelled to behave in this way because of their commitment to the Social Democrat party. They are reluctant to do anything which might weaken the party, because of their commitment and because it is in fact the highest bargaining authority of the trade unions.

They mirror the differences of the rank and file, the personal temperament and characteristics of the people they lead.

They have a morbid respect for formal law, like the Danes generally.

Their differences are a reflection of dissimilarities among industries and among the occupations of the membership, which are asserted in labor leadership.

They differ in their training.

The extent of their training is haphazard and subject to chance as they rise up the labor leadership chain of command. Those who lack preparation are unable to discern long-range goals.

They differ in their willingness to take positions contrary to those of the members. Some of them fail to keep their promises on bargains with employers, some are autocratic, and some enjoy looking for trouble.

Has there been any change in the degree of control the officials exercise on the members? The reply is typically affirmative. "There used to be a time when the labor leader would express all the wishes of the members, including a lot of plain nonsense. . . ." "There are few trade union leaders who would take up a question if they felt the members were wrong. . . ." "Not all of the demands come from the rank and file. They arise out of negotiation among the labor leaders within the federation. . . ."

Without exception, it is felt that the unions have been of considerable help to workers. They have increased the respect accorded the working class, and without them the standard of living would not be so high. When pressures for an economic downturn exist, the unions have succeeded in making the decline less rapid and less steep. What does the labor leader expect from his job? No doubt, power and status are important motives. Some of the respondents, however, stated that the explanation of power as the prime motive of labor leadership is oversimplified and exaggerated. In their words:

I am not too sure that the quest for power is a dominant factor. They are all group minded, conscious of the limitations of opportunities in life, which, in their judgment, organization would tend to overcome. Their salaries are not attractive, and they all started at the bottom at the local level. Like the men in any organization, they like to work themselves up toward the top.

Compared to the routine character of work in the shop, they find their jobs interesting and fascinating. It makes them feel important.

A popular foreign image of Denmark is that of a socialist society in which trade union organization is the predominant power. Consequently, it is interesting to note that among neither the workers nor the industrial relations public group interviewed is this portrait prevalent. Although both expressed the view that the political and economic power of employers and trade unions is fairly equal, their subsequent expressions place the initial generalization in a different perspective. No distinction is made between political and economic influence, in many cases the former being considered the latter *de facto*. The ultimate source of power is to be found among those individuals who are in control of the greatest number of economic resources, and they often outmatch those who control the greatest number of votes. In Denmark, unlike Italy, power accrues in an individual by virtue of the characteristics of the organization he controls, so that the Danes mention organizations more frequently than individuals. The Italian respondents could consider a person powerful by virtue of qualities inhering in him personally, but the Danish respondents could not. Their concept is essentially a materialistic one of respect for organizations which command considerable amounts of financial resources.

In the majority of cases, a particular employer or the employer confederation was mentioned as the most powerful influence in Denmark. In second place is government, or particular organizations in government, such as finance and the central bank. In third is the trade union federation, followed by the farmers' organization. In practically all of the responses, the Danes cited the government, employers, or the trade union federation as having the predominant power, in contrast with the Italians, who tended to cite a particular employer, political figure, or member of the clergy. When a particular union was mentioned in Denmark, it was commonly the General Workers' Union. Following is a typical explanatory response: "The organization which has the greatest amount of monetary resources is really the most powerful. The effective organization of the labor movement is such that a balance of power exists in Denmark. The labor leaders exert the greatest influence among the working classes, but in an accommodation with other groups they have less power. Of course it does change with the issues, the individuals involved, and the shifting situations. I suspect, however, that reference to Denmark as a socialist state is probably a misleading term to a foreigner. Employers in this country are probably subject to less control than in yours, and the fact that they are a political minority does not mean they do not exercise political influence. . . ." Another respondent stated: "There is no distinction between economic and political power. They blend. The exercise of political power has predominantly an economic influence, and the people who exercise it are seeking to promote economic interests. . . ."

These images, in conclusion, provide a framework for the industrial relations systems in both countries. They make their imprint on the structure of these systems and the predispositions of the participants. The manner in which this impression occurs is the subject of the following chapter.

Collective Bargaining
Relationships

A comparative presentation of the labor-employer relations of foreign countries poses the question of how such an analysis should be developed. Its framework may be descriptive, including the characteristics of trade union officials and employers and their behavior toward each other. From these descriptions, different relationships can then be classified into broad types, and the dominant kind of labor-management relationship of a particular country ascertained. Another way may involve the development of the influences behind the relationship, and still another one concentrate on the results of the relationship on both of the parties and on other organizations. Description and influence procedures are difficult to keep apart clearly, the former tending to control and shape the influences which are subsequently recognized in an investigation. However, it seems logical that an analysis of foreign union-management relationships should begin with a description of what they are in the first place.

Several descriptive benchmarks, obtained from the literature on analyzing labor-management relationships, were tried in the field investigations.[1] One was the array of subjects that the parties raise with each other, the level at which these subjects are accommodated, and the degree of penetration of the settlement. It was found that the written collective bargaining agreement is a useful but imperfect source for this information. Such agreements may not be an adequate measure of the array of subjects the parties actually present to each

[1] See the works of Ross Stagner, W. E. Chalmers, and Milton Derber in the Bibliography under Methodological References.

other, nor the actual depth of penetration of these subjects. The precise scope and terms of employment are often not to be found in an official written agreement.

Nor are similar work rules of industrial relations systems of different countries as significant as the manner in which they are made and interpreted.

In Denmark, for example, a wage settlement between a shop steward and the employer, involving a worker or group of workers, would be recorded informally in a meeting report (*mødereferat*) signed by the persons at the meeting. Many such wage settlements exist, together with those on different welfare concessions to workers. The Danes regard these settlements as internal matters outside the formal collective bargaining process between the union and the employer organization. No doubt, these individual agreements have a marked effect on the so-called wage slide, the drift of wages away from formal settlements. American collective bargaining agreements are a more precise record of actual terms of employment than either those in Denmark, which tend to understate, or those in Italy, where for unskilled workers and the South the opposite is the case. However, the relatively greater importance of the formal collective bargaining system in Denmark, compared to Italy, should not be ignored.

Agreements reflect differences in cultural values between countries, the power of the parties, the characteristics of the particular industry which they cover, and the level of formal agreement-making. They are revealing documents in the ratio of employer responsibilities to worker obligations which they specify. Some contracts stipulate what the employer expects from workers more thoroughly than what the latter anticipate from the former. The union may want to talk about other subjects and cannot because of its impotence, or it may have relatively free rein in raising questions over and above those which have a basis in the written agreement. A broad range of subjects at a particular level of agreement-making may indicate, not the dominance of the union in the relationship, but rather a willingness on the part of the employer, for one reason or another, to enlarge the scope of joint decision-making. The examples of labor-management coöperation uncovered in Italy are explainable on these grounds. The degree to which the national agreement specifies in detail the terms of employment provides a clue to the nature of the relationship between employers and labor officials. The Italian agreement is of much greater detail than its Danish counterpart, in both the number of subjects and the depth of particular clauses.

If greater resources had been available for the study, it would have been feasible to determine over a period of time what each party wanted to talk about, the subjects which managed to enter into the agreement, whether written or not, and the desire of the parties regarding the level at which these matters should be discussed. Thus, to use the agreement as an instrument of determining who is dominating the relationship, it would be necessary to ascertain the full scope of the relationship, both formal and informal, the subjects the union desires to discuss, including the level at which it wishes them to be placed, and the changes in scope and substantive terms in the course of time vis-à-vis the demands of the union.

A second complementary description of the union-management relationship may be found in the attitudes each brings to bear against the other. These are both fruitful and economical to obtain. The configuration of attitudes with which each party is disposed to react to the other includes such factors as perception of the other, goals and value standards, concept of role, political and moral sentiments, and extent of union and employer satisfaction in the relations. These items can be obtained through conventional attitude-survey techniques.

A third useful type of description lies in the traits of personality of the particular spokesman for each side in the industrial relations system, and the degree to which these traits conflict with each other. It is difficult to understand Italian labor-management relations without a comprehension of the personality characteristics of the players. Display of temperament and inflexibility are innocuous only when found on one side. And an intimate knowledge, not available to the public, that a particular representative of a union organization has neurotic tendencies may go a long way in explaining what is transpiring in the relationship.

A fourth complementary description is the pressure the parties use on each other and accept on themselves. The instruments of pressure differ in different times and places. A useful pressure-method in one country may be of little value in another. Pressures include not only threats and use of force, but those which parties accept from outside organizations, such as the Church or a political party, and those which they employ singly or jointly on workers.

One way of analyzing the pressures the parties bring to bear on

each other is through the study of the mechanism and the characteristics of the grievances they raise against each other. Here again, it is
precarious to draw generalizations. The extent and the type of grievances raised may be directly associated with a weak union, or they
may not. If Denmark and Italy provide a clue, it would appear that
the use of voluntary arbitration as a terminal point of the grievance
machinery is predicated on a strong union organization's persuading
a reluctant management of the usefulness of such a course of action
in lieu of the uncertainties raised by the possible use of political and
economic pressure. The grievance machinery may also reflect the
attitude of the union leaders toward conflict. Moreover, the same configuration of grievances may be a manifestation of a weak or a strong
union, a highly integrated union-management relationship or a poorly
integrated one, a strong union or a powerful but inept management
giving away the operation of the plant in slow stages, incompetent
union officials or incompetent management executives. And at times
the grievances may be an expression of union politics or simply the
neurotic personality of a particular labor official whose actions may be
inducing management to fight back in order to maintain the efficient
operation of the plant. Consequently, it is difficult to draw neat generalizations either from differences or similarities in the grievance systems
or from the configuration of the grievances which arise therefrom.[2]

A fifth type of description involves the structural characteristics of
the relationship itself. These mechanics include the scope of the bargaining unit, procedure, and points of contact of the parties. The
points of contact between employers and labor leaders in Italy include
the following: (1) at the plant level, principally through the shop
committees, the so-called *commissioni interne;* (2) at the provincial
level, between the local offices of the federation and those of the employers' association, or in rare instances, between the trade union
organization and a particular employer; (3) at the national level,
principally between the coöperating federation and the particular
national union involved and the employers' association. In Denmark,
at the plant level, the relationship is with shop stewards of the different
unions, chief shop steward, production committee representatives, and
on occasion with the union local president; at the national level, with
national unions and the federation on one side, and industry associa-

---

[2] See Sumner H. Slichter, James J. Healy, and E. Robert Livernash, *The Impact
of Collective Bargaining on Management,* Washington: Brookings, 1960.

tion and the combined employer association on the other. A second type of mechanical analysis is the extensiveness of the talks that go on between the parties on an over-all basis and the difference in concentration at the various levels, as well. In Italy, a dominant cause of the weakness of the relationship lies in the fact that only in rare instances are the parties apt to talk to each other in the first place, and when they do, it is generally in an atmosphere of crisis, with huge representations on either side. Generally, the parties in Denmark talk more at the plant level than in Italy.

A sixth facet of description comprises the variables obtained independently. These include plant size, type of ownership of firm, skill-ratio of the workplace, and leadership philosophy of the employer. These materials serve the additional purpose of suggesting influences behind the relationship between employer and trade union.

The second aspect of the problem, the measuring of influences behind the relationship, is more complex. It was found that relationships are affected by a multiplicity of organizations external to the company and trade union organization. Group attitudes are also influenced by the size of the organization, the level of leadership, the range and complexity of economic data with which the parties are confronted, the type of workers the firm is attracting, and the cultural environment in which they work. The education, occupational level, and the level and rate of upward social movement of workers have an important influence, as well.

Another factor, the bargaining power of the parties, sets a potential for the relative dominance of the union and employer and the tone of the relationship between them. While it has an effect on the attitudes of the parties, there are differences in the extent to which they exercise the full use of their power. A trade union may husband its power and later because of a quirk in circumstances decide to use it to its fullest extent. A powerful company may elect to allow the union to dominate the relationship and the setting of employment terms, and cater generally to the institutional needs of the union. Thus one Italian employer granted the union representative some controversial subjects in collective bargaining, partly because of the opposition to them on the part of the employer association. In Denmark, employers' acceptance of trade union values serves to place a restraint on the exercise of their power potential over the union. Another factor affecting this potential is the difference in the economic and social position of the parties and the degree to which that of the labor leaders is stratified. The felt master-servant relationship arising out of this situation, particularly at the plant level, has the effect of the union's deferring to the point of view of the employer. The union representative may not admit as much, but he behaves in this fashion. Moreover, the presence of interested powerful parties such as the Church, the political beliefs of the union representatives, and the community environment influence the extent to which the parties exercise their power on each other. In both Italy and Denmark, the influence of a highly integrated community on peaceful relationships is impressive. What makes predictability difficult in these matters, however, is that the relationship may change quite suddenly, for non-economic reasons difficult to discern unless the investigator possesses an intimate knowledge of the parties.

The field investigations suggest several factors which must be clearly understood in a comparative study of union power on the level of national societies. First, unions have to address themselves to exercising functions arising out of particular expectations and conditions of specific groups of workers. Principal economic forces which make for similarity in the pursuit of such goals are the expectation that the union should obtain for workers a system of accumulating job rights and rising standards, and the degree of similarity in technology and market situations confronting labor organizations of different countries. A principal economic influence making for dissimilarity in methods, goals, and accomplishments is the extent to which full employment exists to make such broad objectives realizable. This array of expectations and environment has a differentiating effect on union power. Second, a distinction exists between the power potential of unions and the degree to which they use such power. For cultural reasons, unless pressed to the contrary by their membership, unions do not use their power to the hilt. The members themselves are likely to accept such cultural restraints, even during periods of adversity. Further, as union power potential increases, the ratio of use to latent potential declines. Third, union power is affected by the methods used, the group against which it is directed, and the goals for which it is employed. And these, of course, as Professor Reder points out, vary with different national societies.[3]

[3] See Melvin Reder, "Job Scarcity and the Nature of Union Power," *Industrial and Labor Relations Review*, XIII, No. 3 (April, 1960), 349–62.

Several inferences are suggested if these generalizations are valid. The power configurations in a national society are intimately associated with its mosaic of values. Differences in power, as is the case between Denmark and Italy, can be greater than is apparent by its use. As Professor Reder suggests, the "wage slide" in a country such as Denmark may be a manifestation of the husbanding of power because of cultural restraints which the unions accept as proper. An analysis of economic power of unions is not meaningful divorced from the particular cultural context out of which it arises. To criticize labor movements for not using their power "properly" or for not "maximizing" their power possibilities is as futile an exercise as berating the thermometer for the temperature it registers.

The burden of being pace-setters in the terms of employment may be an influence causing "tough" relationships between union representatives and employers. Some parties create new interplant inequities by the pace-setting character of their settlements, while the rest have the easier role of closing the gap. In Italy and Denmark, a major role of pattern-maker is played by the metal worker unions.[4] These unions sometimes rely on the existence of intercountry inequities as a basis of seeking to establish new employment terms. Other things equal, the function of having to break through to new standards increases the likelihood of a difficult settlement. When the pace-setters are few and the followers dominate, the general tone of industrial relations may be amicable.

To make the matter more complex, however, a counteracting influence may be the size of the firms involved. The setting of employment terms is more diffused in a large organization, particularly when the top executives are professional individuals and the firm is hiring a professional labor relations director who is likely to bring to bear a moderating influence. Some of the toughest relationships in Italy are with small employers with a baronial philosophy toward the operation of their company.

Consequently, no single variable controls the relationship between the parties in industrial relations. Despite these qualifications, however, the most important single variable ascertained in the setting of

---

[4] In Denmark, the pace-setting role of the Metal Workers is shared with the General and Special Workers' Union. On a particular employer basis, the impact of a new standard set by the Metal Workers' Union is apt to be greater than that of the general laborers' union organization because of the greater difficulty of isolating its effect.

the tone of the relationship is the extent of the disparity in the economic and cultural position of the parties. It is unlikely, for instance, that an integrated relationship will evolve in Italy as it did in Denmark unless the one-sided superiority of the employer in these two respects is curtailed considerably.

Turning to the question of results of the relationship: Does a particular type of accommodation between the union and the employer tend to be identified with a particular set of results? Generally, the array of economic benefits in a relationship manifests a variety of factors, including historical duration, economic mix of the firm and industry, and cultural attitudes toward labor. The same type of accommodation may be attended by different levels of economic benefits, and similar levels of income may be associated with different types of accommodation. If results are measured by wages in particular, they are predominantly a function of differences in capital productivity and product demand, associated with different industries and size of plants. The trade unions in textiles in both Italy and Denmark will probably never succeed in pushing up wages to the level of those in basic steel. A more significant measure of the result of the relationship is the expressed satisfaction of the parties. The degree of expressed dissatisfaction is an indication of the degree of failure in the integration of norms of both sides.

The theory of describing union-management relationships by types relies on several benchmarks. They include such factors as which party is dominating the relationship, to what extent each side is bringing pressures to bear on the other, and what the attitudes of both sides are, including the degree of hostility on either side. Using these criteria, it can be said the relationship in Italy in the main is company dominated, with both the company and union exerting high pressure on each other and with both parties hostile toward each other. In Denmark it is characterized by no dominance by either party, low pressure from both sides, with leader attitudes mutually favorable. In the rest of the chapter, these basic types will be explained in greater detail.

THE RELATIONSHIP IN ITALY

The Setting of the Rules of Work

A traditional and dogmatic society expects people to seek and abide by the thinking of those in power. The function of the leader is to determine what is best for the led, and the duty of the latter is to abide by that determination. Such a society produces inhibitions on upward communication from the bottom and centralization of power at the top. It discourages initiative and independent thought by those who are not expected to indulge in such practices. Authority, in turn, is looked upon with skepticism and suspicion by the led. Institutions, employers, are instruments which should be used to the best advantage with the least amount of personal outlay. In the words of a trade union official, a society is created in which the leaders and the common people try to outwit each other. No sense of community exists. A conviction prevails that those in power are exploiters and that therefore the legitimate role of the led is, by composing cunning evasions, *furberie,* to indulge in some exploiting of their own. A concession to an adversary is a total loss for the one making the concession. The workers look upon an improved term of employment as an extraction long overdue. The employer views their demands as questioning his sense of moral responsibility toward his wards, and when the concession is made, decries the lack of gratitude shown by the workers.

These attitudes prescribe the nature of the conflict in Italian collective bargaining. Juxtaposed against the employer attitude of *l'état c'est moi* is the revolutionary disposition of the labor leader. Humanistic overtones are strong on either side, but what constitutes human benevolence comes into conflict. Neither party is strongly production oriented. The idea of avoiding a strike in order to maintain production in the public interest has not yet taken hold.[5] Moreover, conflict per se is not bad. Indeed it affords a means of self-expression. Conflict, in a sense, is a part of the returns in the collective bargaining process. Thus it can be seen that values not only influence the array of aspirations of a labor movement, but also act as benchmarks in the measurement of achievement.

In Italy, the group determination of terms of employment takes place at three levels. The federation, acting in behalf of all its national unions, has stipulated agreements with the Italian Confederation of Industry (Confindustria) on such matters as cost-of-living wage escalation formulas, meal allowances, and equal pay for equal work for

---

[5] Some unions do try to minimize public hostility in the scheduling of demonstration strikes. These generalizations are somewhat less applicable in the more heavily industrialized North and more so in that part of Italy outside the industrial triangle.

women. At the second level, the various national unions write agreements for an industry group or particular industry with the assistance of the federation. Thus, the three national unions of metal workers write an agreement with the various employer associations in the metal industries. At the third, the procedure is more diverse. The provincial federation may come to an agreement with the provincial office of the employer association in industry, commerce, or agriculture. Agreements also exist at this level between the provincial organization of the federation or a particular trade union and one company. Finally, accords have been stipulated locally between a firm and the members of the plant committee. Generally, the tendency of the unions has been to try to push the level of agreement-making downward, with the employers pulling in the other direction.

In a law which went into effect July 14, 1959, the terms of employment in collective bargaining agreements are extended automatically to both organized and unorganized workers of employers who are not affiliated with the contracting employer associations. The legislation, called the law on the validity *erga omnes* of collective bargaining agreements, was proposed by a former Minister of Labor and supported by the union federations. Actually, the law gives the government the power to establish minimum terms of employment for all workers belonging to a particular *categoria*. In order to establish such standards, the government relies on new "floors" established periodically by collective bargaining agreements. The law was defended in Parliament on the basis that it would implement the right of a worker, guaranteed in the Italian constitution, to a wage "proportionate to the quantity and quality of his work and in any case sufficient to secure for himself and his family a free and dignified existence." The act demonstrates the heavy reliance on law by the Italians in passing what is in effect a minimum-budget criterion of wage determination. Organized labor and employers supported the legislation because their agreements were serving to provide a subsidy to the employers who were not signatories to them. Both had a common interest in eliminating the competitive advantage given "chiseling employers" who did not abide by the national agreements. The law is an instrument of organization of the unorganized on both sides. It remains to be seen whether the automatic extension of a collective bargaining agreement to a party who does not participate in its stipulation will be considered constitutional by the Italian Supreme Court.

As has been stated, the general characteristic of the Italian collective bargaining relationship is employer dominance and hostility of each party toward the other. The subjects and substantive terms of employment, even those for the stronger unions, sound more like the demands of the employer on what he expects of labor than like those of the union on management. At the insistence of Confindustria, bargaining by broad industry groups is the prevailing procedure.[6] A contract may take two or three years to renew after its expiration, while at the plant level the employer may be improving terms of employment unilaterally, despite the wishes of labor leaders to the contrary. Wages set by these national agreements are those which the most inefficient employer in the association is able to pay, while those above the minimum actually being paid are often considered a generous bounty by the employer, rather than the fruits of trade unionism. Thus the exercise of free collective bargaining is severely limited by the practice of bargaining national minimum standards for a multi-industry group and having at the same time a system of comprehensive minimum standards set by law. Such a combination squeezes the free agreement-making process into an area of small significance. National collective bargaining would provide more status to the union leader if it were done by industry rather than by interindustry groups. It would be more realistic for workers and even for management if both were being asked to make adjustments in terms of their own particular problems. The problems of a Fiat company are not quite the same as those of a bicycle shop operated by an artisan and his assistant. The effect of such a system of collective bargaining has been to strain the credulity of workers as to its usefulness, especially those working for large employers whom economies in scale make able to pay wages as much as 80 per cent above those stipulated in the national agreement. Consequently, it can be said that in Italy government and the employer have a greater voice in the setting of employment terms than the free process of collective bargaining itself.[7]

Two key bargains are those covering the metal workers and the textile workers. They are precedent-making in character and become

[6] In 1960, a breakthrough occurred with a settlement in government-owned plants in the electronics portion of the metal workers' group.

[7] The importance of government in setting terms of employment is shown in the provision for family allowance disbursements, which in 1958 were received by six million heads of families and on the average amounted to more than a month's pay per recipient.

the basis, in differing degree, of demonstrating the existence of inter-plant inequities for other workers. The wage levels of these two groups are in contrast with each other, one being among the highest and the other among the lowest in Italian industry. The precedent-making aspect of these bargains, however, is in the change in terms of em-ployment, rather than in their level.

In the bargaining of a new textile agreement beginning in 1958, the employers pointed to the new crisis in the industry in support of the view that minimum wages should be kept frozen. In response, the labor officials stressed the 5 per cent increase in the cost of living, and the three federations carried out jointly a series of *manifestazioni* throughout the country. In the metal industry, the trade union leaders stressed that the production index had risen faster than the index of wages, and they too joined in a series of trade union demonstrations.

The tactics of collective bargaining is a complex affair in Italy. There are three parties on the labor side of the bargaining table, each con-cerned not only with the position of the employer representatives but also with that of the negotiators for the other union federations. None can afford to have the others dominate the negotiations. Demands must take into consideration not only the reaction of the employer but also the possibility of improving the position of one federation at the expense of the others. The CGIL may make an outlandish demand in order to demonstrate the intransigence of the employer. To dead-lock the negotiations, all that needs to be done is insist that nothing else be discussed until the demand is settled. The risk involved in such a position would be to leave to the CISL the opportunity of sign-ing an agreement which might eventually have to be accepted by the CGIL. Since the workers cannot assume strike action on a sustained basis, conflict must take on quick, quasi-insurrectionist proportions. There must be planted in the mind of the employer an awareness of the possibility of continual and unexpected intermittent disturbances.

In such bargaining, the three federations sometimes set aside their ideological differences and coöperate in the writing of new collective bargaining agreements with employers. They agree to joint demands and strike action, although occasionally such accords manage some-how to go awry in their implementation. In 1958, in the metal industries, the federations asked for a substantial wage increase, new clauses on incentive work, a more extensive job-classification system consistent with technological changes, a reduction in hours, with take-home pay remaining the same, a third week of vacation, and the institution of a regular system of collective bargaining at the company level. In addition, particular demands were made for the various subgroups, such as shipbuilding, automobiles, electronics, and basic steel. Negotiations were curtailed because of a procedural question. The employers' association had invited to the negotiations the CISNAL and the splinter union of the CISL at the Fiat company. The CISL, the CGIL, and the UIL refused to recognize the legitimacy of either organization in collective bargaining. Thereupon, the employers postponed all meetings indefinitely in order to review the procedural question raised by the three federations.

The final metal-industry settlement, effectuated by arbitration of a cabinet minister agreed to by the parties, while representing a small change in the terms of employment, increased the status of the labor leaders. The worker could bring his grievance on incentive work to the union if the first step with the *commissione interna* failed to produce a settlement. An agreement was also reached on new definitions for existing job classifications. On the demand for a reduction in the workweek, management agreed to pay overtime for work in excess of forty-four hours at a rate of 7 per cent. The small concessions on incentive systems and job classifications represented a major change in the scope of collective bargaining, to which employer resistance is much greater than in the case of increases in the depth of existing terms of employment.[8]

During the same year, the parties managed to conclude accords in other industries. The rubber industry arrived at an agreement after two years of collective bargaining. Minimum wages were raised 3 per cent, less than the increase in the cost of living, and an agreement was concluded on a job-evaluation system for the industry. The demand for reduction of the workweek to forty hours was dropped. In other accords, the glass industry agreed to an average 3 per cent wage hike, while negotiations in the quarry industry were suspended indefinitely because of wide differences of wages, the unions insisting on 11 per cent and the employers having offered 1.

Two prominent breakthroughs have occurred in the attempt of Italian trade unions to push collective bargaining down to the plant level. The first happened in a large women's clothing firm, Luisa Spagnoli, and the second in the largest candy-manufacturing company in

[8] For the changes in the metal worker agreement, see Appendix E.

Italy, Peruguina. It is significant that, contrary to popular generalizations about family-owned firms, both are family enterprises. Neither of them is in metal manufacturing, but both are in industries where labor costs loom large as a share of total costs. The first agreement, signed by the provincial general secretary of the CISL, constituted a joint acceptance of increased productivity by both parties. The company recognized the union as having a role in increasing plant productivity and agreed to consult with it on any company plans designed to reduce costs. The forms such consultation takes include job evaluation, production premiums, the conversion of work to incentive payment, and the training of employees. The company further agreed to hold regular meetings with the union in order to discuss the implementation of programs covering these matters.[9]

The second agreement is a contract signed both by the CGIL and the CISL on the provincial level in the same province of Italy. It represented a confluence of the Social-Communist federation's casting aside its doctrinaire attitude against company-wide agreements and the failure of the Catholics to gain exclusive recognition at the company. The agreement included several subjects: (1) The determination of work standards. Management agreed to furnish the unions with data on how work is measured and how incentive pay is determined, and to post incentive earnings of workers on a daily basis. (2) Wages to be paid reclassified employees. On the reclassification of piece-rate employees to jobs requiring a period of training, management agreed to stipulate the training period and to pay the worker an increasing portion of the incentive earnings that would normally accrue to the job. (3) The transfer of piece-rate employees to hourly-rated jobs. Such transfers when in the interest of management would be liable to payment of one-half of former incentive earnings of the transferred worker in addition to the regular pay for the job. (4) Grievance procedure. Any employee with a grievance under the agreement can present it to management, either directly through the department head or indirectly through the shop committee. If management fails to resolve the grievance within five days, conciliation would take place between the company and the shop committee for the ensuing ten-day period. If

---

[9] From *Conquiste del Lavoro* (Rome), October 23, 1960. The company also granted a 46-hour week instead of 48, and a pension guarantee of 75 per cent of wages at the time of retirement, including government social security.

there is failure to resolve the dispute, the next step would be between the company and the trade union chosen by the employee. In the event of a settlement in favor of the worker, the company would be liable to back pay up to the date of the filing of the grievance.

While the depth of these settlements is small, the subjects themselves represent a breakthrough in the determination of employment terms on the plant level by the process of collective bargaining. They mark a beginning in wage determination above the not-too-meaningful setting of minimum wages by the national agreements. They are also a start in the direction of joint control of job reclassification of employees and in the development of a grievance procedure in which the trade union takes over the role usurped by the independent shop committee. Finally, these agreements increase the status of the provincial labor leader in his relations with workers, employers, and the whole network of trade union organization in Italy.[10]

Following is a penetrating statement by a federation official on the status of collective bargaining in Italy:

Actually we have only been bargaining for eight years, and our unions are not designed to bargain collectively effectively. The unions are incapable of controlling the labor supply, which is an indispensable part of collective bargaining. Industry came late in Italy, and no specialized craft skills developed. The consequence was a mass of workers shifting from job to job, from one plant to the next, with no company orientation. To avoid their competing with each other, we had to organize them immediately on a horizontal basis. Our unions consequently had no basis in monopoly skills. The quickest way for us to acquire power in this kind of situation was to go into the political arena. Our task now is to remove collective bargaining from the quasi-Fascist method of bargaining on the national level and to alter the function of the union as simply a device to provide legal assistance to workers on their rights under labor legislation.

National union leaders are not categorical about their estimate of the relative influence of employers and unions in collective bargaining. It depends on the industry, the time of negotiations, and the personalities of the parties who are involved in the bargaining. Their responses reflect greater experience in the discharge of the collective bargaining function. They also manifest an appreciation of tactics in formulating demands which can be met by employers in order to avoid a struggle leading to an impasse and no returns at all.

The interviews turned to questions on how the national trade union

[10] In an article appearing in *Politica Sindacale*, III, No. 4 (August, 1960).

official prepares himself to bargain collectively with the employer. The comments below are representative of the substance of the replies. No meaningful differentiations were obtained by federation.

Hold meetings with workers throughout the country first to find out their wishes and then sit down with my colleagues and formulate demands.

Analyze the conditions of the industry first.

Use the higher standards of employment in one plant in order to obtain concessions in another plant.

Consult with the provincial secretaries before formulating demands.

Study the industry and the needs of the workers and then construct realizable goals.

Construct the size of the original demands, depending upon the psychology of the employer.

Make the demand vague to act as a spur to increased employer efficiency.

Determine two things: what you can obtain with striking and what you can obtain without striking.

Formulate demands and then consider yourself fortunate if the employers elect to talk to you.

Use strike demonstrations to test the position of your employer.

No use in preparing to bargain collectively; the employer decides what to give and what not to give.

The national union group complained about the legalistic approach of employers. They tend to react to demands not on their face value but on the basis of whether they are consistent with the spirit of the law. The legal talent of the employers is so formidable as to create a frustrating inability to make an effective counterattack. One official expressed the view that no real collective bargaining takes place. Most of the major agreements are signed in the office of the Department of Labor, where political pressure can be used to induce the employer to sign an accord.

Employers have successfully resisted the attempt of trade unions to use arbitration as the last step in the grievance procedure. The contract of the metal industries group stipulates the use of arbitrators in specific types of grievances. The procedure, however, can be stalemated by the inability to agree on an arbitrator. Key agreements rely on government mediation for settlement, which in most instances means the services of the secretary of labor, or a vice-secretary.

Attitudes toward the Strike

The strike in union-management relations is a particularly difficult instrument to employ in Italy. The insurrectionist and emotional character which the strike frequently assumes in that country makes difficult its use as a means of building up in systematic fashion an increasing groundswell of pressure in behalf of a meeting of minds between employers and labor leaders. The use of the preannounced twenty-four– or forty-eight–hour demonstration strike is not simply a manifestation of the lack of economic wherewithal to take a protracted work stoppage. The strike also assumes the nature of a contest between employer and trade union official for the loyalty of the workers. For example, in a work stoppage during the period of the investigation, company executives were lined up at the entrance to the plant, pleading with the employees to enter the plant and go to work. On the other side of the street were the trade union officials, shouting to the workers to hold their ranks. Periodically, the labor leaders would be picked up in trucks by the police and taken to the *questura* for questioning. Somehow they would manage to return to the picket line in their automobiles to plead again for a show of solidarity. Moreover, a work stoppage too often creates more pressure on the trade union official for a return to work before it collapses than it does on the employer to come to terms. In some instances, as in the case of sharecroppers, orthodox use of the strike would serve no purpose at all. The better tactic is the sudden, unannounced cessation of work during harvest time, passive resistance to employer policies, or the retention of products.[11]

A universal method of trade unionism is the application of pressure on different groups in order to achieve objectives. However, the forms which these pressures take are not the same and cannot easily be placed on some inferior-superior or immaturity-maturity scale of differences. The twenty-four– or forty-eight–hour preannounced demonstration strike in Italy may seem incongruous by American standards. Nevertheless, the insurrectionist character which it assumes becomes an adroit employment of pressure in the light of the peculiar cultural circumstances confronting the labor leader. The lack of collective bar-

---

[11] Since the field investigation, there has been some talk concerning the establishment of strike funds, *casse di resistenza,* in support of the so-called *sciopero a tempo indeterminato,* in which the strike is announced but no termination date fixed.

gaining power and the cultural milieu within which labor relations take place make the American-style strike an unusable weapon.

Table 39 summarizes responses of trade union officials on the purpose of the strike. It is commonly accepted as a means of exerting pressure in order to achieve objectives. The respondents in the CGIL believe the weapon can also be legitimately used against government as

TABLE 39

Opinions of Italian Labor Leaders on the Purpose of the Strike

Attitude	CGIL	CISL	UIL
Positive	12	9	9
Ultimate weapon against employer or government	4	0	0
Way to obtain from bosses what you cannot get otherwise	3	0	0
Way of offering employer choice of strike or settlement	2	0	0
Pressure weapon after collective bargaining has failed	1	5	5
Means of obtaining social and economic changes	1	0	0
Defense of peace and liberty	1	0	0
Means to weaken the position of employer	0	2	2
Means of obtaining clearly defined objective	0	2	0
Way to maintain equilibrium with employers who do not believe in bargaining collectively	0	0	2
Negative	2	4	3
A defensive weapon	2	0	0
An impossible weapon	0	2	2
A two-edged sword	0	2	0
A weapon of exasperation	0	0	1
Total	14	13	12

well as against employers. In their view, government could conceivably seek to force workers to pursue a course of action highly repugnant to them, the only alternative for them being to go on strike. They concede that in the past the CGIL too frequently had asked the workers to go out on strike. However, the error is in the loss of effectiveness because of frequent use, rather than one of principle.

Italian employers were asked: "In your judgment, what function, if any, does the strike have?" Responses differentiate by location of the plant, size of plant, and the particular union with which the employer is confronted. The large northern employer tends to view the announced strike as a legitimate economic pressure weapon, although complaining about its use for political ends. The southern employer finds it generally intolerable and unacceptable. Small employers are more apt to view the strike as a personal affront than are the large employers. From an employer in a Communist belt in north central Italy: "I am fed up with the quickie strikes. They tempt me to use all my power to destroy the union. It would not even be a fair contest. I do not mind a full cessation of production, but the unannounced strikes of a few minutes are intolerable. I cannot plan my work. . . ." From a large metal manufacturer in the same region: "The strike should be restricted by law solely to trade union objectives. And before it is used, the union first must be made to go to a permanent court of arbitration. . . ." From an employer in the industrial triangle: "The Italian strike is not used as a pressure weapon against the employer. It is a demonstration which may provide an emotional satisfaction. It exerts no pressure on the employer. All he has to do is to wait until the demonstration is over. . . ."

The dominant issues in collective bargaining brought out during the interviews are three: (1) bargaining at the company level; (2) reduction in the hours of the workweek to forty; (3) the scope of union-management relations. The majority of the employers in the sample expressed initially the official position of the employer association against company-wide bargaining of agreements. Subsequently, however, some of them stated that company-wide bargaining could have an advantage to the firm. Following are representative expressions:

It will lead to the pirating of labor among employers on the basis of differences in wages.

It has some advantage as a means of bringing together employers and workers. Its disadvantage is that company bargaining may place us in an adverse competitive position.

The unions are not technically qualified to assume such a function.

There should be only national bargaining; anything over the national bargain should be granted individually by the employer, based on individual merit.

Yes, if the bargain is based on the economics of my plant.

It will create serious worker dissatisfaction because of the considerable differences in plant productivity in Italy and the ignorance of the worker as to the causes of differences in productivity.

A major reason given by employers against the practice of company bargaining is the danger of being whipsawed by the union. Italian employers expressed the view that a concession obtained from one employer becomes the basis of seeking additional improved terms of employment from another. The whipsawing effect would be more acute because of the existence of three rival federations competing with each other for membership. Members of the employer association are steadfastly against such a change in collective bargaining procedure. They appear to be concerned with the possible loss of an important function of their organization. A small minority of employers believe that dealing directly with the local representative of the union in the plant has advantages. One employer stated: "I agreed to company bargaining with the union because they wanted it badly. Now I see it as a device of achieving acceptance of decisions made by the company and the union. . . ."

An interesting feature of the responses is the apparent remoteness of collective bargaining for many of the employers. Some people in Rome bargain on wages which they accept on the conviction that their competitors will also pay them. If a grievance arises over existing terms of employment, the local office of the employer association will take care of that matter also. The rare occasions on which they have any relationship with trade unionists are encounters with the members of the shop committee. The dealings with the committeemen, however, rarely could be described as a bargaining relationship of coequals. In all, the employers are seeking to retain industry-wide bargaining, while the unions are attempting to break it down. This paradoxical switch of roles is explainable on economic and status grounds. Company-wide negotiations would increase both the bargaining power and the influence of labor in the eyes of workers and decrease the prestige of Confindustria as an employer organization.

The majority of employer responses on the hours of work are against reduction. The replies are indicative of the universal reasons which employers present in their opposition to a reduction in work hours.

It cannot be done because it increases the cost of production. Overtime should be cut instead, to provide more jobs.

There is not sufficient skilled labor to hire in order to keep the machines busy.

There are not the capital funds needed to buy additional equipment for the additional labor.

It will not work. The employees need more work, not more leisure. They would merely seek part-time employment if the workweek were reduced to five days at forty hours. Or they would squander money in leisure pursuits.

It makes no economic sense. Hours-reduction is the consequence of full employment and wages well above the subsistence level.

We gave our employees a five-day week; but they turned around and obtained part-time employment from employers who do not bother to submit social security contributions for them.

It is still premature; productivity must rise more.

Several employers gave responses favorable to the idea:

I am in favor of the idea, for economic and social reasons. It would increase productivity and provide the worker more time for his family. But we should go slow on it.

It is inevitable and I am planning for it.

I am in favor, but we should have more studies on its impact.

The statement of a CISL provincial secretary to his colleagues on the subject of union-management relations is a revealing document of aspirations. First of all, he stated, the employer should be approached as an equal. The relationship with him is the most important function of the trade union, and any form of subjection or subordination is intolerable. In the second place, the employer should not be approached by preconceived and rigid formulas which could prejudice the course of the relationship with him. Third, it should not be considered that a high frequency and intensity of relationships with employers and employers' associations are negative and unnecessary. On the contrary, they should be viewed as a manifestation of legitimate trade union activity in defense of workers. In this way, the statement continued, fundamental principles of democracy are established. Fourth, the relationship should be based on a knowledge of the problems involved. To present oneself to an employer without adequate preparation would prejudice the very interests of the workers to be defended. The objective of the union-management relationship should be to improve the condition of labor and to understand the nature of the labor problem itself. It is both a means of acquiring knowledge and of solving problems.

The relationship should be both internal and external to the plant, the statement continued. In regard to the former, it should be remembered that an agreement exists on the creation of the *commissioni interne*. Since it has been recognized that these committees are not a completely adequate instrument of defense of the workers' interests, the creation of groups representing the trade union itself should be encouraged. The function of the trade union group should be not the writing of agreements but the analysis of problems arising in the plant and the manner in which the trade union could solve them. The CISL members of the shop committees should not have any relationship with the employer other than that established by the agreement covering such committees. Where the CISL members are in the majority, they should maintain a relationship with the minority solely within the limits of the function of the committee and exercise their role on the basis of defending the interests of all the workers in the plant. If they are in a minority, they should maintain unity in the organization so long as the majority does not make a political instrument of the committee. In any case, they should maintain close ties with either the trade union or the regional federation office.

From the point of view of the union, the external relationship between employer and trade union office is the most profitable. This relationship presupposes a solid tie between the rank and file and the trade union organization, and the existence of a strong national trade union. The writing of agreements should be done on the basis of this external relationship, not by union or shop committee representatives in the plant.

Employer–Labor-Leader Relations at the Plant Level

A noteworthy feature of employer–labor-leader relations at the plant level in Italy is the absence of a mutually acceptable system of communication between them. The basic fact of the relationship at that level is the existence of two hostile groups armed with contrasting values, each suspicious of the intent of the other. The tried instruments of bringing them together, the labor-management production councils, the shop committees, and collective bargaining at the plant level, are defunct, corrupted, and inoperative. Labor leaders and employers have found neither subjects about which they can talk to each other nor a mutually acceptable structure which would make their relationship a routine matter. Consequently, they rarely express to each other through a mechanism of control the fears and expectations they have of each other.

According to an agreement between the labor federations and the employers' association, Confindustria, there are supposed to be shop committees organized in every plant with more than forty employees. Under this accord, the worker representatives on these committees have the function of enforcing the terms of the collective bargaining agreement, overseeing the implementation of the health and safety regulations of the plant, and representing employees in grievances arising between workers and management. The 1951 Italian industrial census lists 10,048 plants which employ more than fifty employees. Of this number, it is estimated by the unions that approximately only one-half have any shop committees at all. The farther south in Italy, the lower is the proportion.

Even in those plants where the shop committee is operating, few employers are aware of its possible use as a means of employee expression. The majority of the employers in the sample expressed indifference or hostility toward the committees. Their members are ignorant of the problems they are supposed to be dealing with. The committeemen instigate workers to pursue a course of action of no interest to either the company or themselves. They try to bargain on new terms of employment, when their function should be to police the national agreement instead. Some employers in the group believe that the committees weaken trade unionism rather than strengthen it, a view shared by the leadership of the CISL federation. This undermining of trade union status is achieved by giving important functions to men not beholden to any labor organization and by correspondingly weakening the ability of the trade union to strengthen its right, in the eyes of workers, to exist. One employer stated that he is happy that the committee in his plant is defunct and would rather deal with a responsible trade union official than with his employees. Such a procedure, he feels, would provide the trade union representative and himself greater freedom of action. A small group expressed the belief that the committees have made a positive contribution to the successful operation of the plant. The substance of their response is that the shop committee provides them with the opportunity of learning the sentiments of their employees, which would not be obtainable otherwise. A major criticism of the quasi-labor officials of these committees is that they do damage to the company because they are politically minded and technically incompetent. The committee was not operative in two of the firms in the sample. Of these two, one employer had strengthened the position of the CISL by signing an agreement with that labor organization, as a result of which the committee became inoperative soon thereafter. His belief is that the communication problem with employees is eased by dealing directly with a single outside trade union official. Generally, the responses reflect the communication void between the employer and employees and the master-servant character of the relationship between the two.

The relative increases in the votes for the CISL candidates for the shop committees have been interpreted as losses in strength for the Communists in the CGIL. Part of these gains, however, are spurious. They reflect in part the increasing ability of the employer to screen potential employees on ideological grounds and to manipulate the candidates for the shop committees. The workers themselves are sensitive to the point of view of the employer. They are inclined to switch their votes for fear of losing their jobs or incurring the displeasure of the employer. Those who turn away from the CGIL in the heat of an inspired shop committee election may be prone to switch back in a subsequent year because of a situation operating against the CISL or the UIL. Votes for both the Communist party and the CGIL are supported by a strong undercurrent of attitudes which are not eradicated by manipulation on the part of either employer or trade union representatives. The effect of such maneuvering may not be a weakening of the left as much as a serious deterioration of trade unionism in general.

There are several ways in which the shop committee can be converted into a docile company union. The members of the committee may be fixed by manipulation independent of the three labor federations. The employer may provide them with facilities, and give them a salary without the requirement of working in the plant, thus furnishing them with a status they would be reluctant to relinquish. Under such conditions, it is difficult not to abide by the employer's wishes and point of view. The committeemen may develop a marked empathy for employer feelings. In addition, department heads may discreetly advise employees how to vote. Votes of the various federations could be analyzed on a department basis, and then by a manipulation of layoff and selection a relative decline could be effectuated in the strength of a particular federation. The employer can also decide to talk only to a particular organization and refuse the others a hearing. He can sign an agreement improving the terms of employment with the federation he favors at a particular moment. Consequently, an employer, if he so desires, can without too much difficulty convert the shop committee into a company union.

It would not be unwarranted to conclude that these committees serve the interests of employers more than they do the trade unions. Their weakness is primarily the responsibility of the federations themselves, who have failed to make them a mechanism of trade unionism and who use them instead as an instrument of providing an annual spectacle of workers being pitted against each other for political reasons. They have evolved into organizations which, while having no right to bargain collectively for new agreements, have not only done so but have acquired a more effective voice than the trade unions in their interpretation.

TABLE 40

Italian Labor Leader Attitudes toward the Possibility of Union-Management Coöperation at the Plant Level
(Per Cent)

Nature of response	CGIL	CISL	UIL
Affirmative	0	27	27
Qualified affirmative	36	60	46
Negative	50	13	27
No response	14	0	0
Total	100	100	100
Number	14	15	11

Table 40 lists responses on whether labor-management coöperation at the plant level is possible. The majority in the CISL–UIL group give either an answer in the affirmative or a qualified *yes* to the item. The majority in the CGIL group do not believe that such coöperation is possible. Representative statements included the following:

From the CGIL:

It is impossible to collaborate with an employer in a capitalistic society, if by that you assume an independent trade union and free collective bargaining. In Italy, the employer chooses the union he wants to negotiate with and then grants concessions as he sees fit. *Il padrone concede ma non contratta.* [The boss grants rather than bargains.] When the employer says the forty-hour week is absolutely out of the question in Italy, that is not bargaining.

We believe a conflict of interests exists between employers and workers But we reject the idea of a permanent war against them and have been trying to discourage our *attivisti* from believing in the concept of total war. It could come about by workers' participating in joint production councils. But the employers view these councils as a means of rubber-stamping their decisions. We want workers to exercise autonomous judgment. The union-management coöperation programs made by the CISL are just scraps of paper.

It is impossible to collaborate with employers in a capitalistic society.

Only on condition that workers participate in management of the plant . . .

It cannot happen in Italy; the employers are not enlightened enough.

From the UIL:

The employer would have to accept the trade union and collective bargaining and thereby give up unilateral decision-making.

It is all right so long as such coöperation does not include bargaining over wages.

Yes, on the basis of mutual responsibility of both parties. But this can be brought about only by the workers' seeing the importance of trade unionism.

From the CISL:

Yes, if it is limited to productivity increases only and not to trade union matters.

It cannot happen in Sicily; the employers are too baronial.

It is possible only if the employers start treating workers like human beings.

The tendency of the young Italian labor movement to create new schisms rather than heal old ones is exemplified in the history of the shop committee of one of the dominant companies of Italy, the Fiat Motor Company. Between 1945 and 1950, the CGIL initiated at the company a number of strikes and demonstrations of a political character. Part of their effect was an increase in the disillusionment of workers about trade unionism. This in turn caused them to look toward the employer for leadership just at the time that the two new federations, the CISL and the UIL, were coming into existence. Although management denies it, the labor leaders in these organizations state that their first representatives on the committee were men who had gained the support of company executives and supervisors. Attempts were made to strengthen their position, these officials state, by making concessions in employment terms through these representatives. These increased benefits raised questions as to the violation of the national agreement covering the shop committees, which did not make them an instrument of collective bargaining of new agreements. They also set the scene for the growth of a benign type of company unionism, and its acceptability to the employees. The CISL members on the committee then split into two groups: those who believed in this type of collaboration with the employer and those who espoused a more militant kind of trade unionism on a national union basis. In 1955, the CISL expelled the former group, but later, in a move the leaders of the federation now consider a blunder, they were again readmitted. The autonomous group, known as the *Arrighiani* after the name of their leader, continued to take positions independent of the CISL. In 1958, after an attempt by Arrighi to remove the CISL adherents from the commission at Fiat, the CISL again expelled them from the union, and this group, with the aid of a member of Parliament belonging to the Christian Workers' Associations, the clergy, and employer representatives, formed an independent union. One effect of this split was the increase in votes for the CGIL shop committee candidates.

A spokesman for the Fiat Company denied that they have organized a company union. The scarcity of strikes and lack of trade union militancy is due, not to the company domination of the plant committee, but to disillusionment on the part of the employees after eight years of continuous strikes and sabotage. "A fatal dichotomy exists in the CGIL between their ideological inclinations and successful trade unionism, and we become tired of being victimized by their ideological exercises. The desire for autonomy and independence on the part of Arrighi is natural in a situation where differences exist between the plant leadership and top trade union officials. The company-wide bargaining that exists in Italy is almost always with the *commissioni interne* and not with the trade union." Asked whether he felt the collective bargaining power of the union could be enhanced if the negotiators were officers of the national union instead of plant employees, he replied that the shop committeemen are more responsive to the needs of the employees. "Part of the lack of militancy is due also to the favorable terms of employment at Fiat. Employee wages average 80 per cent above the minima stipulated in national agreements. The workers have seventeen paid holidays (including one for the patron saint of the city), and fifteen days vacation. In 1956, eight thousand Fiat employees purchased automobiles, compared to several hundred in 1949, and the bicycles some of them ride are being replaced with motorcycles. The problem is one of developing in Italy a new type of leadership that is informed and not demagogic. The changes are slow, but if you come to Italy again after ten years you will see the difference."

Arrighi's position is that the shop committeemen, not the trade union, should do the bargaining at the company level. "We are an organization elected directly by all the workers in the plant. We also know better the problems in the plant and are in a better position to undergo such bargaining. The CISL never told us what labor policies they were proposing. There are some disadvantages to a company union that has no federation support. It really cannot say to Fiat, 'Let us start bargaining.' What if the company should say no?"

Some concluding observations can be drawn on Italian union-management relationships. First, a distinction has to be drawn between the federation leadership and the subordinate leaders, some of whom may be technicians seeking to discharge the relationship successfully on a day-by-day basis. The hostility that may exist at one level should not be inferred to exist in another. The making of denunciatory after-dinner speeches at top levels while the members of a lower level are working together unobtrusively is a custom not uniquely American. On the whole, however, there are no mutually accepted rules of the game which could systematize and stabilize the relationship at the company level, while those at the national level serve best the interests of the organized employers. The instability at the bottom is made greater by the existence of competing labor movements, who are opposing each other on how the rules of the game should be changed, in the face of strong opposition from the employer association.

Second, patriarchal labor relations are still common, although diminishing, in Italy. The relationship in which the employer commits himself morally to providing for his workers in return for their fealty is found more commonly in the South than in the industrial North and may break down with rapid industrialization, increase in size of plants, and full employment. The fact that such a relationship also exists in some degree in the country places of Denmark strengthens the idea that it is a rural phenomenon which disappears with urbanization and large-scale industrial production.

Another characteristic of this relationship is the impotency of the trade unions to effectuate changes of substantial proportions. In Italy this lack of influence is due to the following factors: (1) the split in the labor movement, which serves the interests of the employer; (2) the high rate of unemployment, which makes for a docile labor force subservient to the point of view of the employer; (3) the low level of education and training of workers and the lack of a tradition of independent initiative, fostered in part by the Fascist inheritance and by the Church; (4) the strong pressure-tactics of the Communists, which have the effect of stiffening the position of employers; (5) the lack of technical preparation of trade union officials; (6) the inability of the labor movement to direct a long strike to achieve drastic revisions in the scope and depth of collective bargaining agreements; (7) the ineffectiveness of the national agreement in grappling with actual worker problems in particular plants and the failure to establish company-wide collective bargaining; (8) the marked social-economic differences between labor leaders and employers.

THE RELATIONSHIP IN DENMARK

A feature of the labor-management relationship in Denmark is the high integration of functions of employer and union representatives. Selection of shop stewards, for example, is subject to collective bargaining. The persisting effects of the guild system combine what are considered elsewhere separate management and trade union functions in the duties of one individual who is a member of the union. The "employer" provides work on a contract basis to this individual, who in turn recruits workers into the appropriate trade union and exercises supervisory responsibility over them. He also acts as their shop steward and distributes to them any surplus funds remaining at the termination of the work. What is more, it is conceivable that the workers may lodge a grievance against him at the local union or that some day he may become the *formand* of that union local. While the inroads of large-scale factory production tend to break down this inheritance of the guild system, its pervasive force in the economy serves to make the parties regard each other more as colleagues than as adversaries.

In a sense, Danish employer and trade union organizations can be considered a single group with similar functions, goals, and values. Neither leadership expresses views sharply at variance with those of the other. Their perceptions are similar. Both organizations exert similar pressures on workers. The employer feels trade unionism to be in his interest because it becomes the instrument of putting over his point of view to workers. No sharp contest between them over their respective functions exists, the battle over prerogatives having been resolved before the turn of the century.[12] Functions such as selection and training, normally reserved in the United States for company personnel departments, are performed by the union almost exclusively, and only a small grumble could be heard from the employers questioned on the matter.

The unique relationship between Danish employers and trade union officials suggests that an interpretation of a labor movement has to rely on the broader base of an interpretation of industrial relations. Both exercise considerable joint power. They can sit down and change the wage level of their country in one fell swoop. The union leader is considered not an alien influence but an indispensable part of production organization. Both labor and employer leadership are necessary. No presumption exists that the former could be dispensed with if the latter were to perform in an efficient manner. The personnel function is not employed as an instrument to thwart unionism. A serious conflict over prerogatives is unlikely, not so much because management would be disinclined to seek to bar intrusions in certain types of decision-making as because the trade union officials are disposed not to press hard on the functions of management. In Denmark differences in aspirations between labor and management are smaller than in Italy because the aspirations of management are fewer than its counterpart in Italy and those of the Danish worker greater. Consequently, the respective goals of both parties have been more easily integrated in a manner perceived by both employer and labor leader as preserving their respective interests.

The employer-employee relationship in Denmark is channeled to an extraordinary degree through the union shop steward. He is a key figure in communication between employers and employees and assumes functions which in the United States and Italy would be considered as properly belonging to the supervisor. The worker is more apt to consult the shop steward than the foreman on terms and con-

[12] The rights and responsibilities of the parties are spelled out in their historical peace treaty, the September Agreement of 1899. The federation has moved several times to seek an alteration of the pact. The last change as of this writing occurred in 1960.

ditions of employment. It is not rare for the supervisor himself to find
out about changes of employment terms from the shop steward, much
to his chagrin.

The Setting of the Rules of Work

In many of the industries in Denmark, the employer is confronted
in collective bargaining by a key craft union and by the ubiquitous
General and Special Workers' Union. Although in theory the bargain
over terms of employment is set separately with each union, a particular settlement is looked upon with an eye toward its effect on
agreements covering other workers in the plant. The effect of this
cautious policy of watchful waiting is the pushing-up of settlements
to the economy level and the making of agreements based on an understanding as to what all the major settlements will be. In this jockey-
ing for position, the leaders of the Metal Union and of the General
and Special Workers' Union play strategic roles. The position of the
latter is probably more difficult. Not being on piece-rate systems, generally, the workers in this union cannot obtain increases in their earnings through the manipulation of incentive rates. In addition, the price
of unemployment which might have to be paid as the consequence
of a collective bargaining agreement is more likely to fall on the members of this trade union. The employers view these two unions as pace-
setters and are concerned lest concessions to one of them become the
basis of a general increase in labor costs. In the 1958 settlement, the
newspapers carried a picture of the prime minister and the president
of the General Workers' Union after the signing of the national agreement. In a sense, the photograph symbolizes the pressures confronting
the employers in collective bargaining in Denmark, for the ultimate
negotiator for the trade unions is the Social Democrat party.

In this maneuvering over making key bargains, certain pressures
stand out in significance. The relative differences in the wages of workers of different unions are as important to employers as they are to
labor leaders. Any creation of new differences is a burden that should
be avoided. The lack of exclusive collective bargaining representation,
as it exists in the United States, serves to place in the same plant several
unions, each conscious of any changes in the position of the other. In
addition, in the pursuit of collective bargaining objectives, the trade
union officials are more likely than the employers to maintain the appearance of a common front. The egalitarian spirit in the ranks of the

trade union movement seeks those advantages which can be gained from the individualism among the employers.

Following are typical comments from labor leaders on pressures in collective bargaining.

There are pressures to raise wages based on ability to pay, but it cannot work without having industrial unionism. It is impossible to determine standards otherwise, and besides it will improve the present shortcomings in fact-finding technique on an individual craft union basis.

I do not want government mediation. It forces us to settle for less because the employer, in anticipation of mediation, starts negotiations by saying No to all the proposals. The only advantage occurs when it can be used in saving face when the rank and file is pushing demands which the labor leader realizes cannot be met.

You demand a little more than you can get in collective bargaining. You exert pressures by pointing out inequitable geographical differences. We do not want our demands to hurt the economy, but you must have some sort of improvement in the terms of employment.

In collective bargaining we stress that the employees are orderly, competent, and responsible. The employer knows the workers want the industry to bloom, and therefore we stress that too.

Social differences in community standards are a forceful argument in persuading an employer to improve a term of employment. A plea to change the wage level is too abstract. It is difficult, however, for an employer to rebut the argument that Danish workers "cannot celebrate Christmas in the same manner as other members of the community." The demands are influenced by the changing strength of the membership which stands to the left of the labor leader.

Employers generally feel that they have a stake in bargaining collectively through the employer association. This procedure assures them that new differences between their competitors and themselves in terms of employment will not be established. For several employers, however—in each instance large organizations led by men who started at the bottom—the monolithic kind of collective bargaining of the employer association is not attractive. They prefer to go it alone, rather than see their decision-making ability circumscribed by the bureaucrats of the association. Or they are concerned with the effects on the country of a type of collective bargaining which changes the economy in one fell swoop.

The process of whittling-down union demands begins long before they reach the collective bargaining table. A distinction is drawn in collective bargaining between general and special demands. Control of the former in the trade union organizations is achieved by the labor leaders' informing their membership on the general changes in terms of employment which are likely to be of issue in the signing of the new agreement. The latter are arrived at by the solicitation of expressions of sentiment from the rank and file on particular changes in the terms of employment, which are edited and communicated upward to the national leadership. In this way, demands for the new labor agreement are drawn. While the settlements on particular questions, so called, are likely to be made by the individual national unions, the general issues are more apt to be settled by joint strategy at the federation and employer association level. Consequently, the structure of bargaining is such as to seek some measure of uniformity in changes in general terms of employment and to reconcile pressures for uniformity and moderation from the top leadership of both parties with what the rank and file believes represents its particular needs.

Propelled by these influences, the area of the collective bargaining agreement has been shifting from the individual craft union to the level of the industry and the federation. The pressures of collective bargaining push the trade unions in the direction of industry-wide bargaining despite the reluctance of some of them to move in that fashion. It is in the interest of neither the employer nor the labor leaders to make accords one at a time, because of the uncertainty which such a procedure forces on them. In this unobtrusive shift to industrial union forms, it is likely that a significant number of workers in the General and Special Workers' Union will benefit, because their wages will be more closely geared to those prevalent in the industries in which they are employed. In addition, the advent of industrial unionism is likely to remove the barrier to promotional opportunities in the firm which the craft forms of organization have created.

The progressive editing of demands and the upward shifting of the control of collective bargaining policy serve to make accommodation between the parties easier. The role of the trade union official is not merely that of an agent who transmits all demands that can be mustered within the union organization. Rather, he is expected to modify them in a manner that would increase their acceptability to the employer. Nor is he likely to react with shock at the demands the employer may make on him. Such procedure prevents situations prevalent in other countries, where the manner in which both sides initially confront each other assures the inevitability of conflict between them.

The collective bargaining relationship in Denmark is characterized by a Danish student of labor relations as one of increasing stability within an intricate maze of rules. The parties have a respect for the law. It is said that neither party would approach the other without consciously implementing a particular rule in the course of his behavior. Conflict has declined to small proportions, and the stability of the relationship has ushered in a new trend in long-term agreements. The principals in collective bargaining approach each other within a stabilized bureaucratic system and at times address each other in the *du* form rather than in the formal *De*. Final decisions are made by a handful of men, and in the main the rank and file acquiesce. Trade union officials use statistics furnished by the employer association to make new claims on the employers, and the latter call on the former to curtail the demands of the workers. Although the employer plays the functional role of pointing out the good features of existing employment terms and the labor leader plays his by demonstrating their inequities, their estimates of what the new standards will be are not far apart. In this high integration of top-level goals, the function of the Communist membership is to maintain a certain amount of dissatisfaction with the way matters are. Consequently, the pressures are strong against using the strike as an instrument of agreement. The employees themselves express a reluctance to strike, particularly those working in small organizations and communities. Nor would a worker wish to continue to work for an employer if a grievance persisted on either side.

The wages of a Danish worker change as a result of decision-making by different sets of individuals at various levels of the industrial relationship. The group of individuals making the change is not the same in all cases. The change may come from an increase in the wage minima determined by collective bargaining between the industry association and the national union. These minima are actually base rates plus accumulated cost-of-living adjustments, and can be revised at the termination of an agreement. The second way wages can change is by means of a negotiated general wage increase, which takes place at the level of the federation and the employers' association. A third way is by the setting of new piece rates on a new or altered job. With the exception of the General and Special Workers' Union, it is less painful to effectuate a general wage increase through the administration of the piece-rate system at the local level than it is to negotiate a flat amount of money at the top. The fourth manner in which an employee's earnings can rise is through the automatic operation of cost-of-living adjustments, the criteria of which have been previously agreed to by the parties. An individual adjustment in wages above the minimum between an employer and a particular employee is a fifth way of effectuating wage change. Although such adjustments based on "merit" would be a violation of association rules if put into effect for a group of employees, employers nevertheless do make them. In times of a labor shortage, wages tend to move away from the minima stipulated in agreements to such an extent that the latter merely represents a floor below which wages cannot fall without agreement in the event of economic adversity. It can be seen, therefore, that the actual average wages of workers cannot be determined from those stipulated in collective bargaining agreements.

Consequently, the actual price of labor is determined to a considerable degree by individual bargaining. Its range is controlled by the flexibility left the employer, after the agreement has been signed, to make adjustments without a formal agreement with the union. Since individual bargaining between employer and employee is rare except in the very small firm, these post-bargaining decisions are made more or less unilaterally and are motivated by the desire to control profit margins, retain key employees, and attract new labor. Any attempt by the union to narrow profit margins by increasing labor costs or by controlling prices will be met with strong resistance. Though not to the same degree, these factors are prevalent in both Italy and Denmark. It can be said, therefore, that while these labor leaders join with the employer in an agreement on wages, the actual price of labor tends to be set by the employer at the plant level, based on an appraisal of economic and social forces confronting him. Moreover, a greater tolerance apparently exists in these countries than in the United States for a random individual adjustment of wages apart from the standards set for the group as a whole. To what extent this phenomenon reflects a sympathetic attitude toward the employer point of view on the part of the trade union official or whether it simply represents an inability to muster enough pressures against the practice is not clear.

This tendency of actual wages to be set at the plant level has an effect on the scope of collective bargaining conducted at the top level of labor leadership. The labor leader who makes a settlement on wages of no particular significance to the actual earnings of the membership has done little to improve the terms of employment. The consequence of this type of bargaining, therefore, is to shift national negotiations to hours of work and fringe benefits and to maintain the importance of the union local. To cite an example, it has been traditional policy in Denmark to seek to narrow wage differences between the skilled and unskilled by greater increases to the latter in formal agreements. However, the inducing of a "wage slide" by wage administration at the plant level has the effect of maintaining differences between both groups.

This distinction between the nature of industry-wide agreements in Denmark and Italy and those in the United States should be kept in mind. Except in the case of marginal employers who pay minimum wages set in these agreements, the actual earnings of workers are determined at the plant level by a higher degree of unilateral employer wage-setting than exists for the unionized American employer. To be sure, as far as piece-rate systems are concerned, the local officials in Denmark join with the employer in setting new rates. The method, however, leaves to small, ill-equipped craft unions the job of bargaining out interplant differences with individuals who generally have more resources than they. The Metal Workers are aware of this anomaly and have been willing to forgo national wage increases and concentrate on gearing wages to the productivity of individual plants. As a consequence, the difference in earnings of metal workers in different plants is greater than the difference in the average wages between the skilled and unskilled. In Italy, the issue of company collective bargaining arises primarily because the unilateral wage-setting of the employer over the national minima is a serious threat to the existence of the union. There is a danger that paternalistic relationships will develop as the worker realizes that the union serves no function in determining what his terms of employment are. Such a procedure may insulate the most powerful employers from the effects of collective bargaining.

How can this greater area of permissibility of individual bargaining within the scope of a collective bargaining agreement be explained? For one matter, the fractionalizing of jobs within detailed job-descriptions and its attendant inflexibility for the employer does not exist in either country to the extent that it does in the United States. There is a greater tendency to consider a man as a potential of skills whose monetary value to the employer is not precisely the same as that of another in the same classification. Accordingly, once a minimum is set for an industry or occupation, the employer will resist any tendency to relate wages to jobs rather than to individuals. Thus the slogan "Equal pay for equal work" is contested on the basis that its implementation would mean equal pay for unequal potential. Capacity cannot be determined on the basis of a group standard and should not therefore be subject to collective decision-making. This being so, its measurement should be resolved directly between the employer and the individual worker, and if no agreement can be reached, the latter can elect to withdraw his employment. At least, such is the argument raised by the employer in the setting of individual wages. Under conditions of full employment, such a procedure allows workers to obtain wages higher than those obtainable under a more rigid system of collective bargaining.

The presence of a strong left wing in a union serves to make more difficult a meeting of minds on the extent of a general wage increase. The following statement from a Danish employer is typical: "When I negotiate with Mr. _____, we both know what the wage settlement should be. If he demands two hundred kroner when his Communists are asking for four hundred and he knows he will get sixty, that immediately makes for a difficult settlement. We tell him he is asking for too much, and when he denies it, we know he is being pressed hard by his left wing. The employers then read about the demand and start curtailing their production. This lack of courage in the face of left-wing sentiment is the biggest weakness of trade unionism. . . ."

The handling of disputes arising from existing agreements in Denmark takes place by a system of industry arbitration boards and a higher labor court, Den Faste Voldgiftsret, which has been created by the law. Grievances over the interpretation of the agreement fall within the purview of the industry arbitration boards, while those involving contract violations go to the labor court. Although the distinction between the types is not always clear, the court seeks to interpret jurisdiction in a manner that keeps the bulk of grievances at the industry arbitration level. In any case, the court is the body of last resort on both procedural and substantive matters arising out of contract interpretation.

Cases involving suit for damages for violations of contract are the exclusive jurisdiction of the labor court. The hearing is conducted in a quasi-judicial atmosphere in a high-ceilinged room whose furnishings seem proportioned to humble the labor-management spirit. Smoking is not permitted. Instead of the triangular arrangement typical of American labor arbitration, the parties symbolically sit side by side facing the impartial chairman at the center of a long table. Behind the spokesmen for the employer association and the trade union federation are officials of the union and the employer involved in the dispute. In one hearing which the investigator attended, the representative of the employer association was asking that a fine be imposed on the union for a wildcat strike. The dispute arose out of rehiring by the employer which the union was alleging had been done without recalling previously laid-off employees. The union argued that the workers had reacted spontaneously when they heard that their former fellow workers had not been rehired. The hearing went on quietly, each side presenting its argument with the support of precedent. There were no raised voices, no emotional outbursts, no points of order. No stenographic transcript of hearings was kept. The secretary of the court, sitting to the right of the chairman, took notes. The employer argued that he had the right to discharge, and the union stated that management should have gotten in touch with the union to rehire former employees. A pre-arbitration hearing had previously clarified the issues and had almost produced a settlement which would have avoided the necessity of a formal submission of the dispute to the court. The possible solutions which the chairman suggests in a pre-arbitration hearing become the basis of determining the area of agreement if a formal decision has to be rendered. During the course of the formal hearing, a meeting of minds was sought by the use of recesses to allow negotiation between the parties and ex parte discussions with the chairman. Consequently, the award was not a surprise decision. In this case, the union acquiesced to a fine smaller than the original demand of the employers' association.

The content of such grievances is dissimilar to that in the United States. The Danes do not have the finely divided system of job classifications which creates a considerable number of American grievances. In addition, discharge cases are not subject to the regular grievance machinery. Instead, the employer is required to give to the discharged employee a termination notice proportionate to his length of service in the firm. The common cases which arise are those involving strike action. While the union does not, in the collective bargaining agreement, forgo the right to strike, it cannot strike without adhering to prescribed rules. The effect of such rules is to produce either a strike which invariably enters the grievance machinery, or no strike at all.[13]

The determination of whether the greater collective bargaining power lies with unions or employers is a difficult matter in Denmark. A particular issue may have the full force of the employer association or the federation behind it, while another may be left to an individual employer or a local union. The bargaining of new agreements which provides employers with guarantees against whipsawing tactics by the union and with flexibility in the determination of wages on an individual-employee basis reflects employer interests more than it does those of the trade unions. However, these rules of the game manifest just as much the array of values of the trade unions as they do the ability of the employer to express his point of view in collective bargaining. The highly integrated organization of the employers and their interest in pushing collective bargaining toward deciding new levels of employment for everyone in one fell swoop has the effect of reducing the bargaining power of some unions. Even such cases, however, are dependent on time, particular issues, and industries. Each party seems to have managed to do all that can possibly be done to control the power of the other. The financial, political, and social facts which each side can direct against the other are such that both sides lose equally in the event of a conflict.

This equality of collective bargaining power, consequently, is not explainable on economic grounds alone. The forces which narrow the demands made by the parties in industrial relations on each other and render them highly acceptable are cultural as well as economic in character. Agreement in collective bargaining involves the reconciling of values of the employer and labor leader. To bring about a meeting of minds, the preferences of both have to be reconciled. In comparison with Italy, these opposing value-structures in Denmark are in less conflict with each other. Each party is more inclined to accept as reasonable the preferences and goals of the other. The greater economic power which might accrue to the union in times of high employment becomes diffused by the excellent organization tactics of employers, including their ability to exert on the trade union officials political pressure, despite their minority representation in Parliament. The equal-

[13] For an analysis of the structure of the Danish arbitration system, see Walter Galenson, *The Danish System of Labor Relations* (Cambridge: Harvard University Press, 1952), pp. 106–7 and 226–32. For a translation of the dispute-settlement agreement for the metal workers, see Appendix F.

ity of bargaining power is evidenced by a growing conviction of the futility of striking and the indispensability of mediation. In this balance of cultural and social forces, whoever is the lion at a particular moment in collective bargaining is not inclined to seek the lion's share even though he possesses the power to do so. Neither party finds himself in the position of having to accept a highly distasteful demand made by the other because the price of not doing so would be too great. If the balance of forces is relatively equal, mediation is available to resolve the deadlock, and if it is unequal, restraint does not allow using the difference up to the hilt.

Almost all of the respondents in the sample of national labor leaders believe that the collective bargaining power of the parties is "equal." They base the explanation of equality on two factors: the complete organization of each side and the relatively similar amount of resources each party can direct at the other. In this view, the advantages of bargaining power that accrue to trade unions during a period of high demand for goods are curtailed by employer organization, which minimizes the possibility of employers' competing with each other for the services of labor. "You have to stay in a union if you want a job; we control the labor supply, while the employer has the ability to withdraw all of the jobs from the labor market. If we withdraw labor or if the employers withdraw jobs, we pay similar costs. Under these circumstances, you cannot insist on demands which the other party believes are not reasonable. . . ."

A minority of the group expressed the belief that it is difficult to make a categorical statement on the degree of bargaining power. The extent of bargaining power depends on the stage of the business cycle or the level of unemployment at the time of negotiations. It depends on which side can hold out longer, and that varies with shifting circumstances. Some stated that bargaining power can be discussed only with reference to particular unions; when they are pressed further, however, the term "particular unions" implies the economics of the industry, such as technology and profitability. One labor leader believes that in "socialist" Denmark it is the employers who have the greater bargaining power. "Their power is more organized and more concentrated than ours. Ours is based on democratic consent which places a limit on the decisions we can make. They succeed in pushing up a major issue to the national level, where they can effectively control it in their interest."

Attitudes toward the Strike

With the exception of the time of the successful struggle for recognition in 1899, the periods of postwar adjustments, and the deep depression in the mid-thirties, strike statistics for Denmark show a continual decline to the point where man-days lost to total working time is measured to the fourth decimal place. Their conflicts are of small consequence, and those that occur are often the product of the small left wing of the labor movement. In the old days, the left-wingers used to be the syndicalists, but now the role of dissenter has been assumed by the Communists. Their influence is small, however, and directly associated with the availability of a crisis in the union which can be used as an instrument of rallying the membership behind their leadership.

Danish national labor leaders were asked about their attitudes toward the strike. The preponderant number of positive responses concern its usefulness in creating pressure to effectuate a meeting of minds. The threat of a work stoppage itself is a means of narrowing differences between the parties and of obtaining concessions from the employer.

It is always necessary to obtain at least a small concession from the employer, and it is therefore necessary to threaten a strike when no concessions are forthcoming.

It preserves the employer will to bargain collectively in future negotiations

It is a means of pressing for gains.

It maintains the idea that a work stoppage is possible.

It is a weapon of last resort when collective bargaining fails.

It can be used when it is impossible to obtain an agreement otherwise.

It is a means of changing the position of the employer.

The respondents who expressed such views emphasized the threat of a work stoppage as producing net gains for the union, rather than an actual strike itself.

A noteworthy number of responses express negative attitudes toward the use of the strike weapon.

It is not worth the cost; we know each other's strength.

The consequence of a strike is government intervention, and neither of us wants that. Because of its commercial obligations, the government is compelled to intervene before the strike generates sufficient pressure on the parties themselves.

It is no longer an effective weapon. The threat of a strike forces collective bargaining up to the federation level, and at that point it is a game of politics and not collective bargaining.

A union starting a strike may cause an employer lockout of the entire labor force.

What is the use of striking for a wage increase when you can obtain it in the course of the collective bargaining agreement anyway?

The skepticism of the respondents toward the strike suggests several implications. First, the prevalent sentiment among Danish labor officials is that the employers have succeeded in reducing the effectiveness of the strike by complete organization. Second, even a labor government sympathetic to trade unionism has needs of its own, which supersede those of the organizations on which it relies for support. Third, the strike is no longer an effective instrument of collective bargaining when its use does not serve the immediate purpose of producing an agreement. It causes government intervention long before the parties are ready for a meeting of minds, and the price to be paid for its use is too great in comparison to the improvement in terms of employment it might provide the membership. Fourth, the view of the strike as a manifestation of social failure limits its use. Fifth, when the differences between the parties are small and when tacit agreement exists among them as to the eventual settlement, the strike appears an irrational act. In sum, increasing market, political, and cultural restraints combine to make the strike in Denmark an obsolete weapon for producing collective bargaining agreements.[14]

Employer–Trade-Union Relations at the Plant Level

An agreement between the federation and the employers' association signed in 1947 provides for the creation of joint production committees on the plant level, composed of management and employee representatives in firms above a certain size. Each party is represented by an

[14] On November 18, 1960, the employers' association and the trade union federation signed an agreement limiting further the right to strike and increasing the procedures necessary before a strike can take place. The agreement adds to the responsibility of the federation in preventing strikes not consistent with agreed-to procedures and makes disagreements over the interpretation of these rules subject to arbitration. Of novel importance in the same agreement is the obligation of the employer to advise employees with one year or more of seniority of the basis for their discharge. While Danish trade unions have not by any means circumscribed the right of discharge to the degree achieved by American unions and labor arbitrators, they seemed to be inclined to move in that direction.

equal number of delegates, the company providing a chairman and the union a vice-chairman, generally the shop steward. A tenth-anniversary study of these committees indicates that some 35 per cent of Danish enterprises had such committees in existence and that most of them had been established in the first year of the agreement. Many of them were not holding the four regular meetings a year contemplated by the accord. The small number of meetings was explained by a tendency to solve problems through informal contacts in the plant, reserving the formal committee hearing for problems of broader significance, such as reviews of company accounts. The subjects reported in the study as being handled by these production committees include safety, work studies, technological changes, employment problems, welfare programs, and to a lesser degree, training, education, information, quality standards, and material waste.

The dominant tone of the responses on the question concerning this form of labor-management coöperation is that it is not a success. A newspaper labor reporter interpreted the pessimism of the trade union officials in this fashion:

The committee meets and does nothing. The failure is due to lack of technical preparation by the union and the disinclination on the part of the employer to reveal his finances and future plans. Another factor is the high level of relationships that has existed hitherto between Danish employers and the trade unions. The intensity of the union-management relationship at the plant level found in the United States is not found in Denmark. The problem is one of learning how to deal with each other in a manner different from the employer–shop-steward relationship characteristic of Europe.

The pessimistic views of the trade union officials do not ascribe the failure to any one particular party. Representative responses are given below:

Some employers do not understand the purpose of these committees, but the success of the program depends on the technical preparation of the *klub* members. We are therefore sending them to adult education courses.

The employers do not want to show the balance sheets.

The employers do not want them, and the workers have had bad experiences with them in the past.

The success of those committees depends on the training we provide our representatives to perform their job.

When costs are reduced as the result of the efforts of the committee, the workers want to talk about wage increases, and that is forbidden by the collective bargaining agreement.

Employers are somewhat more optimistic than the labor leaders, though not universally so. Following are representative comments:

I was going to organize one myself before the agreement because it establishes confidence and a knowledge of each other.

They are an effective means of communication between management and the workers.

I could easily talk of the benefits of productivity to the president of the _____ union, but it is quite another matter to do it with his workers.

The General Workers use it as a means of asking for a wage increase, while the skilled workers suggest new machines which they have seen elsewhere that I should buy.

They have some advantage; they tend to localize trouble like a lightning rod. But the workers are not inclined to come forth with production proposals. It is not consistent with their pessimistic attitudes. The more enterprising among them leave Denmark.

It is a lot of nonsense. There is too much talk about toilet facilities and too little on how to increase production.

They just talk [snak].

The worker representatives dare not be objective.

A majority of the employers in the sample group believe union representation at the plant level to be an asset or partial asset. The favorable responses are generally from large firms, while the unfavorable ones come from small organizations or those built from nothing in the lifetime of the respondent. The responses below are typical of each subgroup:

Asset

Gives me the opportunity of uncovering a problem and meeting it head on; never had a wildcat strike in the plant.

Shop stewards have been an instrument of communication with workers for sixty years.

They are helpful in explaining costs to workers.

Means of giving workers status; we meet with shop stewards four times a year and have cake and coffee.

All our relations with the workers are through the shop steward.

They keep down trouble-makers.

They see the interest of the firm more than the workers do.

Most of our forty shop stewards are helpful to the company.

Partial Asset

They are a means of communication, but some of them are not flexible. Some of them lack the courage to tell workers they have to change their behavior. For example, we have a ten-minute coffee break which has become a half-hour. When I point this out to the shop steward, he says it is true it is supposed to be ten minutes but it has gotten to be a half-hour. Both of us continue this way and nothing is accomplished.

Some of them are mediocre. The chief steward is generally intelligent, but the rest are mediocre.

Partial Liability

The frequent elections for shop steward make them improperly trained to do the job.

The shop steward must be technically qualified and have an interest in the company; otherwise he becomes somewhat of a liability to the company. My chief shop steward is a Communist, but even he is interested in the prosperity of the company. So we have similar interests.

Liability

They do not have a long-run point of view.

They are either ignorant or badly trained.

They look at the immediate advantage of a situation instead of planning ahead.

They are vote-conscious like the leaders of the Socialist government and do not have the courage to tell workers what their responsibilities are.

They are not well trained. The job of the man who talks dissatisfaction is always easier than that of the one who talks satisfaction. That is why the role of the labor leader is easier and needs less intelligence and training.

The young ones in particular bring up petty grievances which have no merit.

In conclusion, the employer–labor-leader relationship in Italy is dominated by the employer and is subject to heavy pressure and hostility on both sides. In Denmark, generally, neither party is dominant, low pressure exists on both sides, and the respective sets of leaders act in a manner that is mutually reinforcing. In the Scandinavian country, machinery for dealing with each other is complex and established, compared to Italy, where it is weak and a matter of controversy. In either country, the relationship varies with the size of company, the level of leadership, the economic matrix confronting the parties, the type of workers involved, and whether the parties are pace-setters or followers in collective bargaining. However, it can be said in general that the marked disparity in the economic and cultural position of employer and labor leader in Italy serves to make the employer dominate the relationship between them.

Both similarities and differences exist in the collective bargaining process of these countries. First, both rely on the writing of national agreements in their formal agreement-making. However, the craft structure in Denmark and the greater homogeneity of firms in a particular competitive group make their agreements more meaningful. Second, in both countries, the changes in terms of employment occurring in a particular plant may not be reflected in the national agreements. More informal agreement-making exists in both countries than in the United States, where collective bargaining contracts are a more reliable document of actual employment on an individual basis. To what extent this greater flexibility reflects a sympathetic attitude toward the employer point of view on the part of the labor official is not clear. Third, the periodic push to a new formal standard of employment terms is a more centralized and monolithic affair in Denmark. The egalitarian spirit of that country forces the new standard to be decided in one fell swoop. However, recognition of this tendency should not overshadow the constant haggling taking place at the plant level. At the national level, cultural coercion, centralized bargaining structures, and a strong leadership tend to whittle down quickly any "pie in the sky" demands emanating at the bottom of the organization. Fourth, there are relative differences in the extent to which government, the employer, or collective bargaining are controlling the terms of employment. Fifth, several clues are available to make it possible to detect differences in the bargaining power of employers and labor leaders abroad. They include dissimilarities in the time elapsed in the writing of new agreements, the ratio of employer-responsibility clauses to worker- or union-responsibility clauses in labor contracts, and new breakthroughs in collective bargaining compared to labor leader demands. Sixth, the extent of the detail of a national agreement is partly a measure of the fiduciary relationship existing between employers and workers and their representatives, and partly the degree to which the relationship has become "legalized." Last, both countries have begun to recognize the responsibilities of workers in increasing productivity. However, the mechanical forms of implementing the idea, the measurement of productivity changes, and the form of distribution of its benefits remain obscure.

CHAPTER

8

Conclusions and Implications

The purpose of the field investigations in Italy and Denmark during the period from 1957 to 1959 was to develop a way of analyzing the labor systems of countries of contrasting cultures and institutions. In this concluding chapter, the results of the investigation will be summarized, with remarks on the method of approach, the special situation in Italy, comments on both countries combined, and lastly some general interpretations.

In the course of the investigation, a way of comparing labor systems by developing the differences in labor leader behavior was found. The findings suggest that the important dissimilarities among labor leaders are their array of values, their perceptions, and their estimates of the probability of success for the rank and file and for themselves. These characteristics assert themselves in behavior. Their estimates of situations and goals differ because of differences in such factors as the rate of upward movement in their life cycle, the social origin of their families, and the degree of homogeneity in expectations and fulfillment between them and their followers on the one hand, and for other groups in their society on the other. What constitutes such success in life is not the same in different countries, and its absolute measure is not as important as is the relative difference with which various groups in a country are experiencing it. Moreover, if their organizations are democratic, leaders mirror the values and aspirations of the rank and file in such a way that a study of the one provides clues to the characteristics of the other. This is not to say that both groups are precisely alike. Leaders are more intelligent, more expressive, and have problems that are not the same as those of the membership. Despite this difference, how-

313

ver, a study of labor leaders is an economical inquiry on the cultural milieu of the country in which they operate.

The differences in these cultural and social settings can be systematically described and analyzed by a comparative study of labor leadership in its broadest sense. Such a method provides a more useful structure for the development of international labor movement theory than that resting on British-American premises alone. The findings indicate that comparing value standards with which labor leaders make choices is a fruitful benchmark in developing international differences. This is not to suggest that economic factors are excluded. Rather, the analysis of these cultural differences is a convenient way of assembling the myriad pushes and pulls, including economic forces, which are affecting labor leader behavior, and of discerning relationships between national character and social change. The sample size, limited by financial resources, did not allow extended statistical treatment of the data. And not all the questions raised in the formulation of the project could be answered by an investigation covering Denmark and Italy alone. However, it is hoped that the study can now be extended to other nations, including those in Eastern Europe. The project would be given additional substance by a study of where the effective labor leadership in those countries lies and what its characteristics are.[1]

The experience indicates that it is not sufficient in the study of labor leaders to restrict depth interviews to them alone. The study of labor movements per se is not too meaningful. Employers, politicians, workers, and special segments of the public have to be reached in order to place labor leaders in proper perspective in their country. It is not only labor leaders who exercise the leadership of workers in a society. The allocations of leadership power in different countries are not alike. Workers may look to politicians, employers, intellectuals, or the clergy for guidance in the fulfillment of aspirations. Such leader-follower control may be extremely diffused in a society, and the allocation of functions between the parties not at all the same. The effective labor leaders of Italy are politicians and the clergy as much as trade union

[1] To my knowledge, the only attitudinal studies on labor in the Soviet-type economies are those of the Polish industrial sociologist Adam Sarapata, covering workers and professional employees in his country. The Soviet government was approached on the possibility of performing a study of Soviet worker characteristics. The response from the USSR State Committee on Cultural Relations with Foreign Countries was that the appropriate organizations in the Soviet Union were "not interested now."

officials. In Denmark, they are the trade union officers and the members of Parliament from the Social Democrat party.

Labor leaders, thus, do not operate in isolation. Their influence can be better measured in relative terms with that of other leaders in industrial relations. Their behavior manifests the shifting structure and power of all the organizations that play a part in production and in politics. Their goals, strategy, and methods of performance reflect attitudes of government representatives, employers, and workers. Consequently, a study of labor leadership becomes in fact a study of all the effective leaders of labor.

Such a study is not simply an analysis of the traits of labor leaders. No use is served by this kind of assessment. Rather, labor leadership is accepted as it is. It represents a classification of the behavior of the representatives of the working classes, acting inside and outside their organizations, and the influences associated with such behavior. The goal of such an inquiry is to develop a classification system of similarities and differences and to associate these characteristics with particular types of environments. By so doing, it will be possible to achieve the long-run objective of such a method, predicting the critical characteristics of labor leadership from a systematic analysis of environmental influences existing at a particular time. It rests on the following propositions: (1) What the labor leader does and says are clues to social and economic influences which are pushing labor systems this way and that. (2) This expression may be classified into terms which allow to a substantial degree a valid comparison between countries with differences in culture and development. In this fashion, the behavior controlled by particular patterns of cultural settings differing from one country to the next is converted into benchmarks of labor leader behavior.

Furthermore, such a comparative study marshals the forces affecting trade unionism and industrial relations in different stages of development by depicting systematically the structure of values with which the leadership in the employment relationship is making choices. It clarifies problems with which labor leaders feel they are confronted, by virtue of utilizing the attitudes of individuals in their own and outside organizations. The difficulties inherent in a comparative study of labor are not underestimated, and the suggested approach provides no easy panacea to these problems. It is invaluable, however, as a supplement to conventional methods. For after institutions, historical antecedents, and the condition and returns to workers are analyzed, there still remains the problem of what possible inferences can be drawn from such comparisons without an awareness of the value choices on which they are based.

These value choices present two difficulties: how to control those of the investigator and how to analyze systemically those he is observing. The same terms used in different countries, such as "industrial relations," "labor," "employers," and "strike," do not evoke the same image, and act as barriers to understanding. The use of strike statistics as a basis of comparison is of limited meaning when in one country men find conflict a mark of social failure and in another a form of expression. The importance of such values is not new. What needs to be done, however, is to develop a method of control in a manner that validates intercountry comparisons. Under such circumstances, it would seem to be necessary to concentrate the study of labor abroad first on the systematic assembling of the raw material of behavior rather than to yield to the more attractive course of writing impressionistic essays.

Comparative studies of labor leaders, moreover, are an economical instrument of studying national character and uncovering the locus and power differences of the effective leadership of a society. This leadership may be found in government, trade unions, the Church, or other organizations. The analysis of trade unions cannot be divorced from a concomitant inquiry on political leadership. The term "labor movement" itself is construed, as it is in Scandinavia, to mean the group action of worker representatives in both economic and political spheres. In this fashion, like Santayana's traveler, the observer of foreign labor leadership can recompose in systematic fashion what he sees and carry away a picture that can be recorded into a transmissible fund of knowledge. Such studies can be made an effective way of ferreting out factors which are likely to make for long-term differences in the industrialization process of different countries. They present a summary of dissimilarities in the aspirations and conditions of labor. They provide for participants of labor movements a vehicle in which to express their own points of view in their own words, and thereby reduce the tendency of reporting on foreign labor investigations through the culturally biased eyes of investigators inclined to make an appraisal of European soccer under the rules of American football. Such a method may break down the view of foreign labor movements as an abstract homogeneous mass into associations of different men in different unions, industries, and levels of leadership. It affords the opportunity to re-move comparative labor movement analyses away from the focus at federation headquarters and bring them down to the level of particular plants and locals. By placing the study of labor problems within a cultural climate developed through the perceptions of those involved in them, the method can distinguish new national trends from ebbing influences, which are often given emphasis in the reporting of foreign events.

Lastly, the quantitative and qualitative variables of labor leader-ship provide opportunities for the control and evaluation of policy. These variables can be used to discern relationships between the char-acteristics of leadership and those of environment by developing null hypotheses and by testing for correlations among a variety of such variables. This technique would place us in the position of venturing predictions by expecting a certain outcome from a specified application of a particular variable. The policy implication is that since we know how to produce certain outcomes, then given a particular objective, we could work toward it with some assurance of success if the ap-propriate variables are inserted in the environment.

ITALY

There are pressures in the Italian scene significant enough to cause pronounced changes in the labor system of that country. The trade union organizations are trying to push collective bargaining toward the level of the plant. The shop committee, the Achilles' heel of the Italian labor movement, may become dominated by the trade unions. They are being used by trade unions as a political football and by employers as a gratuitous opportunity to divide and conquer the unions. They furnish for disillusioned workers an annual exhibition of workers pitted against each other in political campaigning which has little to do with the election of qualified representatives. They are an impediment to trade union growth unless the federations curtail their influence and return collective bargaining to the trade union. A revolution is also taking place in the occupational distribution of the working classes. *Mezzadria* is declining and the number of small holders rising. Both sharecroppers and agricultural laborers are moving toward the cities. By region, the movement is from the South to the cities of the industrial triangle. Marginal lands on the hills and mountains are being aban-doned. And the movement is occurring despite the restrictions on labor mobility. This new industrial labor represents a principal force in the future Italian industrial relations system. With these changes, the classical function of the trade union official, essentially that of a social worker, is shifting also. The traditional philosophy of leadership, whether it be that of priest, politician, or trade union official, has been charity to the weak, and loyalty from them in return. It has been epitomized in the Italian expression of the role of trade unionism: *assistenza economica e morale.* The pressures in Italy now may bring changes in this point of view.

Italy is unlikely to succumb to the depersonalization that has occurred in the non-Latin types of Western industrialization. If the individualism and intensive man-to-man relationships of that country persist, Italy will provide the West with a clue on how to avoid the social estrangement that has occurred as a consequence of Western industrialization. So may the view of conflict as a spice of life tend to persist. I cannot imagine Italians adopting to the same extent the Anglo-Saxon view of conflict as an expression of social failure. The same is so for attitudes toward diversity. Non-Latin attitudes toward diversity in life range from the view that it is simply not efficient to the attitude that it is almost subversive. Americans have a compulsion to appear to be at dead center. In Italy no such compulsion exists to any degree.

The American view of the leveling process going on in the industrial relations system of the world seems to imply leveling up to Anglo-Saxon thinking. It suggests that other cultures, such as those of Latin societies, leave something to be desired, but will eventually catch up. On the contrary, it would be tragic indeed if one were to submerge the other in a contest for supremacy. Each has a positive contribution to make. While Anglo-Saxon and Nordic societies can teach the gospel of efficiency and the beneficence of increased production, the Italians can provide clues on how to avoid its price of depersonalization and commercialization of the human relationship. An irreconcilable conflict of ideas would be lamentable. A great contribution can be made by the leaders of the developing countries in seeking to fuse the ideas of these two cultural types. I refer not only to Italy but to the Latin-American countries as well. In a real sense, the Italian cities of Milan and Florence, despite their commercial excesses, juxtaposed against the models of New York and Chicago, provide clues to the benefits which can be derived from such a fusion of ideas. The Italian masses have a genius for establishing an intensively human rapport with each other, regardless of the particular attitude they are expressing. If Americanization kills off this basic need of man, Italy will have lost the opportunity to make her natural contributions to future world society.

Italy makes an ideal country as an anchor point for a massive labor inquiry. She presents a spectrum of economic development from Milan, a jewel of economic development, Italian style, to western Sicily, symbol of medieval exploitation and banditry. As a Latin society, she provides a testing ground of whether her industrial relations system will level up to Anglo-Saxon norms, especially because of her membership in the European community and her increasing exposure to non-Latin forms. She could demonstrate the validity of both the theory of increasing similarity by using economic benchmarks of production forms and consumption and the theory of sustained cultural heterogeneity by criteria measuring values. The measurement of the rising number of television sets and traffic jams would sustain the increasing similarity thesis. The persistent strength of the Italian Communist party, despite the sharp economic advances, would support the persisting dissimilarity thesis. If one were to go to the auto plants of the Italian Fiat, the French Renault, the German plant in Wolfsburg, and manage somehow to obscure the car models and the workers' faces, it would be difficult to distinguish the workers from each other and the technology from Detroit technology, and yet what differences in values and industrial relations forms! If one were to make a comprehensive labor inventory now, and return a decade hence, what would be the cultural and industrial relations forms in these areas? It would be regrettable indeed, if the opportunity which Italy affords for humanizing industrialization is lost. A comprehensive inquiry on her feudal rural labor in western Sicily and her auto workers in Turin would provide clues and should command the highest priority in international labor studies.

ITALY AND DENMARK

A noteworthy basis of differences among Danish and Italian labor leaders is found in their value standards. Religion, social orientation, the relative importance of individualism versus group control, a priori thinking versus pragmatism, these conscious and unconscious benchmarks for making choices give their labor movements a particular kind of thrust and direction. The leaders of different organizations are all discharging the function of crystallizing and guiding the aspirations and achievements of their members in a manner that would strengthen the organization. These functions, however, are performed in a way which is controlled by different sets of standards. They serve as a bond of compulsion between trade union leaders and the rank and file, and the extent of the differences between the standards of labor officials and those of employers prescribes the problems that arise in collective bargaining.[2]

The analysis of the situation confronting these labor leaders, against which values are placed, is rarely a purely objective appraisal of facts. In differing degree, in the case of the Italians, decisions have to be made hurriedly with limited facilities and generally rather imperfect knowledge. Decisions are affected by mental endowment and the level of leadership at which the trade union official is operating, and particularly by their potential impact on rival organizations. These standards of preference of the respondents do not fit into a neat logical order; rarely is the labor leader aware of two distinct steps in the making of decisions. Rather, the criteria represent a haphazard accumulation from life experience which determines at an early stage of his trade union career which of the three organizations is the most compatible with his beliefs.

Neither the Italian nor the Danish labor leaders comprise a homogeneous group within their respective labor movements. Differences in level of leadership, geographical location, and industry affiliation impose on them differing demands, as well as different qualifications and points of view. The primary leaders cannot isolate themselves from the day-by-day pushes and pulls which come from the rank and file.

The characteristics of these leaders differ according to the role they are playing. Secondary leaders have different types of problems. They deal with ultimate sources of power in their society and are more politically conscious. Their relationships are more formal, more ritualistic, and less turbulent. In Italy, this role is differentiated by federation, geographical location, and the position of the trade union official in the trade union or federation structure. The differences among the

[2] For a relating of these findings to the American labor movement, see the analysis of Richard A. Lester, *As Unions Mature* (Princeton, N.J.: Princeton University Press, 1958). On the international level, see Walter Galenson (ed.), *Labor and Economic Development* (New York: John Wiley & Sons, 1959).

Danes are also related to geography, but, more than the Italians, to the particular levels of leadership and the trade unions in which they are found. The explanation in part is the older age of the Danish labor movement and the persisting influence of the guild system which it inherited. The problems of an old trade union organization seem to be more affected by the characteristics of its particular economic environment than those of a young organization faced with the problem of first achieving recognition. Consequently, it is difficult to draw generalizations applicable to all the leaders of a labor movement. To say, for example, that the Italian labor movement is "political" is an oversimplification which removes the differences existing among men required to play different roles because of particular characteristics of community, industry, and level of leadership.

The education and training of the Italians is more heterogeneous than that of the Danes, and their orientation toward particular occupations is negligible. The typical Danish labor leader leaves school at fourteen, serves an apprenticeship lasting approximately four years, and begins his trade union career in the shop in which he finds a job. The education of the Italians ranges from five years of elementary school to a college degree in a profession, with little or no formal industrial training. The Catholics as a group have more education than the Social-Communists. Both begin their careers in the trade unions through affiliation with a political party. The Social-Communists, however, are more worker oriented. They tend to begin their careers as workers and start in the trade unions at the bottom leadership positions, more than the Catholics. From early in life, the Danes as a group acquire a technical orientation related to a particular type of industrial job, in contrast to the Italians, whose education is more classical in scope, whether self-acquired or obtained in the educational system of their country. Moreover, from the point of view of the stresses it creates among them, greater diversity exists among the Italians in both their education and their social origins.

The Italians view as their major responsibility the developing of trade union militancy; the Danes, the servicing of the needs of the membership through the practice of collective bargaining and the exercise of political influence through the Social Democrat party. The Italians stress as part of their responsibilities the importance of allowing the expression of worker sentiments, the Social-Communists more than the other two federations. A noteworthy number of the Social-

Communists conceive of successful leadership as expressing the attitudes of workers through action, compared to the Catholic-Liberal groups, who look upon success to a greater extent in terms of the achievement of short-term objectives. The Dane conceives of his role as mediator between the point of view of the employer and that of workers. Success for the Danish official is in terms of obtaining concessions from the employer in behalf of the membership. In Denmark, the individual is expected to conform more in his behavior to the needs of the group organization. For the Danish labor leader, the employer image is that of a co–decision-maker belonging to an allied group that is looked upon with respect. For the Italians, the image of the employer is that of the authoritative boss, *il padrone,* and that of the employers' association, a group hostile to trade unionism. The Social-Communists' view is even more harsh and more monolithic. A majority feel that it is impossible to collaborate with employers in a capitalistic society, although some gave a qualified *yes* to the possibility of labor-management cooperation.

Both groups of trade union officials want power and prestige. The Danes, however, have succeeded in attaining these goals and are secure in their position. Their organization represents one of the several influential economic and political forces in Danish society. The challenge of rival forces does not exist, and they are not faced with the struggle of holding on to their members.

The Italians have a greater flair for making abstractions. Even those with a few years of formal education have to an extraordinary degree an ability for expression and a priori thinking. They live in a society which places a value on purism and abstract idealism, whereas the Danes live in an atmosphere of pragmatism and group control.

A parallel appears to exist in the types of unions wherein the exceptional labor leaders are to be found. The outstanding men of the Danish labor movement are from the ranks of the metal workers and the unskilled workers. Similarly, in Italy outstanding leadership is found among the metal workers and in organizations of large groups of unskilled workers on the fringes of the community. The first appears to be associated with the type of intellectual endowment that workers in these industries bring to their organization, and the other with exceptional motivational push. Large groups of workers who feel isolated from the community, who may be hostile to it, and who feel a status inferiority, are likely to develop leaders of exceptional talent and drive.

Interestingly enough, while these two sets of leaders may both be exceptional, they have meaningful differences in their standards of value. Neither mediocrity nor exceptional talent, however, is the exclusive characteristic of any one organization. In fact, the outstanding leader of a labor union is often succeeded by an unobtrusive, methodical administrator.

The Danes play quite a different role from the Italians. They are joint decision-makers with management on the terms and conditions of employment. The employers, on their part, feel that the trade union official's role is an indispensable one. His job is to whittle down the demands of the rank and file in cognizance of the point of view of the employer. He accepts the wages system, liberal democracy, and the private control of the means of production. Agreement is more important to him than conflict. If the criteria of a successful labor movement are responsible democratic leadership and joint decision-making through the collective bargaining process, it would be difficult to find a labor movement that would surpass that of the Danes.

The Italians are not joint decision-makers because the employers have not accepted such a policy of determining employment terms. Their role is one of reacting, in some instances violently, to the unilateral decisions of the employer. Real collective bargaining is rare, the term masking employer determination of conditions of employment. Consequently, the Italian trade union official finds himself in the position of acting as the defender of the rank and file against the unilateral acts of the employer. It is difficult for him to stimulate union democracy because of the physiological and psychological states of the worker. He often accepts neither the wage system, liberal democracy, nor the private control of the means of production, and finds conflict more impelling than agreement.

The majority of the Danish trade union leaders are craft oriented. That is to say, they perceive their role as one of controlling the jobs and employment terms of a particular occupation and of progressively increasing the income derived from these jobs. The apprentice craftsmen, whose numbers and selection are controlled by the trade union, are attached to individual journeymen, who alone are eligible for union membership. The necessity of 100 per cent organization of the men in their occupation is quite clear in their minds. They are not too certain, however, of how to react to the shift of jobs away from their craft monopoly. A close relationship exists between these characteristics of the officials and those of the rank and file. Invariably, the former has risen out of the shop in his particular craft. At the local level, it is difficult to distinguish him in temperament and perceptions from the more intelligent workers in the shop. His traits and values reflect the size, craft, and general characteristics of the pool of workers from which he comes. At the national level, there is less identity between leader and rank and file. There the problems and experiences assume a different character. The leader comes in contact with top-level management, government officials, political representatives at the national level, and public groups with functions and responsibilities of broader scope. His values and perceptions, consequently, undergo change as the change in his role takes him further away from his original craft-identification and orientation.

A fraternal bond of impulsion exists in both labor movements between leadership and rank and file. The wall of indifference and suspicion that exists in some labor movements between leaders and membership is found in Denmark only in a very small degree. The workers possess a sense of camaraderie which in Italy transcends the individual trade union. The Italians are labor-movement–conscious, while the Danes are more trade-union–conscious. In both cases, the union is an important part of their lives, not an institution accepted with indifference. This attitude provides a strong unitary thrust to their organizations. A sense of idealism welds together leaders and rank and file. In such an atmosphere, it is difficult for them to understand the existence of corruption in a labor movement.

The differences between Danish and Italian labor leaders are an expression of dissimilarities in the social, economic, and political conditions of labor in their countries and of varieties in the union-management relations they produce. Three types of labor leaders, divided along ideological lines, are found in Italy. Political Catholicism, political anticlericalism, and political Marxism are the dominant forces around which the various sets of labor leaders rally. The three labor movements express attitudes of their membership, the ideological tone of the one being compatible with the outlook of the other. In the exercise of union-management relationships, however, the behavior of these three types is more homogeneous than one might infer from the ideological differences they articulate. The forces toward uniformity emanate from the very labor movement that generates the ideological divisions but feels similar frustrations, and from a more homogeneous group of employers whom they confront in common. In Denmark, differences in effective labor leadership are more narrow, whether found in government, the coöperative movement, the trade unions, or the different political parties. The Danish labor movement is not as sharply divided. Their values and, hence, objectives are more homogeneous. The dissimilarities among labor leaders in that country are more easily constructed on technical grounds and in range of perceptions than in ideology. Ideological differences among labor leaders are much narrower. The Church plays no part in sharpening divisions. Divergencies are expressed in terms of the validity of the thesis of nationalization of industry and comprehensive planning rather than on religious grounds. Orientation ranges from a narrow, confined, craft-outlook to a national point of view. To be sure, they are not all alike in every respect. For example, they differ in enthusiasm for labor education and politics. However, in terms of the organization they administer and the bargaining relationship with the employer, the dominant difference among Danish labor leaders is one of technical orientation to problems.

Union-management relations are integrated and power balanced in Denmark, divisive and employer dominated in Italy. The degree to which each industrial relations party is inclined to accommodate and integrate its role and objectives with those of the other is greater in Denmark. There employers have a voice in the regulation of what in the United States might be considered internal union affairs, while the union discharges duties which might be viewed as inviolate management functions elsewhere. No major contest exists in that country over the exercise of leadership of labor. It is shared by the employers and labor officials and dominated by the latter. Some employers are critical of union monopoly control of skilled labor and its coöperative ventures in manufacturing and distribution. Some seek to remove the unemployment compensation function from the trade unions in the hope of weakening labor organization and the Social Democrat party. The greatest resistance to collective bargaining is directed against organized clerical workers by large industrial organizations and by firms using office workers exclusively. No real struggle, however, exists between employers and trade unions as to their respective roles.

There exists in collective bargaining a phantom area which readily escapes notice. The meeting of minds necessary for an agreement rarely occurs at a formal gathering around the collective bargaining table.

The intercession of a common confidant, the planned "chance meeting" in private of the top officers of negotiating organizations, the shuttling back and forth of an intermediary between parties, the raising of a trial balloon by a "public-spirited citizen," these are devices designed to save face and reach a settlement. The final assembly around the collective bargaining table formalizes an agreement previously arrived at. Such methods come with age and are apparently a custom not exclusively American.

A striking characteristic in the labor relations of Scandinavia in general and Denmark in particular is that the law governing the relationship between labor leaders and employers is passed by the participants themselves outside the halls of legislatures. Although they too have fought the battle over prerogatives, their respective responsibilities have been decided not by the law of legislators but by their own direct agreement.

Such is not the case in Italy. That country has been traveling on a path similar to that of the United States by exposing labor-management relations to the pushes and pulls of statutes and legalistic interpretations. The difference in the approach to hammering out the nature of the labor-management relationship is that Scandinavia has relied on voluntary jurisprudence, while Italy is attracted to legislative jurisprudence. The latter approach is evidence of failure to establish mutual respect and responsibility. And the former is recognition that while a legislature can effectively raise minimum standards of employment, it cannot grapple too successfully with the philosophy and attitudes of parties toward each other.

The predominance of lawyers and politicians in the labor relationship in Italy is basically an indication of chaos. Their primary interest is not the best solution of a technical problem but its impact on themselves and the institutions they represent. The concern of the Italian lawyer is how to win a case by a flood of oratory rather than how to solve a problem, while that of the politician is what a situation means to his political ambitions and his party. However, it would be erroneous to infer that Scandinavian labor relations by rules of "the sense of the meeting" would produce similar results elsewhere. In one country, it might result in an expression of the will and point of view of the community. In another, such an approach might amount to a collusive bilateral arrangement between formerly warring groups. Here, the clue to these divergent tendencies is to be found in the cultural restraints which the parties in Scandinavia place on themselves.

Differences in strike attitudes in the two countries raise questions of measurement and reasons for the dissimilarity. Estimates of differences in the propensity to strike, in terms of the number of workers involved and average working days lost per strike, need supplementation. Important differences exist in both countries in the number of times that workers are asked to go on strike and in the incidence of strikes in particular industries, which partly reflect how a new standard in terms of employment is being set in the economy. Professor Ross estimates that, compared to the Italians, the Danes strike for a longer period of time, while the percentage of workers involved is considerably smaller. His figures also show an important difference between Denmark and the other two Scandinavian countries in working days lost per striker. Differences in strike patterns of Italy and Denmark reflect the following political, economic, and social factors: (1) The dissimilarity in feelings of abhorrence toward social conflict. (2) The stifling of the propensity to strike in Denmark, by the placing of major collective bargaining decisions at the level of the federation, whose leaders are more sensitive than the membership to political pressures against striking. (3) The close margin of political power of the labor party in Denmark, increasing its sensitivity to public opinion and its influence over the trade union officials. (4) Less difficulty for the Italians in making up work lost by their demonstration strikes, compared to the Danes, whose cessation of production due to strikes represents net losses to a greater extent. In Italy, arrangements to perform postponed work are often made before the beginning of the strike. (5) The marked difference in attitudes of Danish and Italian employers toward labor leaders and their unions. (6) The greater acceptance by Danish workers of their social and economic institutions. (7) The leadership rivalry among the three federations in Italy. (8) The snowball effect of strikes in the Danish economy, in which the strike activity of one group of workers may have the effect of producing an increasing number of strike declarations by allied crafts as the strike gathers momentum, and the concomitant tendency of employers to lock out their employees. This explosive potential quickly creates pressures for political intervention before a strike is allowed to take its course. (9) The still-unresolved issue in Italy of the proper scope of collective bargaining. In sum, the Danish strike is more of a trial of staying power in the American tradition. Its greater relative decline in Denmark, compared to the United States, has been caused by such factors as the integration of employer and labor leader functions, the increased and approximately equal costs of striking, for the parties and their ability to agree tacitly as to what the eventual settlement will be, should a strike occur.[3]

The factors behind the differences in the strike statistics for Denmark and the other Scandinavian countries are problematical. The Danish economy is more sensitive than the others to the impact of strikes on its foreign trade. The industrial form of trade union organization in Sweden and Norway may act to increase the duration of their strikes. The Danish machinery for settlement of disputes is also some thirty-five years older than that of Norway and Sweden. The rate of economic change has been faster in these countries, as well.

In a sense, the use of the strike in Denmark as a means of bringing about an agreement has been supplanted by the disquieting contemplation of the price to be paid if one were to occur. The greater sensitivity to public opinion, the economic costs, the political and cultural restraints, and the diffusion of power, all combine in Denmark to create a low propensity to strike.

The political and economic life of Italy is dominated by the large employers and the Church. The employers' philosophy is unilateral decision-making at the work place and government intervention in doses to be prescribed by them. The Church participates in effective leadership either directly through the clergy or indirectly through lay organizations. The farther south in Italy, the more the figure of the parish priest looms large as the effective spokesman of the community. Consequently, a contest goes on among employers, the Church, the trade union movement, and the political parties on the relative influence they should exercise on the aspirations of workers and fulfillment of labor goals.

Moreover, the farther south, the more the employer-employee relationship can be described as patriarchal. In such an association, the employer commits himself morally to providing for his workers in return for their fealty. Such a relationship exists to a smaller degree in the country areas of Denmark and is apparently a rural phenomenon

[3] Arthur Ross, "Changing Patterns of Industrial Conflict," in *Proceedings of the Twelfth Annual Meeting of the Industrial Relations Research Association* (Publication No. 24 of the Industrial Relations Research Association [Madison, Wis., 1960], pp. 146–69.

which tends to break down with urbanization and industrialization of the labor force.

The degree of such employer–labor-leader integration, however, cannot be used as a universal benchmark of evaluation of such relationships. The highly integrated system that exists in Denmark might raise serious questions of public interest in another country. One may also observe the consequence in the long term of an integrated, peaceful relationship. The power balance in Denmark will pose serious opposition to any party trying to make a major change in the rules of the game. There is the question, too, whether the rank and file eventually may become distrustful of such a cozy rapprochement between the parties in industrial relations.

The sets of individuals and institutions whose coercive influence the leaders yield to, in a manner consistent with their preferences, are different. In both countries, labor leaders are often men playing simultaneous roles as trade union officials and politicians. In Denmark, government represents an arm of the trade union movement. In Italy, the attitude toward government still involves to a large degree an image of an alien force. The labor movements of both countries were originally shaped as protest organizations against goal-blocking groups in the society. However, the Danish labor movement has long since passed that stage, while the range of protest in Italy is still great. Italian labor leaders have neither the power nor the prestige of the Danes. They are not co–decision-makers with the employers. There are marked differences in the importance of individual expression and dynamism in the exercise of leadership. They share the importance of having power and prestige, but they differ in the degree to which they possess these attributes and the restraint that should be exercised on them.

To ascribe these differences to specific causes is a difficult matter. The dissimilarity reflects the accumulation of two thousand years of history. The attitudes of Italian labor leaders are related to employer hostility to their quest for status and to their low prestige in their country. Differences in education and training, dissimilarity in outlook within the ranks of labor and between employers and employees as a group, play their part. So do differences in work attitudes. The Danes emphasize the pleasure of work in employment, *arbejdsglaede*, while the Italians do not. The Danes have a sense of accomplishment in performing a job. Italian factory workers feel alienated in their work places. The type of employer is a causative factor, also, but it is not too clear whether the size of firm, type of ownership, kind of industry, or some other factor is involved. In a sense, Danes are also individualistic. They are difficult to coerce to a particular point of view that does not reflect their own. However, this regard for self-assertion evolves in one country into efficient group behavior and pragmatism and into a display of temperament in another. The differences which exist in political outlook in the two countries are in part affected by the way employers deal with the aspirations of labor. This behavior is not solely a matter of wage policy as much as a general approach in handling workers' expectations.

The differences in the perceptions of labor leaders are related to the size of organization, level of leadership, range and complexity of the economic forces with which they are confronted, characteristics of workers their industry attracts, and the cultural milieu in which they work. The scope of the responsibilities of a labor leader has a considerable influence on his breadth of outlook. The same individual with perceptions confined to such details as setting piece rates in his craft union can change radically by assuming broader functions which bring him in contact with the top people of different collaborating and contending organizations. Consequently, it is not solely a matter of particular crafts' and industries' attracting different types of individuals. Their education, specialization, and the institutions which surround them in life experience affect the roles labor leaders play and constantly remold their values and perceptions in dissimilar mix. An association is apparent between the outlook of the labor leader and the extent to which he is experiencing success. This in turn is related to differences in the environment confronting him and to his concept of success, as well. It may be that as the level of economic development in different countries becomes similar, so will the respective outlook of different labor leaders. On the other hand, it may be that the individuals of one society will persist in remaining more group conscious than those of another, and that the latter will resist the array of external forces which are being channeled into their respective organizations. The problem can be studied better by adding more countries to the investigation and by observing trends, particularly in such countries as Italy, where individualism is relatively high and trade union organization low.

The value orientation of the Italian and Danish labor movements tends to be more fraternal and less plant oriented than that of American trade unions. The workers are more conscious of their group association with the working class generally. This attitude asserts itself in the high level of collective bargaining, settlements, and the willingness at times to forgo an improved term of employment not available to an allied group of employees. The egalitarian spirit is a strong motive behind the behavior of their labor movements. An intimate bond of voluntary compulsion among workers and between themselves and their leaders makes incomprehensible to them a situation in which officials of another labor movement use their organizations as instruments of personal gain, or where workers of one plant make decisions whose effect is the destruction of the standards or the jobs of workers in other plants. Their reaction to organization, particularly in the case of the Danes, is more in terms of what is in it for their national group. It explains their criticism of the American labor movement as too "autonomous," not "idealistic," led by "bosses" whose objectives are the improvement of work standards of a worker elite, even if it is at the expense of the working class and the public generally. If typical American labor leaders view the lack of broadly based ideology as a strength, the Danes and Italians consider the absence of national neutral ideals as a weakness which will eventually place the American labor movement in grave difficulties.

To be sure, problems of communication between leaders and rank and file exist in all labor movements. The problems of labor leaders and workers are not precisely alike and neither are their goals. The disorientation between leaders and rank and file in particular and the working class in general may be greater in the United States than it is in Denmark or Italy. The leadership of American workers may be more diffused, less impulsive and effective, and shared more by different elites.

To a considerable degree, the Danes have succeeded in overcoming this crisis of organization. They also have experienced the bureaucratization of leadership, the centralization of power, and the decline of militancy. However, the tone of Danish trade unionism is different from that of other labor movements which have reached similar levels of maturity. To be sure, the administration of unemployment compensation funds by the trade unions is an inducement to remain a member in good standing. On the other hand, the unemployment funds in Norway and Sweden are administered by the State, and membership is high and fraternal. Danish unions are an integral part of community activity and an important way of life for workers. Workers themselves refer to an employee staying out of the union as "antisocial." The unions provide a significant means of upward movement for members with leadership ability, opportunity not obtainable in other fields of economic activity. Thus, in the key Metal Workers' Union, the apprentices who move up a step when they become qualified mechanics and full-fledged union members, eventually become trade union officials and supervisors. In this way, the Danish labor movement is a potent instrument of successful community life, and the success of the able and ambitious tends to be identified with the trade union.

In the matter of political activity, it cannot be said that the Danish labor movement is less politically conscious than the Italian. The Danes are rather more fortunate in having most of the trade union membership in one party, compared to three parties in Italy. Consequently, the price they pay for political activity is less than that of the Italians. In that country, a trade unionism split three ways has been instrumental in losing the structural reforms necessary to make collective bargaining work. The Danes pay for their political activity by a decrease in returns in collective bargaining for particular unions. A delicate balance of political power in Denmark requires the trade unions to exercise restraint in collective bargaining. However, this has been offset by gains through legislation and through status and recognition as a governing force in the country.

For neither labor movement is the choice pure trade unionism or political activity. Both are required by circumstances to pursue methods which place them in both arenas simultaneously. Their problem is how to achieve gains in one without suffering equal losses in the other. This goal is difficult in Italy as long as a strong Communist party attracts the Church into politics and causes a stalemate. In contrast, the diffusion of political and economic power in Denmark and a lack of conflicting ideological groups make this objective easier for the labor movement.

Thus, it can be seen that the extent to which differences between Denmark and Italy are ascribable to "economics" and "psychology" is a baffling question. Labor officials themselves are inclined to see these differences as being molded by external social-economic situations which affect their outlook and behavior. After living in both countries for an extended period of time, one cannot ignore differences in child-rearing, for example, and the impact of such training on eventual man-to-man relationships and economic organization. Can it also be said that the socio-economics are transmitted by parents as part of the total inheritance and that the explanation of differences is essentially deterministic and materialistic? That would be an oversimplification. No doubt a complex, mutually reinforcing, interaction occurs between these two sets of influences. Real differences exist in cultural environment and personality formation. Does the greater homogeneity of thinking of Danish employers and labor leaders cause a more homogeneous economic and social environment, or does the latter cause the former?

Exponents of a global economic theory of industrialization may argue that the dissimilarities between the two countries are ascribable to differences in stages of economic development, while the similarities are accounted for by the "universal imperatives of industrialization." Such a theory of labor would make the economic factor the independent variable and the inexorable force which will eventually eradicate the major differences between the two industrial relations systems.

Do the Italian and Danish data support such a simple theory of development? The evidence does not support such a view. The manner in which the industrialization process and the labor movement began in each country is considerably different. The backbone of Italian organized labor antedates industrialization. Nor can present differences between both countries be ascribable in the main to dissimilar stages in economic development. The similar agricultural proportions in both countries represent a significant portion of the total economic activity. The much older Italian rules of work in agriculture are more extensive and complex than the Danish. To be sure, a considerable amount of Italian economic activity is in an initial phase of development, grappling with the problem of increasing agricultural productivity. However, to describe Italy as "backward" and Denmark as "more advanced" does not square with the industrial-machine and cultural strengths of the Italians. Such phenomena in Italy as labor relations methods and the zest for fractionalized political activity seem to be more cultural than technological. Consequently, while the characteristics of industrialization and labor organization have a mutual effect on each other, it cannot be said that the one is the universal cause of the other.

Worker protest is active in Italy and in Denmark almost extinct. The Italians protest not so much over the process of industrialization as over the insecurity of their lives, their isolation from the main stream of Italian community life, and the unilateral imposition of employment terms. Indeed, they seem to enjoy the act of protest. A contest goes on between different sets of leaders as to who should manage this protest. In Denmark, the protest dissipated when cultural patterns facilitated a quick reconciliation of motivations. In Italy, the leadership comes from employers, the unions, and the Church, the latter two playing a temporizing role. In Denmark, the process is under the co-direction of employers and labor leaders.

Both countries suggest that cultural factors resist technological onslaughts and that late starts in industrialization and enlightened employer and government policies make more effective the resistance against the demands of the goddess of efficiency. Italy suggests further the danger of extending the Protestant acquisitive ethic willy-nilly to non-Anglo-Saxon societies. On balance, the data do not support the idea that cultural differences are ascribable to differences in stages of development. The term "stages" itself prejudges a question which has not yet been resolved. On the contrary, the evidence seems to point to the differentiating impact of cultural systems on the demands of optimum economic organization.

The factors which account for the absence of trade union corruption in these two countries provide clues to the reasons for its presence elsewhere. The solutions to this problem that the responses suggest include the following: (1) a highly motivated rank and file, with a greater interest and participation in their labor organizations because of a conviction their expectations are being fulfilled by their organizations; (2) trade union activity through units small enough for an intimate bond to develop among participating members; (3) industrial activity in geographical areas with a sense of community among the members, which is captured in the performance of the trade union function; (4) a high level of education and awareness among the rank and file; (5) a values system in which the competitive pursuit of material acquisition completes with coöperative values; (6) a homogeneous sense of community in which no major segment of the work force, because of feelings of inferiority and isolation, feels no stake in what the community considers "good" behavior; (7) trade union machinery which provides for greater control and surveillance by the rank and file over their elected leaders.

Lastly, what do these two countries suggest will be the design of future industrial relations systems? It is not likely that conflict in industrial relations will diminish to skirmishes of small importance of uniformity between countries. It is probable that different levels of conflict will persist, because of cultural differences in abhorrence and attraction for it. Conflict may be the spice of life in one country and bad manners in another. It must be assumed that so long as change occurs in industrial life, so will excesses, irrationality, and questioning of existing rules within a particular cultural context. Like human life, industrial relations may be a game whose rules are subject to continual relearning and change of no hard and fast pattern.

IMPLICATIONS FOR INTERNATIONAL LABOR INTERPRETATIONS

Denmark and Italy suggest a number of critical factors which make for diversity in labor systems. These factors create in the initial stages of labor development dissimilarity which tends to persist in subsequent phases.

1) *Diversity of social patterns among workers, labor leaders, and employers.*—These social patterns are created by such factors as differences in socio-economic origins, education and training, and the rate of upward movement of leaders and workers in the industrial relations system. They affect the degree of integration of the community, hostility of employer to labor leader goals, and degree of the master-servant relationship between the parties. They create a mosaic of diverse sentiments and aspirations within the labor movement and in the employer-employee relationships which sets the tone in industrial relations and trade unionism. In Italy, for example, the Communist labor leadership, to a greater extent than its Catholic counterpart, has its origin in the industrial working class, has a lower formal education, and has experienced less three-generation upward social movement. In Denmark, origins are more homogeneous, and, just as important, differences between labor leaders as a group and employers are much smaller. In a sense, the Danish employer association and the labor organization can be considered a single group sharing the implementation of production and distribution goals. In Italy, the diversity of origins and social movement creates a conflicting pattern of optimism-pessimism states and of estimates of the probability of success in life.

2) *Value orientation.*—The behavior of both labor movements is controlled by particular patterns of value orientation. What is un-

desirable in one country may complete for primacy as a legitimate objective in another. Values circumscribe the conclusions which can be drawn from terms of employment, the scope of collective bargaining, the relative power of the parties, attitudes toward conflict, and harmonious relationships. They are a quirk of history, a continuing summation of the experiences of the labor leadership, and they affect both goals and what are to be considered the pertinent facts in a particular situation. In Italy, value orientation prescribes the three labor movements in which the leaders and the led find themselves and their group perceptions of each other. In Denmark, a greater homogeneity of values sustains a unitary labor movement and an integrated labor–leader–employer relationship. Values have to do with concepts of justice, loyalty to political parties, attitudes toward conflict, concepts of what constitutes the good life, and the importance of tradition. Italians generally are social individualists; Danes, social conformists. In Italy, the diversity in the industrial relations fabric sets up a contrasting array of "pertinent" facts and aspirations which have to be reconciled, and which become conflicting benchmarks in the measurement of achievement. Values determine the sets of individuals and institutions whose coercive influence labor leaders will resist or voluntarily yield to in a manner consistent with their preferences. They are, in sum, a haphazard agglomeration of shifts in life experience.

3) *Differences in attitudes toward union democracy.*—In the field investigations, Italian Marxists expressed their view of labor leadership as one arising spontaneously from the rank and file and moving inexorably toward the top. The leader merely reflects the needs and sentiments of workers. His personality structure has little to do with the leadership he exercises. Although his perceptions may be somewhat more discerning than those of workers, the quality of his leadership is an expression of the condition of labor. He interprets rather than leads, and does not influence the members as much as the latter influence him. This concept of leadership suggests that the leader's function is to follow willy-nilly in whatever direction the masses are inclined to go.

4) *Differences in attitudes toward conflict.*—While the Danes view conflict as a failure in the social fabric, the Italians look upon it more as a method of expression. Thus viewed, the returns of a conflict are to be found partly in the conflict process itself.

5) *Characteristics of the employer-employee relationship.*—These characteristics, in which Italy rates high, include the following: (*a*) the extent of inequality of bargaining power between employers and unions; such inequality hindering the process of reconciliation and narrowing down of differences between both groups; (*b*) disparity in the level of education and training of workers and their respresentatives, compared to employers and their representatives; (*c*) the extent to which these two groups are experiencing success in life and the feeling by labor that its frustrations are being caused by the employer; (*d*) employer hostility to labor leader goals, including political objectives; (*e*) the degree to which both groups are unintegrated in the community in the discharge of their functions; (*f*) the disinclination and inability of workers to approach the employer on the basis of group determination of employment terms, including the extent of the prevalence of a pragmatic rather than absolutist approach to such terms; (*g*) the rejection of the employer as a respected leader in society; (*h*) the felt master-servant relationship between the parties.

6) *Differences in motivations of labor leaders in entering the labor movement.*—Motivations range from reformist goals to the technical necessity of filling primary leadership posts in the organization. They may be technically oriented and group oriented in character, as in Denmark, or may arise out of personal frustrations, such as the inability of the sons of the poor to overcome sharp class distinctions, as in Italy.

7) *Differences in labor leader perceptions arising out of role differences.*—Differences in the perceptions of labor leaders appear related to their positions and responsibilities in the trade union and industrial relations structure. Factors include size of organization, the level of leadership and the range and complexity of the economic forces with which the leaders are confronted, the characteristics of workers attracted to the industry, and the cultural milieu in which they work.

8) *Differences in the array of organizations competing for leadership of labor.*—Trade union leaders have differences in status. In Denmark, a single labor movement is exercising exclusive jurisdiction over the leadership of labor. The Communist party is considered an alien force in the community and neurotic in its tendencies. In Italy, labor is propagandized by a host of rival or supplementary economic, political, and religious organizations, some of which are demanding exclusive loyalty as a condition for membership. The Communist party is highly

respectable. Thus, labor leadership may be more diffused, less impulsive and effective, and more shared by different elites from one country to the next.

9) *Differences in experiencing success.*—This factor includes the contrast with which different groups in society are experiencing success in life and the extent and locus of pessimism over the probability of success.

10) *Differences in labor force characteristics.*—The contrasting settings of Italy and Denmark suggest labor force characteristics which affect labor development. They include the following: (*a*) The relationship of land and the masses. The reallocation of land and increase in agricultural productivity achieved in Denmark several decades ago contrasts with Italy, where the problem of labor displacement and resettlement is still in process of resolution. (*b*) The extent to which skilled labor and independent enterprise are symbols of status. (*c*) Differences in worker acceptance and participation in the life of the community. (*d*) Extent of the role of other leaders in the community and the degree of acceptance of such roles by the working class. (*e*) Dissimilarity in opportunities for upward occupational movement, a niche or two above that of the start in the life cycle. The greater the extent of upward occupational movement of the working classes, the greater the conservatism of the labor movement. (*f*) Differences in homogeneity of outlook of workers, a factor directly related to the extent of monolithic structure within the labor movement. (*g*) The degree of acceptance of the employer point of view on the part of the working class. (*h*) Differences in the extent to which union members are conscious of their particular occupations, such occupational consciousness reflecting itself in the extent and kind of political activity which workers find tolerable on the part of union representatives. (*i*) Shifting of trade union expectancies with changes in job status and aspirations, the level of the one being inversely related to that of the other. (*j*) Other things equal, the greater the predominance of skilled, occupation-conscious workers, the more the labor movement would be "optimistic," limited in political scope, and the more technical demands would tend to be placed by workers on the leadership. (*k*) Extent of organizational responsiveness. Workers differ in the degree to which they subject themselves to group action and accommodation. The psychological-economic states of workers may be such as to blunt the thrust behind organization and the exercise of initiative in determining their eco-

nomic destinies. In Italy, the paternalism of the Church, and fascism, unemployment, grinding poverty and low education have contributed to passivity and fatalism in the working classes, factors that immobilize leaders and prevent them from making decisions with the support of collective strength behind them. The condition of labor must be such as to provide a competency and willingness to participate successfully in joint efforts to reach goals in the face of difficult obstacles. A sense of fatalism which makes workers turn their backs to inequities in their society, rather than exciting the ambition to pursue measures on a sustained basis in order to eliminate them, is fatal to labor movement organization. (*l*) Differences in the willingness of the working class to follow "intellectuals." Several concomitants are apparently necessary for acceptance of this type of leadership, as in Italy. They include a sense of respect and deference on the part of the working classes to the man of culture, the individual who has been to the university; a considerable difference between cultural levels of employers and workers, so that the latter seek compensation for the difference by accepting leadership not arising from the work place; and a low level of industrialization and few plants of large scale, out of which arise a decline in the tolerance for such leadership and an increase in the demand for leaders coming out of the work place. The intellectual type of leadership shifts the tone of the labor movement. It tends to become more abstract, more ideological, more subject to schisms over matters of idealistic principle, if a lesson can be drawn from the Italian experience.

These factors make for differences among countries in the ratio of expectations to fulfillment of the labor force. They are indicated by the level of the proportion as well as in distortions created by aberrations of the ratio from unity.

11) *Factors making for spurious comparisons of labor movements.*— These include comparisons of what appear on the surface to be similar structural units of different labor movements but which in fact involve men performing dissimilar roles. The problem of comparison of what may not be homogeneous units raises difficult questions as to the meaningfulness of conclusions drawn from comparing and contrasting headquarters of federations, national unions, and regional and local units. Another facet of this problem of method is the possible injection of bias in the study by virtue of having to jump the language barrier twice for data, once into the foreign language and a second time back into English. The items used for the investigation may inhibit the drawing-

out of latent content in responses, while their conversion into English may inject cultural biases which distort actual differences. Labor movements operate in different cultural environments for which no superior-inferior scale exists. A Danish labor leader behaving like a Dane in the labor movement in Italy and his Italian counterpart performing in his own fashion in Denmark would both be absurdities.

Differences in the time of origin of labor movements also provide a dissimilar array of influences, even though there exists the same desire for power with which to achieve social and economic objectives. In Italy, a major thrust came from a semiliterate proletariat and sub-proletariat with few or no skills. In Denmark, the push came from an old philosophy of monopolist craft-exclusiveness, whose influence has persisted despite the eroding tendencies of mass production. Time also brings to bear a different array of government and employer values. In addition, time upsets the traditional phases of a labor movement of pre-acceptance, acceptance, and retrenchment. Consequently, differences may be reflecting in part the starting point and the number of decades of history behind different organizations. Latter-day labor movements no longer grow up like Topsy. In fact, it has become fashionable for governments and political parties, rather than workers, to organize and shape them by deliberate design.

In summation, juxtaposing Danish and Italian labor movements against the background of American trade unionism suggests generalizations in the interpretations of labor movements. The differences in labor movements cannot be measured by a linear scale of methods or returns to the membership divorced from the value patterns and environments from which they arise. Nor do these values and conditions move toward a common point by a law of increasing similarity. Moreover, it is not sufficient to interpret a labor movement by a systematic analysis of the social and economic condition of workers and their organizations alone. The forces which shape trade unionism are found in part in outside groups, including the general cultural array of leadership in the society and the unorganized workers.

Labor leaders do not operate in isolation. Divorced from their relationships with government and employers, they are meaningless figures. Their influence can be better measured in relative terms with that of other leaders in their society. Their behavior manifests a shifting structure and the relationships of all the organizations that play a part in production and in the accommodation process in the political arena.

Their goals, strategy, and methods of performance reflect values of government representatives, employers, and workers, the unorganized in a sense more so than the organized. Consequently, the shifting cross-currents of influences in a society require that the study of labor movements become a study of comparative industrial relations.

The initial thrusts behind labor movements in different countries are similar. The same desire exists for power with which to achieve social and economic objectives. However, the men involved and their particular goal preferences are not alike. In one country, the thrust may come from a semiliterate proletariat and subproletariat with few skills or none at all. Structural reforms of society may be a pervasive objective. In another country, the thrust may come from a philosophy of monopolist craft-exclusiveness, whose outlook may resist some of the harsh consequences of mass production. By characteristics such as these, a labor movement acquires a particular structure of its own, reflecting the social and economic condition of the working class at the beginning of organization, its array of objectives, and the speed and pattern of subsequent development.

A universal objective of the leaders of democratic labor movements is to assist members in the fulfillment of expectations. In the pursuit of this goal, they are involved in planning, organizing, making decisions, controlling, evaluating, and involving their members in group activity. However, the quality of performance of the leaders of different countries is affected by the interaction of a complex host of dissimilar variables which are in continual ferment in a dynamic society. If they are to remain as leaders, they must develop and adhere in substantial degree to a sensitivity to the point of view of the members of a particular industrial relations system, rather than to that of commentators who decree what in their judgment should be the methods and objectives of a particular labor movement.

The dissimilarities at the beginning and during the course of development differentiate the problems and challenges faced by labor leaders. To view development as an identical progression of increasing maturity may be an oversimplification. Values are not the same, nor can it be presupposed that they narrow down into a pattern of in-crossing similarity by exposure to the same technology. Indeed, values affect technology and push it into an accommodation with human values which may differ from one place to the next. Increasing maturity involves the working-out and integration of different values within a particular society. To the extent that this equilibrium is dissimilar, labor movements will mature in different ways.

Labor movements are generally constrained to become pragmatic in their approach. In the exercise of union-management relationships, the behavior of different ideological groups is more homogeneous than might be inferred from the differences in ideology they articulate. Although ideologies differ, the differences which such orientation are supposed to make in day-by-day objectives are more imagined than real. Ideology is not imposed on the rank and file but must be consistent with the aspirations and outlook of workers. It cannot turn the leaders away from the necessity of providing periodic returns to the membership. It is an instrument of energizing an organization and differs with time, place, education, and culture. The price that labor representatives pay for allowing ideology to deflect them from the problem of sustaining trade-union–consciousness with felt returns by the membership is the loss of a following.

The hackneyed ideologies that labor movements profess may be largely an accident of history. They are a distillation of centuries of events which may have dissimilar impacts in different parts of a country. For the labor leader, they represent convenient approximations of outlook and become the expected attire of office. Their influence on behavior of labor movements, however, is not precisely what appears to be the case at first blush.

The dominance of the federation in trade union structure tends to emphasize ideological differences. The representatives of federations are more ideologically conscious than the leaders of national unions. Workers, by contrast, tend to particularize union energy. The more educated and urbanized they become, the more conscious they are of the use of organization as a device against a particular employer, rather than seeing employers as a group versus the labor movement, each with an inflexible ideological outlook. Accordingly, if the dominance of federations is progressively weakened by a rise in the standards of living, the primary energies of the top leadership are forced toward the improvement of the condition of labor, rather than dissipated in organizational rivalry based on ideological differences.

Comparative analysis of union power suggests several observations. First, the power potential of a labor movement varies with culturally oriented expectations of its members, on the one hand, and the extent to which the environment is conducive to their fulfillment, on the other.

The universal appeal in an industrial society for a system of increasing job status and security tends to make these expectations homogeneous. On the other hand, differences in economic environment, such as technology and market situations, and cultural patterns differentiate the degree to which labor movements muster a potential to seek such objectives. Thus the ratio of objectives to power potential differs in both numerator and denominator from country to country. Secondly, a distinction exists between the power potential of labor movements and the degree to which such capability is used. Varying directly with periods of adversity, unions do not use their full power potential at all times. In the long term, the degree of use depends on the extent to which leaders impose cultural restraints on power. A sense of community, a felt sense of collectivity with employers and society, curtail the use of power. With success, moreover, as union power potential increases, the ratio of use to latent potential decreases.

An important inference follows from these generalizations. The power patterns of an industrial relations system are intimately associated with its mosaic of cultural values. Consequently, a comparative analysis of the power of a labor movement is not too meaningful divorced from the particular cultural context with which it is surrounded.

If unions are heavily committed in the political arena, it is often because they have no other choice. Their problem is not how to remove themselves from politics, but how to organize in a manner that will maximize their political power without weakening their economic influence. Political influence may be indispensable as a supplement to bargaining power and as a means of obtaining initial structural changes through legislation and subsequent increases in minimum standards. Concessions derived by political influence may not be obtainable through the use of economic pressure alone. Consequently, the maintenance of such influence, while at the same time increasing economic power, is the leaders' approach to the problem, rather than the removal of the labor movement from politics.

The synthesis of employer and labor leader functions in some countries strengthens the argument that a labor movement interpretation is essentially an interpretation of industrial relations. In some countries the union leader may be considered not an alien influence but an indispensable part of production organization. Employer and labor leadership may have been reconciled. No presumption exists that the labor leader can be dispensed with, provided the employer performs his job efficiently. The personnel function is not used as a tool of thwarting the growth of trade unionism. A conflict of prerogatives under such circumstances is unlikely, not because management is disinclined to bar an intrusion in certain types of decision-making as much as because trade union officials are disposed to respect what management considers to be its proper functions. In such a relationship, one group is not constantly parrying the circumstances created by the other. No significant contest over the exercise of the leadership of labor exists.

It may be misleading, however, to look upon the degree of employer–trade-union integration as a universal benchmark of "good" labor relations. The highly integrated system which is successful in one country might appear to be a collusive sacrifice of the public interest in another.

With the impulse to associate must come the psychological and physical wherewithal to practice a continuing technical trade unionism. Without such requisites, the pursuit of goals on a sustained basis breaks down. Systematic group control is more difficult in some cultures. Some feel less than others the compulsion to modify and control their actions consistent with a group myth. In one culture, group behavior gives propriety and truth to conduct. In another, no such sanction is automatically bestowed on the organization.

As labor movements grow older, they shift from a determined to a determining stage of behavior. That is to say, they move from a period of reacting and adjusting to the influences in a society shaped by other groups to one in which they acquire sufficient power to exert initiating pressures of their own. However, methods and values do not appear to move toward a common point. Nor can the general reduction of conflict be used as a benchmark of increasing maturity, when conflict is a costly or socially offensive way to reach agreement in one country but part of fulfillment in another.

With age, the interaction between labor unions grows more complex. Organizations become more conscious of the impact of one another's decisions on their respective job-kingdoms and the increase in standards which a particular union acquires for its membership. Changes in terms of employment of different bargaining units become more interdependent. The leader of a labor organization reacts on the basis of how the behavior of other officials is affecting his own position. The effect of this interunion surveillance differs in method and intensity, depending on the array of value standards of the leadership. However, a common problem in strategy for the leader of the labor movement is how to accommodate these growing interrelationships in a manner that will increase his own influence and prestige while keeping the organization intact. The price of his failure to do so is secession by labor unions from the organized labor movement if such withdrawal does not mean self-destruction.

Increased education and sophistication of the rank and file changes their perceptions of leaders and acts as a brake on their power. There is less dependency, less obsequiousness, and less deification. The term "leader" itself becomes inappropriate as the leader's role shifts to that of representative and official spokesman. The style changes from one of manipulating emotions and ignorance to that of technical specialist. Accordingly, the tone of labor leadership in one phase of development may be an anachronism in another.

Trade union economic power is derivative, growing in an expanding economy which provides employment and rising standards which the membership identifies as having been attained because of the existence of the union. Job security and a sense of progress are indispensable in the initial stages of organization. In subsequent stages, however, the combination of employee security opportunities for upward movement and enlightened employer industrial relations policy, forced by labor organization itself, sometimes creates a crisis in organization. The ratio of labor expectations to fulfillment approaches unity. A successful trade unionism generates new preferences, which are manifested in the behavior of employers, government, labor leaders, and workers, increasing the difficulty of gaining new adherents with a will for group activity. Employer and government policies become more benign. The fraternal bonds between labor leaders and membership weaken. Stirring problems yield to methodical bureaucracy. The rise in education and job opportunities and the decline of employer abitrariness and discrimination combine to give workers a sense of upward movement and optimistic outlook. Unless group-consciousness is sustained in some fashion, the initial strong thrust of early organization dissipates.

Consequently, as labor unions increase their influence, they face a decline in new energizing opportunities available to them. Success in maximizing this marginal potential of opportunity depends on the effectiveness with which they gain influence, and the sympathy, neutrality, or hostility they attract to their methods and objectives. Only through gross error can they fail to become influential, for if they fulfill human needs they have at their disposal the largest electorate-group in their society. In the pursuit of this potential of opportunities, trade unions engender conflict which takes no universal form. However, as their prestige increases, the margin of additional opportunities declines. Their influence reaches a plateau and becomes stabilized or even begins to decline, depending upon the impact on their organization of the effects of upward movement on the part of the working classes.

The organizational forms which emerge as this stability of power is reached are not similar for all labor movements. Their structure reflects particular problems and objectives which are not the same. If the labor movement is accepted as an instrument of exercising influence in social and economic affairs, the actions that take place within the organizations and with external groups become bureaucratized. With increasing security in positions of authority, labor leaders become more conservative and more broadly oriented. An increasing integration of labor and management goals may occur as the scope of their relationship and the criteria for altering the terms of employment become resolved. Conflict may decline as the battle over prerogatives subsides and the method for changing employment terms becomes subject to agreement or acquiescence. However, there is no inevitable raising of the level of union functions and a corresponding atrophying of activity at the bottom of trade union organization. It is possible for the top to be pursuing functions of increasing scope and the bottom remain vigorous in union activity. Contract administration does not always become the only important role of the organization, nor does the union structure necessarily become subject to corruption and financial manipulation in the interest of the labor representatives. The latter do not necessarily become fiscal agents whose activity is dominated by the shifting of considerable amounts of money.

Once a society under the push of development provides workers with increasing opportunities for upward movement, labor leaders become faced with the problem of how to maintain group cohesion and identification. They cannot lose sight of the impact of upward movement of workers on their organizations. The success of labor movements is dependent upon fulfillment of member aspirations and the extent to which the members recognize that their organization is playing a role in such fulfillment.

The vulnerable point of a voluntary labor movement is the steady upward movement of workers under enlightened government and employer policies which fulfill their expectations. The forces which tend to forestall this crisis of organization are class-consciousness and idealism among workers; a felt economic and social stake by workers in remaining organized; effective communication between leadership and membership, aided by such structural devices as small local units; and trade union activity which the membership considers an indispensable part of its way of life. The enforced conscription of union members through misleadingly termed union-security clauses during this labor movement phase submerges, rather than solves, the problem of organization.

The approach which labor leaders employ in meeting this challenge of upward movement changes with the rise in the level of education and training of workers. Workers whose higher intellectual level provides them with an independence of spirit cannot be managed in the same way as those still not too far removed from a level of subsistence and paternalistic attachments. The changing quality and tone of labor movements are an expression of the condition of the rank and file. It cannot be said, however, that as workers reach similar levels of intellectual and economic attainment, their organizations would become identical. Each will meet the crisis of organization in its own way.

In conclusion, it would appear that a comparative interpretation of labor should center around the relationships between change on the one hand and the aspirations and fulfillment of labor on the other. A mutually reinforcing relationship exists between the needs of production and the demands of the cultural milieu. Once labor senses and welcomes the possibility of change, a rising ratio of expectation and fulfillment in standards of life provides a major thrust behind changes in production and culture. While the level of the proportion differs among countries, the clue to labor success in all dynamic economies is keeping the ratio close to unity.

Consequently, an international labor theory could well be a comparative theory of the upward movement of labor, an interpretation cutting across national borders being an analysis of the interaction between development on the one hand and the condition of labor within particular cultural contexts on the other. While the ratio of expectations to fulfillment rests on dissimilar levels for different labor movements, they face in common a crisis of organization as it approximates unity and as the organized become inclined to believe that the returns of the denominator can be achieved without labor organization. Such an interpretation places the evaluation of the industrial relations system of a country in terms of the quality of men and consumption it is producing. The eventual payoff of a dynamic system is the extent to which it will create a structure of organization that encourages a free maximum development of human beings, in which man, rather than the system, is the independent variable. What constitutes human fulfillment, however, is not likely to be the same. To place all labor movements into a linear array, therefore, all moving inexorably toward the same type of outcome, may be in error.

The differences in age and values between the Danish and the Italian industrial relations systems provide an excellent opportunity for research in the next decade. Using the benchmarks suggested in this work, such an inquiry would detect changes in the methods of the system, on the one hand, and cultural settings, on the other, and discern the associations between these phenomena. As industrialization of the labor force in Italy continues, will value and structural differences narrow, or will they persist? Will the interindustry-consciousness of Italian workers be supplanted by a more specialized occupation-consciousness? Will the European Common Market produce similar types of industrialization and per capita income among the participating countries, and what will be the effect? In Denmark, what does the move from occupation to industry association portend? By such a study, a hypothesis on the mutually reinforcing effects of economic organization and cultural settings could be examined to determine whether the case is strengthened for a multidimensional cultural or linear economic international theory of labor.

Appendixes

The Method of Studying Labor Leadership

The method relies in the main on a systematic presentation of the expressions of the participants and the special public of industrial relations. These expressions are obtained principally from depth interviews, written questionnaires which serve to supplement and validate responses obtained in interviews, and from labor leaders' statements to other trade union officials and their rank and file. The group includes individual employers, employer associations, social scientists, workers, and individuals proximate to labor and management in and out of government, who by virtue of what they do or fail to do exert an influence on trade unionism and labor relations. The study of this shifting band of influence around the labor leader provides the means of placing him in perspective within his society and of discerning what constitutes outstanding labor leadership in a country, in the judgment of its own opinion-molders rather than that of foreign investigators.

The study seeks to ferret out and account for the similarities and differences among labor leaders. These factors are assembled into two broad categories of *individual factors,* including labor leader traits and characteristics, attitudes, perceptions, value standards, goals, and source of recruitment, together with similar characteristics of the led; and *group factors,* such as duties and role obligations arising from relations with members of their organizations and other groups, methods, decision-making techniques, issues, organization structure, and actual labor leader behavior. All these classifications are closely interrelated. Together with the characteristics of employers and the industrial relations public, they are utilized to provide a comprehensive review of the factors affecting the behavior of labor leaders. The concept of leadership is viewed in its broadest sense, and no restricted analytical design is imposed on the study, since it was not known what point of view would provide the most meaningful interpretations in the comparison of labor.

The methodological question posed for the investigation was the following: Would a research method based fundamentally on interview technique and applied uniformly to different labor movements produce significant interpretative differentiations and associations between countries? The problem was to develop a method which would pull apart the differences among labor leaders and qualify them in a manner that would allow the making of direct comparisons between countries. An analysis of labor leaders alone proved to be inadequate. In order to place labor leaders in proper perspective, the investigation had to be extended to a study of attitudes of employers, workers, and the industrial relations public, and the images these individuals have of trade union officials. With such amplification, the investigation produced meaningful differentiations and associations, and ferreted out the ebbing and swelling influences which are affecting labor leader behavior.

The field investigation uses both a fixed written questionnaire and a guided depth interview. The questionnaire is left with the respondent with a self-addressed envelope, with the request that it be mailed to the address of the individual in charge of the investigation. The exclusive use of written questionnaires met with little success in Italy and still less in Denmark. Exclusive reliance on such questionnaires produces highly questionable results. They may not go beyond initial clichés, and the items are subject to different interpretations. The purpose of the dualistic approach is to analyze comprehensively the similarities and differences between labor leaders and the influences which shape their behavior. The emphasis is placed on what they do and say, rather than on static qualities they may possess. Information sought includes who the interviewee is, his social and occupational origin, how he entered the labor movement, what he thinks of other leaders, his actual duties, role obligations, and the standards by which he makes choices. The respondents in this group included both elected trade union officials, on a sample basis, and elected politicians who receive their support from the labor movement. In sum, the study concentrates on who the labor leader is and what he does rather than on an abstract analysis of the qualities of labor leadership.

The sequence of items is designed with several purposes in view: (1) to begin the interview with disinterested questions of fact and lead into questions of values; (2) to crystallize the major issues that confront the respondents; (3) to postpone until as late in the interview as possible or until the written questionnaire highly abstract questions. However, the sequence is not rigid. It should be broken in the over-all interest of obtaining as much depth in the interview as possible, even at the expense of eliminating some of the questions from the interview. The questions themselves are not definitive. If they are not understood, they are rephrased by the interviewer rather than by an interpreter if one is being used.

The written questionnaire serves several purposes. It collects such facts as biographical information and allotment of working time, and lowers correspondingly the amount of minimum interview time necessary to approximately two hours. Some of the questions are abstract, while others validate responses obtained from the interview. Queries requiring extended reflection of anonymity are placed on the questionnaire. The percentage of returns is high if it is given personally to the respondent by the investigator with the request that it be mailed to him. The written questionnaire proved to be a rich source of information in Italy. The Italians who used it, including Communist members of the CGIL, wrote at length and with candor. The attempt to distribute the questionnaire through the federation offices of the CISL and the CGIL met with little success.

The oral interview is a cross between a simple questionnaire and a non-directed interview. Questions are asked on current issues in the host country and on subjects covering problems, values, objectives, and policies. Flexibility is obtained by improvising and interspersing additional questions, particularly at the beginning. They are used to crystallize an issue or to tap an unanticipated shift in the interview. They may be kept vague and inserted spontaneously throughout the interview and may be designed to establish rapport and to solicit undirected responses from the interviewee on matters which he himself considers important. Several advantages are gained from this mixed type of interview. The relationship with the respondent is established more easily and effectively. Responses are not prejudiced by the rigid manner in which items are posed. In sum, the method maximizes the range of exploration of the greatest number of value characteristics. It also avoids failure in obtaining significant, but unsolicited, responses and provides the greatest degree of revelation of labor leader characteristics. The approach is advantageous despite the occasional protestations that the queries are vague or naïve.

Items seek differentiations in the following areas: (1) motives in joining the labor movement; (2) attitudes toward the respondents' role as labor leaders; (3) labor leaders' attitudes toward other organizations which exert an influence in industrial relations; (4) perceptions of employers; (5) character of their relationship with workers; (6) short-term and long-term objectives and the methods used in achieving these objectives; (7) concepts of success and obstacles the respondents feel stand in the path of success; (8) political attitudes and attachments; (9) social and economic origins; (10) concepts of who is powerful in their society; (11) nature of the collective bargaining relationship; (12) manner in which their working time is allotted; (13) difference in perceptions of problems; (14) perceptions of American trade union-ism; (15) benchmarks used to determine the success or failure of their stewardship; (16) differences in their estimate of the most pressing needs of workers; (17) differences in what they believe to be their role obligations, either because of pressures internal to themselves or those stemming from the rank and file. At the close of the interview, away from the respondent, the investigator and his assistant separately make an estimate of such personality traits as expression, extraversion-intraversion, and energy. These are aligned on the basis of a forced distribution.

To facilitate international comparisons, the labor leaders are classi-fied by level of leadership. These levels anchor around three general points: the first effective organization proximate to the membership; the next higher organization; and the top trade union organization. In Italy the three levels are the provincial organizations, the national union offices, and the federation headquarters; in Denmark, the locals, national unions, and the federation. The sample is not a statistically random one. It is stratified by geography, industrial concentration, and federation. In Italy, all three federations are included. The actual num-ber of interviewees is determined by reaching a point of uneconomic returns in differences within a particular stratification. On the provin-cial level, it was advisable to try to interview the secretaries of the three federations because of the opportunity afforded for cross-checking of responses. The assumption of additional area offices was predicated on the basis of reaching a point where the additional re-sponses were not worth the expenditure of limited funds. In Italy, a total of fifty labor leaders proved feasible, a reasonable replica of the three labor movements having been obtained on the basis of geog-raphy, organizational level, industry concentration, and federation. In Denmark, the number amounted to thirty-five.

The other two groups are the employers and industrial relations segment of the general public. A major purpose of interviewing these groups is to determine their perceptions of labor leaders. The sample in

Italy comprised thirty-five employers and thirty members of the industrial relations public, while for Denmark the figure is twenty-five for each group. The employer sample is stratified by geography and industry. The industrial relations group is sought in the particular towns visited for the purpose of talking to the employers and labor officials. In this respect, the universities are an important source of information and introductions. They are also a helpful springboard in orientation on issues and local problems.

Items for the employers seek differentiations in the following factors: (1) leadership philosophy, in a range running from authoritarian to democratic; (2) attitudes toward labor leaders and trade unionism; (3) influences which employers contribute toward labor leader behavior; (4) background and characteristics; (5) nature of the employer–labor-leader relationship at different levels. In Italy, the principal points of contact are the plant committees, the provincial organizations, the national unions, and the federations; in Denmark, the shop steward, the locals, the national unions, and the federation.

Questions 12 to 16 in the interview schedule are for the purpose of seeking appraisals of trade unionism by employers. The last two of the series were used in Denmark to see to what extent they would produce additional material on the same question. Judgments on the weaknesses of labor leaders are incorporated in the responses made to weaknesses of trade unionism, which contain analyses of trade union structure as such and concepts of labor leadership. Critical attitudes toward labor leaders are also expressed in the reply to the query of the differences among them. This question also produces information on the forces which are creating the differences. A noteworthy association exists between the responses to questions 15 and 16. For example, the employer who sees labor leaders differing in flexibility will state that the quality of a good labor leader is flexibility. From the Danish experience, it appears that queries 12, 13, and 15 are the most fruitful, in that order, while 14 and 16 do not provide any substantial increases in data.

The general classifications for the items covering the industrial relations group are as follows: (1) characteristics of the group; (2) critique of trade unionism and labor officials; (3) perception of the role the employers and trade union officials are playing in their society; (4) proposals for change, if any. Although not presented in this sequence, the items fall into one or another of these general classifications.

Individual workers were interviewed in Italy whenever the opportunity presented itself in the communities visited. The "sample" is not sufficient to obtain analytical differences by geography and occupation.

The interviews in Denmark were conducted on a more systematic basis. The experience suggests that the following objectives should be sought in such interviews: (1) concept of what constitutes a successful life and extent to which the workers expect the trade union to help in its attainment; (2) characteristics they expect in their leadership; (3) relative estimates of who the influential people in their country are; (4) job attitudes; (5) differences in the extent to which they are responding integratively in the organization and the factors which explain these differences; (6) perceptions of employers; (7) extent to which differences are associated with such factors as occupation, age, plant size, geography, and trade union affiliation. A basic objective in these interviews is to assertain the pressures the workers bring to bear on the labor leadership by virtue of what they do or do not do.

The investigator has also to look for action situations which involve labor leaders, employers, and the public. A facet of this analysis is the perception which different leaders have of each other and their relative differences in influence. Consequently, events involving these individuals are an important source of information. A strike, a grievance action, a controversial legislative proposal, all provide opportunities for supplementing the information from the interviews themselves. Therefore, the investigator has to keep abreast of current and significant events in which he can observe his respondents behaving in action situations and keep his travel schedule flexible so as to achieve that purpose.

The sequence of work in the investigation runs as follows: (1) Development of organization charts showing labor leader internal and external relationships. These charts are constructed out of the information developed through discussions with interviewee personnel. Differences will be found among officials as to what constitutes the structure of their organization. (2) Development of current problems, by reading the press and periodicals, by talks with the industrial relations group, and preliminary conversations with labor officials. (3) Development of the sample from information obtained in the first two steps. (4) Interviews, including repeats when necessary.

Coping with the ebullient Italian character raised difficulties. Once a rapport is established, Italians are frank and candid. Deceptiveness and evasion is alien to their character. Under such circumstances, following them becomes a task, once they begin to pour forth their ideas. Ideally, it is best to take down a complete transcript of everything said in the interview. Unless trained in the behavorial sciences, assistants are inclined to determine by themselves what is important and what is not, not making a record of the latter and thus throwing out the baby with the bath water as far as the basic purposes of the interview are concerned. No hard and fast rule can be made, however, as to when to begin note-taking or when it may be prudent to show that one has stopped. In most cases the interviewer should not begin writing immediately, and once begun, it is best to take notes in the foreign language so as not to miss the nuances. On occasion, some of the questions evoke evasiveness or refusal to answer. They may have to do with politics, religion, tactics, and long-term objectives. In general, the Italians are quite free in their responses and more verbose than the Danes.

Numerous changes in the phrasing of the questions occurred in the pilot phase of the study. The difficulty was due in part to the improper phrasing of the Italian and in part to the fact that the concept correctly translated failed to produce any meaningful scaling. Because of differences in issues and the structure of trade unionism and industrial relations, items which scale in one country will not do so in another. With the exceptions of some additional questions tested in Denmark, however, the investigation stayed with basic items as much as possible in order to maintain comparability between the countries. To cite an example, a question on the role of the Church is productive in Italy, but not in Denmark. In Italy, the question was a delicate one for the CISL and one which evoked strong feeling from UIL respondents. The query on the contribution of the Communist party, in the judgment of Communists of the CGIL, reflected bias on the part of the investigator.

Resistance to some of the questions can be broken down by follow-up interviews. The reactions to questions, whether "good" or "bad," are significant commentaries in themselves on felt pressures on trade union officers, coming from their own or outside organizations. With a trade union official sympathetic to the study, added refinement to the questions can be made and additional ones suggested for pertinency in a particular country. Such a liaison is also useful in interpreting responses and uncovering latent meaning. In sum, these matters produce numerous problems in arrangement of the interview schedule which cannot be anticipated prior to arrival in the host country.

The strategic point of investigation of felt labor leader role is approached from different directions. The analysis of working time and workday relationships is one way. Questions are asked on what the respondent feels are his most important problems and responsibilities. Problems are also approached indirectly in terms of what is felt to be the greatest obstacle to the further growth of trade unionism. In the Danish inquiry it was decided to try to force a distinction between problems of the whole organization and those of the respondent's organization in particular. The direct question on what the interviewee considers his role to be proved somewhat abstract for the Danes and a subject for extensive elucidation for the Italians, an interesting reflection of the differences in thought processes between the two. The query on the respondent's idea of success elicits responses associated with role, as does the one on shifts in methods and objectives in the history of the organization.

Meaningful responses are more likely if defensive reactions by the interviewee are not inadvertently provoked. A permissive atmosphere that avoids moralizing on issues and statements should be stimulated. The queries should proceed from those of fact to those requiring a choice of preference. Several questions are used on the same item, and the respondent is not likely to be aware of this. Even if the interviewee speaks English, he should be encouraged to speak in his own language.

Validation is sought in several ways. Questions are pretested with university personnel and labor officials. Anticipated attitudes are expected to be forthcoming in the course of the interviews. Uniform patterns of thinking within classified groups should emerge from a relatively small sample. Corroborative questions are used extensively within the interview and between interview and questionnaire. In addition, marginal interviews within particular stratifications should not produce further significant differentiations. Different sets of interviewees may be participating in the same events, either as colleagues or adversaries. Their comments, accordingly, provide an opportunity of distilling events as they occurred and obtaining different perceptions of the same situation. An interesting aftermath of the interviewing of adversaries was that their differences as pronounced by themselves were more apparent than real. In Italy, such situations occasionally resulted in informal discussion meetings, in one case with explosive results. An external validation is employed also, by the use of statements made by trade union officials to the rank and file and especially to other trade union officials in and outside their organization.

Uniformity in the pattern of thinking within classified groups that emerges from a relatively small sample is striking. A knowledge of the structure of the labor movement and industrial relations and the geographical and industrial dispersion of economic activity is necessary for the construction of a stratified sample. In fixing the number of interviews within each stratification, the point is reached rather quickly where an additional interview does not produce a significant enough differentiation to merit the increased expenditure of time and money. By classifying the respondent as to occupation, education, social origin, geographical location, and group affiliation, it was possible to anticipate the preferences expressed in the course of a marginal interview.

The method is not solely an expression of individual preferences in a static situation. It is capable of developing actual events and dynamic cross-relationships in trade unionism and industrial relations. It constructs problems as the leaders see them, and by repeat interviews of the same individuals, situations which have occurred after the first encounter can be reviewed and the changes in the nature of problems detected in the course of shifting events. In this way, it serves to detect new trends and ebbing influences.

The construction of items with preconceived forced choices is not advisable. General statements are constructed and tested until a phrasing that elicits what the investigator is trying to measure is derived. The responses themselves are then reduced into homogeneous units and assembled into an array of differences. The responses appear to be more dissimilar than is actually the case because of differences in terminology for what is essentially the same idea. By editing, they can be reduced to the point where the differences become relatively fixed. In this manner, dissimilarities in points of view are not obtained through a predetermined system of forced choices, but are developed after all the responses have come in from the field investigation.

Relative differences will occur in the ability to interview various groups in depth. The order of increasing difficulty within countries was labor leaders, employers, and the middle-class, industrial-relations public group. Of the latter, the most difficult was the college professor. He is impeded by what he feels to be his role obligations as an objective analyst and is disinclined to express personal preferences. If he is familiar with the technique, that too acts as an obstacle. The Danes were the more difficult to interview and the industrial relations public most so. The reason for the difference is conjectural. Concern was indirectly expressed in Denmark over how the responses would be used, especially by the middle-class group. (Their response to participation in an attitude survey is often that they have no knowledge of such matters.) It is also apparently more difficult to interview labor leaders with close ties to the party in power, particularly on questions of political policy. The Danes may feel themselves to be in delicate positions of power, a sentiment which may restrain their willingness to express themselves freely. The Italians are generally more expressive and have a *senso di dovere* which makes them feel personally responsible to the interviewer. Sharply contrasting ideological differences with the interviewer may inhibit this characteristic. Generally, however, these qualities of the Italians are an important factor in creating differences betwen the two countries.

In Denmark, after a series of trial operations, workers were reached by means of group interviews in the following manner. After an explanation by the interviewer and his assistant of the purpose of the investigation, the questions were read to the workers and answered one at a time. The interviews were conducted on company premises without the presence of either company or trade union officials. The method proved to be the best alternative to impractical and financially prohibitive personal interviews.

The investigation indicates the importance of developing measurement of differences in the value standards of employers and labor leaders and their perceptions of each other. In seeking this objective, the method relies on current and significant events in industrial relations and the individuals who are playing a part in these events. The particular incident may be the writing of an agreement, the processing of a grievance, or the handling of a legislative proposal. In Italy, coming to a town where a strike was going on or an important meeting of trade union officials taking place provided opportunities to develop cross-relationships among employers and labor leaders.

It was more difficult to pull apart the Danish responses into noteworthy intracountry differences. The ideological dissimilarity in Italy provided the opportunity for a group arrangement which revealed meaningful differences in the data. No such dissimilarity in ideology exists in Denmark. A meaningful arrangement of Danish data is by levels of leadership and by craft. The leaders of organizations with a trade-orientation, such as bricklayers, carpenters, and painters, are distinguishable from the trade unions quasi-industrial in character. A second meaningful classification is union size. In Italy, the responses could best be pulled apart by federation and geographical location. Over-all, the range of the responses was smaller in Denmark.

These results are a measure of cultural differences between a Scandinavian and a Latin society. The Italians are more expressive, tend more to overscore a point in a manner which they allude to as *fare un nerbo un fascio*. The Danes by comparison are terse in their statements and less inclined to express the nuances and subtleties of given situations. Of course there are differences among them in this respect. The leader of the federation in Denmark is not typical of his colleagues in verbiage and facial expressions. Their reserve is also a measure of the fact that the Danes are in power and the Italians are not.

Such a finding is not so much a reflection of a weakness in method as it is one of substance. By any appropriate benchmark of measurement, the Danish labor leaders as a group are more homogeneous than the Italians. Their values, perceptions of events, the concept of the role they are playing, their power differences among themselves and with employers, are more narrow. So are their social origins and their rate of upward movement.

It would be a mistake to force the responses unduly into broader subgroups in order to increase their frequency. To be sure, the reduction of the responses into fewer units increases the opportunity of quantitative comparability and simplifies the tabular presentation. However, by encouraging greater editing on the part of the investigator, it introduces more subjectivity in the study and reduces the qualitative differences in the replies of the respondents. These qualitative dissimilarities should be preserved by retaining as much of the original expression as possible, even at the risk of exposing the frequency of each category to criticism. A balance must be struck between the quantitative advantages of greater simplification and the extent to which the reduction of subgroups causes a loss in qualitative nuances.

The attempt to obtain differentiations in traits was also not too successful in the Danish field investigation. Experience dictated that the simplest and quickest method was best with men who are busy and unwilling to be the subjects of experimentation. At the close of the interview, the interviewer and his assistant independently ranked the interviewee for such traits as expressiveness, extraversion, and control, after a meeting of minds on the definition of these characteristics. Differentiation was sought through a forced distribution. Agreement could be obtained only at the extremes of the list. The greater the number of interviewees introduced in the ranking, the more arbitrary was the listing of those in the middle of the range and the more undiscernible were the differences.

Several observations can be made on trait classifications of labor leaders. (1) While some distribution can be done on the basis of these factors, international comparisons of the rank levels are not meaningful. (2) As expected, the higher the level of leadership, the greater the presence of these traits. (3) The small differentiation in the ranking levels of each trait suggests that too often the same characteristic is being measured. Whatever this characteristic may be, its presence in Denmark is notable in the leader of the Metal Workers and that of the federation, a man who rose out of the ranks of the largest union in Denmark, the General Workers' Union. (4) The relative measure of these traits is subjective and not too meaningful. Even if a more reliable method could be used in this type of investigation, its usefulness is of questionable value. To state that the three leaders of the Metal, Mining, and Transport Workers, for example, are resourceful, expressive, and forceful is a generalization of little significance.

The first step in the analysis of data is assembling and editing the responses into homogeneous categories. A vertical array of the responses to a particular query suggests both the category and a continuum of intensity. What constitutes "least" and "most" in the scale depends on the nature of the item being tabulated. For some items it will be more arbitrary than for others. Each category can be assigned a number of a series whose range depends on the number of different categories. In this way, the responses of a particular leader can be identified and his relative position in the various tabulations ascertained. In the initial tabulation it is best to avoid retaining what the investigator feels is the most significant part of the statement and editing out the remainder. The editing can best be done with the aid of a social scientist in the host country, lest portions of the responses with meaning be discarded. Occasionally the response to one question will be found in the answer to another. Responses will also contain information useful as background material, in addition to that needed for the preparation of tables. These comments often come unsolicited and unanticipated, which strengthens the case for a free type of depth interview.

The next step is the grouping of data on the basis of criteria which may suggest meaningful associations. This is done by trial and error. The benchmark may be age, social origin, level of leadership, geography, or industry. The problem is to determine which group arrangement succeeds in pulling apart the data into meaningful groupings. For the Italian data, the most meaningful arrangement is by federation and level of leadership; for the Danish data, local versus national leadership and type of industry prove to be the most noteworthy. In both countries, if the sample were larger, systematic differences could probably be obtained on the basis of geographical location.

There are several advantages to be gained by this approach. The codification makes possible the eventual manipulation by digital computer technology of data from an increasingly larger group of countries. Cross-tabulations of the responses to different items can be made to determine associations in the range of responses. Profiles of individual officials can also be constructed. The development of a representative profile within groups may serve to narrow the meaningful differences down to a few key indicators and to bring out causal associations more concretely. Like extrapolating the wage structure of a plant from a few key rates, it may be possible to determine the characteristics of a labor movement by the combination of key indicators.

Research assistants employed in the tabulation of data should have both a knowledge of the labor relations of the country of investigation and a sensitivity to the nuances of the foreign language. Without such qualifications, the danger exists that the meaningfulness of responses will be lost when the data are assembled. If such assistance is not available, it is advisable that the data be prepared by the investigator, leaving to research assistance work of routine character only. Central to the problem of converting the responses is the difficult balancing of the original flavor in the foreign language and meaningfulness in English. In its resolution, it cannot be said categorically that the translation should be literal or that it should be idiomatic. Either may be appropriate in particular situations. In listing in tables the various categories of responses, it is advisable to build them around a representative expression within each group. For this reason, it is important that if a translator is used, he translate as literally as possible, leaving the final rendition to the investigator.

The attempt to broaden the industrial relations group to a middle-class sample was not successful. The project tapped sentiment throughout the occupational ladder, with the exception of that heterogeneous group of professional and technical people, administrative employees, sales personnel, and small independent enterprisers known in Europe as the middle class. The pilot responses in either country showed such indifference or pleas of lack of knowledge of trade unionism and industrial relations that it was decided to limit the group in the manner described above.

The use of such attitude surveys for making direct comparisons of the labor leadership of different countries raises many difficult problems. There is the danger that in translation of both questions and responses the emotional content may be lost or exaggerated. The more disparate the culture of the countries in the comparison unit, the more the possibility of distortion. In moving from tentative questions in English to queries in Italian, it was found necessary to tone up the phrasing. The opposite was the case in setting the Danish questions. The item on motivation in entering the labor movement is a case in point. The Italian, literally translated, says: By means of what events did you decide to begin work in the trade union movement? The Danish says more simply: Why did you enter the trade union movement? The first expression is more ornate and more individualistic to one coming from an Anglo-Saxon civilization, but the Italian answering it does not react in the same way. Each expression induced the respondents of a particular country to talk about their motives in entering the labor movement. Such results are achieved by a constant testing and rewording of the foreign expression.

A similar problem exists in moving from the foreign language to English. In the process, it is easy to lose the nuances in the responses and to overestimate or underestimate the emotional intensity. A literal transcription of the Italian responses would carry into the English an emotional pitch which does not exist to the same degree for the Italians. The opposite is true in the case of the Danes. It becomes apparent to the interviewer that they whittle down for the record their actual sentiments about persons, objects, and ideas. For the American reader, too narrow a translation creates an impression of chaos and confusion in one country and peace and tranquillity in the other.

This is not to say that literal translations do not have a function in these studies. They can be used to reflect the temperament and outlook of a people. If, for example, in referring to the function of the Communist party, the Danish trade union official says, "*Holden galden vedlige*," it would be appropriate to translate word for word. The same is so when an Italian labor leader, in referring to the objective of trade unionism, says, "*La tutela degli interessi dei lavoratori.*"

Reports on such investigations could be misinterpreted. It cannot be overemphasized that expression per se is an important value to the Italian, while restraint per se is significant for the Dane. This difference will manifest itself in the phraseology of the responses, and the reader may be inclined to react favorably or unfavorably to them, depending on his own system of values. It is a mistake, for instance, to impute success to the Danes and failure to the Italians from differences in the extent and ease of accommodation in the two countries. Living in Italy over an extended period, one gains the impression that the Italians enjoy conflict situations. For the Italians, *manifestazioni* and the expression of conflicting abstract ideas are as important as the *accomodamenti* between the parties. Neither set of values is "good" or "bad," although one is inclined to think that Americans are more apt to have a favorable reaction to that of the Danes. Herein lies an important cause of differentiation in labor movements, which makes tenuous placing them on a continuum implying different stages of progress in reaching the same level of maturity.

In sum, the major problems of method which the international study of labor leadership raises are related to the question used, the interpretation of response, the use of interpreters, and those created by the characteristics of interviewers and interviewees generally. The translation of queries into a foreign language may inhibit the drawing out of latent content in responses. In tapping an item one desires to measure, such as what the respondent conceives his role to be, it may be necessary to alter the emotional tone of the English up or down.

The problem is to avoid the use of expressions which decrease the likelihood of a personal response and which elicit instead answers whose substance can be found in government and organization literature. The responses, moreover, may have little content to a foreign observer. To an objective informed analyst from the same country as the respondents, the responses may contain considerable meaning.

If an interpreter must be employed, it is important that his presentation to the interviewee be understood and controlled by the investigator. Different interpreters may introduce into responses biases which make the replies uniform or dissimilar because of characteristics which inhere in them and not in the respondents. Consequently, a comparative international study of labor leadership may become a study of the similarities and differences of interpreters. For this reason, their language must be prescribed and kept free from individual interpolations during the course of the interview. The probing should be done by the interviewer himself. While interpreters can be asked to summarize responses from time to time as they are being made, they should also be required to write down the replies verbatim and to furnish the foreign language text to the investigator. Such a restriction, however, may not eliminate the possibility of systematic bias being introduced because of the presence of the interpreter. An interpreter who will not inhibit the interviewee from talking freely should be chosen.

Another problem to be borne in mind is that of determining to what extent a bias exists in the responses because of characteristics of the interviewee or of the interviewer himself. Cultural differences affect the willingness of labor leaders to expose themselves freely to an interview which seeks to ferret out values. A greater resistance to depth interviewing was experienced in Denmark than in Italy. Some respondents may wish to prove to themselves their independence of the interviewer, and some may state what they believe the interviewer would like to hear. Some refer to official sources in their replies. These tendencies become particularly apparent when the replies are cross-checked with each other. Hostility raised by some characteristic of the interviewer or his country of origin may cause the respondent to criticize in an indirect manner or to make certain that his organization appears in the best possible light. This attitude may also reveal itself in apparent inconsistencies in the response. Little of this type of invalidation was encountered among the Communist labor leaders in Italy. When it does appear, it makes itself evident in internal inconsistencies in replies. As a case in point, an Italian respondent spoke generally in warm terms of an adversary, but in the course of the interview made a heated critical evaluation of the same individual.

The newspaper of the Danish Communist party, *Land og Folk,* commented on the study in a front-page article appearing May 3, 1959. Following is a translation of the article:

It is a known matter that USA in the postwar years has mapped most of the Danish community. First in connection with the Marshall loan and later on as a NATO partner, USA's capitalism has had unrestricted admission to public and private offices and enterprises. There is hardly a thing in the Danish community which over the years has not been entered in American index files, and yet one lacked a complete picture of the position in the separate trade unions and that one now seeks to remedy by getting the trade union leaders to answer forty-two indiscreet [*naergaende*] questions. . . . The first questions concern the data of the trade union leader, but he is also asked about his father's and grandfather's occupation. The maternal origin apparently plays no role.

Maybe at first glance the questions seem very naïve and innocent, but it should be remembered that it is precisely the frequently used procedure which the Americans use in their spying activity [*spionagevirksomhed*]. Therefore, most of the trade union leaders will surely choose to throw the whole thing into the wastepaper basket.

Several critical goals are sought in comparative labor leadership research: (1) to derive in a maximum number of respondents personal replies not subject to a self-imposed censorship in contemplation of the attitudes of other persons and organizations; (2) to obtain official sanction for the study, if advisable; (3) to determine accurately the reasons for both the similarities and differences in the responses. Replies may express differences in expansiveness of personalities, candor, or reaction to specific individuals. Respondents whose government or culture is alien or hostile to that of the investigator present special problems in such investigations. There may be a reluctance to coöperate with a foreigner or with an investigator from a particular country. To a considerable degree, the achievement of these goals is dependent on the extent a society imposes group restraints on the expression of individuality on the part of its members.

The seriousness of this problem of group coercion on respondents from different countries is a relative one. Regardless of country, labor leaders are constrained to assume a role consistent with the expectations of those with whom they have associations both inside and outside their organizations. Concern for group deviation can raise methodological difficulties in Scandinavia as much as in Eastern Europe. For not precisely the same reasons, respondents in both cultures may be anxious about what individuals or groups may think of their replies. The felt pressures may come from their own organization or from others, including government. To determine whether this group conformity is "voluntary" or "imposed" by concern for the reaction of others is a difficult but not indispensable task. In any case, it is a mistake to infer that such restraint is to be found only under particular types of government and not under others. It is present in most countries to some degree. Therefore, caution should be exercised lest a comparative study of labor leadership become a study of differences in individuality.

Such obstacles make mandatory several requisites for studies of this type. The use of written questionnaires exclusively is of little value even if a substantial response is obtained. The investigator must be present in the country of study and must guide the depth interview. He has to acquire a knowledge of the language and culture of the respondents and create a sympathetic image of himself in the host country. He also needs the warm support of a respected social scientist in the study country, one on whom he can rely for introductions to individuals in the field of industrial relations and guidance during the course of the study. With the assistance of the social scientist and individuals of influence, he has to develop quietly a chain reaction in behalf of the investigation. An indispensable requisite of labor leadership studies is developing a groundswell of interest in their behalf and confidence in the interviewer. Both take time, patience, and a willingness to follow through despite the inevitable disappointments. Useful insights can be gained in such studies provided, first, that the investigator is deeply immersed in the study of a country before he goes there; second, that he is competent in obtaining the best possible support with interviewees; and lastly, that he has much good luck in his investigation. Unless these requirements are fulfilled, however, the study is likely to fail.

B

COMPARISONS OF SCANDINAVIAN LABOR MOVEMENTS

	Sweden	Norway	Denmark
Per cent labor force organized	60	55	56
Per cent organized in federation	78 *	85 *	96
Number affiliated unions	44	44	70
Type of union organization	Industrial	Industrial	Craft dominant
Level of wage policy control †	Federation	Federation	Federation
Level of control of disputes	National	National	National
Labor court ‡	Yes	Yes	Yes
Workweek	45	45	45
Level of employer control of collective bargaining policy	National	National	National
Labor-management councils	Yes	Yes	Yes
Governing political party	Social Democrat	Labor	Social Democrat
Percentage of Labor party vote §	47.8	48.3	42.1
Representation in Parliament:			
Labor	114	78	76
Conservatives	39	29	32
Center	34	15	38
Liberals	40	15	11
Socialists	—	—	11
Communists	5	1	—
Independents	—	—	6
Christian Democrats	—	12	—
Other	—	—	5
Total	233	160	179

* The disparity with Denmark is due to the organization of white-collar workers outside the federation.
† Generally, the federations maintain control by recommending wage policy to affiliated unions and requesting solicitation of approval for any union desiring to fall out of line.
‡ Employed dominantly in the interpretation of existing contract terms.
§ Figures are based on the general election of 1960 in Sweden and Denmark and the general election of 1957 in Norway. Parliamentary representation is the lower house in Sweden and Norway and the single-house Folketing in Denmark.
Source: Communications from embassies of Sweden, Norway, and Denmark in the spring of 1961.

Interview with Danilo Dolci

Would you please give an account of your work in western Sicily?

Our work, if you would like a definition, consists of the development of a community in a way which makes the population conscious of problems in democratic planning. But I would like to know just how much of our work you would like to be informed of, because the question is quite general. Exactly what would you like to know?

Would you give me some idea, for instance, of your work in Partinico?

Very well. We have sought—after a brief period in which we tried to penetrate into the life of the people—we have tried to single out homogeneous zones from an economic-sociological point of view, and in each of these zones we have looked for the nerve center from which it would be possible to set into motion a more rapid increase in productivity and to verify social phenomena of the area. As a starting point, we opened a pilot center, a center for social and technical-agrarian work. There we have an expert in community development and an agrarian technician who became friends of the people and who try to pinpoint everything that the people can do with their own capacities and everything which the state should do, and to organize to apply pressure to obtain it.

There is also a center for social work at Partinico with an Italian, a foreigner, and three social workers. Two of the social workers work mainly with children, because otherwise the children would remain by themselves in the streets. By means of this work, it is also possible to have a deeper contact with the people. The work with the children was also begun because the assistants were rather young, more capable of working with children than with adults whom they did not understand, since they were not Sicilians.

The agrarian technician, with an assistant, develops experimental stations with peasants who try new methods and crops and who experience greater earnings. Then other peasants learn the new agricultural methods and earn more. Close to this work also are two nurses, who do not seek to compete with the local physicians but try to raise the hygienic standards of the people and create a climate of collaboration and friendship. Each week there are meetings with the peasants—some two, three, or four—in which fundamental problems are discussed. In addition, at Partinico there is a coördination center and a group which is now preparing a plan for the comprehensive development of the whole area, that is to say, of Partinico and all of western Sicily which interests us.

What are the long-run objectives of your work?

The long-term objectives are those of identifying, in collaboration with the people, the most nearly perfect forms of life possible and trying to realize them. I know that this is somewhat general, but, for instance, when I was speaking of a plan, it is not a plan which comes from specialists who work in laboratories or chemists separated from the people. It is made by specialists who work with the people as much as possible. In fact, there are also university professors staying at Partinico with their families; and there is a group specially put together for the work, which, for the sake of brevity, I did not mention before. It is called a group for the discussion of the plan with the population. This group behaves in such a way that the population not only gives its advice and suggestions but also tends to make its own plan as much as possible. It is understood that this is difficult, but I say this in the sense that only if those mountains, those hills, those lakes, and those tastes enter into the plan, will the plan be a dynamic one; one which they desire. It is like preserving their authentic values, while naturally taking from elsewhere that which is good. And above all, there is also this second fact: that if the people understand, they will organize themselves and they will gain. We cannot think ingenuously all we need do is make a plan and it will be realized. In order for it to be realized, the participation of the population is indispensable. Only to the extent that everyone is persuaded of the need for something will the people insist on having it.

How many persons work for you and where do they come from?

There are 51 of us. Half are not Italian. Of the Italians, half are Sicilians. Also, naturally, there are local collaborators who do not work full time for us.

What are your most pressing needs and problems?

Our most urgent needs are men who are both specialists and men. We need, for example, experts in community development, and you know that in Italy there are almost none. We need experts in regional planning; and we do not find any because, as you know, in Italy there are philosophers of economics, philosophers in education, but rarely experts in such problems. Once more, as I was saying, the problem is one of trained individuals. It is possible to have money and not have people. There have been many competent individuals, but they stay only six months, a year; and a job in depth cannot be accomplished in six months or a year. Persons who are capable, not of substituting themselves for the population, but of grasping local values and working in such a manner that these values are born from the population itself— this is the central problem. I will give another example. To break the log jam we need coöperation. But it does not exist. You know in all Italy there is only one real school of coöperation. And we need an expert in coöperation to move along this work.

Where does the money for this work come from?

We have Italian friends who were the first to help, who help primarily at Partinico. Then there is a group of friends, consisting of conscientious objectors, sociologists, scholars. We have supporters in England, Sweden, Switzerland, and elsewhere; and now a group is forming in America.

Why did you enter your present work?

I had studied architecture and I believed that it was really my vocation. But strictly on a professional basis. But then, because of a human need, the more I got to the root of things, the less I felt inclined, in a manner of speaking, to petrify injustices into stone. I felt that if I were to work in that profession, I would have to make homes for the rich, for example, not for the poor, and this did not touch my convictions. I felt the need to do things of which I was completely persuaded. And as my interest in men became greater than my interest in stone, I began to work not only with stone. And then I went to Sicily, to Trappeto, because it was the poorest place I knew, and it seemed to me that, for a young man, the surest thing was to begin to work at the place where men found it difficult even to subsist.

What was the most difficult problem you had to resolve in your work, and what were the circumstances?

In a sense, the greatest problem was this one: to be required to choose between continuing in the way I had for some years, in work of a personal nature, inspired, I would say, by moral reasons exclusively, or, while maintaining these qualitative standards, introducing problems of large scale, inasmuch as I became aware of the fact that in such a complex and vast situation I could not succeed. This passage from work in which I had intimate personal relationships with people to an organized relationship in which my contact with the people was not immediate but through others, and the formation of a work group

—this for me was complex because by nature I was attracted to work of a personal nature.

What criteria can be used to measure the results of your work?

Well, it is easier to measure results from an economic point of view and more difficult to weigh them from an educational point of view. From the economic standpoint, a dam is soon to be constructed by the Southern Development Fund, with the urging of the population; to a considerable extent we have worked on this. And then one can see at Trappeto an economic reawakening, through the efforts of the experimental fields. But it is much more complex to see what is happening in the soul, in the fantasy of the people. It would be necessary to make inquiries into this matter, inquiries which should not be done by us. To have an idea of the attitudes of the people toward us, it would be necessary to make a study and to verify what the different reactions are in different groups and different centers—in different centers, because particular attitudes in part depend upon the operator we have at a center.

What is there in the Sicilian environment which creates obstacles to development?

There is internal resistance among the poor, which is the majority, and external resistance. The internal resistance can be summed up in this fashion. First, a low technical-cultural level. The people have no idea how to create wealth and how to improve themselves. A second difficulty, tied to the first, is that in the area, great value is placed on everyone's minding his own business [*faccia i fatti propri*]. A degree of social withdrawal [*chiusura*] is traditional, you know. And this means it becomes almost an impossibility to stay together, since being with others is a vice. It is true, for example, that the trade union leader is murdered not only because he runs counter to the interests of the Mafia but also because he becomes considered the man who does not mind his own business, who concerns himself with the affairs of others. Therefore, in a sense, his murder represents a reconstitution of morality. As far as external forces are concerned, specific examples are the large property-holdings, the Mafia, the police; and, in a sense, I think that the Church also creates a difficulty in development because of traditional factors, because of its cultural orientation. This could be gone into extensively, but we would be talking at too great length.

Tell me, does a Mafia really exist in Sicily? Who are its members?

I shall only cite some figures. In the period since the war, according to official figures, 580 persons were killed because of the Mafia. Among this group were 39 trade union leaders, and not one of their murderers was found. In almost all cases, a large part of the population knew who he was. I believe these figures are eloquent. As far as the organization is concerned, I would not want to give myself publicity, but in the book published by Einaudi, I devote three chapters to the phenomenon. One is dedicated to the Mafia in the interior toward Mussumeri. Another is devoted to the killing of a trade union leader through the work of the *mafiosi* in the zone of Corleone, where the new Mafia is— quite different from the old. The third is concerned with the Menfi area. They explain what the Mafia consists of, their relationships with the people. Nevertheless, to say just a few words, one should not think of it as an organization similar to banditry, which is external to the people, but as something which is born from the cultural values of the people themselves; in a sense, the power these individuals have is given them by the admiration for power on the part of the people, from old tradition. It is necessary to understand the historical reasons why this happened.

Perhaps you are familiar with the trial of those accused of the murder of the trade union leader Carnevale of Sicily? What happened in that trial?

Nothing happened. There was an appeal made in Naples, and nothing happened there either. And we are afraid nothing will happen, as in the other 38 cases.

I suppose everyone wants to be a success in life. What constitutes success for you in your work?

If all the men of western Sicily could work. If all the children could go to school. If every family shedding tears because of someone who is either in jail or in the hospital, if all these families could be families in fact, if all the population could have a real life, that would be a beautiful thing indeed. If I could contribute to this, it would really be success.

According to Sicilian workers themselves, what are their greatest needs?

I have often asked, and I can answer immediately, sure of interpreting their desires. They are, in substance, work and schooling. I could ask hundreds and hundreds of people, and the replies would be fundamentally two. We do not want charity; we want the opportunity to work.

And what would you say are their aspirations?

I believe that fundamentally the need of work is the foremost. That is the first thing. Often the people of the South are referred to as loafers and that is an absurdity because one must know them intimately to understand their capacity to make sacrifices, to work intensely. This no doubt is the primary need. The others are the needs of men . . . they are men.

What do you believe should be the function of trade unionism?

Your question interests me very much. We were saying that these people have a low technical-cultural level. I'll give you an example, insofar as this relates to trade unions. After the war, there was pressure from the peasants, the result of which was that about 12,000 hectares of land were distributed in the province of Palermo. It was a notable thing, paid for in blood and jail terms for thousands of persons. If side by side with this effort there were another, as, for instance, the possibility of irrigating the land—you know in Sicily an irrigated hectare of land yields as much as four not irrigated—if this effort were made, it would have become known to us that 30,000 hectares could have been irrigated. Then the 30,000 would have become 120,000 hectares of land. This means it is not simply a matter of redistribution of income. It is a matter of increasing productivity. But as the people have difficulty understanding what the possibilities are of increasing production, so do the trade unions, which do not have the technical means to understand, to see. For this reason, a great part of trade union action, a great part of political action, I would say, consists of a clientele relationship [*clientela*], something directorial, something akin to social assistance; but something that resembles trade unionism in the modern sense is difficult to find.

What have been the successes of trade unionism on the island?

In my judgment, the occupation of the *feudi* was important, but I would say in a moral way, rather than economic, because a great part of the land that was distributed was very bad and allotted in insufficient amounts. As I was saying, the slogan of "Land to the peasants" was probably good ten years ago, but now something else is needed. It seems to me the unions are not keeping up with the times. They do not have, first of all, a true function of their own. I understand there is difficulty because trained cadres would be needed to prepare persons; lacking functioning unions—I should say functioning parties—it is like a motor turning madly out of control, like trying to put a hole in water; it is like revolving around oneself, and so it does not take hold; one remains always at the same point. I'll give an example. When at Partinico —where, you know, the Italian state has tried to suppress banditry, spending five billion lire—when at Partinico we sought how the people could live, people whom we could see very well were not bloodthirsty vampires, we became aware that among the people neither individuals, trade unions, nor political groups knew how this could be done. We asked many times. They would tell us: Well, it has always been this way. Then someone said, since the slogan of expropriation was in vogue, that there was a certain *feudo* called Sagana which had to be expropriated. I went to see about this *feudo*. There was water, about 45,000-

000 cubic meters, that was annually going into the sea. That is, there was the possibility of irrigating about 8,000 hectares, and nobody knew it. I say this not to shock anyone, but to mention once more the necessity of raising the technical-cultural level of the people in order that problems may be effectively met, because if the problem is not structured it cannot be resolved.

In your judgment, if there were no unions, would the condition of workers be better, the same, or worse?

It is a good thing that they do exist. They serve to raise the wages, even of the peasants; but in my judgment, their presence is insufficient, not only because they do not exert sufficient pressure, but, as I was saying before, because they do not have the indispensable instruments of trade unionism—that is to say, the means which might indicate to them what must be done. And this is a problem not only in western Sicily, or Sicily, but in Italy generally, I think.

In your view, what are the characteristics of a good leader?

He should be a person who should not only lead but at the same time know how to listen.

What contribution have the political parties made for the workers?

In Sicily we still have a system of political parties dispensing favors, and I am hardly persuaded they serve a function for the people. I also am becoming increasingly aware of the fact that a great number of those with responsible positions in the parties are lawyers, very respectable persons; I have great admiration for them; I would not be here if it were not for them; I would still be in jail, and who knows for how many years? But I am aware that with all their classical training, with all the Greek and Latin they know, they are not always the persons most suited to face a production problem, problems of a social character. I would say they have unconsciously almost a contempt for everything rural, for peasantry, for dung; they believe they can save the world at the Parliament, at the Forum, with speeches. Naturally, I do not wish to generalize. This is an impression we have. They want to introduce oratorical flight as the key to the solution of problems, cunning, the cunning of the "smoke-filled room," and this to me does not seem sufficient. I do not think the situation will be loosened up any until there is the possibility of introducing politics on a scientific basis. On the basis of effective interests, if anything.

What contribution has the Communist party made?

I would prefer restricting myself to western Sicily and not to all of Italy because the discussion would otherwise be much too complicated and much too long. I would risk being imprecise. In western Sicily where we work, it is certain that the greatest force against the Mafia is the Communist party. It is not that people have read Marx, or that they know how to theorize. On one side is the baron and on the other a person who is hungry, and the person who is hungry meets others who are also hungry; they want land and work; and this is the general approach of the party, which has found leaders for them. The party has had, even if it appears paradoxical to those who do not know the situation, a liberalizing function; "liberal" because a situation overwhelmed by the Mafia is an impossible situation. If one can get around, if one can live, it is due to this kind of action. I would also say that insofar as violence is concerned, the greatest education for non-violence did not come from the Church, and I say this not to engage in polemics, because I also have Catholic collaborators in the group, but above all from the left-wing political parties, inasmuch as they have organized the protest of the people, which was once on an individual basis, which could only be the protest of the bandit; they have organized it, not in trade union forms or authentic political activity, but at least in more progressive forms. It is interesting; it would be something to study in depth.

Do you believe the Church has a role to play in the labor problem? If so, what?

Two years ago we began an inquiry to see what could be the relationship between the Church parish and unemployment. In substance, we became aware of the fact that the mentality of the clergy was as follows: The strong live; and for the weak, charity, if that is possible. It is an old traditional mentality which must be done away with entirely. We cannot be content with this.

Are there differences among employers? If so, what are they?

You raise intelligent questions which require serious study. I now can only give you impressions. And they have to be then verified. There is a difference, I think, between those on the coast and those in the interior. Those in the interior are the large proprietors, who often do not live on their property, but have a *gabellotto* as an intermediary. On the coast where the situation is more dynamic, the relationship is more intimate. There the small proprietor has a closer relationship with the peasant who assists him.

In your judgment, what responsibilities do employers have toward their workers?

The large proprietors in the interior do not have any sense of the social function of property. They live elsewhere; the half they get from sharecropping is spent elsewhere; it is not reinvested, as happens elsewhere where the proprietor is an *appassionato*.

What structural reforms do you think are necessary to improve the condition of labor in Sicily?

We were speaking of *mezzadria*. The first thing that should be done, naturally, is to leave the land to the *mezzadro* without paying the proprietor for it. This is the first thing that should be done. Two cannot live on the land. We should experiment with pilot works of a coöperative character in order to realize a new social-economic structure. We should not assume a particular structure. In other words, it is not just a matter of redistribution of income, but one of increased productivity which is tied to rationalization.

Studies in Italy appear to indicate a strong hostility on the part of workers toward their employers. What factors do you believe account for the presence of this hostility?

It is due to a form of behavior typical in backward areas. The people seek the help of others. On one side there is the boss, who is almost the owner of people, and on the other those who have difficulty being self-sufficient individuals, who rely on others for the solution of their problems. This is typical of a backward area.

What should be the relationship between trade unions and political parties?

In my view, they should be entirely distinct things, if we want to progress in the situation. The trade union should represent the precise interests of a particular group of workers, but instead, as you know, in Sicily the trade unions as well as the coöperatives are entirely dependent on political parties. And the parties do not respond to the needs of particular individuals. They are old parties, not founded on particular problems. I say this not to ridicule the efforts they make, which could be considerable. The point of arrival is that it is only necessary to participate in a session of Parliament. It seems to me there is a tendency to be orators, lawyers, to reach for words, and not consider meetings as an opportunity to come up with concrete decisions; it is difficult to find people who think over beforehand what they have to say.

A problem in the American labor movement is that of corruption. What factors do you think account for its absence or presence in a labor movement?

It cannot be said corruption does not exist in the Italian labor movement. One can say that in certain groups, in the larger groups, there is no corruption. But there are some trade union units which are in my judgment not only corrupt but corrupting. It is useless to indicate who and how. It is much more difficult to find corruption in the extreme left wing because participation in left-wing unionism requires considerable courage, and sometimes the leftist parties in Sicily are called parties of conscience, *partiti di coscienza;* very interesting.

In what way can Americans help in your work?

The greatest help is for someone to come and see the situation. We need witnesses. Secondly, if we could find some expert in community development, coöperation, and regional planning. This would be a great help also. Money is important, but important to be wisely invested in men. This is the important thing: men.

Interview Schedules

The interview schedules are the ones which survived from those tested in both countries. Items were discarded for several reasons. They may not have produced meaningful differences within a country or between the two countries. In some cases, items drew a blank. Some were offensive to the point of arousing hostility. And others proved too far removed from my area of interest. Items included in the schedules below were used in both countries unless otherwise indicated. Those used only in Italy are marked (I); those only in Denmark, (D).

TRADE UNION LEADERS

Interview

1. Date of Birth _____.

2. Place of Birth _____.

3. Occupation of father _____.

4. Occupation of paternal grandfather _____.

5. Education _____.

6. What is the purpose of your organization?

7. Please give all the jobs and trade union positions you have had since leaving school and starting work, up to your present position.

8. Why did you decide to work in the trade union movement?

9. What do you feel are your most important responsibilities as a trade union leader?

10. In your judgment, what are the responsibilities of employers toward their workers? What differences, if any, are there among employers? What accounts for the differences?

11. Do you think employers are favorable to trade unions, merely tolerate them, or prefer they did not exist?   Why?

12. Who has more political influence in _____, the employers or the trade unions?   Why?

13. Who has more collective bargaining power, the employers or the trade unions?   Why?

14. (a) What are the pressing problems, if any, in the _____ trade union movement? (b) In your opinion, what are the greatest obstacles to the further development of trade unionism in _____?   (D)

15. What should the relationship be between trade unions and political parties?

16. What are the pressing problems of your workers and your organization that you are confronted with as a labor leader?

17. What has been the contribution of the Communist party to the cause of the workers?

18. What do you conceive the role of the labor leader to be?

19. Do you think that trade unionism has objectives and methods different from what they used to be in the past?   If so, what are they?

20. In your judgment, what is the function of the strike?

21. Certain individuals or groups have more influence in a country than other individuals or groups. What individuals or groups do you believe have the greatest influence in _____?

22. I suppose everyone wants to be a "success" in life. What constitutes "success" for you as a trade union leader?

23. What long-term objectives, achieved either through trade unionism or government legislation, do you believe the labor movement should strive for?

24. (a) Do you believe labor-management coöperation at the plant level is possible in Italy?   (b) If so, how?   (I)
(a) Has the experience in labor-management coöperation to date under the joint production committees been satisfactory or unsatisfactory?   (b) Why?   (D)

25. Do you believe the development of industrial unionism in your country would have a beneficial effect?   Why?   (D)

26. Cite the specific ways in your organization how trade union officials and the membership communicate with each other either directly or indirectly:

    a) at the national organization level
    b) at the local organization level
    c) at the plant level

27. In your judgment, what are the most pressing problems of your country?

What role, if any, do trade unions have in resolving these problems?

28. Whom would you cite as one of the best employers in Italy? One of the worst?   Why?   (I)

29. Do you believe that the trade union federations in Italy should unite? Do you think unification is possible within five years? In what way could unification take place?   (I)

30. Which political party do you think best represents the interests of workers in Italy?   (I)

31. What do you believe should be the objectives of trade unionism?   (I)

32. Do you believe the Church has a role to play in the labor problem? If so, what?   (I)

33. Do you believe that every worker should be required to join a union of his own choosing?   (I)

Questionnaire

1. What do you think is the most important function you discharge as a labor leader?

2. The purpose of this question is to determine the portion of your working time spent in discharging your various functions as a trade union leader. Please consider the entire scope of your duties in terms of both your relations with different people and your responsibilities. Below each item you cite, write the percentage of time spent. The items below are given only as examples and are not intended to be conclusive. Each of the two columns should add to 100 per cent.

Relations	*Responsibilities*
( ) with colleagues (please indicate their titles)	( ) bargaining collectively
	( ) individual grievances
( ) with workers (please indicate how)	( ) correspondence
	( ) attending meetings
( ) with employers	( ) public relations
( ) with employer associations (please indicate which)	( ) other (please list other responsibilities not mentioned above)
( ) individual effort (please list the kind of work you do alone)	
( ) other (please list other relations not mentioned above)	
(100)	(100)

3. Approximately how many hours do you work in the course of a week?

4. You are the leader of a $\dfrac{}{\text{national union}}$ or a $\dfrac{}{\text{local union}}$?

5. What was the most difficult problem that you had to face and resolve in your career as a trade union leader?
What were the circumstances?

6. What aspects of American trade unionism do you prefer ?

7. What aspects of American trade unionism do you find less desirable?

8. In your opinion, what are the criteria which can be used to measure the achievements of trade unionism?

9. In all probability, workers have different needs and goals. There are different methods with which to pursue these needs and goals.
   a) Which of these needs and goals do you believe are the most important?
   b) What method would you employ in obtaining them?

10. After having made a decision on a trade union problem, what criterion would you use in order to determine whether the results have been a success or failure?

11. On what basis would you determine whether a colleague is discharging his responsibilities properly?

12. What obligations do you feel constrained to assume because of your role as a labor leader?
What do you believe your workers expect of you as their leader?

13. Please cite by placing a number after each item the order of importance you feel workers would place the following goals:
   good supervision by the employer
   higher wages
   opportunity for a better job
   employment security
   better physical conditions of work
   improved government welfare programs
   shorter hours of work
   better employer health and welfare benefits
   other (please specify)   (D)

14. In your judgment, what do you think are the characteristics of a "good" labor leader?

WORKER QUESTIONNAIRE (DENMARK ONLY)

1. Date of birth _____.

2. Your present occupation _____.

3. Occupation of father _____.

4. Occupation of paternal grandfather _____.

5. Number of years of school _____.

6. Number of years of apprentice training, if any _____.

7. Please cite what you think should be the characteristics of a "good" labor leader.

    1) _____

    2) _____

    3) _____

    4) _____

8. What responsibilities, if any, do you feel workers have toward their trade unions?

9. Do workers have any responsibilities toward employers?   If so, what are they?

10. What are the most desirable qualities of trade union leaders in _____?

    What, if any, are their less desirable qualities?

11. If there were no trade unions, would you say the terms and conditions of employment would be:

    a) better

    b) about the same

    c) worse

12. How would you evaluate the job your trade union is doing?

    a) excellent

    b) fair

    c) poor

13. Please list in order of importance what you think should be the different functions of trade unions.

    a) _____

    b) _____

    c) _____

    d) _____

14. People often talk of being successful in life. When you talk of being successful in life what do you mean by it?

In what way do you expect your trade union to help you to be successful in life?

In accomplishing this objective would you say your trade union has been

a) very successful   *b*) fairly successful   *c*) unsuccessful

15. Please list what you believe are the greatest aspirations of _____ workers.

    a) _____
    b) _____
    c) _____

16. Do you like your present job?   Why?

17. What did you hope to become when you left school or started work?

18. If you had a son starting out now, what would you advise him to become?

19. Of all the jobs that you have ever had, which job did you like best? Which job did you like least?   Why?

20. Certain individuals or groups have the greatest influence in a community. List in order of importance the individuals or groups which you feel have influence in your community.

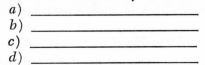

    a) _____
    b) _____
    c) _____
    d) _____

21. If you had to start your work career over again, what would you want to be?

22. In your judgment, should wages be paid on the basis of:
    a) differences in the skill of workers
    b) differences in the productivity of workers
    c) both differences in skill and productivity
    d) should be fairly similar regardless of differences in skill
    e) other (please specify) _____

23. Please cite by placing a number after each item the order of importance to you of the following goals of workers:
    good supervision
    higher wages
    opportunity for a better job
    employment security
    better physical conditions of work
    shorter hours of work

better health and welfare benefits

other (please specify)

24. In what way would you describe how you have been achieving these objectives:

    a) very well

    b) fairly well

    c) not too well and not too badly

    d) badly

    e) very badly

25. Please list all of the jobs you have had since starting work, the time you spent in each job, and the reason why you left the job.

Job	*Time Spent*	*Reason for Leaving*

For Shop Stewards

1. What do you feel are your responsibilities as a shop steward?

2. What are your problems in trying to perform your duties as a shop steward?

3. What do you feel the workers expect of you as their shop steward?

4. What do you feel the employer expects of you as a shop steward?

5. Please list in order of importance all of the functions you perform as a shop steward.

EMPLOYERS

1. Age _____.

2. Occupation of father _____.

3. Occupation of paternal grandfather _____.

4. Industry _____.

5. Number of employees in company _____.

6. Education _____.

7. What are your major problems in the operation of your organization?

8. What are your objectives as an employer?

9. Do employers have functions and responsibilities that are different from what they were in the past? If so, what are they?

10. Do you have any direct relations with trade union leaders? If so, please state the level of leadership, such as shop stewards, regional officials, etc.

11. In your judgment, what responsibilities do employers have toward their workers?

12. What do you believe should be the function of trade unionism?

13. In your judgment, what are the qualities of a "good" labor leader? (D)

14. What would you say are the weaknesses of labor leaders, if any?

15. How do labor leaders differ from each other? What accounts for the differences? (D)

16. What do you think are the weaknesses of trade unions, if any?

17. What factors do you believe account for the absence or presence of corruption in a labor movement?

18. In your judgment, are the union representatives at the plant level an asset or a liability in the life of a company? What is the reason for your choice?

19. To what extent are the trade unions expressing the needs of their members:

　　———— very well
　　———— fairly well
　　———— sometimes well and sometimes poorly
　　———— poorly
　　———— very badly   (D)

20. Studies in Italy appear to indicate a strong hostility on the part of workers toward their employers. What factors do you believe account for the presence of this hostility?   (I)

Studies in Italy appear to indicate a strong hostility on the part of workers toward their employers. (a) Do you feel Danish workers are hostile toward their employers? (b) What factors account for the difference?   (D)

21. In your judgment, what is the best way to improve further the standards of labor in ————?

22. What characteristics of the ———— people do you feel account for the uniqueness of their trade unionism and labor-management relationships?   (D)

23. In what way, if at all, does trade unionism run counter to the well-being of the company?

24. I suppose everyone wants to be a success in life. What constitutes success for an employer?

25. Please cite by placing a number after each item the order of importance you feel workers would place the following goals:
good supervision by the employer
higher wages
opportunity for a better job
employment security
better physical conditions of work
improved government welfare programs
shorter hours of work
better employer health and welfare benefits
other (please specify)   (D)

26. Has the experience in labor-management coöperation to date under the joint production committees been satisfactory or unsatisfactory? Why?   (D)
Do you believe labor-management coöperation is possible in Italy? If so, how?   (I)

27. What do you feel would be an equitable way to determine the general level of wages and the relative differences between the wages of workers?   (D)

INDUSTRIAL RELATIONS PUBLIC

1. Occupation of interviewee _____.

2. Certain individuals or groups have the greatest influence in a country. Please list in order of importance the individuals or groups which you feel have influence in your country.

3. In your judgment, if there were no trade unions, would the conditions of labor be:
1. better
2. about the same
3. worse   (D)

4. What do you think is the proper function of trade unionism?

5. What do you believe are the weaknesses of trade unionism, if any?   (D)

6. Who has more political influence, employers or trade unions? Why?

7. Who has more collective bargaining power, employers or trade unions? Why?

8. People often talk of being successful in life. What do you believe the working class considers being successful in life?

Who are their "heroes," if any? (D)

9. What is the biggest weakness, if any, in trade union leaders?

10. To what extent are the trade union leaders expressing the needs of their membership:

_____ very well
_____ fairly well
_____ sometimes well and sometimes poorly
_____ poorly
_____ very badly (D)

11. Are employers favorable to unions, do they merely tolerate them, or do you believe they prefer they did not exist? (I)

12. In your judgment, what are the most pressing problems in your country?

What role, if any, do you think the trade unions have in the resolution of these problems? (D)

13. In your opinion, what should the relationship be between trade unions and political parties?

14. Studies in Italy indicate a strong hostility on the part of workers toward their employers. Does such hostility exist in Denmark?

What factors account for its absence (or) for its presence? (D)

15. A problem in the American labor movement is that of corruption. What factors do you feel account for its absence or presence in a labor movement?

16. How do labor leaders differ from each other in Denmark?

What factors account for these differences? (D)

17. In your opinion, what characteristics of the Danish people produce a trade unionism different from that to be found elsewhere? (D)

18. What do you think labor leaders expect from their jobs? (D)

19. Do you believe that trade unionism can run counter to the interests of society? If so, how? (D)

Metal Industry
Collective Bargaining Agreements
in Italy and Denmark

The two collective bargaining agreements below include the subject matter of all the clauses and major portions of actual terms of employment. Substantive terms of particular interest to students of American labor relations are translated in full. The translations are designed to achieve a measure of comparability and comprehension for American readers through the use of the jargon of American industrial relations whenever possible. Numbers refer to particular articles of the agreement. The agreements cover the industrial worker elite in each country.

THE ITALIAN AGREEMENT

The contract covers all of Italy and embraces various metal industries listed in the first seven pages of the agreement. Signatories include some eighty employer representatives of various employer associations in the metal industries and the General Confederation of Italian Industry, Confindustria, and delegations from each of the three trade union federations and their respective national unions. The main section covering blue-collar workers contains fifty-one clauses, the remainder of the agreement comprising a section for white-collar workers, one for a special category of production workers, a section common to all employees, and a table of wage rates by geographical areas. Subsequent interpretations of a particular clause are placed into the agreement by the parties as a written clarification (*chiarimento a verbale*). These have not been translated.

Scope of Clause and Term of Employment

1. *Hiring of new employees.*—New employees will be hired through the state employment exchange. Management will inform them in writing of their classification, wage, and date of employment. Before hir-

ing, workers can be obliged to take a medical examination from a company physician. It is to be understood, particularly for small and medium-size plants, that a worker can be employed in other than his job classification if the work so requires.

2. *Hiring of women and children.*— . . . is to be regulated by public law supplemented by agreements which may be made from time to time by the parties. . . .

3. *Documents to be presented by newly hired employees.*— . . . identification card, labor book, social security card, certificate of legal residence are to be presented; in addition, management can require a police certificate not older than 3 months attesting to the non-commission of crimes.

4. *Probationary period of employment.*— . . . a twelve-day probationary period during which time the worker is subject to dismissal without the payment of severance pay . . .

5. *Starting and quitting signals.*— . . . three for starting and one for the end of the shift. . . . Workers are forbidden to cease work before the sounding of the quitting signal.

6. *Hours of work.*—For work in excess of 44 hours in any one week, premium pay of 2 per cent of base pay. . . . The normal workweek terminates at 1300 hours on Saturday. . . . The hours of work are to be counted by the clock of the department or the plant. In continuous shift operations, workers can leave their posts only when relieved by another worker. In exceptional cases when the nature of the work requires the continuous presence of an employee, a worker can be required to remain on the job for a full second shift.

7. *Suspension and interruption of work.*—In cases of interruption of production not exceeding one hour in its entirety in the course of any one day, the worker is entitled to a full day's pay. Interruptions in excess of one hour are subject to the payment of wages only if management retains the worker on the job.

8. *Suspensions and reduction of work.*—In case of a suspension or reduction of work due to factors which concern the entire industry, the parties to this agreement place themselves at the disposition of any agreements which may be made by interested federations on the matter.

9. *Recovery of work lost.*—Work lost for reasons beyond the control of management can be recovered at straight time earnings provided it does not exceed one hour in any one day and is effected within 30 days after the interruption of such work.

10. *Weekly day of rest.*—Workers are entitled to one day of rest each workweek, which would normally be on Sunday. In cases of Sunday work permitted by the law, some other day will be set aside as the day

of rest. Work performed on the normal day of rest will be paid on the basis of a 20 per cent premium for the first two hours and 30 per cent thereafter. . . .

11. *Holidays.*—The agreement recognizes 16 paid holidays plus the day of the patron saint of the town in which the plant is located. Work on such holidays is payable on the basis of 40 per cent premium.

12. *Pay for work in different classifications.*—Work performed in different classifications will be paid for at the highest classification provided the work is typical of such classification. . . .

13. *Temporary job transfers.*—Management has the right to require the performance of work outside of the employee's occupation provided it does not cause a cut in wages or a substantial change in the worker's "moral position" in the plant. After 30 days continuous work in a higher classification, a worker is entitled to be upgraded within that classification. . . .

14. *Women performing work normally done by men.*— . . . to be paid at the rate for men workers. . . .

15. *Regulations for incentive work.*—Work standards should be such as to guarantee to the average worker at least 8 per cent of his base pay. This condition is presumed filled when a group of workers on incentive in the same department reach an average premium of 8 per cent, which does not exclude the revision of the rates in cases where such group of workers have a capacity above normal. . . .

In cases in which workers do not reach a premium of 8 per cent for reasons not due to themselves, their pay will be made to reflect such a minimum. Whenever changes in the method of operation occur, rates will be modified in proportion to the manner in which the change has affected output time. . . .

At the request of the worker, the company will inform him of the method of computation of his incentive pay. . . .

During the period of time in which a worker is off incentive, he will be guaranteed wages not less than 70 per cent of his earnings while on incentive. . . .

The company is forbidden to employ incentive workers having under their direct employ other workers who are directly paid by them. . . .

When an appreciable decline in average incentive earnings has taken place, the *commissione interna* can intercede with management in order jointly to ascertain the causes thereof. . . .

Any disputes concerning the application of this article will be examined under the grievance procedure. . . .

16. *Methods of wage payment.*—Wages are to be paid weekly, bi-

weekly, fortnightly, or monthly, according to plant practice or agreement between the parties. . . .

With such payment, workers will be provided with information including the nature of the firm, the name of the worker, the time period covered by the pay, a breakdown of the components of the wage and all withholdings. . . .

17. *Pay claims.*—Any claims of differences between actual pay and that indicated on the pay envelope or complaints on the quality of money must be made immediately at the time of payment. Purely accounting errors must be claimed within one year of the error. . . .

18. *Vacations.*—Workers are entitled to vacations on the following basis:

1 to 7 years of service	12 days
7 to 15 years of service	14 days
15 to 20 years of service	16 days
Over 20 years of service	18 days

The time of vacations will be established by management consistent with the federation agreement of May 8, 1953, on the function of the *commissione interna,* keeping in mind the desires of the workers and the needs of the firm. . . .

Workers in the employ of the company for less than one year will be given vacations on the basis of one day for every month of employment. . . .

Vacation pay shall consist of net earnings plus 4 per cent for time workers and average earnings for the prior three months' period for incentive workers. . . .

19. *Christmas bonus.*—Workers are entitled to a Christmas bonus equivalent to 200 hours' pay for time workers and the equivalent of one month's earnings for incentive workers. . . .

20. *Length-of-service bonus.*—Workers are entitled to a length-of-service bonus equal to 125 hours of pay after 10 years of employment and 250 hours at the end of 20 years. . . .

21. *Housing indemnity.*—Whenever the place of work is away from housing or public transportation leading to inhabited centers and the distance to the perimeter of such centers is more than five kilometers, an indemnity shall be paid the worker in an amount to be decided by the parties. . . .

22. *Health and safety.*—Management will keep the work place in a manner conducive to good health and safety, consistent with the provisions of the law. . . .

23. *Work clothing.*—Workers performing dirty work shall be provided with special clothing and the means to change at the plant. Work-

ers required to wear special clothing must be provided them by management. . . .

24. *Occupational sickness and accidents.*—The law regarding provisions for safety and assistance is acknowledged. All accidents are to be reported by workers to their superior in order to provide first aid and put into effect the requirements of the law. Any faulty plant operations detected by workers should be reported immediately to appropriate superiors.

The worker's job will be maintained when: (*a*) in case of an occupational illness for the period of entitlement of disability pay under the law; (*b*) in case of an accident up to the time of cure as indicated by a medical certificate.

Workers unable to continue in their former jobs will be reassigned to work more suitable to their capacities.

A worker having an accident is entitled to wages for the day during which the accident occurred.

During the period of job guarantee, length of service and all job rights will continue to accrue and be in force. . . .

25. *Illness and accidents away from the job.*—In case of illness the worker must notify the firm by the second day of absence and transmit a medical certificate within three days of absence. The plant has the right to check such illness by its own physician. Workers are guaranteed rights of recall for six months for length of service up to five years. . . .

26. *Matrimonial leave of absence.*—Workers are entitled to a matrimonial leave of absence of ten days with pay not less than 72 hours hours. . . .

27. *Pregnancy and childbirth.*— . . . to be provided for consistent with law . . .

28. *Military service.*—Workers going into military service are guaranteed their jobs for a period up to a month within the cessation of such service. . . .

29. *Plant discipline.*—The worker is subject to the authority of his superiors. He should be polite to his fellow workers and subordinate to his superiors. Consistent with the personal dignity of workers, supervisors will have relationships with them in a spirit of collaboration and civility. . . .

30. *Improper use of time cards.*—The marking of time cards or the handling of one belonging to another employee is subject to penalty up to discharge. . . .

31. *Absences.*—Absences must be justified within the day following the beginning of the absence except under justifiable circumstances. . . .

32. *Entering and leaving the plant.*—Workers are forbidden to leave

the plant during their shift without authorization. Workers desiring such permission must request it within the first hour of the shift except in special circumstances when it is not possible to do so.

Workers attending courses of study during the evening or on holidays will be granted permission to leave the plant during the period of examinations. . . . A discharged worker is forbidden to enter the plant without authorization. . . .

33. *Use of materials and equipment.*—To provide himself with materials and equipment, a worker must make a request of his immediate supervisor. He is responsible for the proper handling of such material and equipment. . . . Any damage thereof is subject to a charge against pay up to 10 per cent. . . .

34. *Forbidden conduct.*— . . . working in other shops, collections, soliciting signatures, the sale of tickets, without authorization; the solicitation of union dues can be effectuated in the plant outside of working hours. . . .

35. *Disciplinary measures.*—Any infraction of this agreement by a worker is subject to the following penalties depending upon the seriousness of the offense: (1) oral reprimand; (2) a fine not to exceed three hours' pay; (3) written reprimand; (4) suspension up to a maximum of three days; (5) discharge.

36. *Fines and suspensions.*—A worker is subject to fines or suspension for: (1) unexcused absences or leaving one's place of work; (2) beginning work late or ending before quitting time; (3) spoilage of material and work in production; (4) negligence or slowdown in work; (5) appearing for work in a state of intoxication; (6) performing work through the medium of third parties similar to that of the firm; (7) smoking wherever prohibited; (8) performing work in the plant not belonging to the company; (9) committing any act prejudicial to discipline, morals, health and safety of the plant. . . .

37. *Discharge.*—(A.) Infractions subject to dismissal without warning and with dismissal pay: (1) minor cases of insubordination; (2) damage to material or equipment; (3) the performance of work not belonging to the company without the permission of management; (4) abandoning the work post by employees having custodial and watchman duties; (5) unexcused absence in excess of four consecutive days or absences repeated three times in the course of a year on the day following holidays or vacations; (6) a conviction subject to a jail sentence; (7) recurring offenses listed under Article 37. . . .

(B.) Infractions subject to dismissal without warning and without dismissal pay: (1) major cases of insubordination; (2) theft of plant property, sketches, designs and other documents belonging to the company; (3) deliberate damage to material and equipment; (4) imperiling the safety of others or the safety of equipment by abandoning one's work post; (5) smoking at the risk of the safety of persons or equipment; (6) executing without permission a substantial amount of personal work; (7) indulging in altercations with other employees in the departments of the plant.

38. *Dismissal notification.*—Workers discharged for reasons outside the scope of Article 37 or resignations by the worker himself are subject to notification depending on length of service. . . . Any party not making such a notification must pay the other an indemnity equivalent to the number of days of warning. . . .

39. *Discharge length-of-service pay.*—Workers discharged for reasons outside of the scope of Article 37 are entitled to an indemnity calculated on the basis of Articles 2120 and 2121 of the civil code and the following norms. . . . [The discharge pay ranges from four to fifteen days, based on length of service.]

40. *Indemnity pay for workers who quit.*—Workers who quit voluntarily are entitled to a percentage of indemnity pay stipulated in Article 40 of this agreement. . . .

41. *Death pay.*—In case of death of the employee, indemnity pay will correspond to that indicated in the civil code.

42. *Job classifications.*—Workers employed in metal plants and second-group basic steel plants are divided into the following job classifications on the basis of definitions as specified in the agreement:

Skilled workers [*operai specializzati*]: . . . tool-makers, riggers, pattern-makers, calibrators . . . ;

Semi-skilled workers [*operai qualificati*]: maintenance mechanics, machine-cleaners, sheet metal workers, carpenters . . . ;

Specialist laborers [*manovali specializzati*]: machine-tenders, solderers, distributors of equipment, firemen, varnishers, furnace-tenders . . . ;

Common laborers [*manovali comuni*]: janitors, material-handlers.

Women:

First category: women who perform work characteristic of semi-skilled male workers . . . ;

Second category: women who tend machines or do bench work . . . ;

Third category: women who perform cleaning work and movement of goods . . . also those performing work not requiring any particular skill or experience. . . .

43. *Subdivisions of the work force in basic steel plants.*—Workers

are divided into two groups, consisting of those in direct production and those who perform indirect production. [For example, those who load and tap furnaces are considered direct production workers.] . . .

44. *Minimum hourly rates of pay.*—Minimum hourly rates of pay are those appended to this agreement.

45. *Base pay of steel workers.*— . . . Base pay shall consist of the rate stipulated by this agreement plus additions, if any, derived from company-wide agreements or from unilateral acts of the company. . . .

In the case of installation of new plants or modifications to existing plants, base pay shall be determined on the basis of equivalent jobs in the firm. When the new installation involves a newly constructed plant for which this extension of rates cannot be made, base pay will be set on the basis of rates found in similar plants subject to mutual agreement of the parties. . . .

46. *Indirect production in basic steel plants.*—The following operations are considered to be indirect production. . . . Whenever productive work during the course of a shift is interrupted for indirect production, employees performing such work will be paid their base pay plus a minimum of 85 per cent of their average incentive earnings at the time the shift to indirect production is made. . . .

47. *Changes in earnings due to variations in the size of work crews.*— Whenever changes in earnings to individual workers are caused by changes in the composition of work crews, grievances thereunder can be raised under the procedure stipulated in Article 10, Part IV, of this agreement.

48. *Substitutions for absent workers in work crews.*—Whenever it is not possible to provide for a substitution for an absent employee in a work crew, the members of the crew shall share the base pay of the absent employee. . . .

49. *Regulations governing intermittent jobs or those calling for guard and custodial duties.*— . . . workers in such jobs can be hired up to a ten-hour day and a normal workweek up to 60 hours. . . . Custodial employees living on the plant premises will have terms of employment regulated on an individual basis, subject to consultation with a union should the employee so desire.

50. *Transfers.*—Workers on temporary assignments away from their normal place of work will be treated in the following terms:

Lunch pay will be granted when such a transfer provides them with time off for lunch of less than 40 minutes or less than the time granted workers in the plant. . . . Lunch pay is not to be paid when a meal is regularly provided workers in the plant in which the employee has been temporarily transferred.

This article does not apply to workers whose jobs require constant movement, such as telegraph, telephone, and power-line employees. The base pay of such workers is 30 per cent above the minimum wages stipulated in the agreement. . . .

In the case of temporary transfers from one plant to another of the same company in the same community, the provincial organizations will make agreements to provide for such cases on a company-by-company basis. . . .

The parties are in agreement that the above article is intended to be a minimum and not to be used as a means of allowing reductions in cases where individual employees are receiving more favorable terms of employment.

Section II

Regulations Covering Workers Belonging to a Special Category

1. *Definitions.*—Special-category workers as defined below are subject to special provisions indicated in the agreement: (1) those performing jobs superior to those in the highest worker classifications; (2) those performing confidential and responsible duties not normally assigned to workers; (3) those who supervise the work of a group of employees and who assume technical responsibility for such work.

Such workers are divided into two classes: (1) those who must exercise a certain amount of initiative with respect to the results of operations; and (2) those whose labor is technically more complex than employees in the regular classifications. . . . An example of the first would be the worker in charge of a rolling mill and of the second an employee in charge of a work crew.

2. *Hiring.*—

.   .   .   .

3. *Probationary period of employment.*—Probationary period is not to exceed one month. Lesser periods must be agreed to in writing. . . .

4. *Movement from regular classifications to a special category.*—
. . . Such workers are entitled to privileges accruing to those whose employment is terminated and are to be considered as new employees with the exceptions as provided below: . . .

5. *Hours of work.*—The hours of work shall be regulated as those for clerical workers in Part III of the agreement.

6. *Overtime, night, and holiday work.*—The provisions of Article 12 above are applicable, with the following exceptions. . . .

7. *Suspension or reduction of hours of work.*—The provisions of Article 3 of the agreement covering clerical workers are applicable. . . .

8. *Recovery of work lost.*—

.   .   .   .

9. *Length-of-service increases.*—The provisions of Article 15 of the clerical employees' agreement are applicable. . . .

10. *Vacations.*—

Length of Service	Amount
Up to five years	15 days
6 to 12	20 days
13 to 20	25 days
More than 20	28 days

The length of service obtained in a worker classification is valid to the extent of 50 per cent of such service. . . .

11. *Sickness and accidents.*—In the event of sickness and accidents, employees are entitled to reëmployment on the following terms: . . .

12. *Dismissal and resignation notifications.*—The employment relationship cannot be terminated by either party without notification under the following terms. . . .

13. *Length-of-service pay for workers who quit voluntarily.*—Employees who quit voluntarily are entitled to a length-of-service bonus as follows: [the length-of-service bonus payable ranges from 50 to 100 per cent of monthly wages depending upon the years of employment].

A complete indemnity is payable to male workers over 60 years of age and women workers over 55. . . .

14. *Length-of-service pay for discharged workers.*—In case of termination of employment by the company not within the scope of Article 28 of the agreement covering clerical workers, the employee is entitled to a length-of-service bonus as follows: [an increasing percentage of monthly wages based on years of employment].

15. *Disciplinary measures.*—Disciplinary measures applicable to clerical employees apply also to special-category workers. . . .

16. *Terms of employment similar to those for clerical employees.*—The following terms of employment for clerical employees also apply to special-category workers. . . .

17. *More favorable terms of employment for individual employees.* — . . . the parties to the present agreements do not intend to substitute less favorable terms of employment by virtue of this national agreement. . . .

18. *Monthly wages.*—Minimum monthly wages are those appended to this agreement.

Regulations Covering Clerical Employees

1. *Hiring of new employees.*—The hiring of clerical employees will be made through the employment exchange, consistent with law. The employer will provide a newly hired employee the following information in writing: (1) the place in which he will work; (2) the date of employment; (3) the work duties and category to which he has been assigned; (4) starting terms of employment; (5) length of his probationary period; (6) any other terms agreed to. . . .

2. *Hiring of women and children.*— . . . shall be consistent with the law. . . .

3. *Documents to be presented.*—

. . . .

4. *Types of clerical employees.*—Clerical classifications are as follows:

(1) first-class clerical employees [*impiegati di concetto*] with technical and administrative duties, with functions of directing work forces or which call for specific technical preparation, who must exercise judgment and independent initiative within the limits of directives of management . . . ;

(2) general clerical employees [*impiegati d'ordine*] divided into two groups: (*a*) stenographers, record-keeping clerks, copyists, file clerks, bookkeeping clerks . . . ; (*b*) those whose clerical duties require no training or experience.

5. *Promotion from a worker to a clerical classification.*—In the case of a shift from a worker to a clerical classification in the same firm, the worker has the rights accruing him upon resignation as an industrial worker and is considered to be hired ex novo with length of service accruing only for computing length-of-service pay equivalent to 20 per cent. . . .

6. *Promotion from the special-category classification to clerical employee.*—

. . . .

7. *Probationary period.*—First-class clerical employees will have a period of probation not to exceed six months; and three months for those of other categories. . . .

8. *Hours of work.*—The normal hours of work are those specified by law. For work in excess of 44 hours, up to a maximum of 48, employees will be paid in addition to their regular salary one-half of their minimum wages. . . .

9. *Suspension or reduction of work.*—Consistent with interfederation

norms . . . in case of suspension of work or reduction of work hours
. . . the monthly salary will remain the same. . . .

10. *Weekly day of rest.*—

. . . .

11. *Holidays.*—

. . . .

12. *Overtime, night, and holiday work.*—Work in excess of 8 hours
in any one day and 48 hours in any one week will be paid for at a
premium rate of 25 per cent. . . . Work on holidays will be paid for
at a premium of 40 per cent. . . .

13. *Pay for work in different classifications.*—

. . . .

14. *Assignment of work.*—Clerical employees must be assigned to
duties within their classifications. . . .

15. *Length-of-service increases.*—Clerical employees are entitled to
a 5 per cent increase in wages every two years after 20 years of age,
regardless of any individual merit increases. . . .

16. *Indemnity for the handling of funds.*—Clerical employees whose
normal work consists of the handling of funds have a right to an indemnity equivalent to 6 per cent of minimum scales of the particular
category.

17. *Method of payment of wages.*—Clerical employees shall be paid
at the end of each month. . . .

18. *Pay claims.*—

. . . .

19. *Vacations.*—Clerical employees are entitled to a vacation on
the following basis:

Length of Service	Number of days
1 to 2	15
2 to 10	20
10 to 18	25
Over 18	30

20. *Christmas bonus.*— . . . 30 days pay . . .

21. *Housing indemnity.*—

. . . .

22. *Treatment in case of sickness or accidents.*—

. . . .

23. *Matrimonial leave of absence.*—

. . . .

24. *Pregnancy and childbirth.*—

.   .   .   .

25. *Military service.*—

.   .   .   .

26. *Obligations of clerical employees.*—Clerical employees should perform their work in a manner consistent with the duties inherent in their jobs and in particular: (*a*) observe the hours of work; (*b*) apply themselves assiduously and diligently to the work assigned them, consistent with the agreement and the orders of their superiors; (*c*) maintain an absolute secrecy in the interests of the company, not profit at the expense of the company nor undertake activities contrary to the production interests of the company, and not abuse by acts of disloyalty information derived in the course of employment. In its turn, the company agrees not to place restrictions on the professional activities of the clerical employees exceeding the limits of this agreement or that provided by the law; (*d*) take care of their work place, furniture, objects, machines, and equipment placed in their trust.

27. *Absences.*—

.   .   .   .

28. *Discipline.*—Misconduct by clerical employees can be punished according to its gravity by: (1) oral reprimand; (2) written reprimand; (3) a fine not to exceed three hours' pay; (4) suspension, not to exceed five days; (5) discharge with indemnity but no warning; (6) immediate discharge without indemnity.

Clerical employees are subject to immediate discharge without indemnity pay who commit moral or material damage to the company or who commit actions in the course of employment which constitute crimes under the law. . . .

29. *Dismissal and resignation notices.*—

.   .   .   .

30. *Discharge length-of-service pay.*—

.   .   .   .

31. *Indemnity pay for employees who quit.*—

.   .   .   .

32. *Indemnity pay for deceased workers.*

.   .   .   .

33. *Wages.*—Minimum monthly salaries are those listed in the attached table of this agreement.

Common Part of the Agreement

1. *Seniority.*—The interruption of work due to reduction or suspension of operations does not constitute a break in service.

2. *Methods of wage payment.*—Workers are to be paid on a time basis or under one of the following forms of wage payment: (1) individual incentive; (2) group incentive; (3) other forms of incentive. . . . As a means of increasing production through increased worker productivity, the parties recognize the opportunities to extend incentive systems. In cases where such extension is not possible, all workers on time rates are to be paid 4 per cent of their minimum contract wages or salaries. . . .

3. *Plant cafeterias.*—Keeping in mind the great variety of situations existing in plants, which make general regulations difficult, it is agreed that existing cafeterias will be maintained by employers, except in the case where local or company agreements effectuate other arrangements.

4. *Personal inspections.*—Workers cannot refuse to be subjected to an inventory of company property or to personal inspections at plant exits. . . . Inspection of women must be conducted in separate quarters and by female personnel only. . . .

5. *Wage differentials for work in malaria zones, high altitudes, and underground operations.*—Workers in non-malaria zones transferred to malaria areas must be paid an indemnity to be agreed to among the union organizations in the particular area. . . . A differential shall also be paid for work exceeding 1500 meters in altitude or in underground operations. A worker can refuse employment in a malaria zone without prejudice.

6. *Consignment of documents to employees at the termination of employment.*—

.   .   .   .

7. *Certificate of employment consigned to workers.*—

.   .   .   .

8. *Transfer or conversion of a company.*— . . . does not determine normally the termination of the employment relationship. In such a case, the worker maintains with the new principals all acquired rights, including length of service, category, job assignment, and other obligations deriving from this agreement.

9. *Special regulations.*—In addition to this agreement, workers must inform themselves of any regulations established by management, provided such norms do not modify or limit those derived from this agreement and from others which may be in effect.

10. *Claims and disputes.*—Recognizing the possibility of a direct

settlement between interested parties, individual and group grievances will be resolved as a first step between management and the *commissione interna* and in the absence of such an agreement through the respective trade union organizations.

Collective agreements on the interpretation of this agreement shall be examined by the respective territorial organizations and in the absence of an agreement by the respective national organizations.

11. *More favorable terms of employment.*— . . . by the present agreement, the parties do not intend to substitute more favorable terms of employment actually in effect not deriving from national agreements. . . .

12. *Duration of the agreement.*—This agreement will be in effect from 10 March 1956 until 31 December 1958, and will be renewable from year to year if not terminated on the basis of a three months' notice prior to its lapse by registered letter. In case of such notification of termination, the contract will remain in force until substituted by a new national agreement.

13. *Posting of contract.*—The present agreement together with eventual internal regulations shall be posted in each plant.

Whenever the undersigned organizations of workers, together with employer associations or artisans, should make an agreement on terms of employment less onerous than those in this contract, such terms when agreed upon by interested organizations in a particular area will be automatically extended to other firms with similar characteristics and who are affiliated with the General Confederation of Italian Industry.

Major Amendments Effectuated in the 1959 Agreement

1. Duration of the agreement: three years.

2. An average increase of 5.5 per cent in minimum wages.

3. In the case of grievances arising out of incentive work, the employee has the right to bring them before the *commissione interna.* If no settlement is made, the trade union can intervene in his behalf.

4. A similar procedure to apply, in the case of grievances arising out of the job classification assigned a worker by management.

5. Minimum incentive pay increased from 8 to 10 per cent.

6. Premium pay for work between 44 and 48 hours is increased from 2 per cent to 7.

7. The length-of-service requirement for vacations is reduced. A worker with one to three years of service is now entitled to twelve working days' vacation. Corresponding reductions are made for those with greater length of service.

8. Premium pay for holiday work increased from 40 to 50 per cent.

9. Length-of-service bonus is made more liberal, so that it becomes payable at the 10th, 15th, and 20th year of service, with the provision that additional payment be given workers with over 20 years of service who have already received the length-of-service bonus.

10. Clerical employees with a college degree will be automatically assigned to the second category if they are given responsibilities consistent with their education.

11. The agreement stipulates procedure for further discussion of the "equal pay for equal work for women" issue.

12. The agreement also stipulates procedure for further talks on the length of apprenticeships in the industry.

THE DANISH AGREEMENT

The contract is an agreement between the Iron and Metal Industries Employers' Association and the Central Organization of Metal Workers, effective March, 1958.

Scope of Clause and Term of Employment

1. *The coöperation clause.*—For each plant or place of work, employees shall choose a shop steward who will act as their representative with the employer or his representative.

When one or a group of workers desire to do so, either because of a felt grievance or for some other reason, the shop steward is obligated to state their claims or suggestions to the employer, but only if the matter has not been settled satisfactorily by the supervisor.

The shop steward can make suggestions or complaints to the employer about the hygienic conditions in the plant and precautions that should be exercised to prevent accidents and minor injuries.

If a satisfactory arrangement is not possible, the shop steward is free to bring the case to his trade union and the work must go on undisturbed until a decision is made by management.

The trade union agrees in recommending that workers and employers coöperate in an effort to modernize work places and promote production. With this purpose in mind, the employer is bound to call upon the suggestions of the shop steward and to call shop steward meetings once every three months to discuss production and similar matters and to provide information about future employment conditions in the firm. Special meetings can be convened at the request of either party by indicating the questions they wish to discuss.

Shop steward meetings will not generally be held during work hours, and an honorarium of nine kroner will be paid the shop steward for each meeting, including special meetings called by the employer.

Should the employer desire to hold such meetings during working hours, such arrangement should not cause a loss of wages for the shop steward.

The shop steward has the right to complain about unreasonableness concerning hiring and discharge.

The employer federation agrees to discuss such questions with the central organization as are consistent with the above paragraph, when the central organization judges that special circumstances make it reasonable to do so.

2. *Election and discharge of shop stewards.*—The shop steward must be elected from among the skilled workers (members of the trade union), who have been employed for at least 18 months during the previous two years at the place of work in question. Where less than five exist, no shop steward is to be elected unless the parties jointly wish so. A shop steward elected during a period of greater employment ceases to be one when the eligible workers become fewer than five for a period of three months, unless the parties desire that the position be retained.

The shop steward election is to be held among those employed by the firm during the time of the election and is valid only when more than half of the employees have voted for him. The trade union executive board is obligated to see that this provision is kept.

A shop steward election is not valid unless approved by the trade union and the central organization.

The parties agree that if the employer organization feels a protest against a shop steward election is valid, it has the right to complain to the trade union.

The parties agree that in plants where there are four or more shop stewards it might be suitable to elect a representative among their number who, in common questions of planning working hours, hygiene, canteen, holidays and similar subjects, can be the chief shop steward of all the workers. The employer or his representative is not allowed to interfere in any questions concerning the normal functions of the shop steward in their respective parts of the work shop.

The parties also agree that when an extra shift of at least five workers of the trade union is established in which the shop steward does not participate, he may select a substitute who can act in his behalf in obtaining information and resolving disagreements, or when circumstances do not allow, in bringing the case to the shop steward. The name of this substitute must be given the employer.

The discharge of a shop steward must be based on cogent reasons only and must be preceded by a two months' warning. If the discharge is due to lack of work, the duty of warning is not controlling.

If the union feels a dismissal is not warranted, the other party will be bound by the decision of the labor court.

3. *The organization of* klubs.—If workers establish a *klub* or something similar in a firm, the shop steward must be selected as its chairman.

4. *Duties of shop stewards.*—It is the duty of the shop steward, both to his organization and to the employer, to maintain and promote coöperation [*godt samarbejde*] at the work place.

In the discharge of his tasks, the shop steward is not allowed to leave his work, or confer with workers during working hours, unless a request exists under Paragraphs 1, 7, and 8 of the agreement and in each case an agreement has been reached with the representative of the employer.

5. *Agreements and* klub *laws.*—Agreements made by workers concerning the work or other circumstances of the firm must not be inconsistent with existing agreements. Such agreements must be brought to the knowledge of the shop steward and the executive board of the trade union for acceptance, which in turn will inform the central organization. Without executive board acceptance, such agreements are invalid.

6. *Keeping of working hours.*—Workers are not permitted to miss fixed working hours without good reason; it is also the duty of all workers to make the most of tools and machines.

The trade union agrees that an employer can expect its employees to work without a break, that they be at their work places at the beginning of the shift, and that toilet facilities and dressing rooms be provided at the time clocks.

7. *Piece-work agreements.*—Piece-work contracts are to be made after free negotiations between the employer or his representative and the workers to whom the piece-work contract is offered, in such a way that the making of any single piece-work contract cannot be prejudiced or prevented by a *klub* decision. . . . Nor can a worker be forbidden to discuss his rate with fellow workers. . . .

If an agreement cannot be reached, each party is entitled to call on the shop steward to take part in further negotiations.

If no agreement can be reached, the work must be performed at a price 15 per cent less than the average piece rate at the place of work in question within the previous three months. . . .

Schedules of wages and fixed piece rates are terminable by either party on two months' notice until the first of the month, unless another agreement has been made.

On renewal of the above-mentioned schedules and piece rates, the parties may make arrangements about the duration and terms of notice. . . .

8. *Overtime.*—The Central Organization of the Metal Workers of Denmark and the Metal Industry Employers' Association agree that under certain circumstances overtime work may be required. . . .

The amount of overtime work usually is to be arranged between the employer and the individual worker in consideration of the special circumstances of the firm. An individual worker, however, is not allowed to perform overtime work in excess of 16 hours in four consecutive weeks or in excess of six hours in any one week.

When it is urgent to do so, management and the shop steward can agree to overtime work in excess of 16 hours in four weeks, but not in excess of six hours in any one week. . . .

9. *Arbitration clause and shop regulations.*—The arbitration agreement in force is the "Regulations for Handling of Industrial Disputes in the Iron Industry of September, 1902," revised 1947, and the Shop Instructions are the "Common Shop Instructions" of March, 1958.

10. *Relation between the foreman and the trade union.*—Whereas the trade unions accept that foremen with fixed salaries who comply with the rules laid down in the "September Agreement" of 1899, in their capacity as employer representatives shall not join the trade unions, the employer organizations on their part shall not allow the appointment of additional foremen with the purpose of claiming that the persons in question must resign from the trade union organizations.

11. *Right of prosecution of the parties.*—In each case, whenever one of the parties after necessary proof judges that these common decisions are not being fulfilled, it has the right of prosecution of the other party; the latter is bound to give its fullest coöperation in the investigation and preparation of the case.

12. *Graduated wage schedule for apprentices.*—

. . . .

13. *The training of apprentices.*—

. . . .

14. *The recognition of apprentices.*—Skilled workers are those who have served their apprenticeship and who have received their journeyman's certificate, or those who have been recognized by the employers' association and the trade union, according to the regulations applicable thereto.

When grinders, pressmen, and silverplaters have worked for three years in the trade and have proof of such work, they shall be looked upon as skilled workers. Unskilled workers at shipyards are able to obtain recognition as skilled workers in accordance with the agreement between the employers' association and the union, dated April 11, 1956.

15. *Membership in the trade union.*—No trade union organization is allowed to admit a worker as a skilled member unless such worker has proved his identity by presenting his journeyman's certificate, or, as far as grinders, pressmen and silverplaters are concerned, is able to present proof of having worked for three years on the skill. The Danish Union of Mechanics and Fitters is allowed to admit such workers as skilled members, who have not had a proper apprenticeship, but are recognized as skilled workers according to the rules agreed upon between the employers' association and the trade union, dated April 11, 1956.

The trade union is to give each skilled member a membership book containing the journeyman's full name, the name of his instructor, the length of apprenticeship, and the date of the journeyman's certificate. For skilled members who are admitted without taking a journeyman's test, the membership book must contain information about employment which forms the basis of recognition as skilled workers.

In the admission of members other than the skilled-worker organizations, it must appear clearly from the membership book that the person in question is not a skilled worker in that skill and what special training the person in question has had.

Amendment: It is realized that the trade unions are not able to take on any obligations in accordance with Paragraph 15, Section 1, above, in the case of foreigners who are transferred to the organization in question from similar foreign organizations.

Both parties admit the sense of having the full name of the members of the trade union and the length of apprenticeship in the membership book and will try as much as possible to achieve this goal.

16. *Proof of being a skilled worker.*—In the case of skilled workers seeking employment in a firm belonging to the employers' association, the presentation of the membership book is sufficient proof of being a skilled worker in the event the journeyman's certificate is not presented.

17. *Investigation of violation of regulations.*—In each case, when one of the parties after necessary investigation has judged that these rules governing skilled workers are not being fulfilled, the other party is obligated to assist in the investigation and coöperate in the satisfactory arrangement of the case.

18. *Working hours.*—From the first workweek after 1 March 1958, the normal week will be 47 hours (from 48 hours); from the first work-

week after March 1959, 46 hours, and after 1 March 1960, 45 hours.

19. *Dismissal regulations.*—For workers who, without any other break in service than that mentioned below, have been employed in the same firm for a period mentioned below, to be counted from age 21, the following dismissal notice is valid:

2–3 years	7 days
4–5 years	14 days
Over 5 years	21 days

For time of notice ordinary days are counted, whereas for compensation in lieu of notice only lost workingdays are calculated.

The following is not counted as a break in service: illness reported within 24 hours; military service; rest after childbirth according to factory law; interruption of work caused by the stopping of machines, lack of material, or lack of work, provided the employee accepts work when it is offered. For a period of unemployment of more than 14 days caused by lack of work, only the first two weeks are counted for the purposes of computing seniority.

For absence because of illness in excess of 3 months, continuous military service, or rest after childbirth, only the first three months are computed for the purposes of seniority.

Workers who resume employment within one year of layoff will recover all their previous seniority. If the worker provides proof that he had no work during the prior two years, the one-year period shall be extended to two.

The layoff notice is not applicable in ship repair work of less than two weeks' duration, unemployment caused by a work stoppage . . . or by *force majeure*. . . . Dismissal notices are also not applicable in the performance of work outside of the area of the firm.

In case a worker according to the above regulations is laid off improperly, or if such worker leaves the firm without giving at least three days' notice, the offending party will pay an amount of money equivalent to his hourly rate plus cost-of-living bonus for the number of days involved.

Amendment: In spite of the worker's obligation to provide notice of quitting, the employer should not refuse to make an agreement to the effect a worker can leave his employ immediately if the worker proves that he is being offered a permanent job or similar.

Any existing agreements on dismissal notice are not affected by this agreement.

20. *Wages.*—For all skilled workers under the agreement between

the Central Organization of Metal Workers and the Iron and Metal Industries Employers' Association the minimum wage is 105 ore per hour and for time work 157 ore per hour.

For unskilled workers the minimum rate shall be 103 ore per hour and the time rate 157 ore per hour. . . .

THE PAY FOR MORE SKILLFUL AND MORE TRUSTED WORKERS SHALL BE REGULATED IN EVERY SINGLE CASE BETWEEN THE WORKER AND THE EMPLOYER OR HIS REPRESENTATIVE WITHOUT INTERVENTION FROM THE TRADE UNION OR ITS MEMBERS. . . .

21. *Minimum rates of pay.*—The Employers' Association agrees that members of the Danish General Workers' Union in the following job classifications will be given an addition of 27 ore per hour to the minimum rates stipulated above. . . . Molders, permanently employed crane operators, drivers of trucks and motor vehicles, riggers, and drillers when they are employed in the building department of the shipyards.

These increases are valid continuously in the above job classifications; the higher agreed-upon minimum hourly rates are payable when the worker is skilled in the field in question and in any case after he has been employed for three months within the work.

22. *Other wage questions.*—Melting-furnace firemen will receive an increase of 175 ore per day unless the rise is covered by an agreement having a provision for such work. General workers employed in shipyards in foundry operations will receive a raise of 1 ore over the minimum rate. . . .

In building and iron construction work each worker is to receive an increase of 35 ore per hour.

Contract and building operations either inside or outside the firm performed by workers for either contractors, master artisans, or the firm itself, do not fall within the scope of this agreement. Small work of this type will fall within the scope of this agreement.

23. *Wages and regulations governing young workers between the ages of 14 and 18.*—

.   .   .   .

24. *Aged and infirm workers.*—Old and infirm workers, and those whose working capacity has been reduced because of accidents may work for a pay lower than the minimum, according to agreement between the employer and worker concerned. The trade unions are entitled to protest against abuse of this rule according to the Regulations for the Handling of Industrial Disputes.

25. *Pay for holidays falling during the workweek.*—Workers em-

ployed at least three months are entitled to the following pay for holidays:

Men	25 kroner
Women	20 kroner
Workers under 18	10 kroner

26. *The pay week.*—The pay week terminates Saturday, and wages are to be paid not later than the following Thursday, and if a holiday, on the day before.

Amendment: For members of the Danish General Workers' Association, payment is to take place during working hours, when such is the existing practice and in other places in as short a time after working hours as possible.

27. *Daily benefit in case of accidents.*—In case of accidents on the job causing absence from work in excess of three days, the employer will pay the following daily sums, beginning with the seventh day after the accident until the compulsory insurance becomes effective:

Adult male workers	12 kroner
Adult women workers	9 kroner
Workers under 18	4 kroner

It has to be proved by a valid health insurance certificate that conditions for the payment of the daily allowance are present.

Existing agreements providing for a greater allowance or an allowance payable sooner are not invalidated by this agreement.

Wages to be paid in the course of an illness are regulated by those rules previously agreed to December 21, 1956.

28. *Vacations.*—Workers have the right to an annual vacation in accordance with the law of March 31, 1953. The vacation is to consist of one and a half working days for each month of work during the year prior.

If the vacation amounts to 12 days or less, it must be given in its entirety during the period between May 2 and September 30, as far as possible, and in connection with three Sundays.

Vacations exceeding twelve days have also to be given continuously, but can also be given outside the vacation period. When production considerations make it desirable, the portion of the holiday in excess of twelve days can be given as separate off-days. . . . Vacations in each firm can be carried out either by closing or by giving workers successive vacation periods. The firm must circulate not later than April a list in which each worker will indicate his time preference.

The employer will fix vacations consistent with these preferences as much as possible and will notify workers no later than one month before the beginning of the period.

In firms where vacations are given successively, a worker who was employed for a period of less than one year can request time off in proportion only to his reduced vacation pay. No such request can be made in firms which shut down during the vacation period.

The holiday year is to be computed from April 1 to March 31. Workers have a right to vacation pay equivalent to 6.5 per cent of all collected wages, not including reimbursement for transportation or boarding expenses.

A worker incapacitated because of illness up to three months is entitled to vacation pay, if he has been employed for at least one year. If incapacitated because of an accident, the one year of employment does not obtain.

The right of vacation pay according to the above agreement has to be proved by a valid health insurance certificate.

Complaints from workers concerning employer calculation of vacation pay must take place at the time of presentation of the pay envelope.

A worker who changes his employment during the course of the vacation year will be given at the time of his termination from employment a card stating his name, his length of service during the vacation year with his previous employer, vacation pay paid the employee, as well as vacation pay and number of days of entitlement. . . .

A worker with accumulated vacation rights can claim them from his prior employers, provided proof is furnished that the worker will take his vacation. . . .

A worker with vacation rights who, by virtue of military service, illness, shift to independent business or work in the home (women), stay abroad, or imprisonment, is prevented from taking his vacation during the vacation period, will be given his vacation pay. . . .

Entitlement of a halfday or more is to be considered a full day. . . .

A worker who uses his vacation period at another place of employment will lose his entitlement during the following vacation year. . . .

Vacation compensation not cashed before the termination of the current vacation year (March 31) is lost.

In the event of death, vacation compensation reverts to the estate of the deceased.

Vacation pay not cashed before the end of the vacation year reverts to the vacation fund. . . .

The parties agree that vacation pay is to be considered part of wages and that failure of payment can be the object of legal proceedings against the employer in question.

Any dispute arising over the vacation rules can be dealt with under the "Rules for the Handling of Trade Disputes."

Existing vacation regulations are not to be reduced by virtue of this agreement.

29. *Funerals and days off.*—

. . . .

30. *Cost-of-living allowance.*—The parties agree to the following cost-of-living allowance as of March 1, 1958:

Men workers and skilled women	207.0 ore per hr.
Unskilled women over 18	159.1 " " "
Men workers under 18	83.0 " " "
Unskilled women under 18	83.0 " " "
Beginners	46.0 " " "

[The agreement specifies taking a look at the price index twice a year, on February 1 and August 1. For every 6 points rise in the index, it specifies an increase of 5 ore for men workers and skilled women workers, and 2 ore for workers under 18. Unskilled women workers are divided into two groups, one receiving 5 ore and the other 3.3 ore.]

The Danish Agreement of 1902 for Settling Disputes in the Iron and Metal Industry

Agreement
for the Settling of Labor Disputes in the Iron and Metal Industry
Mutually Agreed Upon
By
The Central Organization of Metalworkers in Denmark and
The Almagamation of Employers in the Iron and Metal Industry
in Denmark.
September 1902
Re-edited in July 1947 in accordance with the Legal Practice
that has developed on the basis of said
Regulations.

ART. 1.

In case of disagreement of a professional character [*baglig karakter*] between an employer belonging to the Amalgamation, or between the Amalgamation as such, on the one hand, and one or more Members, a Section or a Union belonging to the Central Organization, or the Central Organization as such, on the other hand, conciliation through a Conciliation Committee shall be attempted when it has become evident that the disputed matter can not be settled by negotiation between the directly interested parties and after both the Employers' and the Workers' Organizations have been informed of the names of the disputing parties and the subject-matter of the dispute at hand.

The Conciliation Committee consists of a representative of the Amalgamation and a representative of the Central Organization, or of the organization in question under the latter. The Committee shall meet with the disputing parties as soon as possible; if in Copenhagen, within

3 week-days; if in the provinces, within 5 week-days from the date on which the opposing organization has received information about the disputed matter.

If at all possible, a conciliation meeting must be held in the place of employment where the dispute arose, and the conciliation members shall seek to bring about a settlement of the dispute through negotiation between the parties.

The conciliation members shall see to it that brief minutes of the proceedings are taken; they shall sign same and send a copy to each of the parties and to both Organizations.

ART. 2.

Simultaneously with one of the Organizations requesting conciliation, it must notify the opposing Organization of the name of the person who will undertake conciliation in its behalf. Thereafter it is incumbent upon the opposing Organization to convey, as soon as possible, to the complainant Organization a similar communication as to the name of its representative at the conciliation proceedings.

The time and place of the meeting shall be fixed by mutual arrangement between the offices of the Organizations.

ART. 3.

If no settlement of the dispute is obtained by conciliation, one or the other of the Organizations may refer the dispute to a Ten-Man Committee composed of 5 members from each Organization.

The Ten-Man meeting shall be held as speedily as possible; if in Copenhagen, at the latest 3 week-days after the opposing Organization has received a request to that effect, and if in the provinces, at the latest 5 week-days after that has occurred. At the Ten-Man meeting held in Copenhagen a settlement of the dispute will be sought through negotiations between the Organizations. Brief minutes of the proceedings shall be taken, and shall be signed by both Organizations.

ART. 4.

If no agreement is reached by this procedure either, it is incumbent upon the Organization mentioned in Art. 3, that wishes the disputed matter to be referred to the Court of Arbitration, to inform the opposing Organization thereof—within a time-limit of 3 weeks—whereupon the latter is obliged to communicate its stand on this matter, within the same time-limit.

When the Organizations have agreed on referring the dispute to the Court of Arbitration, the parties to the dispute bind themselves to

submit to the award of the Arbitration Court and waive their right to
seek a judgment of their dispute through the regular judicial channels.

ART. 5.

The Court of Arbitration is composed of 7 members.

When a case has been appealed to the Court of Arbitration each
of the two Organizations shall designate 3 members for the Court.
Notifications of the names of the members thus selected must be ex-
changed immediately upon their selection. The two Organizations
jointly select an umpire who stands outside of both Organizations. If
the Organizations cannot agree on an umpire they must request, within
a time-limit of 3 days, the President of the Permanent Court of Arbitration to designate one. The request to the President of the Permanent
Court of Arbitration must contain information as to which persons
have been suggested as umpires in the course of the negotiations between the two Organizations.

The umpire selected or designated, and who must declare himself
willing to accept the task, shall act as President of the Court and direct
its proceedings. He shall convoke the members of the Arbitration Court
as soon as possible and see to it that the documentation submitted in
the case up to that time be laid before the Court.

ART. 6.

If an award does not obtain a majority, the umpire shall decide the
question in dispute, and an award must be at hand not later than 14
days after the case was admitted for decision.

The award must include a provision as to the time-limit within
which it is ordered to be carried out. The award shall be communicated in writing to both Organizations, who will forward it to the disputing parties for their further information.

ART. 7.

The Court of Arbitration decides on its own all questions concerning
business routine and matters of order not determined by these present
regulations.

The President also participates in the voting, and a simple majority
decides the outcome, independently of the number of persons present.

ART. 8.

Should a member of the Court be prevented from attending, this
member must personally see to it that an alternate be convoked for
the imminent meeting. If such convocation is omitted or remains with-

out result, this, however, shall not affect the quorum of a session of the Court.

ART. 9.

If it transpires that a member of the Court of Arbitration is a party in the case, or becomes a party in it during its trial, he must step down and an alternate will take his place.

ART. 10.

Each of the two Organizations is entitled to have a secretary attend, and take down a report of, every session convoked in accordance with the present arbitration rules.

ART. 11.

Prior to the handling, as determined by the present regulations, of a dispute that has come up between the Organizations or their members, neither party is allowed to cause a work-stoppage of any kind (blockade, lockout or strike).

ART. 12.

The present regulations do not curtail the right of the two Organizations or their members to participate, without prior conciliation and arbitration, in a work-stoppage which has been decreed, respectively, sanctioned, by the Confederation of Danish Employers [Dansk Arbejdsgiverforening] or the Confederation of Danish Trade Unions [De samvirkende Fagforbund] (*cf.* Agreement of September 5, 1899, Paragraph 2).

ART. 13.

The present arbitration regulations remain valid until they are denounced—with 3 months' notice—by one of the undersigned Organizations. However, cases, the trial of which started in the Arbitration Court before the arbitration regulations, after due notice, became invalid, shall be carried through to their termination in accordance with the present regulations.

Copenhagen, July 17, 1947.

For the Central Organization of Metalworkers in Denmark:

HANS RASMUSSEN

For the Amalgamation of Employers in the Iron and Metal Industry in Denmark:

AXEL VON DER LIETH

Trade Unions Affiliated with Italian Federations

CONFEDERAZIONE ITALIANA SINDACATI LAVORATORI (CISL) [33]

Clothing Workers' Federation
Food, Sugar, and Alcohol Workers' Federation
Chemical and Petroleum Workers' Federation
Construction Workers' Federation
Workers of Extractive Industries Federation
Book Workers' Federation
Italian Federation of Metal Workers
Italian Federation of Public Service Workers
Unitary Federation of Workers of the Theater
Textile Workers' Federation
Italian Federation of Salaried Agricultural Workers and Technicians
National Federation of Sharecroppers
National Federation of Tenants and Landowners
Federation of Workers of Commercial Services
Bank Workers' Federation
Italian Federation of Local Public Service Employees
Italian Federation of Hospital Trade Unions
National Federation of Employees of Public Corporations
Post and Telegraph Workers' Union
National Elementary School Union
Italian Trade Union of Workers of Local Offices and Post-Telegraph
   Agencies
Italian Federation of Tax Services and Underwriters
Italian Federation of State Workers
Telephone Workers' Union
Transport Workers' Federation
Railroad Workers' Union
Sea, Air, and Fishing Industries Workers' Federation

Port Workers
Federation of Bus and Tram Workers
National Union of Pensioners
Federation of Artists and Professionalists
Federation of Italian Physicians
Federation of National Associations of Discharged Military Officers

CONFEDERAZIONE GENERALE ITALIANA DEL LAVORO (CGIL) [45]

Metal Workers' Federation
Textile Workers' Federation
Chemical Workers' Federation
Construction Workers' Federation
Extractive Industries Federation
Ceramic Workers' Federation
Food Workers' Federation
Printing and Paper Workers' Federation
Clothing Workers' Federation
Sugar Workers' Federation
Hat Workers' Federation
Petroleum Workers' Union
Union of Fishermen
Tobacco Shop Workers' Union
Federation of Workers of the Theater
Federation of Telecommunication Workers
Gas Workers' Federation
Federation of Aqueduct Workers
Railroad Workers' Union
National Federation of Bus and Tram Workers
Sea Workers' Federation
Air Transport Workers' Federation
Port Workers' Federation
National Union of Porters
National Union of Navigation Workers
Federation of Agricultural Workers
Sharecroppers' Union (Coloni e Mezzadri)
Federation of Commerce Employees
Hotel Workers' Federation
Federation of Traveling Salesmen
Barbers' Federation
Newspaper Workers' Union
Federation of State Employees
Post and Telegraph Workers' Federation

Federation of Local Public Service Employees
Hospital Workers' Federation
Federation of Medical Workers
Federation of Managers of Public Corporations
Federation of Employees of Credit Associations
Bank Employees' Federation
Federation of Firemen
Consumption Goods Tax Collectors' Employees
National Union of Painters
National Union of Painters and Sculptors
Peddlers' Association

UNIONE ITALIANA DEL LAVORO (UIL) [51]

Italian Union of Land Workers
National Union of Salaried Agricultural Workers (Braccianti Salariati)
National Union of Technical Employees
Alliance of Independent Farmers (Coltivatori Diretti)
Italian Union of Electrical Workers
Italian Union of Chemical Workers
Italian Union of Metal Workers
Italian Union of Textile Workers
National Union of Miners
National Federation of Construction Workers
National Union of Newspaper Workers
Italian Union of Railroad Workers
National Union of Bus and Tram Workers
National Federation of State Employees
National Union of Defense Employees
National Union of Army Employees
National Union of Navy Employees
National Union of Air Force Employees
Italian Union of Post and Telegraph Workers
National Union of Local Public Service Employees
National Union of State Monopoly Employees
Italian Federation of Theater Employees
Italian Union of Bank Workers
Italian Union of Petroleum Workers
Italian Union of Paper and Graphic Arts Workers
Italian Union of Food Workers
Italian Union of Commerce Employees
Italian Union of Hotel Workers
Italian Union of Gas Workers

Italian Union of Transport Workers
Italian Union of Pensioners
Italian Union of Glass, Ceramic, Abrasives Workers
Italian Union of Wood Workers
Italian Union of Fishermen
Italian Maritime Union
National Federation of Port Workers
Italian Union of Insurance Workers
National Union of Boarding School Employees
Italian Union of Hospital Workers
Italian Union of Sugar Workers
National Union of INAM Employees (National Sickness Insurance Institute)
National Union of INAIL Employees (National Industrial Accidents Institute)
National Union of INADEL Employees (National Insurance Institute for Municipal Employees)
National Union of INPS Employees (National Social Insurance Institute)
Italian Union of Clothing Workers
Italian Union of Air Communication Employees
Union of Italian Artists
Autonomous Union of Peddlers
Italian Union of Traveling Salesmen
Italian Union of Telephone Workers
Italian Union of Tax Collectors

Trade Unions in Denmark [1]

TRADE UNIONS AFFILIATED WITH THE SAMVIRKENDE FAGFORBUND

Union	Membership
General Workers	246,900
Commerce and Office Workers	72,315
Iron and Machine Workers	62,388
Women Workers	42,609
Textile Workers	20,325
Tailors	18,403
Municipal Workers	18,238
Slaughterhouse Workers	13,654
Joiners	13,459
Carpenters	12,809
Wood Industry Workers	11,863
Painters	11,370
Bricklayers	11,313
Railway Workers	10,346
Electrical Workers	8,637
Administrative Employees	8,572
Tobacco Workers	8,165
Bakery and Confectioners	7,424
Bookbinders and Container Workers	7,247
Shoe Workers	5,810
Maritime Workers	5,211
Garden Workers	5,135
Domestic Workers	4,856
Saddle Makers and Upholsterers	4,383
Dairy Workers	3,537
Sheet Metal Workers, Plumbers, and Pipefitters	3,475

[1] As of December 31, 1956. Source: *Lommebog For Arbejdere*. Copenhagen, 1958.

Union	Membership
Ceramic Workers	3,056
Molders	2,716
Boiler and Machine Tenders	2,547
Locomotivemen's Association	2,288
Paper Industry Workers	2,200
Skilled Kitchen Employees	2,058
Gold and Silver Workers	1,808
Prison Workers	1,792
Seamen	1,769
Confectionery and Chocolate Workers	1,706
Lithographers	1,610
Special Workers	1,580
Ship Carpenters	1,565
Hotel and Restaurant Workers	1,500
Coach Makers	1,418
Millworkers	1,190
Hat and Furriers	1,153
Iron and Metal Workers	1,036
Watch and Optical Workers	828
Tanners	801
Private Railroad Employees	800
Stone Industry Workers	598
Brushmakers	584
Glaziers	557
Rope Makers	504
Glass Workers	342
Chimney Sweepers	322
Locomotivemen	277
Glove Makers	267
Riggers and Sail Makers	260
Coppersmiths	253
Lighthouse Workers' Association	236
Bridge Erectors	204
Coopersmiths	202
Artists	159
Metal Pressmen	144
State Mental Hospital Stewards	134
Divers	130
Stucco Workers	45

ORGANIZATIONS OUTSIDE THE SAMVIRKENDE FAGFORBUND

Union	Membership
Brewery Workers	6,019
State Telephone Workers	4,423
Musicians	3,948
Milk Industry Workers	1,932
Coastal Restaurant Employees	1,038
Barbers	991
Hospital Workers	735

Bibliography
Index

Selected Bibliography

ITALY

Adams, John Clarke. "Italy," in *Comparative Labor Movements*, ed. Walter Galenson. New York: Prentice-Hall, 1952.

Alasia, Franco, and Danilo Montaldi. *Milano, inchiesta sugli immigrati.* Milan: Feltrinelli, 1960.

Archibugi, Franco. "Recent Trends in Women's Work in Italy," *International Labour Review*, Vol. LXXXI (April, 1960).

——. *Panorama delle relazioni industriali nell' epoca del'automatismo.* Sixth Meeting of the Conference on Problems of Automation. Rome: National Research Council, 1956.

Associazioni Cristiane Lavoratori Italiani. *La classe lavoratrice si difende.* Milan: ACLI, 1953.

Branco, Giorgio. *L'associazione sindacale.* Milan: Giuffrè, 1960.

Calca, Terna E. *L'agricoltura nello sviluppo delle economie arretrate.* Milan: Giuffrè, 1954.

Candeloro, Giorgio. *Il movimento sindacale in Italia.* Rome: Edizioni di Cultura Sociale, 1950.

Carocci, Giovanni. "Inchiesta alla Fiat: indagine su taluni aspetti della lotta di classe nel complesso Fiat," *Nuovi Argomenti*, Nos. 31 and 32 (March–June, 1958).

Cavalli, Luciano. "I metalmeccanici," *Notiziario di Sociologia*, Vol. I, No. 2 (May–June, 1958).

——. *La gioventù del quartiere operaio.* Genoa: F.lli Pagano, 1959.

——. "Politica e tempo libero nel quartiere operaio," *Notiziario di Sociologia*, Vol. I, No. 1 (March–April, 1958).

——. *Quartiere operaio.* Genoa: SAGA, 1958.

Centro Democratico di Cultura e di Documentazione. *L'industrializzazione del mezzogiorno.* Rome: Centro Democratico, 1956.

Clough, Shepard B., and Carlo Livi. "Economic Growth in Italy: An Analysis of the Uneven Development of North and South," *The Journal of Economic History*, Vol. XVI, No. 3 (September, 1956).

Confederazione Italiana Sindacati Lavoratori. *Il sindacato e l'organizzazione di fabbrica.* Rome: CISL, 1955.

——. *Il sindacalismo democratico.* Rome: CISL, 1959.

——. *Il sindacato democratico per lo sviluppo della società italiana ed europea.* Rome: CISL, 1959.

——. *Le relazioni umane e sociali nelle aziende.* Quaderni di Studi e Documentazione, No. 3. Rome: CISL, 1957.

Dal Pane, Luigi. *Storia del lavoro in Italia.* Milan: Giuffrè, 1944.

DeAngeli, Franco. *Lavoro e retribuzione.* Turin: Boringhieri, 1960.

427

Diena, Leone. *Gli uomini e le masse*. Turin: Einaudi, 1960.

DiSimone, G. M. "Sviluppo economico del mezzogiorno e sviluppo economico italiano," *L'Industria*, No. 3 (1960).

DiVittorio, Giuseppe, Giulio Pastore, Italo Viglianesi, *et al. I sindacati in Italia*. Bari: Laterza, 1955.

Dolci, Danilo. *Inchiesta a Palermo*. Turin: Einaudi, 1956.

Fegiz, Luzzatto. *Il volto sconosciuto dell'Italia, dieci anni di sondaggi DOXA*. Milan: Giuffrè, 1956.

Galeotti, Guido. *Problemi del mezzogiorno*. Rome: Centro Democratico di Cultura e di Documentazione, 1955.

Giugni, Gino. "The Structure of Collective Bargaining in Italy," *Industrial and Labor Relations Review*, Vol. X (April, 1957).

Gradilone, Alfredo. *La storia del sindacalismo*. Milan: Giuffrè, 1959.

Grasso, Pier Giovanni. *Gioventù del metà secolo*. Rome: AVE, 1952.

Gualtieri, Humbert L. *The Labor Movement in Italy*. New York: Vanni, 1946.

Hildebrand, George H. "The Italian Parliamentary Survey of Unemployment," *American Economic Review*, Vol. XLV, No. 5 (December, 1955).

———. "The Postwar Italian Economy: Achievements, Problems, and Prospects," *World Politics*, Vol. VIII, No. 1 (October, 1955).

International Social Security Association Bulletin. *Family Allowances in Italy*. Geneva: ISSA, January–February, 1959.

Istituto Centrale di Statistica. *Sommario di statistiche storiche italiane 1861–1955*. Rome: ISTAT, 1958.

La Palombara, Joseph. *The Italian Labor Movement: Problems and Prospects*. Ithaca, New York: Cornell University Press, 1957.

Lutz, V. "Italy as a Study in Development," *Lloyds Bank Review*, Vol. LVIII (October, 1960).

Neufeld, Maurice F. *Italy: School for Awakening Countries*. Ithaca, New York: New York State School of Industrial and Labor Relations, 1960.

New York University Graduate School of Business Administration. "The Economic Position of Italy," *New York University Bulletin No. 203* (October, 1957).

Papi, Giuseppe. *Teoria e politica dello sviluppo economico*. Milan: Giuffrè, 1954.

Pizzorno, Alessandro. *Il tempo libero e i lavoratori*. Florence: La Nuova Italia, 1960.

Preti, Luigi. *Lotte agrarie nella valle padana*. Turin: Einaudi, 1955.

Rassegna di Statistiche del Lavoro. *Il lavoro in Italia nel 1958*. Rome: Confindustria, 1959.

Rossi Doria, Manlio. *La scuola e lo sviluppo del mezzogiorno*. Rome: Opere Nuove, 1960.

Sanseverino, Luisa Riva. *Diritto del lavoro*. Padua: CEDAM, 1952.

Toldo, Antonio. *Il sindacalismo in Italia*, 2nd ed. Milan: Centro Studi Sociali, 1953.

Tremelloni, Roberto. *Storia dell'industria italiana*. Turin: Einaudi, 1947.

———. *Storia recente dell'industria italiana*. Milan: Garzanti, 1956.

DENMARK

Bukdahl, Jørgen, Aage Heinberg, *et al. Scandinavia Past and Present*. 3 vols. Arnkrone: Edvard Henriksen, 1959.

Buhl, Jens. "Dansk Arbejdsret," *Jern og Metal,* No. 11 (1959).

Danish Employers' Confederation and Danish Federation of Trade Unions. *Regulations Governing the Sick Leave Fund.* Copenhagen: Langkjaersbogtrykkeri, 1956.

Danish Employers' Confederation. *The Danish Employers' Confederation.* Copenhagen: The Federation, n.d.

Danish Federation of Trade Unions. *The Danish Federation of Trade Unions.* Copenhagen: The Federation, 1955.

Danske Selskab. *Employers and Workers, Development and Organization of the Danish Labour Market.* Copenhagen: Det Danske Selskab, 1956.

Dreyer, Erik. "Forligsinstitutionen gennem 50 aar," *Socialt Tidsskrift,* Vol. XXXVI, No. 3 (1960).

Hansen, Bent, and Gösta Rehn. *On Wage Drift, A Problem of Money Wage Dynamics.* Stockholm: Svenska Tryckeriaktiebolaget, 1957.

Jensen, Eiler. "Diamond Jubilee in Denmark," *Free Labour World,* No. 93 (1958).

Johnson, Dudley W. "Wage Escalators and Inflation in Denmark," *Journal of Political Economy,* Vol. LXVIII (April, 1960).

Jørgensen, Anker. "Større medindflydelse-hvordan," *Løn og Virke,* Vol. LV, No. 2 (1959).

Knudsen, Jens Risgaard. "Arbejdere og funktionaerer maa sikres større indflydelse," *Stof og Saks,* No. 6 (1959).

Ministries of Labour and Social Affairs. *Historical Background of Social Welfare in Scandinavia.* Copenhagen: The Ministries, 1957.

——. *Health Insurance.* Copenhagen: The Ministries, 1958.

——. *Employment Injuries Insurance in Denmark.* Copenhagen: The Ministries, 1955.

——. *Welfare of the Aged.* Copenhagen: The Ministries, 1957.

——. *Social Status of Women in Denmark.* Copenhagen: The Ministries, 1958.

——. *Unemployment Insurance.* Copenhagen: The Ministries, 1957.

——. *National Assistance.* Copenhagen: The Ministries, 1957.

——. *Housing.* Copenhagen: The Ministries, 1958.

——. *Holidays with Pay.* Copenhagen: The Ministries, 1959.

Nielsen, Einar. *Indførelse i arbejdsretten.* Copenhagen: Forlaget Fremad, 1956.

Philip, Grethe. "Hvad 3000 Maend Uden Skoleksamen blev til," *Socialt Tidsskrift,* Vol. XXXI, No. 1 (1955).

Stolitz, G. *Arbeidstidsproblemer, En økonomish analyse.* Oslo: Oslo University Press, 1958.

Urban Coöperative Union. *The Coöperative Movement in Denmark.* Copenhagen: Central Coöperative Committee, 1951.

Wendt, Frantz. *The Nordic Council and Coöperation in Scandinavia.* Copenhagen: Bianco Luno A/S, 1959.

Willerslev, Richard. "Arbejdernes økonomiske kaar gennem 100 aar," *Løn og Virke,* Vol. LIII, No. 20 (1957).

METHODOLOGICAL REFERENCES

Ackoff, Russell L. *Design of Social Research.* Chicago: University of Chicago Press, 1953.

Chapin, Stuart F. *Experimental Designs in Sociological Research,* rev. ed. New York: Harper, 1947.

Duijker, G. C. G., and N. H. Frijda. *National Character and National Stereotypes.* New York: Humanities Press, 1961.

Festinger, Leon, and Daniel Katz. *Research Methods in the Behavioral Sciences.* New York: Holt, Rinehart and Winston, 1953.

Goode, William J., and P. K. Hatt. *Methods in Social Research.* New York: McGraw-Hill, 1952.

Gordon, Thomas. *Group Centered Leadership.* Cambridge: Riverside Press, 1955.

Gross, Edward. "Dimensions of Leadership," *Personnel Journal,* Vol. XL, No. 5 (October, 1961).

Hemphill, John D. "Group Factors in Leadership," *Journal of Social Psychology,* Vol. XXXII (1950).

Kluckhohn, Clyde, Henry A. Murray, and David M. Schneider. *Personality in Nature, Society, and Culture.* New York: Knopf, 1955.

Morris, Richard T., and Melvin Seeman. "The Problem of Leadership: An Interdisciplinary Approach," *American Journal of Sociology,* Vol. LVI (1950).

Palmer, Gladys L. "Attitudes Toward Work in an Industrial Community," *American Journal of Sociology,* Vol. LXIII, No. 1 (July, 1957).

Scott, E. L. *Leadership and Perceptions of Organization.* Research Monograph No. 82, Bureau of Business Research. Columbus: Ohio State University Press, 1956.

Siegel, Sidney. *Nonparametric Statistics for the Behavioral Sciences.* New York: McGraw-Hill, 1956.

Stagner, Ross, W. E. Chalmers, and Milton Derber. "Guttman-Type Scales for Union and Management Attitudes Toward Each Other," *University of Illinois Bulletin,* Vol. LVI, No. 54 (March, 1959).

———. "Environmental Variables and Union-Management Accommodation," *University of Illinois Bulletin,* Vol. LV, No. 82 (July, 1958).

———. "Uniformities and Differences in Local Union-Management Relationships," *Industrial and Labor Relations Review,* Vol. XI, No. 1 (October, 1957).

Stogdill, Ralph M., and Alvin E. Coons. *Leader Behavior: Its Description and Measurement.* Columbus: Ohio State University Personnel Research Board, 1956.

Stogdill, Ralph M., E. L. Scott, and W. E. Jaynes. *Leadership and Role Expectations.* Research Monograph No. 86, Bureau of Business Research. Columbus: Ohio State University Press, 1956.

Stogdill, Ralph M., and Carroll L. Shartle. *Methods in the Study of Administrative Leadership.* Columbus: Ohio State University Personnel Research Board, 1955.

Index